Contents

Chartered Accountants Ireland Code of Ethics

The Chartered Accountants Ireland Code of Ethics applies to all aspects of a Chartered Accountant's professional life, including dealing with corporation tax issues, capital gains tax issues, capital acquisitions tax issues and stamp duty issues. The Code of Ethics outlines the principles that should guide a Chartered Accountant, namely:

- Integrity
- Objectivity
- Professional Competence and Due Care
- Confidentiality
- Professional Behaviour

As a Chartered Accountant, you will have to ensure that your dealings with the tax aspects of your professional life are in compliance with these fundamental principles. Set out in **Appendix 4** is further information regarding these principles and their importance in guiding you on how to deal with issues which may arise throughout your professional life, including giving tax advice and preparing tax computations.

Overview of Tax System

Learning Objectives

In this chapter you will learn:

- how the administration of our tax system is structured and the role of the Revenue Commissioners;
- how different types of taxpayers are identified;
- how different types of income are classified;
- some key definitions; and
- essential data on income tax rates and bands.

1.1 Introduction

The main taxes levied in Ireland may be classified as **taxes on income** and **taxes on transactions**.

The main taxes on **income** are Income Tax and Corporation Tax, while the main taxes on **transactions** include Value Added Tax, Customs & Excise Duties, Stamp Duty, Capital Gains Tax, and Capital Acquisitions Tax.

A further distinction is also made between **Direct taxes, Indirect taxes** and **Social Contributions**.

Direct taxes are typically taxes on earned income or wealth, e.g. Income Tax, Corporation Tax and Capital Gains Tax.

Indirect taxes are typically taxes or levies on transactions or production, e.g. VAT, Stamp Duty, Customs and Excise Duties, Carbon Tax and Capital Acquisitions Tax.

Social contributions are levies that are paid into social security funds or schemes.

Income tax is generally assessed on the **worldwide income** of **Irish resident** persons. Non-residents are, in general, liable only to the extent that they have income arising in Ireland. Irish corporation tax is levied on the worldwide income of companies resident in Ireland for tax purposes and on the trading income of non-resident companies to the extent that it arises in Ireland. A non-resident company is liable to **income tax** on **Irish source income** if it is not trading in the State through a branch or an agency.

1.2   Legislation

Income and corporation tax law is based on legislation contained mainly in the **Taxes Consolidation Act 1997 (TCA 1997)** and the annual **Finance Acts (FA)**. Certain detailed tax rules relating to the legislation are set out in regulations that are issued by the Revenue Commissioners under powers conferred by the foregoing legislation. Relevant tax case law and tax practice also plays an important role in putting tax legislation into effect. Decisions from the **European Court of Justice** and **EU Directives** are also influential and binding once enacted into Irish legislation. EU consent is also required where tax measures support an industry sector or region.

1.3   The Revenue Commissioners, Inspectors, Appeal Commissioners and Collector General

Responsibility for the care and management of both **direct** and **indirect** taxes rests with the Office of the Revenue Commissioners. The Revenue Commissioners are a division within the Department of Finance and overall control rests with the Minister for Finance.

- The board of the **Revenue Commissioners** consists of three Commissioners who are appointed by An Taoiseach.
- **Inspectors of Taxes** are appointed by the Revenue Commissioners and are deployed throughout the country in four regional divisions and a separate Large Cases Division. They are responsible for the efficient operation of the Irish tax system by issuing tax returns and other forms for completion, by issuing assessments to taxation, examining tax returns completed by taxpayers and agreeing taxpayers' liabilities.
- The **Collector General** is appointed by the Revenue Commissioners and he is responsible for the efficient collection of taxes, including the pursuance of unpaid taxes.
- **Appeal Commissioners** are appointed by the Minister for Finance and adjudicate between Inspectors of Taxes and taxpayers on matters of disagreement.

1.3.1   Regional Divisions and Large Cases Division

The country is divided up into four regional divisions as follows:

1. **Border Midlands West** which covers Galway, Sligo, Leitrim, Donegal, Louth, Monaghan, Cavan, Mayo, Westmeath, Offaly, Longford & Roscommon
2. **Dublin**
3. **East South-East** which covers Meath, Kildare, Wicklow, Wexford, Carlow, Waterford, Tipperary, Kilkenny & Laois
4. **South-West** which covers Cork, Limerick, Kerry & Clare

Each region looks after all tax aspects of the taxpayers in their region. Business taxpayers are generally dealt with in the district where their business is managed and controlled. Non-business taxpayers are dealt with in the region where they live. Each region is further divided up into Revenue districts covering different geographical areas.

The **Large Cases Division** is a separate division that deals with large companies and very wealthy individuals regardless of where they are living or where their businesses are located.

1.3.2 Appeal Commissioners

Where assessments to tax are under appeal and cannot be finalised due to a dispute between the Inspector and the taxpayer, then the Inspector will list the case for hearing before the Appeal Commissioners, who will effectively act as judges between the Inspector of Taxes and the taxpayer and/or his agent. The decision ("determination") of the Appeal Commissioners is final and conclusive unless either the taxpayer or the Inspector is dissatisfied with the decision given. If dissatisfaction is expressed within the appropriate time limits then additional appeal procedures are available to both parties. **(See Chapter 9).**

Cases heard before the Appeal Commissioners are held *in camera*. Determinations, which do not identify the taxpayer, are published from time to time.

1.4 Classes of Taxpayer

Income tax is assessed on the following persons (the term "person" for tax purposes includes individuals, corporate bodies and trusts):

1. Individuals
2. Individuals in partnerships
3. Trusts
4. Non-resident companies are liable to income tax on certain types of income, such as rents arising in Ireland.

Income tax is levied on income applicable to the above classes of taxpayers. It may be assessed by **direct self-assessment** (i.e. profits of a sole trader) or by **deduction at source** from an individual's income (i.e. employees under the PAYE system).

1.5 Classification of Income

If a person's income is assessed directly, it must first be **classified according to the source** from which it arises under the Schedule system used by the Irish Revenue. For example, an individual's total income may be categorised as Trading Income, Employment Income and Investment Income. Special rules apply for calculating the taxable income from **each** source and for determining the **timing** of the tax charge.

Under the Schedule system the various sources of income are classified as follows:

Schedule D
- **Case I**   Trading income
- **Case II**   Income from vocations and professions
- **Case III**   Investment income and income from foreign employments and possessions, provided they have not suffered Irish standard rate income tax at source.
- **Case IV**   Republic of Ireland deposit interest that has suffered deposit interest retention tax (DIRT). Income not taxed specifically under Schedule E or F or under any other Case of Schedule D and income received under deduction of Irish income tax at the 20% standard rate.
- **Case V**   Rents and income from property in the Republic of Ireland.

Example 2:

Martin and Mary are married and jointly assessed for 2012. Martin's income is €7,000 and Mary's income is €48,000. Their tax credits are €4,950. Compute their income tax liability for 2012.

Income Tax Computation of Martin and Mary for 2012

		Martin €	Mary €	Total €
Total Income		7,000	48,000	55,000
TAX PAYABLE: (Married Persons)	Mary - first €41,800 @ 20%		8,360	8,360
	Martin - total €7,000 @ 20%	1,400		1,400
	Mary - balance €6,200 @ 41%		2,542	2,542
Gross Income Tax Liability		1,400	10,902	12,302
Less: Tax Credits				(4,950)
Net Tax Due				7,352

Questions (Chapter 1)

(See Solutions to Questions at the end of this textbook.)

1 Overview of Tax System

1.1 Pat and Una

Pat's income for 2012 is €15,000 and he is married to Una whose income is €47,000. They are jointly assessed and their tax credits are €6,600.

Requirement
Compute their income tax liability for 2012.

1.2 Paul and Jason

Paul and Jason are civil partners and jointly assessed for 2012. Paul's income is €47,000 and Jason's income is €41,000. Their tax credits are €3,300.

Requirement
Compute their income tax liability for 2012.

1.3 Sean Paul and Norah

Sean Paul earned €88,000 and is married to Norah who is a home carer with no income. Their tax credits were €5,760.

Requirement
Compute their income tax liability for 2012.

Residence and Domicile

2

Learning Objectives

In this chapter you will learn:

■ the importance of the concepts of residence and domicile in assessing taxes;
■ the difference between residence, ordinary residence and domicile;
■ the implications of residence, ordinary residence and domicile in the calculation of taxable income;
■ the concessions available for individuals entering or leaving the country during the year of assessment; and
■ the rule relating to the domicile levy.

2.1 Introduction

The extent to which an individual's income is liable to irish income tax depends on three criteria:

(i)   the individual's **residence**;
(ii) the individual's **ordinary residence**; and
(iii) the individual's **domicile**.

In simple terms, an Irish tax resident is liable to irish income tax on his/her worldwide income. A non-resident is liable to Irish income tax on his Irish income only.

Before looking at the tax implications of the above in detail, it is necessary to examine the meaning of the terms "residence", "ordinary residence" and "domicile".

2.2 Residence

An individual's residence is determined for **each tax year separately**. Generally, an individual will be **resident** in Ireland for a tax year if he/she is either:

■ present in Ireland for a total of **183 days or more** during that tax year; *or*
■ present in Ireland for a total of **280 days or more** in the **current and previous** tax years,

provided that where an individual is present in the State (i.e. Ireland) for only **30 days or** less in a tax year,

- he will not be Irish resident in that year; *and*
- no account will be taken of that period in calculating the aggregate of 280 days over two tax years.

An individual is present in Ireland for a day if he is in Ireland at **any time during that** day (with effect from 1 January 2009) or if he is in Ireland at the **end** of the day, i.e. at midnight (for 2008 and all prior years).

Test to establish Irish Residency (other than election)

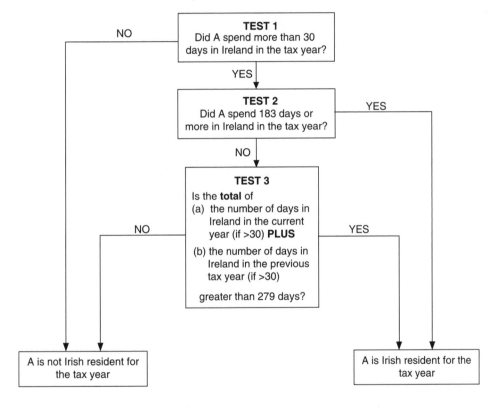

2.3   Election to be Resident

An individual may **elect to be** Irish resident for a tax year if:

- he is not resident in Ireland in the tax year; *and*
- he satisfies the Revenue that he is in Ireland with the intention and in such circumstances that he will be resident in Ireland for the next tax year.

An individual might elect to be Irish tax resident for the following reasons:

- to qualify for full tax credits;
- to avail of Ireland's network of double taxation agreements; *or*
- to qualify for joint assessment. The Irish Revenue's view is that **both** the individual and their spouse must be Irish resident to qualify.

Example:
Anne jets between her home in Barbados and her retreat in West Cork. She spends the following number of days in Ireland over the following tax years:

Year	Days
2009	Nil
2010	100
2011	125
2012	165

YEAR 2010

Test 1:	Does Anne spend more than 30 days in Ireland in 2010?
Answer:	Yes, therefore go to Test 2.
Test 2:	Does Anne spend 183 days or more in Ireland in 2010?
Answer:	No, therefore go to Test 3.
Test 3:	Is Anne's total number of days in Ireland in 2010 and 2009 greater than 279?
Answer:	100 days in 2010 and 0 days in 2009. No, not greater than 279 days. Anne is not resident in 2010.

YEAR 2011

Test 1:	Does Anne spend more than 30 days in Ireland in 2011?
Answer:	Yes, therefore go to Test 2.
Test 2:	Does Anne spend 183 days or more in Ireland in 2011?
Answer:	No, therefore go to Test 3.
Test 3:	Is Anne's total number of days in Ireland in 2011 and 2010 greater than 279?
Answer:	125 days in 2011 **plus** 100 days in 2010. Total days in Ireland 2011 and 2010 = 225. No, not greater than 279 days. Anne is not resident in 2011.

YEAR 2012

Test 1:	Does Anne spend more than 30 days in Ireland in 2012?
Answer:	Yes, therefore go to Test 2.
Test 2:	Does Anne spend 183 days or more in Ireland in 2012?
Answer:	No, therefore go to Test 3.
Test 3:	Is Anne's total number of days in Ireland in 2012 and 2011 greater than 279?
Answer:	165 days in 2012 **plus** 125 days in 2011. Total days in Ireland 2012 and 2011 = 290. Yes, greater than 279 days. Anne is Irish resident for 2012.

2.4   Ordinary Residence

An individual's ordinary residence is determined for each tax year separately. An individual is ordinarily resident in Ireland for a tax year if he has been resident in Ireland for each of the **last three tax years**.

An individual does not stop being ordinarily resident in Ireland unless he has been **non resident** for the preceding **three tax years**.

Example:
Tom comes to live in Ireland from the US on 1 May 2008. He leaves permanently on 28 January 2012.

Tax Year	Resident	Ordinarily Resident
2008	Yes > 183 days	No
2009	Yes > 183 days	No
2010	Yes > 183 days	No
2011	Yes > 183 days	Yes (resident for previous three years)
2012	No – fails 30 day test	Yes

Tom will continue, until 2014, to be ordinarily resident in Ireland. He will cease to be ordinarily resident when he has been non-resident for three years, i.e. 2015.

2.5   Domicile

Domicile is a legal term. The main idea underlying the concept is **home**, the permanent home. Generally a person is domiciled in the country of which he is a national and in which he spends his life. However, the equating of domicile to home must be treated with care as, in certain circumstances, a person may be domiciled in a country which is not and never has been his home. A person can have two homes but he can only have **one domicile**.

2.5.1   Domicile of Origin

An individual is **born** with a domicile known as his domicile of origin. A child at birth acquires the domicile of his father. If his parents are not married, he acquires the domicile of his mother. An individual can **reject** his domicile of origin and he can **acquire** a new domicile. In order to abandon the domicile of origin, the individual must prove conclusively that he has **severed all links** with the country in which his domicile of origin lies. A domicile of origin cannot be lost by a mere abandonment. It can only be lost by the acquisition of a domicile of choice.

2.5.2   Domicile of Choice

A domicile of choice is the domicile that any independent person (e.g. an individual who has attained 18 years of age) can acquire for himself by a combination of **residence** and **intention**. To acquire a domicile of choice, an individual must establish a physical presence in the new jurisdiction and have an intention to reside there indefinitely. A domicile of choice can be abandoned. This will involve either the acquisition of a new domicile of choice or the revival of the domicile of origin.

2.5.3   Domicile of Dependence

The domicile of dependent persons (children less than 18 years, incapacitated persons) is **dependent** on the domicile of someone else other than themselves.

Three general points regarding domicile require special attention:

1. a person cannot be without a domicile;
2. a person cannot possess more than one domicile at any time; and
3. an existing domicile is presumed to continue until it is proved that a new domicile of choice has been acquired.

2.6   Impact of Residence, Ordinary Residence and Domicile

2.6.1   Resident and Domiciled

Such an individual is liable to Irish income tax on his **worldwide personal income**, irrespective of where it is earned and whether or not it is remitted to Ireland.

Example: Pat, a single man, has the following sources of income in 2012.	€
Salary paid by Irish co	75,000
Dividends from Spanish Co	10,000
Rent received from USA (not remitted)	5,200
Total income	90,200

Pat is resident and domiciled in Ireland. Therefore, he is liable to income tax on his worldwide income of €90,200 regardless of where it arises or whether it is remitted into Ireland.

2.6.2 Resident and Domiciled but not Ordinarily Resident

An Irish domiciled individual who is resident but not ordinarily resident in Ireland (e.g. an Irish citizen who has been living abroad for many years and who has returned) is liable to income tax on:

1. any income arising in Ireland; *and*
2. foreign sourced income.

Prior to 2010, such an individual was taxable on the remittance basis in respect of foreign income.

Example: Patrick, an Irish citizen, returned to Dublin in May 2012 after a five year secondment to his employer's parent company in Dubai. He has the following sources of income in 2012:	€
Salary paid by Dubai parent Co (to May 2012)	60,000
Salary paid by Irish Co (June to Dec 2012)	40,000
Rent received on Dubai apartment (June to Dec) (remitted)	9,000
Dubai deposit interest (paid Oct 2012) (not remitted)	4,000
Patrick is domiciled (Irish citizen) and resident (> 183 days) in Ireland for 2012 but is not ordinarily resident (as he was non-resident for 2011, 2010 and 2009). As Patrick qualifies for split year residence, he is therefore liable on:	
	€
Salary paid by Irish Co. (June to December 2012)	40,000
Dubai rent	9,000
Dubai deposit interest	4,000

2.6.3 Resident but not Domiciled

An individual who is resident but not domiciled in Ireland is liable to income tax in full on:

1. any income arising in Ireland; *and*
2. other income (excluding employment income) arising outside of Ireland **but only** to the extent that it is **remitted into** Ireland; *and*
3. income from an office or employment, insofar as that income relates to the performance, **in the State**, of the duties of that office or employment (irrespective of where it is paid or whether it is remitted into Ireland or not).

FA (No. 2) 2008 introduced a limited **Special Assignee Relief Programme (SARP)** for higher paid executives coming to work in Ireland for the first time (**section 825B TCA 1997**). This has been amended a few times since its introduction and was further amended in FA 2012.

Special Assignee Relief Programme (SARP) – effective 1 January 2012

Where a *relevant employee*:

1. is resident in the State for tax purposes and is not resident elsewhere, *and*
2. performs in the State the duties of his employment with a *relevant employer* or *associated company*, *and*
3. has *relevant income* from his *relevant employer* or *associated company* which is not less than €75,000,

then the relevant employee, on making a claim, will be entitled to a **deduction** of a *Specified Amount* **for the first five years** from the income, gains or profit of the employment with the relevant employer or associated company.

   The *Specified Amount* **is calculated at 30% of income between €75,000 and €500,000 and consequently exempts this amount from income tax but not from PRSI and USC.**

Relevant Employee

A relevant employee is a person who:

1. was a full-time employee of the relevant employer for the whole of the 12 months immediately before his arrival in the State and exercised the duties of his employment for that relevant employer **outside** the State; *and*
2. arrives in the State in any of the tax years 2012, 2013 or 2014, at the request of his or her relevant employer, to:
   a. perform in the State the duties of his employment for that employer, *or*
   b. to take up employment in the State with an associated company, *and*
3. performs the duties of his employment in the State for a **minimum** period of **12 consecutive months** from the date he takes up residence in the State; *and*
4. was **not resident** in the State for the **five tax years** immediately **preceding** the tax year in which he first arrives in the State for the purposes of the employment.

Relevant Employer

Relevant employer means a company that is incorporated and tax resident in a country with which Ireland has a double taxation agreement, or an information sharing agreement.

Associated Company

Associated company means a company that is associated with a relevant employer within the meaning of section 432 TCA 1997.

Relevant Income

While all income and emoluments are subject to income tax, the *relevant income* definition assesses whether a person can **qualify** for SARP by having *relevant income* greater than €75,000. Relevant income includes all the relevant employee's income, profits and gains from the employment, but excludes the following:

1. benefits in kind and perquisites;
2. bonus payments (whether contractual or not);
3. termination payments;

4. shares or share-based remuneration; and
5. payments in relation to restrictive covenants.

In effect, *relevant income* will be the base salary.

Note that the *relevant income* definition is **only** for the purposes of assessing whether the person can qualify for SARP and **is not relevant in calculating the actual relief, i.e. the** *Specified Amount.*

Example:
Mary Watson, an American citizen, was sent to work in the State in January 2012 by a relevant employer and had the following sources of income in 2012:

	€
Salary paid by US parent	150,000
Bonus paid by US parent	70,000
Benefit in Kind	4,000
Total Income	224,000
Less: Tax deducted under the PAYE system	(81,500)
After tax income	142,500

SARP Relief:
  (a) Relevant Income > €75,000
     Salary €150,000 > €75,000 ⇨ eligible for SARP relief
  (b) Calculation of **Specified Amount:**

Total Income:	224,000
Less: lower threshold	(75,000)
	149,000
Specified Amount @ 30%	**44,700**

Total Income	224,000
Less: Specified Amount	(44,700)
Taxable Income	179,300

Ms Watson will need to make a claim for a tax repayment of €18,327 (€44,700 @ 41%).

Situation Prior to 1 January 2012
Prior to the introduction of SARP in 2012, a limited **Remittance Basis** applied in respect of **employment** earnings not remitted into the State.

Limited Remittance Basis – effective 1 January 2010 to 31 December 2011
As these provisions were introduced for a three year period effective 1 January 2010, any individuals who already made a claim under Section 825B TCA 1997 can continue to claim this relief to the end of the three year period.

Where a *relevant employee*:

1. becomes resident in the State for tax purposes for the first time,
2. is required by his *relevant employer* to exercise the duties of his employment in the State for the first time,
3. exercises those duties in the State on behalf of the relevant employer or associated company of the relevant employer for a period of at least **1 year,** *and*
4. while so exercising those duties, continues to be paid *relevant emoluments* from abroad by his relevant employer,

then, at the end of the tax year in which the emoluments are paid, the employee may apply to Revenue to have the tax due on the relevant emoluments computed for the tax year on the full amount of the **greater of:**

1. the relevant emoluments earned and received in or remitted to the State, *or*
2. an amount equal to €100,000 plus 50% of the relevant emoluments in excess of €100,000,

and any tax already deducted from the relevant emoluments in excess of the tax due as so computed shall be repaid on foot of a claim from the employee. Note that PAYE paid in the State is deemed to have been remitted.

Relevant Employee
A relevant employee is a person who:

1. is resident in the State for tax purposes, *and*
2. who is not domiciled in the State, *and*

prior to becoming a resident in the State:

(a) was resident in an **EEA State** (EU Member States and Iceland, Norway and Liechtenstein) or in a country with which Ireland has a double taxation agreement, *and*
(b) was employed in that country by the same relevant employer or associated company of the relevant employer, *and*
(c) had exercised the greater part of his employment in that country.

Relevant Employer
Relevant employer means a company that is incorporated and resident in an **EEA State** or in a country with which Ireland has a double taxation agreement.

Relevant Emoluments
Relevant emoluments are emoluments paid by the relevant employer or an associated company which are chargeable to tax under Schedule E and have been subject to PAYE.

Example:
Steve Brown, an American citizen, was sent to work in the State in 2011 by a relevant employer and remitted €50,000 of his salary to Ireland in 2012:

	€
Salary paid by US parent	220,000
Less: Tax deducted under the PAYE system	(74,800)
After tax income	145,200
Remitted to the State in 2012	50,000
(a) Amount Remitted	50,000
PAYE paid (deemed remitted)	74,800
Total	124,800
(b) €100,000 + (50% (€220,000 − €100,000))	160,000

Mr Brown will be assessed on the greater of (a) and (b) above, i.e. €160,000 instead of his gross salary of €220,000. A claim for a tax repayment for the tax paid on the difference of €60,000 will need to be made by Mr Brown.

2.6.4 Not Resident and not Ordinarily Resident

An individual who is not resident in Ireland is liable to income tax only on income arising in Ireland. In addition, a non-resident individual is not generally entitled to tax credits and reliefs. The domicile of such a person is not relevant.

2.6.5 Not Resident but Ordinarily Resident

An individual who is not resident in Ireland but is ordinarily resident in Ireland is liable to Irish tax on his worldwide income **except for**:

1. income from a trade or profession, no part of which is carried on in Ireland;
2. employment that is carried on **outside** the State (incidental duties may be carried on in the State); and
3. other foreign income which in any year of assessment **does not exceed €3,810**.

Example:

Mary Rose, an Irish citizen, who is single, emigrated to Canada in May 2010. Apart from an annual two week holiday she has not returned to Ireland. She has the following sources of income in 2012.

	€
Salary paid by her Canadian employer	90,000
Rent received from letting her house in Canada (not remitted)	15,000

She is non resident for 2010 and 2011, but is still ordinarily resident for 2012. Therefore she is liable to income tax on the Canadian rent since it is in excess of €3,810 but not her Canadian salary as the employment was exercised wholly outside Ireland.

2.7 Split Year Residence

As outlined above, an individual is Irish resident or non-resident, as the case may be, for a full tax year.

Section 822 TCA 1997 provides that an individual can be treated as Irish resident for **part** of a year only in certain circumstances.

2.7.1 Year of Arrival

An individual who:

1. has not been resident in Ireland in the preceding tax year,
2. arrives in Ireland in the current tax year,
3. is resident in Ireland in the current tax year (i.e. 183 days or more), and
4. satisfies the Revenue that he is in Ireland with the intention of and in such circumstances that he will be Irish tax resident in the following tax year,

will be treated as Irish resident only from **the date of his arrival** in the State as far as **employment income** is concerned. However there is no apportionment of tax credits, allowances or tax bands.

Example:

Simon, a single man, has lived in London all his life.

His employer sends him on a three-year secondment to Ireland. He arrives on 1 June 2012. His salary from his UK employer is his only income. In 2012, his salary was €66,000 and was paid to him in the UK.

His basic personal tax credit was €1,650 and his employee tax credit was €1,650 for 2012.

Will Simon qualify for split year residence?

Q.   Is he resident in 2011?
A.   No.

Q.   Did he arrive in 2012?
A.   Yes

Q.   Is he resident in 2012?
A.   Yes, under the 183 day rule.

Q.   Does he intend to be resident in 2013?
A.   Yes.

Simon, therefore, qualifies for the split year residence: he will be treated as resident from 1 June 2012. His Irish income tax liability will be as follows:-

Schedule D Case III		
€66,000 × 7/12ths =		*€38,500*
Tax:		
€32,800 @ 20%		€6,560
€5,700 @ 41%		*€2,337*
		€8,897
Deduct tax credits:		
Basic personal tax credit	€1,650	
Employee tax credit	€1,650	(€3,300)
Net tax liability		€5,597

2.7.2 Year of Departure

An individual who is:

1.   resident in the current tax year, **and**
2.   satisfies the Revenue that he is leaving the State other than for a temporary purpose with the intention and in such circumstances that he will not be resident in the next tax year,

will be treated as resident only up to **the date of departure** as far as **employment income only** is concerned.

Example:
Brian, a single man from Dublin, leaves to work in Boston on 1 May 2012. He has signed a three-year employment contract with a US firm.

His basic personal tax credit was €1,650 and his employee tax credit was €1,650 for 2012.

His income in 2012 is as follows:

Irish salary	€18,500
PAYE deducted	€3,530
US salary	€30,000

Will Brian qualify for split year residence?

Q. Is he resident in 2012?
A. Yes, under the 280 day rule.

Q. Is he leaving Ireland for other than a temporary purpose?
A. Yes

Q. Does he intend and is it likely given the circumstances of his departure to the US, that he will not be resident in 2013?
A. Yes.

Brian, therefore, qualifies for the split year concession. His Irish income tax liability for 2012 will be as follows:

Schedule E		
Irish salary		*€18,500*
Tax @ 20%		€3,700
Deduct tax credits:		
Basic personal tax credit	€1,650	
Employee tax credit	€1,650	(€3,300)
Net tax liability		€400
Less: PAYE deducted		(€3,530)
Tax refund due		(€3,130)

Brian is not taxed on his US employment income and receives full personal tax credits.

2.8 Domicile Levy

Section 531AA TCA 1997 introduced a levy from 1 January 2010 to ensure that individuals who are domiciled in Ireland would make a contribution to the Exchequer irrespective of their residence status. FA 2012 removed the requirement that the individual had to be a "citizen of Ireland". The domicile levy applies to an individual:

1. who is domiciled in Ireland in that tax year, *and*
2. whose world-wide income for the tax year is greater than €1 million, *and*
3. whose final Irish income tax liability is less than €200,000, *and*
4. who has Irish property with a market value exceeding €5 million at 31 December.

The amount of the levy is **€200,000**. Irish income tax paid by an individual will be allowed as a credit against the domicile levy. However, taxes paid overseas on the world-wide income are not allowed as a credit. Irish property does not include shares in a company (or a holding company) **carrying on a trade**, but includes all property **situated in Ireland** to which the individual is beneficially entitled in possession at 31 December. The market value is the price at which the property would sell on the open market and does not take into account any charges or mortgages taken out against the property.

The levy operates on an individual basis, i.e. if jointly-assessed spouses both meet the conditions above, the levy is payable by both spouses. The tax is payable on a self-assessment basis on or before 31 October in the year following the valuation date, i.e. 31 December each year.

Questions (Chapter 2)

(See Solutions to Questions at the end of this text.)

2   Residence and Domicile

2.1   Hank

Hank is a US citizen seconded to work in Ireland for two years. He arrives on 19 May 2010 and leaves on 1 May 2012. He does not leave the country during that period.

Requirement
Establish Hank's residence status for each year.

2.2   Kenji

Kenji is a Japanese citizen seconded to work in Ireland for a two-year period. He arrives on 17 December 2009 and leaves on 16 January 2012. He does not leave the country during the period of his secondment.

Requirement
What is Kenji's residence status for each year?

2.3   Aurore

Aurore is a French woman who has been seconded from France to work in Ireland for three years. She arrives on 1 February 2011 and leaves on 10 January 2014. Her French employer continues to pay her salary in France of €3,000 per month and an additional €2,000 per month in Ireland.

Requirement
What is Aurore's residence status for each year?
What advice would you give Aurore and her employer in connection with her residence status and salary payment?

2.4   Mr Harris

Mr Harris is married and has the following sources of income for 2012:

	€
Irish rents	37,000
US dividends	4,000

Tax was deducted by the lessee of €7,400 on the gross rent received of €37,000 in 2012.
Mr Harris is not Irish domiciled and is not resident or ordinarily resident in Ireland.

Requirement
Calculate Mr Harris's income tax liability for 2012.

2.5 H. Klaus

Mr Klaus, a German citizen, was sent to work in Ireland in May 2012 by his company, Flow GmbH. He had the following sources of income in 2012:

	€
Salary paid by German parent	250,000
Benefit in Kind	2,500
Bonus payment	20,000

Requirement
Calculate Mr Klaus's entitlement to relief under SARP.

Classification of Income

3

Learning Objectives

In this chapter you will learn:

- how income is classified for tax purposes according to its source;
- how to distinguish between the different types of income and, in particular, self-employed income versus employment income;
- the basis of assessment for each of the different types of income;
- the special rules associated with the commencement and cessation of trading in a year of assessment;
- the distinctions between and classification of unearned and passive income, e.g. bank interest, dividends and rental income; and
- the definition of employments and the rules regarding the assessment to tax of employment income, benefits-in-kind, commencement, termination and retirement payments.

3.1 Cases I and II – Schedule D

3.1.1 Introduction

Income tax is charged on profits or gains arising from any **trade** (Case I) or from any **profession** or **vocation** (Case II). The tax treatment and computational rules for Cases I and II are practically identical and are therefore considered together.

Persons chargeable to tax under Case I would include shopkeepers, manufacturers, farmers, etc., while the charge to tax under Case II would extend to self-employed individuals carrying on professions or vocations (whether as single individuals or in partnership) such as doctors, solicitors, architects, accountants, dramatists, and jockeys. The latter two are regarded as vocations rather than professions.

3.1.2 Definitions of "Profession", "Trade" and "Vocation"

Profession

The term "profession" is not defined in TCA 1997 and accordingly one must therefore look at decided tax cases to help clarify the term. The following considerations are relevant in determining whether or not a profession exists:

1. Is the taxpayer a member of a professional body?
2. Does the professional body:
    (a) Limit admittance to membership to persons who have successfully completed examinations and/or undergone a period of specified training?
    (b) Prescribe a code of ethics, breach of which may incur disciplinary measures against the member?
3. Does the occupation require mainly intellectual skill?
4. Is his/her relationship with clients in the nature of contracts **for** services, rather than contracts **of** service (e.g. employments)?
5. Examples of individuals regarded as carrying on a profession would include teachers, doctors, opticians, actors, and journalists.

Vocation

In decided tax cases, the word "vocation" has been compared with a "calling". Decided tax cases have held that the following are vocations:

- a bookmaker;
- a dramatist; and
- a jockey.

Trade

Section 3 TCA 1997 defines "trade" as including *"every trade, manufacture, adventure or concern in the nature of trade"*. The question of whether or not a trade is carried on is a **question of fact** rather than a point of law. The courts have held this definition to include profits or gains arising from trading in the normal sense of the word but also from **isolated** transactions and activities. Profits from farming and from dealing in development land are assessable under Case I.

3.1.3 "Badges of Trade"

Guidance as to what constitutes "trading" is available from case law and from a set of rules drawn up in 1955 by the **UK Royal Commission on the Taxation of Profits and Income**. These rules, known as the **Badges of Trade**, have been approved by the Irish Courts. The six "Badges of Trade" listed by the Commission are as follows:

1. **The Subject Matter of the Realisation**
    The general rule here is that property, which does not give its owner an income or personal enjoyment merely by virtue of its ownership, is more likely to have been acquired with the object of a trading transaction than property that does, e.g. the principal private residence of an individual is more likely to have been bought for the purposes of his and his family's personal enjoyment rather than for the purposes of a trading transaction.

2. **Length of the Period of Ownership**
    As a general rule, property acquired for a trading or dealing purpose is realised within a short time after acquisition. However, there may be many exceptions to this rule.

3. **Frequency or Number of Similar Transactions by the Same Person**
   If the individual completed a number of transactions involving the same sort of property in succession over a period of years or there have been several such realisations at about the same date, a presumption arises that there has been a dealing in respect of each, i.e. that they were trading transactions.

4. **Supplementary Work on or in connection with the Property Realised**
   If the property is improved or developed in any way during the ownership so as to bring it into a more marketable condition, or if any special marketing efforts are made to find or attract purchasers, such as the opening of a sales office or a large scale advertising campaign, then this would provide some evidence of trading. Where there is an organised effort to obtain profit, there is likely to be a source of taxable income. However, if nothing at all is done, the suggestion would tend to go the other way.

5. **The Circumstances Responsible for the Realisation**
   There may be some explanation, such as a sudden emergency or opportunity calling for the realisation of cash, which may eliminate the suggestion that any plan of dealing prompted the original purchase, i.e. in the case of "an unsolicited offer that cannot be refused".

6. **Motive**
   Motive is extremely important in all cases. There are cases in which the purpose of the transaction is clearly discernible. Circumstances surrounding the particular transaction may indicate the motive of the seller and this may in fact overrule the seller's own evidence.

It is, however, important to appreciate that the "whole picture" must be taken into account, so that the weight given to the various factors may vary according to the circumstances. Furthermore, it is important to recognise that any given factor may be present to a greater or lesser degree, and that the absence (or presence) of any single factor is unlikely to be conclusive in its own right.

There are a number of significant tax cases which consider this matter:

- The **profit motive** was considered in the UK case of ***Erichsen v. Last*** (1881) when the judge defined trading as "where a person habitually does and contracts to do a thing capable of producing a profit, and for the purpose of producing a profit, he carries on a trade or business".
- The matter of **supplementary work** was considered in the UK case of ***Martin v. Lowry*** (1927) where the judges referred to the "mantle of trading" which the merchant donned as a result of the elaborate selling organisation he employed to sell his aeroplane linen to the public.
- Lord Sands in the UK case of ***Rutledge v. Inland Revenue*** (1929) considered the subject matter of the realisation in this case which was a consignment of toilet paper which Lord Sands considered must be bought for resale and so be "an adventure in the nature of the trade" under the terms of the relevant legislation.
- The case of ***Jenkinson (HMIT) v. Freedland*** (1961) brought a note of sobriety to the badges 'however' as the judge reminded us that "the facts of each case must be considered not merely the motive of acquisition, and conclusion arrived at" but that "the true position is that all facts in each case must be considered".

3.1.4 Basis of Assessment Cases I and II – Schedule D

The income assessable under Cases I and II is normally based on **the accounting period of 12 months ending during the year of assessment** e.g. profits earned by a trader for the year end 30 June 2012 are assessed in the tax year 2012.

There are, however, special provisions when a trade or profession **commences** or **ceases** business.

3.1.5 Commencement Years

The date on which a trade commences is a question of fact. The ***Birmingham & District Cattle By-Products v. Inland Revenue*** (1919) case established some tests which are still used to determine when a trade actually commences. These can be summarised as follows:

- The date when premises are acquired?   NO
- The date when staff are hired?   NO
- The date when supplier contracts are signed?   NO
- The date when raw materials/stock is received?   YES

First Year

The basis of assessment for the first tax year is the **profit from the date of commencement to the end of the tax year**. If the accounts of the individual do not coincide with this period, then the assessable profit is arrived at by **time apportionment**.

The first year of assessment is always the tax year during which the trade or profession commenced.

Example
Mr Jones commenced to trade as a builder on 1 July 2011 and prepared accounts for 18 months to 31 December 2012.

In this case, Mr Jones will be assessed under Case I as a builder for 2011 on the basis of the profits from 1 July 2011 to 31 December 2011. These will be arrived at by time-apportioning the 18 months results to 31 December 2012, i.e. the amount assessed for 2011 will be 6/18ths of the total profits for the period.

Second Year

(a)   If there is a 12-month accounting period ending in the second tax year and it is the only accounting period ending in that year, assess the taxable profits of that 12 month accounting period.

Example:
Donna commences to trade on 1 June 2011
Accounts are prepared for the year ended 31 May 2012
Taxable profits for year ended 31 May 2012 = €24,000
Accounts are prepared annually to 31 May.

Tax Year		Period	Calculation	Taxable Profit
2011	(1st year)	1/6/11–31/12/11	€24,000 × 7/12ths	€14,000
2012	(2nd year)	1/6/11–31/5/12	€24,000 × 12/12ths	€24,000

(b)   If there is an accounting period **other than one of 12 months** ending in the second tax year and it is the only accounting period ending in that tax year and the trade had commenced not less than 12 months before that date, assess the taxable profits of the year ending on that date. (You may add two or more accounting periods to get this 12 months)

Example:
Lisa commences to trade on 1 May 2011.
Accounts are prepared for the 17 months ending 30 September 2012
Taxable profits for the 17 months ending 30 September 2012 = €68,000
Accounts are prepared yearly to 30 September thereafter.

Tax Year		Period	Calculation	Taxable Profit
2011	(1st year)	1/5/11–31/12/11	€68,000 × 8/17ths	€32,000
2012	(2nd year)	1/10/11–30/9/12	€68,000 × 12/17ths	€48,000

(c) If there are **two or more accounting periods** ending in the second tax year, and the trade commenced not less than 12 months before the later date, assess the taxable profits of the year ending on the **later** date. (You may add two or more accounting periods to get this 12 months)

Example:
Rose commences to trade on 1 July 2011.
Accounts are prepared for the 10 months ending 30 April 2012
Taxable profits for the 10 months ending 30 April 2012 = €10,000
Accounts are prepared for the 8 months ending 31 December 2012
Taxable profits for 8 months ending 31 December 2012 = €6,000

Tax Year		Period	Calculation	Taxable Profit
2011	(1st year)	1/7/11–31/12/11	€10,000 × 6/10ths	€6,000
2012	(2nd year)	1/1/12–31/12/12	€10,000 × 4/10ths+	
			€6,000 × 8/8ths	€10,000

(d) In any other case, assess the actual profits for the tax year.

Example:
David commences to trade on 1 November 2011
Accounts are prepared for the 8 months ending 30 June 2012
Taxable profits for 8 months ending 30 June 2012 = €32,000
Accounts are prepared for the year ending 30 June 2013
Taxable profits for year ending 30 June 2013 = €46,000
While there is an accounting period ending in the second tax year, 2012, David did not commence to trade at least 12 months before this date. Accordingly, for the second tax year, David is taxed on the actual profits arising in that tax year.

Tax Year		Period	Calculation	Taxable Profit
2011	(1st year)	1/11/11–31/12/11	€32,000 × 2/8ths	€8,000
2012	(2nd year)	1/1/12–31/12/12	€32,000 × 6/8ths +	
			€46,000 × 6/12ths	€47,000

Third Year
The basis of assessment for the third year of assessment is **the accounting period of 12 months ending during the tax year**, i.e. if 2012 was the third year of assessment for a sole trader and he prepared a set of accounts for the 12 months to 30 September 2012, then these accounts would form the basis for tax year 2012 (subject to the option discussed below).

Option

If the actual profits of the **second** tax year are less than the profits assessed under the rules outlined above, then the difference can be deducted from the taxable profits of the third year.

Example:		Profit
Date of commencement 1 July 2010		
Accounts for 12 months to 30 June 2011		€52,000
Accounts for 12 months to 30 June 2012		€48,000
Accounts for 12 months to 30 June 2013		€30,000
Computation:		**Final Assessment**
First Year of Assessment 2010		
Profit period 1/7/2010 to 31/12/2010, i.e. €52,000 × 6/12ths		€26,000
Second Year of Assessment 2011		
12 month accounting period ending 30 June 2011		€52,000
Third Year of Assessment 2012		
12 months accounting period (basis period) ending 30 June 2012		€48,000
Assessable profits		
Amount assessed in second year (2011)	€52,000	
Less: actual profits for the second year (€52,000 × 6/12ths) + (€48,000 × 6/12ths) =	€50,000	
Excess		(€2,000)
Final assessment 2012: €48,000 – €2,000 =		€46,000

Fourth and Subsequent Years

The basis period for any particular year of assessment will normally be the accounting period of 12 months ending during the tax year. The taxpayer has no options for these years.

3.1.6   Cessation Years

The date on which a trade ceases is when all its trading stock has been sold or when it ceases to manufacture (although it continues to purchase products to resell). This is demonstrated by the case of *Gordon and Blair Ltd v. Inland Revenue* (1962) where a brewery was held to have ceased the trade of manufacturing beer and commenced the trade of selling beer.

Final Year

The final year of assessment is based on the profits from the beginning of the tax year to the date of cessation, i.e. if the taxpayer ceases on 31 August 2012, the last year of assessment will be 2012 so the 2012 assessment will be based on the actual profits from 1 January 2012 to 31 August 2012. Accounting period profits are time apportioned where necessary.

Penultimate (second last) Year

The profits assessable for this year are those of an accounting period of 12 months ending during the year of assessment. However, the assessment for the penultimate year must be revised to the actual amount of profits for that year if this yields a higher figure.

Where an assessment has to be revised and an additional tax liability arises, the obligation is on the taxpayer to include it in the self-assessed tax return in the year in which the cessation occurred.

Example:
J. Jones, who traded as a butcher for many years, retired on 30 June 2012. The results for the last few years of trading were as follows:-

Year ended 30/9/2010	Profit	€36,000
Year ended 30/9/2011	Profit	€48,000
9 months to 30/6/2012	Profit	€45,000

Computation:
Final Tax Year 2012
Basis of Assessment: 1/1/2012 to 30/6/2012
   €45,000 × 6/9ths   €30,000

Penultimate Year 2011
Original Assessment based on profits
   year ended 30/9/2011   €48,000

Revise to Actual if Actual Profits × €48,000:
Actual profits 2011:
   €48,000 × 9/12ths + €45,000 × 3/9ths   €51,000

3.1.7 Short-lived Businesses

Where a trade or profession is set up and discontinued within three tax years and the profits on which the individual is assessed for the three tax years exceed the actual profits arising in the same period, the individual may elect to have the profits of the second last year of trading reduced to the actual profits arising. By electing to reduce taxable profits for the second last year to actual, the individual is taxable on actual profits for all three years. An election for this treatment must be made before the specified return date for the year of cessation.

Example:
M. Ryan commenced trading on 1 July 2010 and ceased trading on 31 March 2012. The Case I profits for these years were as follows:

Year ended 30 June 2011	Profit	€65,000
9 months ended 31 March 2012	Profit	€30,000

Computation:
First Year of Assessment 2010

Profit period 1/7/2010 to 31/12/2010, i.e.
   €65,000 × 6/12ths   €32,500

Second Year of Assessment 2011
12 month accounting period ending 30/6/2011   €65,000

Last Year 2012
Actual 1/1/2012 to 31/3/2012
€30,000 × 3/9ths   €10,000

Second Year Excess:

Amount assessed in second year (2011)	€65,000	
Less actual profits for 2011		
(€65,000 × 6/12ths) + (€30,000 × 6/9ths) =	€52,500	
Excess		(€12,500)

(continued overleaf)

Final assessment 2012: €10,000 – €12,500 =	€NIL

In the absence of any relief in this case, the individual would be taxed on profits of €107,500 for the three tax years whereas actual profits arising in the three years were only €95,000. If the individual elects to be taxed on actual profits arising in the second year, i.e. 2011, he would be assessed as follows:

2010: Actual as above	€32,500
2011: Elect for actual €65,000 × 6/12ths + €30,000 × 6/9ths	€52,500
2012: Actual (with no second year excess as second year taxed on actual) €30,000 × 3/9ths	€10,000
Profits assessed for three years	€95,000

3.1.8 Post Cessation Receipts

Income received after a trade has ceased (e.g. bad debts recovered) is assessed under Schedule D Case IV (net of any post cessation expenses). Unused capital allowances from the ceased trade may be offset against the income. The Case I/II cessation assessments are not adjusted.

3.1.9 Change of Accounting Date

There are also special provisions when a trade or profession changes its accounting date which are not examinable at CAP 1.

3.1.10 Revenue Concession in Death Cases

A trade or a profession is treated as being **permanently discontinued** on the death of the person carrying on the trade even if his personal representative or successors continue on the trade after his death. Accordingly, the death of a person will normally trigger the **Case I and II cessation provisions** as outlined above. However, Revenue will, by concession, allow a trade to be treated as a **continuing** one where the trade is continued on by the **deceased's spouse or civil partner**. In such a case, provided the deceased's spouse or civil partner elects for such treatment, the cessation provisions are not applied to the deceased and the commencement provisions are not applied to the deceased's spouse or civil partner. If the election is made for the year in which the trader dies, Case I profits for the year of death are apportioned between them on a time basis.

Before making the election outlined above, the liabilities of the deceased and the surviving spouse or civil partner should be calculated on the basis that the trade is a continuing one and also on the basis of the cessation and commencement provisions being applied to see which basis will result in the lower tax liability.

3.1.11 Partnerships

A partnership is regarded as a single unit for the purposes of determining tax-adjusted profits.

How partners are assessed
For the purposes of tax assessment, each partner's share of the total profits is treated as **personal** to that partner, as if they arose from a **separate trade or profession**.

As a consequence, commencement and cessation rules apply to each partner **individually** when he enters/leaves the partnership. For taxation purposes, a partnership continues no matter how many partners are admitted or leave, provided there are **at least two partners at all times**, one of whom was a partner immediately prior to the admission of a new partner. A partnership **ceases** to exist when:

- the business ceases, *or*
- only one partner remains (i.e. sole trader), *or*
- a completely different set of partners takes over from the old partners.

The "**precedent partner**" arranges for the firm's tax computation to be prepared and submitted to the partnership's Inspector of Taxes. This partner is resident in the State, and

- is the first named partner in the partnership agreement, *or*
- if there is no agreement, the first named partner in the partnership name, e.g. Smith, Jones & Company.

If no partner is resident in the State, the agent or manager of the partnership who is resident in the State is deemed to be the precedent partner.

The 1890 Partnership Act defines "partnership" as "the relationship which exists between persons carrying on a business in common, with a view of profit".

3.1.12   Other Items

Interest on Capital

Interest on capital is a distribution of profit and is, accordingly, a disallowable expense in computing the partnership firm's profits or losses for a period.

Interest on capital must, however, be carefully distinguished from interest paid by the partnership in respect of a loan made to the partnership by an individual partner. Such interest, provided the funds borrowed had been used for the partnership business, would be an allowable Case II deduction.

Salaries

Salaries paid to a partner are treated in the same manner as drawings taken out of a business by a sole trader, i.e. they are disallowed for Case II computation purposes.

Rent Paid to a Partner

If a partner beneficially owns the premises from which the partnership is operated and lets the premises on an arm's length basis to the partnership, then the rent will be allowed as a deduction in computing the partnership profits and the landlord partner will be assessed personally under Case V on the rental income.

Sole Trader to Partnership

When an individual, who previously operated as a sole trader, commences to carry on the business in partnership with one or more others, then he is deemed to have ceased his old trade (and the cessation provisions will apply) and a new trade is deemed to commence from the date of commencement of the partnership.

Anti-avoidance

Section 1008 TCA 1997 states that the tax-adjusted profits of a partnership **must**, for tax purposes, be apportioned **fully** between the partners each year, with these profits being taxable at the partners' **marginal tax rates**. This section was introduced by **FA 2007** to counter the practice of not apportioning tax-adjusted profits between partners (for tax purposes), as any amounts not apportioned were chargeable to tax at the standard rate only on the precedent acting partner.

3.2 Case III – Schedule D

3.2.1 Income Assessable

Income tax under Case III is assessed on the following sources of income:

- Interest, annuities and other annual payments, wherever arising, provided it is receivable **without** the **deduction of tax at source** at the standard rate, **nor** does it suffer **Deposit Interest Retention Tax (DIRT)**.
- United Kingdom dividends received by Irish resident shareholders. An individual is assessed on the **cash amount received** exclusive of any tax credit. Under the terms of the Irish/UK double tax agreement, the dividend may be taxed in the UK. There is **no entitlement** to a repayment of this tax credit.
- Income arising from foreign securities and possessions to the extent that it has **not suffered Irish tax at source** or upon encashment.
  Examples are:

  - Dividends and interest from United Kingdom companies,
  - Rents from property situated abroad,
  - Interest from foreign securities, and
  - Income from foreign employments or businesses.

  In practice, most foreign dividends, with the **exception** of dividends paid by United Kingdom companies, do suffer Irish income tax on encashment and accordingly do not fall within the scope of Case III.
- Interest on most Government and Semi-State securities, where interest is paid **without** deduction of tax.
- Dividends paid on Credit Union ordinary **share** accounts. Dividends and interest paid on Credit Union deposit accounts (known as "special share accounts") are liable to DIRT and are therefore assessable under Case IV.
- Income arising to any person as a **member** of the **European Parliament** is chargeable to tax under **Case III** where the income is payable out of money provided by the budget of the **European Union**. Where the income is payable out of money provided by the Irish State, it is chargeable to tax under Schedule E. (Section 127A TCA 1997)
- All discounts
- Deposit interest from EU financial institutions - late filing only.

  With effect from 1 January 2005, interest received by an individual on a deposit account with an EU bank, building society, credit union or Post Office (or the EU equivalent of one of these institutions) will be subject to tax at the same rate as deposit interest received by individuals from lending institutions in Ireland **provided** the tax due on such interest is paid **on or before** the due date for the filing of the individual's income tax return. Such interest will be regarded as income chargeable to tax under **Case IV**.

3.2.2 Basis of Assessment

The basis of assessment for income falling within Case III is the **actual income** arising in the year of assessment.

3.2.3 Exempt Interest

The following interest is exempt from income tax:
- Interest or bonuses arising to an individual from Savings Certificates, Savings Bonds and National Instalment Savings Schemes with An Post.
- Interest on savings certificates issued by the Minister for Finance.
- Interest on overpayments of tax.
- Interest paid on certain government securities to persons who are not ordinary resident and/or domiciled in the State.

3.3 Case IV – Schedule D

This was originally a "sweeping up" case to catch any profits or gains not falling under any of the other cases of Schedule D and not charged under any other Schedule. In recent years, however, legislation has tended to use Case IV for charging certain specific items.

3.3.1 Income Assessable under Case IV, Schedule D

Republic of Ireland Building Society, Credit Union and Bank Deposit Interest
Deposit interest from Republic of Ireland banks, building societies and credit unions, where the interest is paid or credited to ordinary deposit accounts on an annual or more frequent basis, and **is subject to DIRT.**

The DIRT rates are as follows:

Period	Rate of DIRT
6 April 2001 to 31 December 2008	20%
1 January 2009 to 7 April 2009	23%
8 April 2009 to 31 December 2010	25%
1 January 2011 to 31 December 2011	27%
1 January 2012 onwards	30%

Any other deposit account, opened after 23 March 2000, where the interest is credited at intervals exceeding 12 months, e.g. a fixed term deposit account for say, two years, with interest payable on maturity, is subject to DIRT at the **prevailing rate plus 3%**, i.e. 30% and 33% respectively for the tax years 2011, 2012 and onwards.

Note: There is no further tax due on this income but it must be included in an individual's proforma income tax computation. This is because it is income liable to tax and could affect reliefs that are subject to restrictions based on income, e.g. 5% restriction for covenants, 10% restriction for permanent health insurance. It may also be liable to PRSI but is not liable to the Universal Social Charge (USC).

To ensure no further tax is due, an additional tax band equal to the rate of DIRT is included in this computation and the gross amount of the interest taxed at this rate. DIRT paid is included as a non-refundable tax credit.

Relief is available whereby deposit interest can be paid, **without the deduction of DIRT**, to individuals over 65 whose total income does not exceed the relevant tax exemption limits and to those permanently incapacitated upon the completion of the relevant declaration form (Forms DE1 and DE2).

Income Received under Deduction of Income Tax at the Standard Rate

Certain types of income are received under deduction of income tax at the standard rate (20%). Examples include **covenants, patent royalties, interest** paid by a company to an individual and interest payments by one individual to another individual.

The **gross** amount is assessed and a **refundable tax credit** is given for the income tax deducted at source.

Example

Mary Jane pays €8,000 net each year to her Aunt Monica under a seven year deed of covenant. She is 85 and in excellent health. Her only other income is her DSP Old Age Pension of €11,908. Her non-refundable tax credits were €1,895. Calculate Monica's income tax liability for 2012.

		€	€
Case IV covenant income	€8,000/0.8	10,000	
Schedule E DSW pension		11,908	21,908
Taxed as follows:			
21,908 @ 20%		4,382	
Less Non-refundable tax credits		(1,895)	
Less Refundable tax credits	€10,000*20%	(2,000)	
Income tax due		487	

Refund of Pension Contributions

If a director or employee has made contributions to a Revenue approved superannuation scheme and subsequently receives a refund of his contributions, the refund is assessed to tax under Case *IV* at the standard rate of tax. The administrator of the scheme deducts this tax at source at the time of the refund. The net amount received by the employee is treated as **exempt** and is not included in his income tax computation.

Retirement Lump Sum Benefits

Amounts in excess of the maximum lifetime retirement **tax-free lump sum** of **€200,000** in respect of pension benefits taken on or after 1 January 2011 will be subject to tax in two stages. The portion between **€200,000 and €575,000** will be taxed **under Case IV** at the **standard rate** of income tax in force at the time of payment. Any portion above that will be taxed under Schedule E at the recipient's marginal rate of tax.

Post Cessation Receipts of a Trade or Profession

Post-cessation receipts generally arise where a person dies and money earned by him is not received until after his death. These receipts, less any expenses, which would be allowable under Case I/II rules, are assessed to tax under Case IV.

Transfer of Right to Receive Rent

Where, on or after 6 February 2003, an individual receives a capital sum, the consideration for which is:

- The transfer to another person of the right to receive rent *or*
- The grant of a lease where another person is entitled to receive rent under the lease the capital sum received is taxable as income under Case IV in the year in which the person becomes entitled to the capital sum, or the year in which the capital sum is received, if earlier.

Profits from Unknown or Unlawful Activities

Profits arising from unknown or unlawful activities may be assessed as miscellaneous income under Case IV.

Deposit Interest from EU Financial Institutions

With effect from 1 January 2005, interest received by an individual on a deposit account with an EU bank, building society, credit union or Post Office (or the EU equivalent of one of these institutions) will be subject to tax at the same rate as deposit interest received by individuals from lending institutions in Ireland **provided** the tax due on such interest is paid **on or before** the due date for the filing of the individual's income tax return.

Other Investment Income

■ *Special Term Accounts*

With effect from 1 January 2002, an individual may open a Special Term (deposit) account that attracts a favourable tax treatment. The tax treatment of these accounts depends on the term of the investment as follows:

A *Medium Term Account* – the individual holder may not withdraw any deposits (except interest) from the account within **three years** from which the date the deposit was made.

A *Long Term Account* – the individual holder may not withdraw any deposits (except interest) from the account within **five years** from the date the deposit was made.

The following exemptions from tax apply in respect of these accounts:

The first €480 of interest paid in respect of a medium term account and the first €635 of interest paid in respect of a long term account in the tax year is not subject to DIRT and is not taken into account in calculating an individual's income tax liability.

Interest received in excess of the €480/€635 limits is subject to DIRT. This excess interest is also not taken into account in calculating an individual's income tax liability.

However, if the deposit holder is **aged 65** or over, or is **permanently incapacitated**, he may include the interest in his income tax computation for the purpose of obtaining a refund of DIRT **OR** he may make a declaration seeking the interest to be paid gross (see **Section 3.3.3** below).

■ *Shares in lieu of dividend from non quoted Irish resident companies*

The amount of cash dividend foregone is taxable as Case IV income and Dividend Withholding Tax is ignored.

3.3.2 Basis of Assessment

The basis of assessment for income falling within Case IV is the actual income arising in the year of assessment, i.e. if Case IV income arises in June 2012, then this income will be taxable in 2012. Generally, unless tax legislation specifically states otherwise, income is taxable only when **received**. Accordingly, Case IV income is generally taxed on a **receipts** basis.

3.3.3 Deposit Interest Retention Tax (DIRT)

If the amount of DIRT deducted is greater than the individual's income tax liability on this interest, **no refund** is due **unless**:

■ the individual (or spouse, if married) is aged 65 or more; *or*
■ the individual (or spouse, if married) is permanently incapacitated during the year of assessment.

The income exemption limit is also increased by the gross interest assessable. The interest received must always be included in an individual's income tax computation. This is because it is income **liable** to tax and could affect reliefs that are subject to restrictions based on income. It may also be liable to PRSI. Income subjected to DIRT is not liable to the USC.

FA 2007 introduced relief whereby deposit interest can be paid, **without the deduction of DIRT**, to over 65s whose total income does not exceed the relevant tax exemption limits and to those permanently incapacitated, upon the completion of the relevant declaration form (Forms DE1 and DE2) (see www.revenue.ie).

3.4 Case V – Schedule D

3.4.1 Income Assessable under Case V

The following income is assessable under Case V:

■ Rents in respect of any premises or lands in Ireland, i.e. offices, shops, factories, land etc.
■ Receipts in respect of an easement (right over land, e.g. a right of way). An easement includes any right in, over or derived from any premises in the State.
■ Certain premiums received for the granting of a lease.

3.4.2 Basis of Assessment

Tax is charged under Case V on the income arising during the year of assessment. The rent taken into account is the amount receivable in the tax year **whether or not** it is actually received. However if the taxpayer claims and proves that the whole or part of a rent was not received due to it being irrecoverable because of:

■ the default of the person liable; *or*
■ because the taxpayer waived payment of the rent without consideration and in order to avoid hardship,

then the rent not received is **excluded** from the Case V computation.

3.4.3 Commencement and Cessation

A Case V source does not commence until **rental income arises**, not when the property is acquired. A Case V source does not **cease** until the property is **disposed** of. There are no other special commencement or cessation rules for Case V income.

3.5 Schedule E

3.5.1 Income Assessable under Schedule E

The following classes of income are subject to taxation under Schedule E:

- Emoluments from all offices and employments. Examples include: directors' fees, salaries, wages, bonuses and commission paid to employees.
- Private pensions and annuities. Examples include pensions paid to former directors, employees or their dependants.
- Benefits-in-kind and perquisites. Examples include: benefits derived from the use of a company car; the provision of rent-free accommodation to an employee; holiday vouchers and preferential loans.
- Certain lump sum payments deriving from an office or employment, either before its commencement or after its cessation. Examples include: inducement payments; non-statutory redundancy payments; round sum expense allowances; ex-gratia and compensation payments on retirement and dismissal.
- Income arising to any person as a **member** of the **European Parliament** is chargeable to tax under Schedule E where the income is payable out of money **provided** by the **Irish State**. Where the income is payable out of money provided by the budget of the **European Union**, it is chargeable to tax under **Case III Schedule D. (Section 127A TCA 1997)**
- **Treatment of flight crews. Section 127B TCA 1997** provides that any income arising to an individual, whether resident in the State or not, from **any** employment exercised aboard an **aircraft** that is operated:
    - in international traffic, *and*
    - by an enterprise that has its place of effective management in the State,
  is chargeable to tax under Schedule E.
- Social welfare benefits **taxable** under Schedule E include:
    - State Pension (Contributory)
    - State Pension (Transition)
    - State Pension (Non-contributory)
    - Contributory Widow's, Widower's or Surviving Civil Partner's Pension
    - Contributory Guardian's Allowance
    - Ilness Benefit
    - Invalidity Pension
    - One Parent Family Payment
    - Non Contributory Widow's, Widower's or Surviving Civil Partner's Pension
    - Non Contributory Guardian's Pension
    - Social Assistance Allowance for Deserted Wives
    - Social Assistance Allowance for Prisoners' Wives
    - Carers Allowance
    - Blind Person's Pension
    - Occupational Injuries Benefit
    - Disablement Benefit
    - Jobseekers (formerly Unemployment) Benefit*
      The first €13 per week is not taxable.

■ Social welfare benefits **not taxable** under Schedule E include:
- Jobseekers (formerly Unemployment) Assistance
- Maternity Benefit
- Children's Allowance
- Bereavement Grant
- Disability Allowance
- Family Income Supplement
- Persons in receipt of Jobseeker Benefit due to "short-time employment" (e.g. where an individual's normal working week is cut to say three days). The benefit received for days of unemployment is exempt.

3.5.2 Meaning of "Offices" and "Employment"

Office

The term "office" is not defined but has been held under tax case law to mean:

"A subsisting permanent, substantive position, which has an existence independent of the person who filled it, and which went on and was filled in succession by successive holders."

Employment

The **distinction** between an **employee** and a **self-employed** person is not set out in tax legislation. In general, case law has determined that an employee is a person who holds a post and who has a **contract of service** with his employer, which basically involves the relationship of master and servant.

A self-employed person will provide services under a **contract for services**. Whether or not a person is an employee or a self-employed person will normally be clear from the facts of the particular case. However, sometimes the distinction between an employee and a self-employed person is not entirely clear and, accordingly, the issue has been the subject of a number of cases.

The UK case of ***Market Investigations Ltd v. Minister of Social Security*** **(1969)** established a fundamental test which has been quoted in subsequent cases. It established the fundamental test: "Does the person performing the services perform them as a person in business on his own account?"

If the answer is Yes, then the contract is a contract for services; if No, then there is a contract of services.

If an individual is found to be performing the services as a person in business on his own account, then this indicates that the individual is self employed rather than an employee.

The Irish case of ***Henry Denny and Sons Ltd T/A Kerry Foods v. Minister for Social Welfare*** (1998) follows this test and established three other tests to determining control, integration and economic relations to see which type of contract existed.

The ***Denny*** case involved an examination of the employment status of supermarket demonstrators/merchandisers of food products. The court found that the demonstrators were in fact employees rather than self employed.

The Employment Status Group devised these tests to determine employee or self-employed status:

1. **The terms of the contract**

   If, under the terms of the contract under which the person provides his services, he is entitled to holiday pay, sick pay, pension entitlements, company car or other benefits, he is more likely to be an **employee** rather than self-employed. If the contract provides that the person is required to work fixed hours on particular days, then he is more likely to be an employee, although this is not always the case.

2. **The degree of integration of the person into the organisation to which his services are provided**

   The greater the degree of integration into the organisation, the more likely the person is to be regarded as an employee.

3. **Whether the person provides his own helpers**

   If the individual is free to hire others to do the work he has agreed to undertake and he sets the terms under which such persons are employed, this is more indicative of a self-employed person rather than an employee.

4. **Whether the person provides his own equipment**

   If a person provides significant pieces of equipment to carry out the work he has agreed to undertake, this is also indicative of a self-employed person rather than an employee.

5. **The extent of the control exercised over the individual**

   Generally, a self-employed person will have more control over the work he does than an employee in terms of how, when and where it is to be carried out.

6. **The degree of responsibility for investment and management**

   A person who is responsible for running a business, who uses his own capital and is responsible for determining the running and expansion of a business, is clearly a self-employed person. This is essentially the test described above, which examines if the person is performing the service as a person in business on his own account.

7. **The degree of financial risk taken**

   An individual who risks his own money by, for example, buying assets and bearing their running costs and paying for overheads and large quantities of materials, is more likely to be self-employed. Financial risk could also take the form of quoting a fixed price for a job, with the consequent risk of bearing the additional costs if the job overruns. However, this will not mean that the worker is self-employed unless there is a real risk of financial loss.

8. **Opportunity to profit from sound management**

   A person whose profit or loss depends on his capacity to reduce overheads and organise his work effectively is likely to be self-employed.

See Revenue's Code of Practice *"Report of the Employment Status Group PPF"* at Appendix 2.

3.5.3 Basis of Assessment – Schedule E

All income taxable under Schedule E is assessed on the **actual income** of the year of assessment, **irrespective** of the tax year in which it is actually paid and **regardless** of whether taxed under PAYE or not.

For example, a salesman may earn and be paid a salary for the tax year 2012 and is subsequently paid a commission in February 2013 in respect of his sales during the tax year 2012. Despite the fact that the commission is not received until 2013, it is still a Schedule E emolument for 2012 i.e. the tax year in which it was **actually** earned. It should be noted that when calculating an employee's income tax liability, the credit given for PAYE paid is the PAYE deducted from emoluments paid in the tax year, regardless of the year in which the emoluments paid are taxable. Therefore, PAYE deducted from commission paid in February 2013 in respect of sales made during the tax year 2012, will be given as a credit in calculating the salesman's tax liability for 2013 even though the commission paid is taxable in 2012.

Special Treatment of Company Directors

In practice, the basis of assessing company directors under Schedule E is by reference to the amount charged in the company's audited accounts which end during the actual tax year. Additional salary voted to directors will generally be reflected by way of an amended P60.

3.5.4 Assessment in Respect of Benefits-in-Kind

"Benefits-in-kind" are defined as:

- Living or other accommodation
- Entertainment
- Domestic or other services
- Other benefits or facilities of whatever nature provided by an employer to an employee (or director) and are chargeable to income tax under Schedule E. The liability to tax also applies in respect of benefits provided by an employer for an employee's or director's spouse, family, servants, dependants or guests. In addition "perquisites", i.e. remuneration in non-money form, which are convertible into money or money's worth are also chargeable to income tax under Schedule E.

Examples of benefits-in-kind are the use of a company car, loans at a preferential rate of interest, free or subsidised accommodation.

Examples of perquisites are medical insurance premiums, payment of club subscriptions and vouchers.

3.5.5 Commencement/Inducement Payments

Payments received in connection with the commencement of an employment are **taxable**, under Schedule E, as emoluments of the new office or employment where the payment is made under the terms of a contract of service or in consideration of future services to be rendered. However, where it can be shown that the payment is **compensation** for the loss of some right or benefit as a result of taking up the new employment, the payment may not be taxable.

Inducement Payments

An employer may pay a prospective employee a lump sum in order to induce him to accept an office/other position or as compensation for giving up some valuable right as a result of accepting the position. The question as to whether the payment is taxable under Schedule E as an emolument of the new office/employment has to be decided based on the facts and the true nature of the agreement.

For example, in the UK case of *Glantre Engineering Ltd v. Goodhand (HMIT)* (1983) an inducement fee was paid by a company to a chartered accountant working for an international firm of accountants to enter into the company's services. In the case, it was held that the payment was made to obtain the accountant's services in the future and therefore taxable under Schedule E.

Payments made as compensation for, and as an inducement to, the employee to give up a personal advantage before employment is taken up are not taxable.

For example in *Pritchard v. Arundle* (1972) an allotment of shares was given by a company to persuade a chartered accountant in practice to work for the company. In this case, it was held that the fee was not in the nature of a reward for future services but an inducement to give up an established position and status and therefore not taxable under Schedule E.

In the case of *Jarrold v. Boustead* (1963), inducement payments to rugby union footballers for the permanent loss of their amateur status upon signing on as professional footballers for rugby league were held not to be taxable.

In *Riley v. Coglan* (1967), an amateur player received a signing on fee on joining a rugby league club as a professional, a proportionate part of which was refundable if he did not continue to serve the club for the period stipulated in the agreement. The payment was held to be a reward for future services and therefore liable to tax under Schedule E, distinguishing **Jarrold V. Boustead** (1963).

3.5.6 Termination Payments

Special taxation rules apply to lump sum payments made to employees after the termination of their employment. These are commonly referred to as "Golden Boots" (compensation payments) or "Golden Handshakes" (ex gratia payments).

Section 123 TCA 1997 imposes a charge to tax under Schedule E on payments made after an individual has retired or been dismissed from office. The charge covers payment to holders of offices, or employments, whether made by the employer or by a third person, and include payments to the executors or administrators of a deceased person (except as outlined in **Section 4.5.2**).

The actual date(s) of payment of the lump sum(s) is irrelevant. The legislation deems the payment to have been made **on the date of termination** of the employment. Any assessment for income tax arises in the tax year in which the employment terminated.

The charge also extends to payments made to the spouse, civil partner or any relative or dependent of a person who holds or has held an office or employment, or to any person on his behalf (except as outlined in **Section 4.5.2**).

Section 201(8) TCA 1997 introduced a life-time tax free limit on termination payments of €200,000, in respect of any payment made on or after 1 January 2011. This €200,000 limit is reduced by any exempt payment which an employee may have previously received.

Payments **in kind** are chargeable on their value at the time they are given, e.g. a present of a company car, say, at a valuation of €4,000 would be included with the termination payment. Any contribution from the employee towards the cost may be deducted.

Pay in lieu of notice which is payable under the terms of the employee's contract is taxable as normal remuneration. Pay in lieu of notice, which is not provided for under the terms of the employee's contract, is treated as a termination payment.

Holiday pay is treated as regular salary and does not form part of the termination payment.

Payments to which section 123 TCA 1997 applies come within the scope of PAYE, but relief is given under section 201 TCA 1997 with the result that tax is charged only on the **excess of the payment** over the **higher** of the following:

1. Basic Exemption;
2. Increased Exemption; or
3. Standard Capital Superannuation Benefit (SCSB).

Furthermore, the income tax liability on the **taxable portion** of the lump sum is the **lower** of the following two amounts:

1. income tax calculated on the basis of treating the taxable portion of the lump sum as additional Schedule E income for the year of assessment in which the employment ceased; *or*
2. income tax calculated on the basis of applying, to the taxable portion of the lump sum, the taxpayer's average rate of income tax for the three years of assessment immediately prior to the year of termination. This is also known as "Top Slicing Relief".

3.5.7 Retirement Lump Sum Benefits

Under certain Revenue approved pension schemes, taxpayers can receive a retirement lump sum tax free. **Section 790AA TCA 1997** states that the maximum **lifetime** retirement **tax-free lump sum** will be **€200,000** in respect of benefits taken on or after **1 January 2011**. Amounts in excess of this tax-free limit will be subject to tax in two stages. The portion between **€200,000 and €575,000** will be taxed (**under Schedule D Case IV**) at the **standard rate** of income tax in force at the time of payment, currently 20%, while any portion above that will be taxed (**under Schedule E**) at the recipient's **marginal rate of tax**.

The figure of €575,000 represents 25% of the new lower **Standard Fund Threshold** of **€2.3 million**. The standard rate charge is "ring-fenced" so that no reliefs, allowances or deductions may be set or made against that portion of a lump sum subject to that charge.

Although tax-free lump sums taken after 7 December 2005 and before 1 January 2011 are unaffected by the new rules, they will count towards "using up" the new tax-free amount. In other words, if an individual has already taken tax-free retirement lump sums of €200,000 or more since 7 December 2005, any further retirement lump sums paid to the individual on or after 1 January 2011 will be taxable. These earlier lumps sums will also count towards determining how much of a lump sum paid on or after 1 January 2011 is to be charged at the standard or marginal rate as appropriate.

Exemptions
Lump sum payments in the following circumstances are **completely exempt**:

- Any payment arising on the termination of an office or employment by the holder's death (but not payments on death after retirement).
- Any payment made on account of injury or disability.
- Lump sums received by employees on retirement under certain Revenue approved pension schemes. FA 2011 restricts this amount to a lifetime limit of €200,000 effective 1 January 2011.
- Payments to approved pension schemes.
- Certain allowances to members of the Defence Forces and under Army Pension Acts.
- Statutory redundancy payments.
- Payments to certain officers of the State as compensation for the extra cost of having to live outside the State in order to perform their duties.
- Lump sum payments made to employees under certain company restructuring schemes involving agreed pay restructuring.

3.5.8 Share Option Schemes

Share options arise when employees or directors are granted an option to acquire shares in their employer's company or its parent company, at a fixed price, at some time in the future.

The tax treatment of share options used to depend on whether they were granted under **Unapproved Share Option Schemes** or **Approved Share Option Schemes**. However, **section 10 FA 2011** has removed the income tax exemptions available for options received under Approved Share Option Schemes where the right was received on or after **24 November 2010. From 1 January 2011**, all share option schemes will be taxed as Unapproved Share Option Schemes.

(a)   Unapproved Share Option Schemes
   If the employee has been granted a share option by reason of his employment, under general Schedule E principles, a taxable emolument arises. **Section 128 TCA 1997** contains the income tax and capital gains tax rules that apply to share options granted to an employee or director on or after 6 April 1986.

   A person who realises a gain taxable by virtue of section 128 is deemed to be a **chargeable** person for self-assessment purposes for that year, unless an Inspector of Taxes has exempted him from filing a return.

Thus, a person whose income normally consists only of Schedule E salary and who pays all his tax under the PAYE system is required to file a return in accordance with the **self-assessment** system.

Short Options < Seven Years

Short options are options that must be exercised **within seven years** of being granted. Short options are charged to income tax in the year the option is **exercised** on the difference between the price paid (the option price) for the shares and the market value of the shares at the **date of exercise** (date shares acquired). Universal Social Charge (USC) and PRSI are also payable on the difference where the exercise date is on/after 1 January 2011. However, employer and employee PRSI (but excluding USC) will not apply where share-based remuneration was the subject of a written agreement entered into between the employer and employee **before** 1 January 2011.

Long Options > Seven Years

Long options are options capable of being exercised **more than seven years** after being granted. Long options are taxed:

- In the year the option was granted (on the difference between the market value of the shares at the **date of grant** and the option price) *and*
- In the year the option was exercised (as above) – but the shareholder is entitled to a **credit** for tax paid on the earlier charge on grant.

Relevant Tax on Share Options (RTSO)

- Where share options are exercised on or after 30 June 2003, the employee or director must pay **RTSO within 30 days** of the date of exercise.
- **Form RTSO1** must be completed and forwarded **with payment** to the office of the Collector General **within 30 days**.
- Tax is due at the **marginal** rate of income tax (currently 41%). Where a person's total income for the year is liable only at the standard rate of income tax, an application may be made to the Inspector of Taxes to pay at the lower rate. This must be done and the RTSO paid within 30 days of exercise.
- USC and PRSI are payable on the options effective from 1 January 2011.

Restricted Shares

If there is any restriction on the employee's ability to sell the shares acquired under an employee share option, the Revenue accept that the benefit received by the employee is less valuable. Accordingly, where there is a **genuine restriction** on the employee's ability to sell the shares, the taxable gain is reduced depending on the number of years for which the restriction will apply, as follows:

Number of Years of Restriction on Sale	% Reduction in Taxable Gain
1 year	10%
2 years	20%
3 years	30%
4 years	40%
5 years	50%
>5 years	60%

Capital Gains Tax (CGT)

A CGT charge may also arise on the disposal of the shares. The base cost for CGT is the cost of the option (if any), plus the price paid for the shares on the exercise, plus any amount charged to income tax.

(b) **Approved Share Option Schemes (ASOS)**

ASOS are schemes for which Revenue approval, in accordance with Schedule 12C TCA 1997, has been received.

Prior to 1 January 2011, under an ASOS, employees were not chargeable to income tax on the receipt of the right/option or on the gain realised by the exercise of that right/option, but were instead chargeable to CGT on the full gain (i.e. the difference between the amount paid for the shares and the sale amount received) on a disposal of the shares, provided certain criteria were met.

Section 10 FA 2011 amended Section 519D TCA 1997 to remove the income tax exemption in respect of

- the **receipt** of the right/option where the right was received on or after 24 November 2010; and
- any **gain** realised by the exercise of a right where the gain was realised on or after 24 November 2010.

Section 897 TCA 1997 states that an employer is obliged to return details of all benefits, non-cash emoluments and payments, and pension contributions provided to directors and certain employees that have not been subjected to PAYE. **Form P11D** must be returned by **31 May** of the year following the tax year.

FA 2010 (Section 897B TCA 1997) introduced a new reporting requirement making it mandatory for employers to file returns regarding shares and other securities awarded to directors and employees before **31 March** of the year following the tax year **(Form RSS1)**. It applies as and from **1 January 2010** in respect of shares awarded on or after 1 January 2009.

3.6 Schedule F

3.6.1 Income Assessable under Schedule F

Dividends and certain other distributions paid by **Irish resident** companies to individual shareholders are liable to tax under Schedule F. Dividends received by Irish resident individuals are received after the deduction of **Dividend Withholding Tax** (DWT) at the standard rate of tax. The recipient can claim an off-set for DWT against his tax liability and, where DWT exceeds his tax liability, the balance will be refunded.

Matters to be Treated as Distributions
- Dividends paid by a company including a capital dividend.
- Shares in lieu of dividends. A quoted company issues a number of shares which have a value, at the date of distribution, equal to:
  - The dividend forgone, **reduced by**
  - An amount equal to income tax at the standard rate on the amount of cash forgone.

The amount taxable in the hands of the shareholder is the full amount of the gross dividend forgone, and credit is given for the DWT.

Note: Where the distributing company is a **quoted** *(i.e. on the Stock Exchange) company, the shareholder is taxed on this distribution under* **Schedule F**. *Where the distributing company is unquoted, the shareholder is taxed under* **Case IV Schedule D**. (see **Section 3.3.1.**)

- Any distribution out of assets in respect of shares (except any part that represents a repayment of capital).
- Redemption of bonus shares and bonus debentures.

Exempt Dividend Income

Dividends paid by Irish resident companies in certain circumstances can be completely exempt from income tax in the hands of the shareholder. In the case of such dividends they are completely ignored and are not brought into the income tax computation.

The following types of dividend qualify for this exempt status:

- Dividends paid by companies from **profits arising** from the occupation of **woodlands**, managed on a commercial basis, with a view to the realisation of profits.
- Dividends paid out of **patent income**, which qualified for exemption from tax in the hands of the paying company. Shares in respect of which such dividends are paid, must satisfy some very restrictive conditions if dividends are to be exempted and, in practice, do not often arise. **Section 26 FA 2011 amended section 234 and section 141 TCA 1997 and abolished this exemption for payments made on/after 24 November 2010.**

3.6.2 Basis of Assessment

The amount assessable on the individual is the amount received **in the tax year plus DWT** (i.e. the **gross** amount of the distribution).

The date on which the dividend is **paid** determines the tax year, irrespective of the accounting year's profit out of which the dividend was declared.

Questions (Chapter 3)

(See Solutions to Questions at the end of this text.)

3   Classification of Income

3.1   Ms Lola

Ms Lola commenced trading on 1 June 2011 and makes up accounts to 31 May. Her trading results are as follows:

	€
1/6/2011–31/5/2012:	48,000
1/6/2012–31/5/2013:	39,000
1/6/2013–31/5/2014:	37,200

Requirement
Compute Ms Lola's Case I assessments for the first four years.

3.2   Mr Charlie

Mr Charlie commenced trading on 1 May 2011 and makes up accounts to 31 October.
His trading results are as follows:

	€
1/5/2011–31/10/2011:	44,800
1/11/2011–31/10/2012:	54,400
1/11/2012–31/10/2013:	53,600
1/11/2013–31/10/2014:	46,400

Requirement
Compute Mr Charlie's Case I assessments for the first three years.

3.3   Jim – Commencement

Jim commenced practice as a solicitor on 1 May 2011. Tax-adjusted profits for the opening years were as follows:

	€
1 May 2011 to 30 April 2012	48,000
Year ended 30 April 2013	60,000
Year ended 30 April 2014	9,600

Requirement

Compute Jim's Case II assessments for the first four tax years.

3.4 Donna Ross – Commencement

Donna Ross resigned from her job at AIB to sell children's clothing full time on e-bay. She provided you with the following information:

P45 showing gross pay from 1 January to cessation on 30 April 2012 of €20,300 with PAYE deducted of €3,902.

She tells you that she has traded on e-bay part time for a "few" years. She sold only household items or sale bargains picked up while shopping. She estimates that her sales were €5,000 in 2010 and her costs were minimal since the items sold were "lying about the house". She used the family computer and packed the product in her garage. In 2011, she spotted a market opportunity when she bought a job lot of designer childrens' clothes for €10,000 and sold them on e-bay individually for €20,000 in just one month! This prompted her to quit her job and start trading. Her tax-adjusted profit for the year ended 30 April 2013 was €179,400.

Donna is a 32-year-old single parent.

Requirement

Compute the income tax payable by Donna for 2012 and 2013 assuming personal tax credits of €4,950 for 2012 and €3,300 for 2013.

Advise Donna, with reasons, if her e-bay activity for 2010 and 2011 is taxable.

3.5 Cessation – Ms Dora

Ms. Dora ceases trading on 31 December 2012. She made up her accounts annually to 31 May. Her trading results were as follows:

	€
Year ended 31/5/2010:	64,000
Year ended 31/5/2011:	72,000
Year ended 31/5/2012:	9,600
Period ended 31/12/2012:	12,000

Requirement

Compute Ms Dora's Case I assessments for the last three years.

3.6 Cessation – Mr Diego

Mr Diego ceases trading on 31 May 2012. He made up his accounts annually to 31 July. His trading results were as follows:

	€
Year ended 31/7/2010:	32,000
Year ended 31/7/2011:	60,000
Period ended 31/5/2012:	40,000

Requirement

Compute Mr Diego's Case I assessments for his last three tax years.

3.7 Alex

Alex, a single man, traded for many years as a butcher. He retired on 30 September 2012 and he started work for Fagan Organic Lamb as a salesman. His tax-adjusted profits for the periods to the date of cessation were as follows:

Year ended 30/9/2011:	24,000
Year ended 30/9/2012:	240,000

His P60 for 2012 showed gross pay of €15,000 and PAYE paid of €3,485.

Requirement
Compute the income tax payable by Alex for 2012, assuming tax credits were 3,300 and advise if any changes are needed in other years.

3.8 J. Cog

J. Cog retired on 30 September 2012 from his newsagency business after trading for 40 years. His profits for the immediate years prior to cessation were:

	€
Year ended 31 October 2009:	40,000
Year ended 31 October 2010:	65,000
Year ended 31 October 2011:	64,000
11 months to 30 September 2012:	24,000

Requirement
Calculate J. Cog's assessable profits for the last four years of assessment.

3.9 AB Partnership

A and B have traded as partners sharing equally for many years. They prepare accounts each year to 30 September. On 1 October 2008 they take in C as a partner and from that date profits are shared as follows:

A - 2/5ths B - 2/5ths C - 1/5th

Tax-adjusted trading profits were as follows:

	€
Year ended 30/9/2008:	20,000
Year ended 30/9/2009:	25,000
Year ended 30/9/2010:	30,000
Year ended 30/9/2011:	30,000
Year ended 30/9/2012:	35,000

On 30/9/2012, A left the partnership and, from that date, B and C share profits and losses equally.

Requirement
Calculate the assessable profits for A, B and C for the years 2008 to 2012 inclusive.

3.10 June, Mary and Karen

June, Mary and Karen had been carrying on a business for many years sharing profits in the ratio 40:30:30. Karen retired on 30 June 2009 and was replaced by Jill. The profit sharing ratio remained unchanged.

   Louise was admitted to the partnership on 1 July 2011, from which date profits and losses were shared equally by all the partners. The partnership ceased to trade on 31 December 2012, when the business was transferred to a limited company.

   The tax-adjusted profits of the partnership were as follows:

	€
Year ended 30 June 2008:	40,000
Year ended 30 June 2009:	60,000
Year ended 30 June 2010:	54,000
Year ended 30 June 2011:	50,000
Year ended 30 June 2012:	36,000
Six months ended 31 December 2012:	20,000

Requirement
Calculate the assessable profits for the years 2009 to 2012 for all the partners.

3.11 Maeve

Maeve, who is widowed, is in receipt of the following sources of Irish income (dividend income received net of DWT in 2012):

Company	Dividend
	€
Tyson Limited	17,520
Holyfield Manufacturing Limited	1,600
	19,120
Deposit interest received net in the tax year 2012	
	€
Permanent TSB Bank	6,300
Credit Union Interest	1,200
"Long-term" account Interest	720
	8,220
Social Welfare Contributory Widows Pension	11,976

Requirement
Compute her 2012 income tax liability. Her personal tax credits are €2,190.
Assume DIRT of 30% for the full year 2012.

Computation of Taxable Income

4

Learning Objectives

In this chapter you will learn:

- how taxable income is calculated under each head of charge;
- which expenditures are permissible as a deduction in arriving at taxable income;
- the tax treatment of partnerships; and
- the tax treatment of income already subjected to tax at source.

4.1 Trade and Professional Income – Cases I and II – Schedule D

4.1.1 Introduction

A taxpayer, carrying on a trade or profession, will prepare accounts based on commercial and accounting principles, to arrive at his net profit for a particular year. However, the net profit per the accounts **is not the taxable profit**, as the Income Tax Acts (now TCA 1997) have their own set of rules for determining the taxable profit of a person carrying on a trade or profession. Accordingly, the net profit per an individual's accounts will inevitably need **adjustment** to arrive at **"Tax-adjusted"** profits for income tax purposes.

Net Profit Per Accounts

ADD/DEDUCT

Adjustment for amounts not allowable for tax purposes

EQUALS

Tax-adjusted Profits

ADD

Other Income

EQUALS

Total Income

DEDUCT

Allowances and Reliefs

EQUALS

Taxable Income

4.1.2 Allowable and Disallowable Items

There are two fundamental principles in deciding whether an item is properly included in a Profit and Loss Account when calculating a Case I or II Adjusted Profit or Loss:

1. The distinction between capital and revenue. If an item is of a **capital** nature, it must be **disallowed** in computing profits for income tax purposes.
2. Even if an item is of a **revenue** nature, it **may still** be specifically disallowed by statute as a deduction in computing trading profits.

4.1.3 Capital v. Revenue Receipts

Capital Receipts and Expenditure (including Profits and Losses) are **not assessable** under income tax as they are usually assessable under **capital gains tax**.

When deciding for tax purposes whether a receipt is capital or revenue, the following general rules apply:

Capital Receipt

The proceeds from the sale of fixed assets (i.e. assets which form part of the permanent structure of a business) is a capital receipt.

Revenue Receipt

The sale of circulating assets (i.e. assets acquired in the ordinary course of a trade and sold) is a revenue receipt.

There are five basic principles:

1. Payments for the sale of the **assets** of a business are *prima facie* **capital** receipts.
2. Payments received for the destruction of the recipient's **profit making apparatus** are receipts of a **capital** nature.
3. Payments in lieu of **trading receipts** are of a **revenue** nature.
4. Payments made in return for the imposition of substantial restrictions on the **activities** of a trader are of a **capital** nature.
5. Payments of a **recurrent** nature are **more likely** to be treated as **revenue** receipts.

Income/Gains not taxable under Cases I and II Schedule D

(a) Profits on sale of fixed assets

Profits or gains on the disposal of fixed assets or investments are **exempt** from income tax.

(b) Grants

Employment grants paid by the IDA, Enterprise Ireland, or FÁS are exempt from income tax. **Capital** grants on fixed assets (i.e. IDA grants) are exempt from income tax.

(c) Investment Income

- Irish dividends – taxable under Schedule F
- UK dividends – taxable under Case III, Schedule D
- Deposit interest received – taxable under Case IV, Schedule D.

(d) Interest on Tax Overpaid

Interest on tax overpaid is exempt from income tax.

(e) Rental Income

Rental income is taxable under Case V, Schedule D.

4.1.4 Capital v. Revenue Expenditure

Capital expenditure is **not** a deductible expense when calculating net trading profits for income tax. Where capital expenditure or capital losses (e.g. loss on sale of fixed assets) have been deducted in computing accounts profits, they will be **disallowed** when computing profits for tax purposes. However, certain allowances for wasting capital assets may be deducted after tax-adjusted Case I profits have been ascertained, i.e. **capital allowances**.

Note the judicial statement of Lord Cave in the case of *British Insulated and Helsby Cables v. Atherton (1926)*, which is frequently used by the courts to assist them to resolve the problem of whether expenditure is of a revenue nature, and therefore allowable, or of a capital nature, and therefore disallowed:

"When an expenditure is made, not only once and for all, but with a view to bringing into existence an asset or an advantage **for the enduring benefit of a trade ...** there is very good reason (in the absence of special circumstances leading to an opposite conclusion) for treating such an expenditure as properly attributed not to revenue but to capital".

4.1.5   Allowable and Disallowable Case I and II Deductions

Disallowable Deductions

The main statutory provision disallowing expenditure is **section 81 TCA 1997**. This contains specific provisions disallowing various types of expenditure, the most important of which are:

- Expenditure **not wholly and exclusively** laid out for the purposes of the trade. (This is the general deductibility test applied for Case I and Case II purposes).
- Maintenance of the parties and their families and private or domestic expenditure.
- Rent of any dwelling house **not used** for the trade.
- Any sum expended **over and above** repairs to the premises, implements, utensils or articles employed for the purposes of the trade or profession.
- Any loss not connected with the trade or profession.
- Any capital withdrawn from, or employed as, capital in the trade or profession or any capital employed in improvements to premises occupied by the trade or profession.
- Debts, other than bad debts, or a **specific** estimation of doubtful debts.
- Any annuity or other annual payment (other than interest) payable out of the profits or gains.
- Any royalty or other sum paid in respect of the use of a patent.
- Any consideration given for goods or services, or to an employee or director of a company, which consists, directly or indirectly, of shares in the company or a connected company, or a right to receive such shares.
- Any sum paid or payable under any agreement with a connected person, resident outside of the State, as compensation for an adjustment to the profits of the connected person. Transfer pricing adjustments can only be obtained under double taxation agreements or through EU Convention mechanisms.

Expenses Commonly Disallowed

1. **Expenses or losses of a capital nature:**
   - Depreciation
   - Loss on sale of fixed assets
   - Improvements to premises
   - Purchase of fixed assets.

   Note that capital allowances may be claimed on certain wasting assets.

2. **Applications or allocations of profit:**
   - Income tax
   - Transfers to a general reserve
   - Drawings.

3. **Payments from which tax is deducted:**
   - Royalties

4. **Expenses not wholly and exclusively laid out for the purposes of the business:**
   - Private element of certain expenses
   - Rental expenses (allowable against Case V rents)
   - Charitable and political donations and subscriptions

■ Life assurance premiums on the life of the taxpayer or his spouse
■ Fines and penalties.

5. General provisions

In the past, general provisions for future expenditure which had not been incurred were not allowable for tax purposes. However, in 2001 the Revenue issued a statement in which they stated that provisions made **in accordance with FRS 12** would be allowed for tax purposes **if** the following conditions were satisfied:

■ The trader has a present obligation to incur the expenditure as a result of a past action;
■ The amount of the provision required can be determined with a reasonable degree of accuracy; *and*
■ The expenditure in respect of which the provision is made, would be an allowable deduction in deducting profits, e.g. a provision for capital expenditure would not be allowable.

6. Other

(a) Bad debts

Bad debts written off – **allowable**

Bad debts recovered – **taxable**

Increase in a **specific** provision for bad debts – **allowable**

Decrease in a **specific** provision for bad debts – **taxable**

Increase in a **general** provision for bad debts – **not allowable**

Decrease in a **general** provision for bad debts – **not taxable**

(b) Premiums on short leases:

If the taxpayer carries on a trade or profession in a premises leased for a period of less than 50 years, a proportion of any premium paid on the lease is allowable in computing the profits of a trade or profession.

The amount allowable on the premium paid =

$$\text{Premium} \times \frac{51 - \text{Duration of the lease}}{50}$$

spread over the life of the lease.

Example:

On 1 June 2012 James rents a premises from Mr White for 25 years, at a rent of €2,000 per month, subject to a premium of €20,000.

Allowable premium:

$$€20,000 \times \frac{51 - 25}{50} = €10,400$$

2012:

Allowable premium (€10,400 × 1/25th × 7/12ths)	€243
Rent paid (€2,000 × 7)	€14,000

2013:

Allowable premium (€10,400 × 1/25th)	€416
Rent paid (€2,000 × 12)	€24,000

(c) Entertainment expenses:

General entertainment expenses incurred are **completely disallowed**. Expenditure on **staff** entertainment is allowable, provided its provision is not incidental to the provision of entertainment to third parties.

(d) Legal expenses regarding:

Debt recovery – allowable

Acquisition of assets – not allowable

Renewal of short lease – allowable

Product liability claims and employee actions – allowable.

(e) Repairs:

Replacement/redecoration repairs not involving material improvements are allowable.

Expenditure on improvements/extensions, new assets etc. is not allowable

As a general rule, expenditure incurred on **repairs** to buildings is deductible as a normal Case I or Case II expense. The concept of repair is that it **brings an item back to its original condition**. In this connection, the following particular points are critical:

(i) The expenditure must have **actually** been incurred. For instance, provisions for work to be done in the future are not allowable, as clearly the expenditure has not been incurred (unless the conditions outlined in relation to general provisions at (5) above are satisfied).

(ii) The term "repairs" does **not include** improvements and alterations to premises. In this connection, it is not possible to claim a revenue deduction for the portion of the improvements or alterations which would represent the cost of repairs that could otherwise have been carried out.

(iii) The replacement of a capital asset or the "entirety" will not be treated as a repair. This would cover, for instance, the reconstruction of a trader's premises.

The test to be applied is really whether or not the repair entails the **renewal** of a **component part** of the entirety. If it does, it will be regarded as a repair. On the other hand, if it is regarded as the **renewal of an entirety**, it will be treated as a capital expenditure.

A separate identifiable portion of a building or structure may be regarded as an **entirety** in its own right and, accordingly, its replacement would be disallowed. A practical test is whether or not they are of **sufficient size and importance** to be regarded as an entirety. Examples of entireties from case law include the following:

■ Replacement of a large chimney situated apart from other factory buildings.

■ A ring in an auction mart.

■ A stand in a football ground.

■ A barrier which protects a factory against the overflow from an adjoining canal.

It appears that it is necessary to show that the item which has been replaced is **ancillary** to the complete building. In practice, the accounting treatment adopted and the total cost involved may be important factors.

Repairs to newly acquired assets In *Odeon Associated Theatres Limited v. Jones* (1971) it was held that the expenditure on repairs to a newly acquired asset may be deductible provided at least that:

■ the cost is properly charged to a revenue account in accordance with the correct principles of commercial accountancy; *and*

- the repairs are not improvements; *and*
- the expenditure is not incurred to make the asset **commercially viable** on its acquisition; *and*
- the purchase price was not **substantially** less than it would have been if it had been in a proper state of repair at the time of purchase.

(f) Leased motor vehicles

Cars leased before 1 July 2008:

In the case of a leased vehicle, where the list price exceeds the limit prescribed, a proportion of the lease hire charges are disallowed.

$$\text{Lease hire charges} \times \frac{(\text{List price} - \text{relevant limit})}{\text{List price}}$$

The relevant limit is €24,000 for the period 2007 to 2012.

Cars leased on or after 1 July 2008:

FA 2008 introduced a new scheme whereby leasing charges allowances are limited by reference to the CO_2 emissions of the cars. The CO_2 categorisations and allowances are as follows:

Vehicle Category	CO_2 Emissions (CO_2g/km)	Leasing Charges Restriction
A/B/C	0g/km up to and including 155g/km	$\text{Lease hire charge} \times \dfrac{(\text{List Price} - \text{Relevant Limit})}{\text{List Price}}$
D/E	156g/km up to and including 190g/km	$\text{Lease hire charge} \times \dfrac{(\text{List Price} - (\text{Relevant Limit} \times 50\%))}{\text{List Price}}$
F/G	191g/km and upwards	Lease hire charge disallowed

Example:
Joe, who is self-employed and prepares annual accounts to 30 September, leased a car on 20 July 2011, when its retail price was €25,000. Lease charges of €6,000 are included in Joe's accounts for year-end 30 September 2012. Joe has agreed with the Inspector of Taxes that 1/3rd of the usage is private. Joe's car falls into Category D.

Lease Charges:	€6,000
Less: Private element 1/3rd	(€2,000)
Business element	€4,000

Disallowed lease payment:

$$\text{€4,000} \times \frac{(\text{€25,000} - (\text{€24,000} \times 50\%))}{\text{€25,000}} \qquad = \qquad \text{€2,080}$$

2012:
Lease charge disallowed (€2,000 + €2,080)   =   €4,080

(g) Interest on late payment of tax:

Interest on late payment of any tax (including VAT, PAYE, etc.) is not allowed in computing tax-adjusted profits.

(h) Patent fees:

Fees incurred in obtaining, for the purposes of a trade, the grant of a patent or the extension of the term of a patent are allowable.

(i) **Redundancy payments:**

Statutory redundancy payments are specifically allowable. Amounts in excess of statutory entitlements are unlikely to be deductible where a cessation of trade has taken place but would be allowed if the trade continued.

(j) **Renewal or registration of trade marks:**

Expenses on renewal or registration of trade marks are specifically allowable.

(k) **Capital payments for 'know how':**

Payments of a capital nature to acquire technical or other information for the purpose of the trade are specifically allowable as a Case I expense. There are two exceptions to this rule as follows:

- No deduction is allowed where the know how is acquired as part of the acquisition of the **whole or part** of another business.
- No deduction is allowed where the purchase of the know how is from a **connected** party, unless the acquiring company exploits it in the course of a trade.

(l) **Expenditure on scientific research:**

The full amount of any non-capital expenditure on scientific research is allowable as a deduction in computing the profits of a trade. In addition, sums paid to establishments, approved by the Minister for Finance, to carry on scientific research, and sums paid to Irish universities to enable them to carry on scientific research, are also deductible. This rule applies **whether or not** the payments are **related** to the existing trade presently being carried on.

(m) **Accountancy/taxation fees:**

Normal accounting, auditing and taxation compliance costs are allowable. **Special costs** associated with Appeal Hearings are likely to be **disallowed** following the decision of *Allen v. Farquharson Brothers*, where the costs of employing solicitors and counsel in connection with an appeal against income tax assessments were disallowed.

(n) **Pre-trading expenses:**

Under section 82 TCA 1997, an allowance **may** be claimed in respect of pre-trading expenses in the case of a trade or profession (commencing after 22 January 1997) **provided** that the expenses:

- were incurred for the purpose of the trade or profession; *and*
- were incurred within three years of commencement; *and*
- are not otherwise allowable in computing profits.

Where an allowance is granted for pre-trading expenses, it is treated as if the expenditure was incurred **on the date** on which the trade or profession **commenced**.

Examples of qualifying pre-trading expenses include accountancy fees, market research, feasibility studies, salaries, advertising, preparing business plans and rent.

These pre-trading expenses are deductible against the income of the trade. If the expenses exceed the income and there is a loss, this loss cannot be offset against other income but can only be carried forward against future income of the same trade.

(o) **Long-term unemployed**

Wages and Salaries

Revenue Job Assist allows employers to claim a **double deduction** for **wages/salaries** paid in respect of certain employees who have been unemployed for 12 months or more. It can last for a period of up to three years from the date the employment commences, provided the employee is still employed by the employer. There is no limit to the number of 'qualifying employees' the employer can take on under the scheme, provided they take up 'qualifying jobs'.

Employers PRSI

The Employer Job (PRSI) Incentive Scheme exempts employers from liability to pay Employer PRSI contributions – 8.5% or 10.75% of gross pay for certain employees. Qualifying jobs created will benefit from the exemption for 12 months from the date the employment commences. The scheme criteria are as follows:

- The employee concerned must be on the FÁS *Work Placement Programme* for at least three months or getting one of the following social welfare payments for a continuous period of at least six months:
  - Jobseeker's Benefit or Jobseeker's Allowance
  - One-parent Family Payment
  - Disability Allowance.
- The job must be full-time (at least 30 hours per week) and must be new and additional – employers will not be allowed to substitute existing employees to avail of the scheme;
- The employer will be required to furnish an up-to-date Tax Clearance Certificate;
- Employers will be limited to a maximum participation rate of 5% of their existing workforce or, for smaller companies, a maximum of five new jobs;
- The job must last for six months or more. If it does not, the PRSI exempt amounts will have to be repaid by the employer.

(p) Key-man insurance

Key-man insurance is insurance taken out by an employer in his/her own favour against the death, sickness or injury of an employee (i.e. the key-man) whose services are **vital** to the success of the employer's business.

In general, premiums paid under policies insuring against loss of profits consequent on certain contingencies **are deductible** for tax purposes in the period in which they are paid. Correspondingly, all **sums received** by an employer under such policies are treated as **trading receipts** in the period in which they are received. Key-man insurance policies qualify for this treatment where the following conditions are satisfied:

- the sole relationship is that of employer and employee;
- the employee does not have a substantial proprietary interest in the business;
- the insurance is intended to meet loss of profit resulting from the loss of the services of the employee, as distinct from the loss of goodwill or other capital loss; and
- in the case of insurance against death, the policy is a short term insurance providing only for a sum to be paid, in the event of the death of the insured, within a specified number of years. Short term generally means five years but, in practice, if all other conditions are satisfied and the policy cannot extend beyond the employee's likely period of service with the business (i.e. not beyond his term of contract or beyond retirement age), then a longer term policy will qualify.

4.1.6 Taxation Treatment Different to Accounting Treatment

Finance Leases

Assets leased under finance leases may be included as fixed assets in accounts, and interest and depreciation for such assets included in the profit and loss account.

For tax purposes, capital allowances **may not** be claimed in respect of such assets. Instead, a deduction is given for **gross lease payments** made, i.e. interest plus capital. The adjustments to be made to the accounts profit for finance lease assets are as follows:

- add back interest and depreciation charged in respect of finance lease assets; *and*
- give a deduction for gross lease payments made.

Pension Contributions

Ordinary annual contributions by an employer to a **Revenue approved** pension scheme for the benefit of his employees are **allowable** for tax purposes in the year in which they are **paid**. Thus, any **accruals** in respect of ordinary annual pension contributions due which have been included in arriving at accounts profit will have to be disallowed.

If an employer makes a **special contribution** to a Revenue approved pension scheme and the total amount of the special contributions made in the year **does not exceed** the **total ordinary annual contributions** paid in the year, relief is given for the special contributions in the year in which they are paid. If, however, the total amount of the special contributions paid **exceeds** the total ordinary annual contributions paid, relief for the special contributions made is **spread forward** over a number of years. The number of years over which relief is given is calculated by dividing the total special contributions paid by the total ordinary contributions paid. If the factor produced by this calculation is between one and two, relief is given over two years; otherwise, the factor is rounded to the nearest whole number.

Example:

An employer makes the following pension contributions in 2012:

Ordinary Annual Contribution (OAC)	€10,000
Special Contribution (SC)	€27,000

As the SC made **exceeds** the OAC, relief for the SC will be **spread forward**. The **number of years** over which relief is given is calculated as follows:

$$\frac{\text{Special Contribution}}{\text{Ordinary Annual Contribution}} = \frac{€27,000}{€10,000} = 2.7 \text{ rounded up to } 3$$

Relief for the SC will be given over **three years**. In the first two years, the amount of relief given will **equal the amount of the OAC** with the balance of the relief given in the third year. Accordingly relief for the SC of €27,000 made in 2011 will be given as follows:

Tax Year	Relief Given
2012	€10,000
2013	€10,000
2014	€ 7,000

Ordinary Annual Contribution less than €6,350

If the amount of the OAC is less than €6,350, in calculating when relief for a SC is due, the amount of the OAC may be assumed to be €6,350.

Example:

An employer makes the following pension contributions in 2012:

Ordinary Annual Contribution (OAC)	€5,000
Special Contribution (SC)	€8,000

As the OAC is less than €6,350, for the purposes of the calculation, the OAC is taken to be €6,350.

$$\frac{\text{Special Contribution}}{\text{Ordinary Annual Contribution}} = \frac{€8,000}{€6,350} = 1.26$$

As 1.26 is between one and two, relief is given over two years as follows:

Tax Year	Relief Given
2012	€6,350
2013	€1,650

4.1.7 Computation of Tax-adjusted Profits

In order to arrive at "Tax-adjusted" Case I/II trading profits, the following procedure should be adopted.

Step 1: Start with the **net profit** per the Profit and Loss Account.

Step 2: Add, to the net profit, any expenses charged in the accounts that are **not allowable deductions** for income tax purposes e.g. depreciation.

Step 3: Add any trading **income that has not been credited** in arriving at the net profit per the accounts.

Step 4: Deduct any expenses which **have not been charged** in the accounts and which the TCA 1997 allows to be deducted.

Step 5: Deduct receipts that are of a **capital nature** and those that are chargeable under **another Schedule or Case**, e.g. deposit interest, profit on sale of motor vehicle, etc.

Example:

Mr Bailey has operated a sports goods shop for ten years. The Profit and Loss Account for this business for the year ended 31 December 2012 is as follows:

Profit and Loss Account for the year ended 31 December 2012	Notes	€	€
Sales			313,759
Less:			
Cost of Sales			226,854
Gross Profit			86,905
Add:			
Deposit interest received		1,300	
Profit on sale of equipment		580	1,880
			88,785
Less Expenses:			
Wages and PRSI	1.	45,000	
Rates	2.	2,200	

(continued overleaf)

Insurance	3.	8,100	
Light and heat	2.	850	
Telephone	4.	970	
Repairs	5.	3,400	
Motor and travel expenses	6.	5,440	
General expenses	7.	4,575	
Loan interest	2.	9,000	
Bank interest and charges		3,260	
Depreciation		4,450	87,245
Net Profit for the year			€1,540

Notes to the Accounts:

1. Included in Wages are:

	€
Salary to self	20,000
Salary to wife	2,000
Own PRSI	800
Bonus to staff	2,500

2. In March 2007, Mr Bailey purchased, for €100,000, the shop premises in which the business had been carried on for the previous three years. Since 2007, the top floor, which is a self-contained flat, has been occupied free of charge by Mr Bailey's elderly father who takes no part in the business. 20% of the rates, property insurance, light and heat relate to the flat, which represents 10% of the value of the whole property.

   The loan interest relates to interest paid on a loan taken out for the purchase of the premises.

3. Analysis of Insurance Charge

	€
Shopkeepers' all-in policy	1,400
Retirement annuity premiums for self	3,000
Permanent health insurance for self	2,400
Motor car insurance	800
Property insurance	500
	8,100

4. Telephone/home expenses

   Telephone costs include Mr Bailey's home telephone and 25% of the total charge is for personal use. Mrs Bailey carries out most of her bookkeeping duties at home and a special deduction of €156 is to be allowed for costs incurred in carrying out these duties at home. This item has not been reflected in the Profit and Loss Account.

5. Included in the Repairs Charge are:

	€
Purchase of display stand	500
Repairs to shop front	600
Plumbing repairs	800

6. Analysis of Motor and Travel Expenses

   Included in the motor and travel expenses is the cost of a trip to London to a sport goods' wholesale exhibition. Mr Bailey attended the exhibition on two days and then spent a further five days visiting friends and relatives. Details of the expenses are as follows:

	€
Air fare	140
Hotel bill (for seven days)	400
Entertaining overseas exhibitor	100
	640

(continued overleaf)

The remainder of the expenses relate to Mr Bailey's motor car, which had a market value of €25,000 when first leased on 1 March 2010. It is a category C Emissions car.

	€
Lease of car	2,880
Running expenses	1,920
	4,800

His annual travel (in km) was made up of:

Personal	9,600
Business	19,200
Home to business	3,200
Total	32,000

7. Analysis of General Expenses

	€
Covenant to church (net)	405
Donation to church building fund (includes full-page advertisement in magazine – €200)	1,000
Subscriptions to trade association	350
Accountancy fee	1,100
Branded sponsorship of "open day" at local golf club	900
Entertainment – customers	520
Entertainment – staff Christmas party	300
	4,575

Computation of Case I Tax-adjusted Profits for the Year ended 31 December 2012

	Notes	€	€
Net Profit per Accounts			1,540
Add Back:			
Depreciation		4,450	
Wages and PRSI	1.	20,800	
Rates (20%)		440	
Insurance	2.	5,500	
Light and heat (20%)		170	
Loan interest (10%)		900	
Telephone (25%)		242	
Repairs	3.	500	
Motor and travel expenses	4.	2,949	
General expenses	5.	1,725	37,676
			39,216
Deduct:			
Deposit interest		1,300	
Profit on sale of equipment		580	
Mrs Bailey business telephone		156	(2,036)
Adjusted Case I Profits			**37,180**

Note 1. Wages and PRSI

	€
Salary to self	20,000
Own PRSI	800
Disallowed, as these are drawings	20,800

Note 2. Insurance

Retirement annuity premiums for self	€3,000
Permanent health insurance for self	€2,400
Property insurance (20%)	€100
Disallowed	€5,500

(continued overleaf)

The restriction in respect of the motor car insurance is included in note 4.

Note 3. Repairs
Display stand is capital expenditure – disallow

Note 4. Motor and Travel

	€
Leasing charges	2,880
Running expenses	1,920
Motor car insurance	800
Cost per accounts	5,600
Total travel (in km)	32,000
Personal mileage	(9,600)
Home to business	(3,200)
Business	19,200 km (60%)

DISALLOW:

	€
Private Element Car:	
€5,600 × 40% =	2,240

Lease restriction Car:

$$€2,880 \times 60\% = €1,728 \times \frac{(25,000 - 24,000)}{25,000} = \quad 69$$

As the car is a category C emissions car, no further restriction applies.

	€
Air fare and hotel bill (none allowable because of duality of purpose*)	540
Business entertainment	100
Motor and travel disallowed	2,949

The strict position is that because the expenditure was not incurred "wholly and exclusively" for the purpose of the trade, none of the expenditure is allowable. In practice, however, it would normally be acceptable to claim a deduction for a proportion of the total expenditure equal to the business element e.g. 2/7ths.

Note 5. General Expenses

	€
Covenant to church	405
Donation to church building fund	
(excluding magazine advertisement)	800
Entertainment – customers	520
	1,725

The sponsorship of the "open day" at the local golf club would be allowable as advertising.

4.1.8 Partnerships

Apportionment of Tax-adjusted Profits
The partnership firm will prepare an annual Profit and Loss Account, which will be the basis of a tax-adjusted profits computation. Case I and Case II rules regarding allowable and disallowable expenses are applied in arriving at the firm's tax-adjusted profits figure. The only unusual feature is that partners' **salaries/drawings/wages are not allowable** as they are an **appropriation of profit** (i.e. effectively the same as the drawings of a sole trader). Similarly, **interest paid on partners' capital accounts** is not an allowable deduction in arriving at the tax-adjusted profit.

The tax-adjusted profits of the partnership are divided among the partners in accordance with:

- the specific terms of the partnership agreement regarding **guaranteed salaries and interest on capital**; and
- the **profit-sharing ratio** that existed during the accounting period.

Example:
Smith and Jones are in partnership as engineers for many years, sharing profits 60/40. The Profit and Loss Account for this business for the year ended 30 April 2012 is as follows, after allowing for salaries and interest on capital payable to the partners under the partnership agreement:

Profit and Loss Account for the year ended 30 April 2012	Notes:	€	€
Gross Fees			200,000
Less:			
Overheads		50,000	
Salaries paid to partners	1.	41,000	
Interest paid on partners capital accounts	2.	13,000	
Rent paid to Smith for partnership premises		35,000	
Entertainment expenses		15,000	154,000
Net Profit for the year			46,000
Note 1: Salaries			
Smith		18,000	
Jones		23,000	
		41,000	
Note 2: Interest paid on Capital Accounts			
Smith		6,000	
Jones		7,000	
		13,000	

Computation of Case II Taxable Profits 2012	€	€
Net Profit per Accounts		46,000
Add Back:		
Salaries paid to partners	41,000	
Interest paid on partners capital accounts	13,000	
Disallowed entertainment expenses	15,000	69,000
Assessable Profit 2012		**115,000**

Apportionment of Assessable Profit	*Total* €	*Smith* €	*Jones* €
Salaries	41,000	18,000	23,000
Interest paid on capital accounts	13,000	6,000	7,000
Balance (apportioned 60:40)	61,000	36,600	24,400
Case II Taxable Profits 2012	**115,000**	**60,600**	**54,400**

4.2 Case III – Schedule D

4.2.1 Introduction

As outlined in **Chapter 3**, income falling under Case III is the actual income arising in the year of assessment. Income which is received gross, i.e. without the deduction of tax, is taxable on the amount that **accrues** over the year of assessment.

4.2.2   Deductions Available

As Case III income is generally pure income profit, it is not normal to have deductions when computing the amount of assessable Case III interest and dividend income.

4.2.3   Computation of Case III Income

As previously stated, interest received from the EU equivalent of a bank, building society, Credit Union or Post Office is subject to tax at the **DIRT rate** (see **Section 3.3.1**) at 20% up to 31 December 2008, 23% to 7 April 2009, 25% up to 31 December 2010, 27% for year 2011 and 30% from 1 January 2012, provided the tax due is **paid** on or before the due date for the filing of the individual's income tax return and the interest included as Case IV. All other interest income (from outside EU) is included as Case III in the income tax computation and taxed at the individual's marginal rate of tax.

Example:
Brian, who is single, is a self-employed architect. In 2012 he had Case II income of €100,000. During 2012 Brian also received interest of €1,800 from a Spanish deposit account. Brian pays his full tax liability for 2012 on or before 31 October 2013 (the due date for the filing of his 2012 income tax return). His tax credits were €1,650.

Income Tax Computation 2012

Income:	€	€
Adjusted Case II income	100,000	
Case IV income	1,800	
Taxable Income		101,800
Tax Calculation:		
€32,800 @ 20% =	6,560	
€1,800 @ 30%	540	
€67,200 @ 41% =	27,552	34,652
Less:		
Personal Tax Credit		(1,650)
Tax payable 2012		**33,002**

If the interest received by Brian had been in respect of a deposit account with a bank in the Cayman Islands (i.e. **outside the EU**), or if he had not paid his income tax liability for 2012 on or before 31 October 2013, the tax payable for 2012 would be as follows:

Income Tax Computation 2012

Income:	€	€
Adjusted Case II income	100,000	
Case III income	1,800	
Taxable Income		101,800

Tax Calculation:			
	€32,800 @ 20% =	6,560	
Balance	= €69,000 @ 41% =	28,290	
	€101,800		34,850
Less:			
Personal Tax Credit			(1,650)
Tax payable 2012			**3,200**

An additional €198 would be payable, being the difference between tax at the deposite interest income rate of 30% and tax at the higher rate on the deposit interest received, i.e. €1,800 × (41% –30%) = €198.

4.3   Case IV – Schedule D

4.3.1   Introduction

As outlined in **Chapter 3**, income falling under Case IV is the **actual** income received in the year of assessment. Income is therefore generally taxed on a **receipts** basis.

4.3.2   Special Treatment of Income Subject to DIRT

Deposit interest from Republic of Ireland banks, building societies and credit unions, where the interest is paid or credited to ordinary deposit accounts on an annual or more frequent basis, is subject to Deposit Interest Retention Tax (DIRT) at a rate of 30% (from 1 January 2012). Any other deposit account, opened after 23 March 2000, where the interest is credited at intervals exceeding 12 months, e.g. a fixed term deposit account for say two years with interest payable on maturity, is subject to DIRT at the rate above plus 3%, i.e. 33% for the tax year 2012.

How to include DIRT Income in the Income Tax computation:

Step 1:   Gross up the net interest received by dividing by 0.70 (i.e. 1 minus the 30% rate)

Step 2:   Add a new rate band for Case IV Interest income @ 30% for the amount of the gross interest.

Step 3:   Include the DIRT credit (i.e. 30% of gross interest) as a non-refundable tax credit.

Example:
Joe, who is single, is employed by a local supermarket. His gross salary for the tax year 2012 was €36,000 (PAYE €4,572) and he received net interest on his AIB Deposit Account of €750. This was subject to DIRT at 30%. His tax credits for 2012 are the personal tax credit of €1,650 and the employee tax credit of €1,650.

Income Tax Computation of Joe for 2012

Income:		€	€
Schedule D Case IV:			
AIB (€750 × 100/70)		1,071	
Schedule E		36,000	
Total Taxable Income			37,071
Tax Calculation:			
€1,071	@ 30% =	321	
€32,800	@ 20% =	6,560	
€3,200	@ 41% =	1,312	
€37,071			8,193
Less: Non Refundable Tax Credits:			
Basic personal tax credit		1,650	
Employee tax credit		1,650	
DIRT paid (€1,071 @ 30%)		321	(3,621)
Tax Liability			4,572
Deduct: PAYE paid			(4,572)
Net Tax Due			**NIL**

4.3.3 Deductions Available

Income tax legislation gives no guidance as to what expenses are deductible in computing Case IV profits. However, in practice, the general rule is that any expenses incurred in earning the Case IV income will be treated as allowable deductions.

4.3.4 Case IV Losses

Case IV losses may be set against Case IV profits of **the same year** of assessment or, alternatively, set against Case IV profits of **subsequent** years.

4.3.5 Computation of Case IV profits

Example 1:
John and Brigid Murphy had the following income for 2012:

John Murphy	€
Salary (gross)	50,000
PAYE deducted	(10,312)
Bank ordinary deposit interest (net)	2,336
Credit Union interest	
– Deposit account (net)	176
– Medium term share account	295
Brigid Murphy	
Salary (gross)	32,000
PAYE deducted	(3,100)
Bank interest received	
– Ordinary deposit account (net)	190
– Long term account	785
Their non-refundable tax credits are:	
– Married couple tax credit	3,300
– Employee tax credits – €1,650 × 2	3,300

Income Tax Computation 2012

Income:	€	€
Schedule D Case IV:		
– John Murphy (note 1)	3,589	
– Brigid Murphy (note 2)	<u>271</u>	3,860
Schedule E		
– John Murphy	50,000	
– Brigid Murphy	<u>32,000</u>	<u>82,000</u>
Total Taxable Income		**85,860**

Tax Calculation:			
€3,860	@ 30%	1,158	
€65,600	@ 20%	13,120	
<u>€16,400</u>	@ 41%	<u>6,724</u>	21,002
€85,860			

(continued overleaf)

	€	€
Less: Non Refundable Tax Credits:		
Married couple tax credits	3,300	
Employee tax credits	3,300	
DIRT paid (€3,860 @ 30%)	<u>1,158</u>	<u>(7,758)</u>
Tax Liability		13,244
Deduct: PAYE paid		
– John Murphy	10,312	
– Brigid Murphy	<u>3,100</u>	<u>13,412</u>
Tax Refund Due		<u>**(168)**</u>

Note 1:
John Murphy

Bank ordinary deposit interest (net)	2,336
Credit Union interest	
– Deposit account (net)	176
– Medium term share account*	<u>Nil</u>
Interest net	2,512
Interest gross (€2,512 × 100/70)	**€3,589**

Note 2:
Brigid Murphy

Bank ordinary deposit interest (net)	190
– Long term account*	<u>Nil</u>
Interest net	190
Interest gross (€190 × 100/70)	**€271**

* Medium term share account interest is exempt as it is less than €480. Although Brigid pays DIRT on the excess of her long term share account, this amount should not be included in the income tax computation either.

Example 2:

Mary Byrne is a widow aged 66 who has been incapacitated for a number of years. Her son Peter has executed an annual covenant of €5,000 in her favour. Her only other source of income is her pension of €25,000 (PAYE €1,500). Her personal tax credits for 2012 are €2,435 and her employee tax credit is €1,650.

Mary Byrne - Income Tax Computation 2012	€	€
Income:		
Case IV Schedule D (gross covenant income)	5,000	
Schedule E – pension	<u>25,000</u>	
Total/Taxable Income		<u>**30,000**</u>
Tax Calculation:		
€30,000 @ 20% =	<u>6,000</u>	
Tax Liability		6,000
Less: Non Refundable Tax Credits		
Personal tax credits	2,435	
Employee tax credit	<u>1,650</u>	(4,085)
Less: Refundable Tax Credits		
Tax deducted by Peter on payment of covenant	1,000	
PAYE paid	<u>1,500</u>	(2,500)
Tax Refund due		<u>**(585)**</u>

4.4 Rental Income Case V – Schedule D

4.4.1 Introduction

As outlined in **Chapter 3**, income taxable under Case V is the Irish rental income **receivable** in the year of assessment.

4.4.2 Premiums on Short Leases

Prior to the passing of FA 1963, it was possible for a landlord to avoid being taxed on income from let property by letting the property at a large "once-off" premium in the first year and charging a nominal rent thereafter. The "once-off" premium was treated as a capital receipt and was not within the charge to income tax. FA 1963 introduced legislation so that a certain proportion of a premium on a "short lease" is taxable under Case V. The 1963 legislation is now embodied in **section 98 TCA 1997**.

Calculation of Taxable Portion of Premium

Where a landlord receives a premium on the creation of a "short lease" (i.e. the duration of the lease does not exceed 50 years), he will be treated as receiving an amount **by way of rent** (in addition to any actual rent) as computed by the following formula:

$$\text{Premium} \times \frac{51 - \text{Duration of the lease}}{50}$$

Example:
On 1 June 2012 Mr White rents a premises to Mr Blake for 25 years, at a rent of €2,000 per month, subject to a premium of €20,000.

Taxable portion of Premium:

$$€20{,}000 \times \frac{51 - 25}{50} = €10{,}400$$

Case V assessable 2012:	€
Taxable portion of premium	10,400
Rent receivable (€2,000 × 7)	14,000
Total assessable	**24,400**
Case V Assessable 2013:	
Rent receivable (€2,000 × 12)	**24,000**

4.4.3 Allowable Deductions

The following amounts may be deducted from the gross rents receivable (**section 97 TCA 1997**):

- Rent payable on the property (e.g. ground rent).
- Rates payable on the property (e.g. water rates, refuse, etc.).
- The cost of goods or services which the landlord is obliged to provide and for which he receives no separate consideration (e.g. gas, electricity, waste disposal).
- Cost of repairs, excluding improvements and items treated as capital expenditure.
- Cost of insurance, maintenance and management of the property.

■ Loan interest (following a change in FA 2009, with effect from 7 April 2009, only 75% of the loan interest on a residential property is allowable) on money borrowed for the purchase, improvement or repairs to the property, but interest charges incurred prior to the first letting are not deductible.

Where, on or after 6 February 2003, interest accrues on a loan taken out to acquire a residential premises from a spouse, such interest is not deductible. In this context "spouse" does not include a legally separated or divorced spouse.

For the tax years 2006 onwards, a deduction for loan interest will **not be allowed** unless the landlord **registers all tenancies** that exist in relation to that property with the **Private Residential Tenancies Board (PRTB)**, in accordance with the **Residential Tenancies Act 2004**.

■ Accountancy fees incurred in drawing up rental accounts and keeping rental records.
■ Mortgage protection and life assurance policy premiums paid on or after 1 January 2002.
■ Wear and tear allowances may be claimed on the cost of fixtures and fittings for furnished lettings. The rates are as follows:

Expenditure Incurred	Wear & Tear Rate	Basis
Pre 1/Jan/01	15%	Straight Line
1/Jan/01 to 3/Dec/02	20%	Straight Line
4/Dec/02 onwards	12.5%	Straight Line

Allowable expenses are normally deducted on an **accruals basis** rather than on a paid basis. In order to be deductible, the expense must be incurred **wholly and exclusively** for the purpose of earning the rent and must be **revenue** rather than **capital** in nature. Expenses incurred in respect of a property **before** the first lease commences in respect of that property (other than legal and advertising expenses) are **not deductible**. In the case of interest and rent, **no deduction** is allowed for either interest or rent payable in respect of a period before the property is first **occupied** by a lessee.

Non Principal Private Residence Charges (NPPR) and Household Charge payable to local authorities are not allowable as a deduction against Case V income.

Expenses incurred **after** the termination of a lease are not deductible. However, expenses incurred **after** the termination of one lease **and before** the commencement of another lease in respect of the property are deductible provided the following three conditions are satisfied:

1. The expenses would **otherwise** be deductible;
2. The person who was the lessor of the property **does not occupy** the premises during the period when the property is **not let;** and
3. The property is let by the **same lessor** at the end of the period.

4.4.4 Rent-a-Room

Where an individual rents out a room (or rooms) in a "qualifying residence" and the gross income received (including sums arising for food, laundry or similar goods and services) **does not exceed €10,000 per annum**, this income will be **exempt** from income tax. It is also not liable to PRSI or USC but it must be included in an individual's income tax return. In determining whether the limit has been exceeded for the tax year, no deductions for expenses incurred are made. Where the income **exceeds €10,000**, the **entire** amount is taxable.

A "qualifying residence" is a residential premises situated in the State which is occupied by the individual as his or her sole or main residence during the year of assessment.

Room rentals under this scheme **will not affect**:

- mortgage interest relief available to the individual who qualifies for relief; or
- principal private residence relief for CGT purposes on the disposal of the house.

Where the room or rooms are rented out by more than one individual, the €10,000 limit is divided **between** the individuals.

An individual may, if they wish, elect to have any income/losses from this source assessed under the normal rules for rental income (e.g. if there is a rental loss on the room).

Exclusions:

Rent-a-room exemption will not apply where:

1. the room is rented to a child of the individual or the civil partner of the individual renting the rooms **(FA 2012); or**
2. where the individual receiving the rent (or a person connected to them) is an office holder or employee of the person making the payment (or someone connected to them) **(section 216A TCA 1997).**

4.4.5 Rents Paid to Non-residents

Rents paid to a non-resident person must be paid under **deduction of tax** at the standard rate (currently 20%), and the tax paid over to the Revenue Commissioners. Failure to deduct tax leaves the tenant liable for the tax that should have been deducted.

4.4.6 Case V Losses

Case V losses incurred in a year of assessment can be carried forward **indefinitely** and used against **future** Case V profits. Unutilised Case V losses may **not be set off** against any other type of income. A net profit or loss is computed for each property **separately** for the particular tax year. The profits/losses are then aggregated to arrive at the total profit/loss for the tax year.

Section 384 TCA 1997 provides that Case V capital allowances arising in a year are to be deducted against Case V income arising in that year **in priority** to Case V losses that are brought forward from a prior year.

If a property is let otherwise than on an arm's length basis and the rent receivable is insufficient to cover expenses, any loss arising is to be carried forward until the property is re-let on a commercial basis. Tax relief is therefore not available for those losses against rental profits from other properties.

4.4.7 Computation of Case V Income

Example:
John Black has owned rental properties for several years. You are given the following information about the properties owned during the tax year 2012.

(continued overleaf)

Property A

	€
Rent receivable	40,000
Expenditure incurred:	
Insurance (for all of 2012)	1,200
Repairs (incurred December 2012)	400
Interest on loan to acquire the property	36,000

This property is let on a 10-year lease which commenced on 1 April 2012. A premium of €20,000 was payable on commencement of the lease. The property was acquired on 1 January 2012 for €450,000 with a bank loan taken out on the same date. This is a commercial property.

Property B

	€
Rent receivable	9,600
Expenditure incurred:	
Insurance	280
Painting exterior	740
Repairs to door and alarm following burglary	1,250
NPPR	200

Property B is a residential property which was let at €800 per month on a two-year lease which commenced on 1 January 2011. The tenant left suddenly in December 2012 leaving rent owing for the month of November and December. Mr Black subsequently found out that the tenant had emigrated to Australia and has written off the rent owing as a bad debt. The property was re-let to another tenant in February 2013.

Property C

	€
Rent receivable	6,000
Expenditure incurred:	
Insurance	500
Construction of conservatory (May 2012)	12,400
Interest	15,000
NPPR	200

Property C had been let until 30 November 2011 at €1,000 a month. It was vacant until re-let on a one year lease from 1 September 2012 at €1,500 a month. This is a residential property.

Property D

	€
Rent receivable	30,000
Expenditure Incurred:	
Interest	25,000

Mr Black acquired property D from his wife in 2006 for €450,000. Mrs Black had inherited the house from her mother in 2006. Mrs Black used funds from the sale of property D to Mr Black towards the cost of a new house purchased by Mr and Mrs Black as their principal private residence.

Case V **Assessment 2012**	Notes:	Prop. A €	Prop. B €	Prop. C €	Prop. D €
Rent received/receivable	**1.**	40,000	8,000	6,000	30,000
Income element of premium	**2.**	16,400	0	0	0
Gross rent		56,400	8,000	6,000	30,000
Deduct:					
Insurance	**3.**	900	280	500	0

(continued overleaf)

NPPR	5.		0	0	
Repairs/painting		400	1,990	0	0
Loan interest	4.	27,000	0	11,250	0
Total deductions		28,300	2,270	11,750	0
Net profit/(loss)		28,100	5,730	(5,750)	30,000

Case V Assessable 2012

Total €58,080

Note 1

Property B	€
Rent receivable	9,600
Less amount written off as bad	(1,600)
Total rent	8,000

Note 2

Property A

Taxable portion of premium: $€20,000 \times \dfrac{51 - 10}{50} = €16,400$

Note 3

Property A

Expenses incurred before first letting are disallowed (3/12ths)

Insurance allowed $€1,200 \times 9/12\text{ths} = €900$

Note 4

Property A

Expenses incurred before first letting are disallowed (3/12ths)

Loan interest allowed $€36,000 \times 9/12\text{ths} = €27,000$
Commercial – no 75% restriction,

Property C

Interest incurred between lettings is allowable.However as it is a residential property, interest after 7/4/2009 is restricted to 75% of the amount charged.

$€15,000 \times 75\% = €11,250$

Property D

Interest incurred after 6/2/2003 not allowable, as property was acquired from wife.

Note 5

Non-principal Private Residence (NPPR) charge is not allowable.

4.5 Employment Income – Schedule E

4.5.1 Introduction

As already outlined in **Chapter 3**, income from all offices and employments, pensions and annuities, benefits-in-kind and perquisites, and certain lump sum payments, deriving from an office or employment is assessable to income tax under Schedule E in respect of the actual income of the year of assessment.

4.5.2 Treatment of Termination Payments

Payments to which this Section applies come within the scope of PAYE, but relief is given under section 201 TCA 1997 where tax is charged only on the **excess of the payment** over the **higher** of the:

1. Basic Exemption;
2. Increased Exemption; *or*
3. Standard Capital Superannuation Benefit (SCSB).

Basic Exemption
Section 201 TCA 1997 provides relief in the form of a **basic exemption of €10,160 plus €765 for each complete year of service** in the computation of the taxable portion of the lump sum received.

Increased Exemption
Schedule 3 TCA 1997 provides for an **increase in the basic exemption** by an **additional €10,000** where the taxpayer claiming relief has not lodged a claim for relief from taxation in respect of a lump sum payment received on the termination of an office or employment in the previous 10 years.

If, under a Revenue approved superannuation scheme, the taxpayer receives or is entitled to receive a tax free pension lump sum, then the **additional exemption** is **reduced** by the amount of the pension lump sum up to a maximum of €10,000.

Advance permission must be obtained from Revenue in order to pay an amount tax free equivalent to the increased exemption.

Standard Capital Superannuation Benefit (SCSB)
A relief, known as the Standard Capital Superannuation Benefit (SCSB), may be deducted in computing the amount chargeable to income tax if it is **greater** than the basic exemption.

It is calculated as follows:

$$\frac{\text{Last Three Years Remuneration}}{\text{Three}} \times \frac{\text{No. of Complete Years of Service}}{15 \text{ Years}}$$

Note:
1. Last three years remuneration is to the **date of the termination of the office** or employment i.e. not the remuneration for the last three tax years.
2. Where the period of employment was **less than three years**, the amount of the last three years remuneration is replaced by the **full remuneration** earned by an individual throughout the period of employment, and the average figure is computed based on that lesser period.
3. The SCSB calculated under the above formula **must be reduced** by any **tax-free lump sum received or receivable** under a Revenue approved Pension Scheme (excluding refunds of personal contributions by the employee to such a scheme).
4. Only **full years** of service are taken into account, e.g. if an individual was employed for 10.5 years, only 10 years is used for the purpose of the fraction.
5. The definition of a tax-free lump sum received or receivable under a Revenue approved pension scheme includes the **actuarial value** of any **future** lump sum which may be received from the pension scheme. This applies both for the increased basic exemption and for the SCSB.

Lifetime Tax-Free Limit

Section 8 FA 2011 amended **section 201 TCA 1997** to introduce a new **lifetime** aggregate tax-free limit of **€200,000** in respect of payments made on/after **1 January 2011**. However the amendment also provides that the €200,000 limit will be reduced by the aggregate of any **prior** tax-free payments (including Basic Exemption and SCSB deductions) which have been received, thus ensuring that the maximum lifetime tax-free termination payment cannot exceed €200,000.

Top Slicing Relief

A refundable tax credit, known as "Top Slicing Relief", can reduce the income tax liability on the **taxable portion** of the lump sum. It is calculated as follows:

$$A - \left(P \times \frac{T}{I}\right)$$

where,

A = the tax due on the lump sum if taxed in the normal manner;
P = the **taxable** portion of the lump sum payment;
T = the total **income tax payable** for the previous three years of assessment; and
I = **taxable income** for the previous three years of assessment.

Example:

James Smith was an employee of Games Ltd. for 30.5 years. He was made redundant by the company on 30 September 2012 and received €90,000 as a termination payment. Mr Smith is married and his spouse has no income. His credits include the married credit of €3,300 and the employee credit of €1,650.

His salary from 1/1/2012 to date of redundancy 30/9/2012 was €45,750 gross (PAYE paid €5,030). His previous three years taxable income and tax liabilities were:

	2011 €	2010 €	2009 €
Taxable Income	42,000	40,000	38,000
Tax liability	5,400	4,820	4,100

Mr Smith's last three years remuneration as an employee was;

Y/E 30/9/2012	€52,250
Y/E 30/9/2011	€48,000
Y/E 30/9/2010	€39,500

Mr Smith has never received a termination payment before and will be entitled to a tax-free lump sum of €8,000 from an approved superannuation fund.

Basic Exemption Calculation: €

Basic exemption:			10,160
Years of service:	30 × €765	=	22,950
			33,110
Increase in basic exemption:		10,000	
Less: tax free pension lump sum		(8,000)	2,000
Total basic exemption			**35,110**

(continued overleaf)

SCSB Calculation:

$$\frac{€52,250 + €48,000 + €39,500}{3} \times \frac{30 \text{ Years}}{15 \text{ Years}}$$

$$€46,583 \times \frac{30}{15} \qquad = \qquad 93,167$$

Less: tax free pension lump sum	(8,000)
Total SCSB	**85,167**

The SCSB deduction is taken as it exceeds the increased basic exemption of €35,110 which would otherwise be available in this case.

James Smith
Income Tax Computation 2012

	Notes:	€	€
Schedule E:			
Salary			45,750
Termination payment		90,000	
Less: SCSB		85,167	4,833
Taxable Income			**50,583**
Tax (Married couple-one income):			
41,800 @ 20%		8,360	
8,783 @ 41%		3,601	11,961
Less Tax Credits:			
Basic personal tax credit		3,300	
Employee tax credit		1,650	(4,950)
Net Tax liability			7,011
Less:			
PAYE paid		5,030	
Top slicing relief	1.	1,405	(6,435)
Tax due			**576**

Note 1:
Top Slicing Relief:

$$A - \left(\frac{P \times T}{I}\right)$$

A = Tax due on taxable portion of the lump sum = €4,833 @ 41%	€1,982
P = Taxable portion of lump sum = (€90,000−€85,167)	€4,833
T = Tax payable for the previous three years (€5,400 + €4,820 + €4,100)	€14,320
I = Taxable income for previous three years (€42,000 + €40,000 + €38,000)	€120,000

$$€1,982 - \left(€4,833 \times \frac{€14,320}{€120,000}\right) = €1,405$$

4.5.3 Treatment of Retirement Lump Sum Benefits

Under certain Revenue-approved pension schemes, taxpayers can receive a retirement lump sum tax free. **Section 790A TCA 1997** states that the maximum **lifetime** retirement **tax-free lump sum** will be **€200,000** in respect of benefits taken **on or after 1 January 2011**. Amounts in excess of this tax-free limit will be subject to tax in two stages. The portion between **€200,000 and €575,000** will be taxed (**under Case IV Schedule D**) at the **standard rate** of income tax in force at the time of payment, while any portion above that will be taxed (**under Schedule E**) at the recipient's **marginal rate of tax**.

The figure of €575,000 represents 25% of the new lower **Standard Fund Threshold** of **€2.3 million**. The standard rate charge is "ring-fenced" so that no reliefs, allowances or deductions may be set or made against that portion of a lump sum subject to that charge.

Although tax-free lump sums taken after 7 December 2005 and before 1 January 2011 are unaffected by the new rules, they will **count towards** "using up" the new tax-free amount. In other words, if an individual has already taken tax-free retirement lump sums of €200,000 or more since 7 December 2005, any further retirement lump sums paid to the individual on or after 1 January 2011 will be taxable. These earlier lumps sums will also count towards determining how much of a lump sum paid on or after 1 January 2011 is to be charged at the standard or marginal rate as appropriate.

Example 1:
John Bartlett retired in January 2012 and was paid a retirement lump sum of €800,000 on 31 January 2012. This is the first such lump sum he has received. He is charged to tax as follows:
- the first €200,000 is exempt;
- the next €375,000 is taxed at the standard rate for 2012; and
- the balance, i.e. €225,000, is taxed at his marginal rate for 2012.

If John receives any future retirement lump sum, it will be subject to tax at his marginal rate in the year it is paid.

Example 2:
David Murphy is paid a retirement lump sum on 1 July 2012 of €400,000. He had previously received a retirement lump sum of €220,000 on 1 January 2007. The earlier lump sum has "used up" David's entire tax-free limit of €200,000 so that all of the lump sum taken on 1 July is taxable. Even though the earlier lump sum is not taxable, it affects the rate of tax applying to the later lump sum. David is charged to tax on the following:

	€
Lump sum received 1 January 2007	220,000
Lump sum received 1 July 2012	400,000
Total received	620,000

The earlier lump sum has "used up" the €200,000 tax free limit, and €20,000 of the €375,000 is taxable at the standard rate.

Lump sum taxable:

	€
At the standard rate – Case IV Schedule D	375,000
Less: amount "used up" in earlier lump sum	(20,000)
Taxable at standard rate	**355,000**
Taxable at marginal rate – Schedule E:	
Lump sum	400,000
Less: amount taxable at standard rate	(355,000)
Taxable at the marginal rate	**45,000**

Note that the amount taxable is only the total of the lump sum received in 2012.

4.5.4 Valuation of Share Option Benefits

Share options arise when employees or directors are granted an option to acquire shares in their employer's company or its parent company, at a fixed price, at some time in the future.

The tax treatment of share options used to depend on whether they were granted under Unapproved Share Option Schemes or Approved Share Option Schemes. However, section 519D TCA 1997 removed the income tax exemption available for options received under Approved Share Option Schemes where the right was received on or after 24 November 2010. From 1 January 2011, all share option schemes are taxed as Unapproved Share Option Schemes.

Unapproved Share Option Schemes

1. **Short Options < Seven Years**

   Income tax, PRSI and USC are charged on the difference between the option price paid and the market value of the shares at the **date of exercise**.

Example:

On 1 June 2006 James Doyle was granted an option, by reason of his employment, to acquire 5,000 shares in LoCo Ltd. at €2 per share. The option must be exercised before 1 June 2012. No consideration was paid for the granting of the share option. James exercises his option on 1 May 2012 and acquires 5,000 shares at €2 each. The market values of the shares at the relevant dates are as follows:

		€
	1 June 2006	12,500 (5,000 × €2.50)
	1 May 2012	17,500 (5,000 × €3.50)

Taxable Gain 2012:	€
Market value of the shares on 1 May 2012	17,500
Less: Option price paid (5,000 × €2)	(10,000)
Gain	7,500

This gain is chargeable to tax, PRSI and USC under Schedule E in 2012. No taxable gain arises in the year of grant of the option even though the option price was less than the market price of the shares at that date.

---

2. **Long Options > Seven Years**

   Income tax is charged on the difference between the market value of the shares at the **date of grant** and the option price, **and** on the difference between the option price paid and the market value of the shares at the **date of exercise**. The shareholder is entitled to a credit for tax paid on the earlier charge on grant.

Example:

On 1 June 2006, James Doyle was granted an option, by reason of his employment, to acquire 5,000 shares in LoCo Ltd. at €2 per share. James has until 1 June 2015 to exercise this option. No consideration was paid for the granting of the share option. James exercises his option on 1 May 2012 and acquires 5,000 shares at €2 each. The market values of the shares at the relevant dates are as follows:

	€
1 June 2006	12,500 (5,000 × €2.50)
1 May 2012	17,500 (5,000 × €3.50)

Paul paid income tax at the marginal rate (42%) in 2006, and at 41% in 2012.

(continued overleaf)

	€
Income Tax Gain 2006:	
Market value of the shares on 1 June 2006	12,500
Less: Option price	(10,000)
Gain	2,500
Income Tax Gain 2012:	
Market value of the shares on 1 May 2011	17,500
Less: Option price paid	(10,000)
Gain	7,500
Taxable @ 41%	3,075
Less: Tax paid in 2006	(1,050)
Tax payable 2012	2,025
Income tax on each gain is payable within 30 days.	

4.5.5   Valuation of Benefits-in-Kind

General Rule

Except where there are **specific statutory valuation rules**, the amount of the taxable benefit ("notional pay") liable to PAYE, PRSI and USC is:

A.   For **benefits-in-kind**, the higher of:
1.   the cost to the employer of providing the benefit, *or*
2.   the value realisable by the employee for the benefit in money or money's worth,
   Less: any amount made good/refunded to the employer by the employee.

B.   For **perquisites**, which are benefits readily converted into cash (e.g. vouchers), the amount assessable is the amount the employee can realise, on conversion, rather than the cost of providing the perquisite.

   It is the employer's responsibility to calculate the value of the benefit and collect the PAYE, PRSI and USC due thereon through the payroll when the benefit is given.

Specific Statutory Valuation Rules

Specific statutory valuation rules must be used to determine the taxable value in relation to the following benefits:

1.   The transfer of ownership of property,
2.   The free use of property without transfer of ownership,
3.   The provision of living or other accommodation,
4.   The provision of cars, vans and bicycles, and
5.   The provision of preferential loans

1.   Transfer of Ownership of Property

Where the employer gives an asset to the employee/director that the employer has previously used, the **market value of the asset at the date it is transferred** to the employee/director is taken to be the benefit-in-kind (BIK).

   If, on the other hand, the asset is purchased by the employer and not used before being given to the employee, then the **cost to the employer** will be the BIK.

2.   The Free Use of Property without Transfer of Ownership

If an asset of the employer (excluding accommodation) is available for use by the employee personally, the benefit to be assessed on the employee must include the annual value of the use of the asset in addition to any day to day outgoings connected with the asset. With effect from 1 January 2004, where an employer provides an asset (other than premises, land or motor vehicles) for use by an employee, the annual value of the use of the asset is deemed to be **5% of the market value** of the asset at the date the asset was first provided by the employer. If, however, the employer pays an annual rent or hire charge in respect of the asset and the amount paid by the employer exceeds 5% of the market value of the asset, that amount is the taxable benefit.

Example:
On 1 May 2012, an employer acquired an antique dining room table and chairs for €15,000 for an employee's house. The table and chairs remain in the ownership of the employer.

Tax Year	Calculation		Taxable Benefit
2012	(€15,000 × 5%)	× 8/12ths	€500
2013	€15,000 × 5%		€750

Where an employer provides an employee with the use of an asset which has been used or depreciated since the employer acquired it, the annual value of the use of the asset is deemed to be 5% of the market value of the asset when first provided to any employee.

Example:
An employer acquired a dining room table and chairs for €20,000 in 2006 which were used in the employer's premises for entertaining clients. On 1 July 2012, the table and chairs, which were then valued at €12,000, were given to an employee for use in his own home. The table and chairs remain in the ownership of the employer.

Tax Year	Calculation		Taxable Benefit
2012	(€12,000 × 5%)	× 6/12ths	€300
2013	€12,000 × 5%		€600

---

3. Provision of Living or Other Accommodation

Where accommodation is owned and provided by the employer for use by an employee, the value of the benefit to the employee is the aggregate of:

- The annual value of the premises (including land) and
- Any outgoings (excluding the cost of acquisition) incurred by the employer in connection with the provision of the accommodation.

The **annual value** is the annual rent which the employer might reasonably expect to obtain if the property were rented on an arm's length basis, and on the basis that tenant undertook to pay the usual tenant expenses and the landlord undertook to bear the cost of repairs, insurance and other expenses necessary to maintain the premises in a state to command that rent.

Generally, Revenue will apply a rule of thumb of **8% of the market value** of the accommodation supplied as being the annual letting value. However, where a vouched lower figure is available (e.g. an auctioneer's estimate), this may be used for the annual letting value.

Example:

Harry, who earns €25,000 per annum, is supplied with a company apartment by his employer. The apartment originally cost €60,000 and its current market value is €120,000. His employer pays the following expenses in relation to the upkeep of the apartment:

	€
Insurance	600
Housekeeping supplies	1,500
Management charge	900
Heating and light	1,100
	4,100

The BIK assessable on Harry would be as follows:

	€
Annual letting value: 8% × €120,000 (market value)	9,600
Add: expenses paid by the employer on behalf of Harry	4,100
Schedule E BIK	13,700

€13,700 would be added to Harry's other Schedule E income in arriving at his total tax liability.

If Harry was obliged to contribute, say, €1,500 annually to his employer, in consideration for the accommodation being put at his disposal, this would be deducted from the benefit-in-kind of €13,700 in arriving at the net benefit assessable on him of €12,200.

Exemptions

A taxable benefit will **not** arise where an employee (excluding directors) is **required**, by the terms of his employment, to live in accommodation provided by the employer in part of the employer's business premises, so that the employee can properly perform his duties ("better performance" test) and either:

- the accommodation is provided in accordance with a practice which, since before 30 July 1948, has commonly prevailed in trades of the class in question as respects employees of the class in question; *or*
- it is necessary, in the case of trades of the class in question, that employees should reside on the premises.

In practice, it is accepted that the "better performance" test is met where:

- the employee is required to be on call outside normal hours; *and*
- the employee is in fact frequently called out; *and*
- the accommodation is provided so that the employee may have quick access to the place of employment.

Examples of such employees include: a Garda, who has to reside at the station in a country village; chaplains and governors in prisons; managers or night care staff in residential or respite centres; caretakers living on the premises.

4.   Provision of Cars and Vans

(a)   Company Cars

Where a car is available for the **private** use of an employee, the employee is chargeable to PAYE, PRSI and USC in respect of that use.

A "car" means any mechanically propelled road vehicle designed, constructed or adapted for the carriage of the driver, or the driver and one or more other persons and **excludes**:

- A motor-cycle (i.e. a vehicle with less than 4 wheels) where the weight does not exceed 410kg
- A company van, and
- A vehicle of a type not commonly used as a private vehicle and unsuitable to be so used.

The value of the benefit is calculated by reference to the "**cash equivalent**" of the private use of a company car, **less** amounts made good by the employee to the employer.

To arrive at the cash equivalent, the employer must first apply a **business kilometre-related percentage** to the **Original Market Value (OMV)** of the car supplied as per the tables below.

Annual Business Kilometres	Cash Equivalent (% of OMV)
24,000 or less	30%
24,001 to 32,000	24%
32,001 to 40,000	18%
40,001 to 48,000	12%
48,001 and over	6%

FA 2008 (No. 2) introduced a revised method of calculating the cash equivalent by reference to the CO_2 emission category of the car. However, this revised method, which was to be effective for cars provided on/after 1 January 2009, is still subject to a commencement order by the Minister for Finance and is therefore ignored for the purpose of this text.

Step 1: Calculate the Original Market Value (OMV) of the car
The OMV of the car is the price (including any customs duties, VAT, VRT), which the car might reasonably have been expected to fetch, if sold in the State immediately before the date of its first registration.

Generally, the **OMV** is taken to be the **list price** of the vehicle, **including VAT** and **VRT**, at the time of **first registration**. In cases where:

- an exceptionally large discount was obtained (a fleet discount), *or*
- the discount cannot be determined (e.g. car traded in against a new car) *or*
- the car in question was purchased second-hand,

claims in respect of discounts are limited to the discounts **normally available** on a single retail sale on the open market. Discounts **in excess of 10%** will not normally be accepted unless there is documentary evidence available to support such a discount in respect of a single car sale. It should be emphasised that the **valuation for second-hand cars** is still the **OMV** of the car and **not** the **second-hand cost** of the car.

Step 2: Calculate the cash equivalent using the appropriate percentage, having ascertained the business kilometres for the year.
Business kilometres means kilometres incurred by the employee which he is **necessarily obliged to incur in the actual performance of the duties of his employment** (e.g. kilometres travelled incurred in driving to work and returning home is not business kilometres but personal). The total kilometres for the year should be reduced by a minimum of **8,000 private kilometres** to arrive at business kilometres. The employer may accept lower levels of private kilometres, but only where the employee can provide documentary evidence in this regard.

Example:
Sarah is provided with a company car from 1 January 2012. The OMV of the car is €25,000. Sarah did a total of 36,800 kilometres for 2012.

Benefit-in-Kind:	€
Total kilometres	36,800
Less: private element	(8,000)
Business kilometres	28,800
Percentage applicable	24% (24,000 to 32,000 km)
BIK (cash equivalent):	25,000 @ 24% = €6,000

Alternative Calculation for Employees with Low Business kilometres Employees whose annual business kilometres do not exceed 24,000 kilometres may reduce their cash equivalent by 20% where the following conditions are satisfied:

- the employee works at least 20 hours per week;
- the employee travels at least 8,000 business kilometres per annum;
- the employee spends at least **70%** of his or her working time away from the employer's premises; and
- a logbook detailing the employee's business kilometres, business transacted, business time travelled and date of journey, is kept and certified by the employer as correct.

Example:
Joe drives 16,000 business kilometres per annum. The OMV of the company car is €20,000. The car was first provided in 2010. Joe satisfies all the conditions above.

Benefit-in-Kind:	€
€20,000 × 30% =	6,000
Less: 20% reduction	(1,200)
BIK	4,800

Step 3: Company Car not available for a full year
If the employee is provided with the car for only part of the particular tax year, the business kilometre thresholds and the cash equivalent percentages used should be adjusted by the following fraction:

$$\frac{\text{No of days in the year the car was available to employee}}{365}$$

Example:
Alison is provided with a car with an OMV of €25,000 for the first time on 1 July 2012. Her business kilometres for the period 1 July to 31 December 2012 is 16,320 kilometres.

Fraction adjustment: $\frac{184 \text{ days (1/7 to 31/12/12)}}{365 \text{ days}}$ 0.5041

Multiplying 0.5041 by each kilometre figure and % in the table above the revised table becomes:

Annual Business Kilometres	Cash Equivalent (% of OMV) (Category C)
12,098 or less (24,000 0.5041)	**15.12%** (30% 0.5041)
12,098 to 16,131 (32,000 0.5041)	**12.10%** (24% 0.5041)
16,131 to 20,164 (40,000 0.5041)	**9.07%** (18% 0.5041)
20,164 to 24,197 (48,000 0.5041)	**6.05%** (12% 0.5041)
24,197 and over	**3.02%** (6% 0.5041)

Benefit-in-Kind: €25,000 @ 9.07% = €2,267

Change of Car This calculation will also be used in a year where there is a **change of car**, as the annual business kilometre thresholds and the cash equivalent percentages must be calculated for each car **separately**.

Practically, it is simpler to **annualise** the employee's business kilometres and use the original table to determine the correct % to use. In this example, kilometres of 16,320 for 184 days is equivalent to 32,374 kms for 365 days (16,320/184 × 365 = 32,374). As 32,374 falls into the category 32,000 to 40,000 business kilometres the appropriate % is 18%. The employee's taxable benefit for 2012 is therefore €25,000 × 18% × 184/365 = €2,268.

Step 4: Amounts reimbursed by employee to employer.
The cash equivalent is reduced by any amount which the employee reimburses to the employer in respect of any part of the costs of providing or running the car. In order to qualify as a deduction, the costs must be made good **directly by the employee to the employer** (i.e. if Joe pays for his own petrol, there is no deduction. If Joe's employer pays for the petrol, and Joe reimburses his employer, then Joe is entitled to a deduction for the reimbursement).

Where the employee makes a contribution to the employer towards the cost of the car, the amount of the contribution is **deducted** from the cash equivalent in the year in which the contribution is paid. If the contribution **exceeds** the cash equivalent in that year, the excess is carried forward and offset against the cash equivalent the following year.

Example:
Paul's employer provides him with a car with an OMV of €30,000 on 1 July 2012. Paul reimburses his employer €500 annually towards the cost of the car on 1 August 2012. Paul travels 19,200 business kilometres annually.

Benefit-in-Kind:		€
2012	€30,000 × 30% × 6/12ths	4,500
	Less: Amount reimbursed	(500)
	BIK 2012	4,000
2013	€30,000 × 30%	9,000
	Less: Amount reimbursed	(500)
	BIK 2013	8,500

(b) Company Vans

Where a van is made available to an employee for his private use, the employee is taxable on the cash equivalent of the benefit of the van, reduced by any amount which the employee is required to, and actually, makes good to the employer in respect of the cost of providing or running the van. The "cash equivalent" of the benefit of a van is **5% of the OMV** of the van. The business kilometre-related percentage does not apply to vans. OMV is calculated in the same manner as for cars.

A van means a mechanically propelled road vehicle which:

- is designed or constructed solely or mainly for the carriage of goods or other burden; and
- has a roofed area or areas to the rear of the driver's seat; and
- has no side windows or seating fitted in that roofed area or areas; and
- has a gross vehicle weight not exceeding 3,500 kilograms.

If the employee is provided with the van for part only of the particular tax year, then the cash equivalent is reduced on a pro rata basis, i.e. if the van is provided for five months, then only 5/12ths of the cash equivalent is taken.

Exemption from benefit-in-kind
The private use of the van will be exempt from BIK if:

- the van is necessary for the performance of the duties of the employee's employment;
- the employee is required, by the person who made the van available, to keep the van at his private residence, when not in use;
- apart from travel between the employee's private residence and workplace, other private use of the van is prohibited by the employer; *and*
- the employee spends at least 80% of his time away from the premises of the employer.

Car and van pool exemption
No benefit will be assessed on an employee in respect of a car or van that is in a "pool" available for employees generally. A car or van will be treated as belonging to a "pool" where:

- the car/van must have been made available to, and actually used by, **more than one** employee and it is not ordinarily used by any one of the employees to the exclusion of the others; *and*
- any private use of the car/van made by any of the employees is merely incidental to his business use; *and*
- it is not normally kept overnight at the home of any of the employees.

5.   Provision of Preferential Loans
A "preferential loan" means a loan, made by an employer to an employee, a former or prospective employee or their spouses, in respect of which no interest is paid, or interest is paid at a rate lower than the "specified rate". It does not include any loan made by an employer to an employee in the course of his trade, on an arm's length basis, where normal commercial rates of interest are charged.

The specified rates for tax year 2012 are:

Qualifying home loans	5%
All other loans	12.5%

The difference between the interest actually paid by the preferential borrower during the particular tax year and the amount of interest calculated at the specified rate, and any waiver of interest, is treated as a perquisite chargeable to PAYE, PRSI and USC under Schedule E.

Example:
Christopher is employed by a bank and has been advanced the following non-mortgage loans:

a. €10,000 interest free loan
b. €20,000 loan at the rate of 4.5% per annum
c. €30,000 loan at the rate of 13% per annum

Interest due in respect of the €20,000 loan for the year ended 31 December 2011 amounting to €900, was unpaid at 31 December 2011, and was waived by his employer during the tax year 2012.

(continued overleaf)

The amounts treated as perquisites under Schedule E and included as Christopher's income for the tax year 2012 will be as follows:	
	€
Loan No. 1 – €10,000 12.5% deemed interest rate	1,250
Loan No. 2 – €20,000 (12.5%–4.5%)	1,600
Loan No. 3 – Not a preferential loan (rate not less than 12.5%)	<u>Nil</u>
Total	<u>2,850</u>
Interest waived during 2012 by employer	<u>900</u>
Amount assessable as a Schedule E perquisite for 2012	<u>3,750</u>

6. Other Benefits

(a) Benefits on Death or Retirement

The expense of providing any pension, lump sum, gratuity or other like benefit to be given on the death or retirement of a director or employee is **exempt**. The exemption is only given to the extent that the provision is for the benefit of the director or employee himself or for his spouse/civil partner, children, or dependants. This exemption would, for instance, cover normal pension and retirement scheme payments, and death-in-service payments, made by the employer on behalf of the employee.

(b) Medical Insurance

The benefit, which is subject to PAYE, PRSI and USC is the gross premium (i.e. the amount paid to the insurer PLUS the tax relief at source (TRS)) payable by the employer on behalf of the employee. The employee may claim a standard rate tax credit in respect of the gross premium. Medical check-ups, which an employee is **required** to undergo by his employer who pays for them, are not a taxable benefit.

(c) Expense Allowances

(i) Round Sum Expense Allowance

In general, a round sum expense allowance advanced to an employee to be disbursed at his discretion is regarded as taxable Schedule E income (i.e. a perquisite). It is then open to the employee to make a formal claim for a deduction against this income in respect of the actual expenses incurred by him in the performance of his duties including capital allowances.

(ii) Employee Motor Expenses

Where an employee uses his **own private car** for business purposes, his employer may reimburse him for allowable motor expenses by way of a flat-rate kilometric allowance. If the employee bears all motoring costs and is reimbursed for the business element of motoring costs by his employer at rates which do **not exceed** the **Civil Service rates**, then such costs may be paid **tax free** by the employer and are not taxable in the hands of the employee. The employer does not have to seek prior approval from the Revenue for the tax-free payment of costs in line with Civil Service rates, provided the employer operates a satisfactory system of control over the payment and keeps adequate records.

(iii) Employee Subsistence Allowances

Where an employee performs the duties of his employment while temporarily away from his normal place of work, or while working abroad on a foreign assignment, his employer may reimburse the employee for actual expenses incurred or, alternatively, may pay the employee a flat rate subsistence allowance to cover costs incurred by the employee. Where the employee pays all subsistence expenses and is reimbursed for these expenses by a flat-rate subsistence allowance, then such an allowance may be paid **tax free** by the employer and is not taxable in the hands of the employee, provided the allowance paid is **in line** with prevailing **Civil Service subsistence rates**.

The employer **does not** have to seek prior approval from the Revenue for the payment of such tax-free subsistence allowances, provided the employer notifies the Revenue that it pays subsistence allowances in accordance with Civil Service rates, and that the employer operates a satisfactory system of control over the payment and keeps adequate records.

Where the employee's job is such that travel is an integral part of the job (e.g. a sales representative), or where the employee carries out much of his duties at the premises of his employer's customers, his "normal place of work" is regarded as the **employer's** business premises.

(iv) Removal/Relocation Expenses

An employer may make the payment or reimbursement of certain removal/relocation expenses, incurred by an employee in moving house to take up employment, free of tax. The employer must ensure that the following conditions are satisfied:

- the reimbursement to the employee, or payment directly by the employer, must be in respect of removal/relocation expenses actually incurred;
- the expenses must be reasonable in amount;
- the payment of the expenses must be properly controlled; and
- moving house must be necessary in the circumstances.

Expenses that can be reimbursed free of tax are those incurred **directly** as a result of the change of residence and include such items as:

- auctioneer's and solicitor's fees, and stamp duty arising from moving house;
- removal of furniture and effects, and insurance on items in transit or in storage;
- storage charges and cleaning costs of stored items;
- travelling expenses on removal;
- temporary subsistence allowance while looking for accommodation at the new location;
- rent (vouched) for temporary accommodation for up to three months.

With the exception of any temporary subsistence allowance, all payments must be matched with receipted expenditure. The amount reimbursed or borne by the employer may not exceed expenditure **actually incurred**. Any reimbursement of the **capital cost** of acquiring or building a house or any **bridging loan interest** or loans to finance such expenditure would be **subject to tax**. The concession applies to relocations within the same organisation and relocations in order to take up a new employment.

(d) Meals and Meal Vouchers

(i) Canteen Meals

Where free or subsidised meals in staff canteens are provided and **available to all employees,** a taxable benefit **does not** arise. If the facility is not available to all employees, the running costs of the canteen must be apportioned between the employees entitled to use the canteen and taxed as a benefit.

(ii) Meal Vouchers

Where an employer provides luncheon or meal vouchers to employees, a taxable benefit **does arise** on the **face value** of the vouchers (except for the first 19c per voucher).

(e) Crèche or Childcare Facilities
  (i) Employer-provided facility
      Prior to 1 January 2011, employer-provided childcare facilities were exempt from BIK, subject to certain conditions. **Section 120A TCA 1997** removed the BIK exemption for such facilities, effective from 1 January 2011. Therefore, where an employer provides free or subsidised childcare facilities for employees, a taxable benefit now arises.
  (ii) Independent facility
      Where an employer merely pays for, or subsidises, the cost to an independent crèche or childcare facility, the cost borne by the employer **is a taxable benefit**.

(f) Sports and Recreational Facilities
  (i) Facilities provided on the employer's premises
      Where sports and recreational facilities are made available on the employer's premises and are **available to all employees**, a taxable benefit **does not** arise. If the facilities are not available to all employees, the running costs must be apportioned between the employees entitled to use the facilities and taxed as a benefit.
  (ii) Corporate Membership paid by the employer
      Where a corporate membership to sports and recreational facilities is paid by an employer on behalf of an individual employee or specified employees, the amount paid must be apportioned equally among all the employees who are entitled to and indicate an intention to participate in the scheme, and be taxed as a benefit.

(g) Professional Subscriptions
  Prior to **1 January 2011**, where an employer paid a subscription to a professional body on behalf of an employee, or reimbursed the employee who had paid such a subscription, a taxable benefit **did not arise** if membership of that professional body **was relevant** to the business of the employer.

  Section 118 TCA 1997 removed this exemption effective from **1 January 2011** and, accordingly, any such payments are now a taxable benefit and must be included in remuneration as a benefit-in-kind.

  However, where the professional subscriptions can be claimed by the employee as a tax deduction under **section 114 TCA 1997** as a *"wholly, exclusively and necessarily"* incurred expense of the employee in the performance of his employment duties, Revenue will not seek to have such subscriptions taxed as BIK where:
  - there is a **statutory requireme\nt** for membership of a professional body;
  - there is a requirement for a **practising certificate** or licence; *or*
  - membership of the professional body is an **indispensable condition** of employment **and** the duties of the employment requires the employee to exercise that profession and the employee so exercises such a profession.

For example, where a legal practice employs a solicitor to act in that capacity and the employee cannot practice as a solicitor unless he is a member of the Law Society of Ireland, then the annual subscription to the Law Society paid by the employer is not deemed to be a BIK. However, where the solicitor is employed by the legal practice as its Human Resources manager and it is not an indispensable condition of that employment that the employee is a member of the Law Society (though the employer deems it desirable), payment by the employer of such a subscription is taxable as a BIK. (Reference: *Revenue eBrief 19/11.*)

(h) Course or Exam Fees

Where an employer pays, or refunds, an employee for the cost of any course or exam fee, these will not be treated as a taxable benefit if the course undertaken is **relevant to the business** of the employer, where it leads to the acquisition of skills or knowledge which are:

- **necessary** for the duties of the employment; *or*
- **directly related** to increasing the effectiveness of the employee's or director's present or prospective duties in the office or employment.

(i) Examination Awards

Where an employee is given an award for passing an exam or obtaining a qualification no taxable benefit arises provided:

- the examination/qualification bears some relationship to the employee's duties; *and*
- the award is of an amount that can reasonably be regarded as a reimbursement of the expenses likely to have been incurred in studying for the qualification or sitting the examination.

(j) Staff Discounts

Discounts given by employers on the purchase of goods by an employee, are **not** regarded as a taxable benefit if the sum paid by the employee **is equal to or greater than the cost** to the employer of acquiring or manufacturing the goods.

However, where goods are sold **below** the employer's cost, the **difference** between that cost and the price paid **is a taxable benefit**.

(k) eWorking Employees

"eWorking", according to the Revenue, is a method of working, using information and communication technologies, in which the work that is carried out is **independent** of location. This includes working from home on a **full-time** or **part-time** basis. eWorking involves working, for substantial periods, outside the employer's premises, logging onto the employer's computer remotely, sending and receiving e-mail or data remotely and developing ideas, products or services remotely.

The Revenue outlined the following practices with regard to eWorking employees:

- Where computers or other ancillary equipment such as printers, fax machines, etc. are provided by the employer, **primarily for business use**, to enable the employee to work from home, **no taxable benefit** will arise in respect of **incidental** private use.
- No taxable benefit will arise in respect of the provision of a telephone line for business use.
- No taxable benefit will arise in respect of office furniture or similar equipment provided where it is used primarily for business use.
- The employer may make a payment of up to **€3.20 per day tax free** to an employee to cover additional heating and electricity costs. If actual expenditure incurred by the employee exceeds this amount, the employee may make a claim for a Schedule E tax deduction in respect of the excess.

Note that these arrangements **only apply to eWorking employees.** They do not extend to employees who, in the normal course of employment, bring some work home in the evenings, etc.

(l) Provision of computer equipment, high-speed internet access, second home telephone in employee's home and the provision of mobile phones.

Where, **for business purposes**, an employer provides an employee with any of the above and the employer bears the cost of installation and use, no taxable benefit will arise where **private use is incidental** to the business use of the item.

(m) Travel Passes

Where an employer provides an employee with a monthly or annual travel pass for use on bus, train, light railway (e.g. LUAS and DART) and commuter ferries, the pass is not treated as a taxable benefit, provided the pass is for use on a licensed passenger transport service. Section 118B TCA 1997 provides that an employee may "sacrifice" salary in exchange for the travel pass benefit.

(n) Car Parking

While car parking facilities provided by employers for employees are **not treated** as a taxable benefit, **FA (No. 2) 2008** introduced a parking levy for employer provided parking spaces in the major urban areas of Cork, Dublin, Galway, Limerick and Waterford, which is still subject to a Commencement Order by the Minister for Finance, and is therefore ignored for the purpose of this text.

(o) Employee Security

Costs and expenses incurred by an employer, or incurred by an employee and reimbursed by an employer, in the provision of an asset or service for the improvement of the personal security of the employee, is not treated as a taxable benefit if the necessity for the provision of the security service is due to a **"credible and serious threat"** to the employee's physical security which arises **wholly or mainly** from his employment, e.g. a key-holder in a bank.

An "asset" in this context includes equipment or a structure, but does not include any mode of transport, or a dwelling or grounds attached to a dwelling.

(p) Staff Entertainment

Staff Christmas parties and special occasion inclusive events or meals are not a taxable benefit where the cost involved is **reasonable**.

(q) Long Service Awards

A taxable benefit will **not arise** in respect of long-service awards where the following conditions are satisfied:
- The award is made as a testimonial to mark long service of **not less** than 20 years,
- The award takes the form of a tangible article of reasonable cost,
- The cost does **not exceed €50** for **each year of service**, and
- No similar award has been made to the recipient within the previous five years.

This treatment **does not apply** to awards made in cash or in the form of vouchers, bonds etc. Such awards are fully taxable.

(r) Provision of a bicycle

A taxable benefit will **not arise** in respect of the first €1,000 spent on or after 1 January 2009 on a bicycle and related safety equipment to an employee for the purpose of travelling to/from work or between jobs where the following conditions are satisfied:
- claim is made only once every five years;
- an employee may "sacrifice" salary in exchange for the benefit (but must repay within 12 months); and
- electrically assisted pedal cycles are not covered.

(s) **Company Shares/Share Awards**

From **1 January 2011**, the benefit accruing to an employee from the receipt of shares and other securities awarded to employees in their employer company, or its parent company, is a **taxable benefit** and must be included in remuneration as a BIK. The benefit is therefore subject to PAYE, EE PRSI and USC. **Note that it is not subject to employer PRSI.** Prior to 1 January 2011, the benefit was not taxed as a BIK but had to be returned on the employee's return of income form (thus avoiding any charge to PRSI or the health levy). Note that gains or benefits on **share options** are subject to self-assessment and are not taxable under the PAYE system as a benefit-in-kind.

(t) **Company Credit/Charge Cards**

Where the card is provided by the employer **exclusively** for business usage, any stamp duty or membership fee paid by the employer is **not** a taxable benefit. Where, however, the card can be used for **private** purchases or payments, any payments **not repaid** by the employee **are** taxable benefits and subject to PAYE, PRSI and USC.

(u) **Provision of Newspapers, Periodicals, etc.**

Where an employee is provided with free newspapers, periodicals etc. which are **generally related** to the employer's business, a taxable benefit does **not** arise.

(v) **Exceptional Performance Awards/Staff Suggestion Schemes**

Where an employer has schemes in place to reward exceptional performance or staff suggestions, any awards received under such schemes, whether cash or gifts/vouchers, **are** taxable benefits.

Procedures for Collecting Tax on Benefits

1. Benefits received from an employer by an employee whose **total remuneration** (including BIK) is **€1,905** or more in a tax year are taxable. Where the employee is a **director**, the benefits are taxable **regardless** of the level of remuneration.
2. Income tax due on benefits must be collected through the operation of PAYE on the taxable value of the benefit (see below).
3. PRSI, USC and employer PRSI are also due on the benefits and must be collected by the employer through the PAYE system.
4. The notional pay liable to PAYE/PRSI/USC in respect of benefits must be the **best estimate** that can reasonably be made by the employer at the time the benefit is being provided.
5. A benefit with a value **not exceeding €250** is not subject to PAYE/PRSI/USC. However, no more than one benefit given to an employee in a tax year will qualify and, where a benefit **exceeds €250**, the **full value** of the benefit is subject to PAYE/PRSI/USC.

4.5.6 Expenses Allowable under Schedule E

In order for an expense to be deductible from an employee's or director's Schedule E income, it must be shown that it was incurred **"wholly, exclusively and necessarily in performing the duties of the office or employment"**. The test is extremely difficult to satisfy in practice as:

■ the employee or director must be **necessarily** obliged to incur the expense; *and*
■ the expense must be wholly, exclusively and necessarily incurred; *and*
■ the expense must be incurred in the **actual performance** of the duties.

It will be noted that **all of the above tests** must be satisfied. The difficulty of satisfying the tests is obvious in considering the dicta of Judges in deciding cases. For instance, Judge Vaisey said, in the case of *Lomax v. Newton,* that the rules are notoriously rigid now and restricted in their operation. He observed:

"An expenditure may be necessary for the holder of an office without being necessary to him in the performance of the duties of that office. It may be necessary in the performance of those duties without being exclusively referable to those duties. It may perhaps be both necessarily and exclusively and still not be wholly so referable. The words are indeed stringent and exacting, compliance with each and every one of them is obligatory for the benefit or relief to be claimed successfully."

Restriction of Schedule E Expense Deduction in respect of Lease Payments on Cars costing more than €24,000.

In the case of a leased vehicle, where the list price exceeds the limit prescribed, a proportion of the lease hire charges are disallowed. The steps involved in calculating the disallowed lease costs are as follows:

Step 1: The proportion of lease payments relating to personal usage is disallowed. As the vehicle is not owned by the taxpayer, no capital allowances are available.

Step 2: When the otherwise allowable expenses have been established under Step 1, they are further reduced by the following amount:

$$\text{Business Portion of Lease Hire Charges} \times \frac{(\text{* Retail Price of Car} - \text{Relevant Limit})}{\text{Retail Price of Car}}$$

*This represents the retail price of the car at the time the lease was signed (taking into account any cash discount available).

The relevant limit is **€24,000** for leasing expenses incurred in the basis period 2007 to 2012.

Section 380L TCA 1997 introduced a new scheme whereby leasing charges allowances are limited by reference to the CO_2 emissions of the cars, for cars first leased on or after 1 July 2008. The category reflects the adjustment to be made to the relevant limit above.

Category A – C	Use relevant limit irrespective of retail price.
Category D – E	Take 50% of the lower of the relevant limit or car retail price.
Category F – G	No allowance available.

Example:

Joe Jones, who is a salesman, leases his own car to carry out his duties under his contract of employment. The Category D car was first leased on 1 January 2010 when its retail price, after cash discount, was €25,000. Joe incurred lease charges of €8,000 in 2012 and 80% of his mileage was related to his employment.

	€
Lease charges	8,000
Less: Private element 20%	(1,600)
Business element	6,400

(continued overleaf)

Disallowed lease payment:

Car Category A/B/C: $\dfrac{€6,400 \times (€25,000 - €24,000)}{€25,000}$	256
Car Category D/E: $\dfrac{€6,400 \times (€25,000 - (€24,000*50\%))}{€25,000}$	3,328
Car Category F/G: No allowance	6,400

Disallowed lease payment for Joe Jones:	
Private element of lease charges	1,600
Restriction Category D car	3,328
Total lease payment restriction	4,928

4.6 Schedule F

4.6.1 Introduction

As outlined in **Chapter 3**, dividends and other distributions paid by Irish resident companies after the deduction of Dividend Withholding Tax (DWT) are liable to tax under Schedule F.

4.6.2 Computation of Schedule F Income

The amount assessable on the individual is the amount received in the tax year plus DWT.

Example:

Jane Conway, who is single, received the following Irish dividends from LXX plc in respect of their accounting year ended 31 March 2012:

Interim dividend (net) paid 30 September 2012	€2,640
Final dividend (net) paid 1 May 2013	€1,360

Jane also had Schedule E income of €33,500 for 2012 (PAYE deducted €3,500). Her personal tax credit was €1,650 and her employee tax credit was €1,650.

Jane Conway Income			
Tax Computation 2012	**Notes:**	**€**	**€**
Schedule E:			
Salary			33,500
Schedule F:			
Net dividend received 2012	**1.**	2,640	
Dividend Withholding Tax deducted		660	
Gross Schedule F income			3,300
Taxable Income			36,800

(continued overleaf)

Tax:

32,800 @ 20%	6,560	
4,000 @ 41%	1,640	8,200
Less Tax Credits:		
Basic personal tax credit	1,650	
Employee tax credit	1,650	(3,300)
Net Tax liability		4,900
Less:		
PAYE paid	3,500	
Dividend Withholding Tax	660	(4,160)
Tax due		740

Note 1:
Net dividend received €2,640 × 100/80 = Gross dividend of €3,300.

The dividend is not apportioned so the dividend paid on 30 September 2012 is taxable in full in 2012.

Note also that the accounting year's profit, out of which the dividend is paid, is irrelevant. The date of the payment of the dividend determines the tax year. Therefore the dividend paid on 1 May 2013 is assessable in 2013.

Questions (Chapter 4)

(See Solutions to Questions at the end of this text.)

4   Computation of Taxable Income

4.1   Joseph Murphy

Joseph Murphy is a trader. He prepares accounts annually to 31 December. His Profit and Loss account for the year ended 31 December 2012 was as follows:

	Notes:	€		€
Salaries	1	61,864	Gross profit	112,500
Travelling	2	17,512	Discounts received	7,349
Commissions		7,236	Dividends from Irish Co	2,813
Interest on late payment of VAT		1,121	Interest on National Loan Stock	2,250
Interest on late payment of PAYE		1,238	Deposit interest	170
Depreciation		13,793	Profit on sale of fixed assets	5,063
Bank interest		4,008		
Subscriptions	3	1,225		
Repairs	4	6,480		
Bad debts	5	2,475		
Legal fees	6	1,069		
Accountancy fees		2,250		
Net profit		9,874		
		130,145		130,145

Note 1: Salaries include a salary to Mr Murphy of €7,500 and a salary paid to his wife of €5,000 for her work as secretary.

Note 2: Travelling expenses include €1,000 for a holiday trip by Mr and Mrs Murphy.

Note 3: **Subscriptions:**

	€
Political party	75
Local football club	50
Traders association	500

(continued overleaf)

Trade papers	200	
Old Folks Home	150	
Sports club	<u>250</u>	
	<u>1,225</u>	

Note 4 **Repairs Account**

	Dr. €	Cr. €
Opening provision for repairs		855
Expenditure during period	2,335	
New extension to office	3,000	
Charge to Profit and Loss account		6,480
Closing provision	<u>2,000</u>	<u> </u>
	7,335	7,335

The closing repairs provision represents a general provision for expenditure not yet incurred.

Note 5 **Bad debts account**

	Dr. €	Cr. €
Opening provision – general		5,100
Bad debts recovered		2,675
Bad debts written off	2,275	
Charge to Profit and Loss account		2,475
Closing provision – general	<u>7,975</u>	<u> </u>
	10,250	10,250

Note 6 **Legal Fees**

	€
Bad debts recovery	60
Sale of freehold	<u>1,009</u>
	1,069

Requirement

You are required to compute Joseph Murphy's Case I taxable profits for 2012.

4.2 Andy Reilly

Andy Reilly operates a consultancy business providing technical advice. He has carried on business for many years and makes up annual accounts to 31 December. The following information is relevant:

His Profit and Loss account for the year to 31 December 2012 is set out below:

	€	€
Fees charged		178,000
Less: Direct costs:		
Technical salaries and employment expenses	64,000	
Stationery and printing	4,000	
Repairs to equipment	980	

(continued overleaf)

Professional indemnity insurance	370	
Motor vehicle expenses (Note 1)	6,250	
Depreciation – Equipment	2,500	
– Motor vehicles	3,000	(81,100)
		96,900

Deduct overheads:

Rent, rates and property insurance	11,000	
Repairs to premises (Note 2)	6,500	
Lighting and heating	1,100	
Office salaries	7,200	
Telephone and postage	400	
Advertising	800	
Entertaining (note 5)	3,900	
Bad debts (Note 3)	550	
Defalcations (Note 4)	6,000	
Successful claim by client not covered by insurance	2,500	
Andy Reilly's drawings	20,000	
Depreciation – office equipment and fittings	900	(60,850)

Net profit before taxation: 36,050

The following information is relevant:

1. €4,000 of the total motor vehicle expenses relate to Andy Reilly's car; 40% of Andy's total travel in his car is on business. The other motor expenses relate to sales representatives' cars, all of which cost €19,000.
2. Repairs to premises include the charge for constructing two additional garages adjoining the firm's buildings for the sales representatives' cars. This amounted to €3,150.
3. The bad debts charge includes a credit for the recovery of a specific debt amounting to €350 and the creation of a general bad debt reserve amounting to €275.
4. The defalcations were traced to staff and were not covered by insurance.
5. The charge for entertainment is comprised of the following:

	€
Private holiday for Andy Reilly (June 2012)	1,200
Tickets for Andy Reilly and his friend to All Ireland football final	300
Staff Christmas party	1,200
Business meals with customers	1,200
	3,900

Requirement
Compute Andy Reilly's Case I tax-adjusted profit for 2012.

4.3 Tony

Tony set up business as a car dealer/garage proprietor on 1 October 2011. His first accounts were made up for the 15 month period ended 31 December 2012 and subsequently to 31 December each year. The first two sets of accounts show the following results:

		15 months to 31/12/2012 €	Year Ended 31/12/2013 €
Sales – Cars		250,000	200,000
Sales – Workshop		100,000	90,000
		350,000	290,000
Direct costs			
Cost of cars sold		211,500	168,300
Salesman's salary and commission		15,000	13,000
Workshop labour and parts		62,500	66,000
		289,000	247,300
Gross profit		61,000	42,700
General and administrative costs			
Accountancy		1,500	1,250
Advertising		900	1,100
Bad debts	(Note 1)	2,500	400
Depreciation		3,000	2,400
Drawings		15,000	12,000
Entertaining	(Note 2)	1,500	700
Insurance		5,000	4,000
Interest	(Note 3)	18,000	14,000
Legal fees	(Note 4)	400	600
Light and heat		2,250	1,800
Office staff salaries		10,600	8,500
Postage, telephone and stationery		1,500	1,200
Sundries	(Note 5)	1,250	650
Travel expenses	(Note 6)	1,950	1,500
		65,350	50,100
Net loss		(4,350)	(7,400)

Notes:		15 months to 31/12/2012 €	Year Ended 31/12/2013 €
1.	**Bad debts**		
	General provision	2,500	–
	Bad debt written off	–	900
	General provision no longer required	–	(500)
		2,500	400
2.	**Entertaining**	€	€
	Hospitality for representatives of car manufacturer during negotiations for supply of cars	800	–
	Entertaining customers	700	700
		1,500	700

(continued overleaf)

3.	**Interest**	€	€
	Interest on loan from car manufacturer to buy stock	9,500	7,000
	Interest on bank loan to establish business	8,500	7,000
		18,000	14,000
4.	**Legal fees**		
	Advice on supply agreement with car manufacturer	250	200
	Recovery of outstanding debts	–	200
	Defending customer claim refaulty car	150	200
		400	600
5.	**Sundries**		
	Security	500	300
	Drinks at staff Christmas party	150	150
	Subscription to trade association	200	200
	Political donation	100	–
	Charitable donation (eligible charity)	50	–
	Interest on late payment of VAT	250	–
		1,250	650
6.	**Travel expenses**		
	These expenses contain no disallowable element		

Requirement:

(a) Compute the Schedule D Case I profit for the 15 months ended 31 December 2012 and the year ended 31 December 2013.
(b) Calculate Tony's Case I taxable profits for 2012.

4.4 John Smith

John Smith commenced trading on 1 May 2012. The Profit and Loss account from 1 May 2012 to 30 April 2013 shows the following information:

	Notes:	€	€
Sales		201,230	
Less: Cost of sales		140,560	
		60,670	
Interest received	1.	390	
Gross profit			61,060
Expenses			
Wages	2.	23,500	
Motor expenses	3.	1,860	
Depreciation		1,250	
Rent and rates		12,800	
Leasing charges	4.	4,300	

(continued overleaf)

Repairs	**5.**	3,900	
Telephone		800	
Bank interest and charges		3,800	
Sundry expenses	**6.**	3,400	
Insurance	**7.**	<u>2,630</u>	<u>58,240</u>
Net Profit for the year			**<u>2,820</u>**

Notes:

1. Interest received

	€
Post Office Savings Certificates	390

2. Included in wages charges are:

	€
Wage to Mrs Smith (wife), as book-keeper	1,800
Wages to self	5,200
Accrued bonus for sales assistants	500
Own PRSI	200

3. Motor Expenses

Motor expenses relate solely to Mr Smith's own motoring and include a €100 fine for careless driving. 60% of total travel by car is for business purposes. Motor insurance has been included under the insurance charge.

4. Analysis of Leasing charges (all operating leases)

	€
Lease of till	300
Lease of shelving	1,200
Lease of Mr Smith's car	<u>2,800</u>
	4,300

The motor car had a market value of €25,000 when first leased on 1 May 2011. It has an emissions rating of Category D.

5. Repairs

	€
Painting outside of shop	1,000
Repairing shop front damaged in accident	1,300
Insurance claim re above accident	(900)
Extension to shop	1,500
General provision for repairs	<u>1,000</u>
	3,900

6. Sundry Expenses

	€
Trade subscriptions	250
Interest on the late payment of income tax	120
Covenant to church	
(4th annual net payment)	260
Covenant to son at university	
(3rd annual net payment)	710

(continued overleaf)

Christmas party for staff	560
Accountancy	1,500
	3,400

7. Insurance

	€
Business "all-in" policy	270
Motor car	300
Retirement annuity premiums – single	500
Retirement annuity premiums – annual	600
Life assurance	460
Keyman life assurance on salesman	500
	2,630

Requirement

You are required to compute John Smith's adjusted trading profits for income tax purposes for the year ended 30 April 2013.

4.5 *Polly Styrene*

Polly Styrene has been in business for many years manufacturing shoes and she makes up her accounts to 31 December each year. Her Profit and Loss account for the year ended 31 December 2012 was as follows:

	Notes:	€	€
Gross Profit			170,000
Less:			
Wages and salaries	1.	90,000	
Light, heat and telephone	2.	6,000	
Postage and stationery		500	
Repairs and renewals	3.	5,000	
Legal and professional fees	4.	3,000	
Bad debts	5.	2,000	
Travel and entertainment	6.	2,500	
Bank interest	7.	3,500	
Royalties		25,000	
Insurance		3,000	
Freight		4,000	
Sundries	8.	3,500	
			148,000
Net Profit			**22,000**

Notes:

1. **Wages and Salaries**
   Includes €8,000 for Polly Styrene.

2. **Light, Heat and Telephone**
   This includes €1,500 for light, heat and telephone at the residence of Polly Styrene. 1/6th is business related.

3. **Repairs and Renewals**

Painting and decorating	1,600
Extension to shops	1,400
Provision for future repairs	2,000

4. **Legal and Professional Fees**

Debt collection	1,200
Accountancy	1,500
Surveyors fees re abortive purchase of premises	300

5. **Bad Debts**

Trade debts written off	2,800
Bad debt recovered	(200)
Decrease in general reserve	(600)

6. **Travel and Entertainment**

Car expenses (Note)	1,500
Christmas drinks for employees	400
Entertaining customers	600

   Note: The car cost €32,000 and was bought in 2008. Private use is 1/3rd.

7. **Bank Interest**

Bank interest	1,500
Lease interest	2,000

   Polly leased plant and equipment through ACC Commercial Finance under a three year finance lease. The total repayments for the year were €18,600.

8. **Sundries**

Advertising	1,551
Trade protection association	100
Political party subscription	1,000
Parking fines	49
Rubbish disposal	300
Donation to St. Luke's Institute of Cancer Research (Note)	500

   Note: St. Luke's Institute of Cancer Research is a charitable organisation, which is an "approved body" for charitable donations relief purposes

Requirement

You are required to calculate the Schedule D Case I taxable adjusted profit for 2012.

4.6 Jack and John (Partnership Apportionment)

Jack and John are in partnership as accountants for many years. The Profit and Loss account for the year ended 30/4/2012 was as follows:

		€	€
Gross fees			200,000
Less:	Overheads	100,000	
	Jack's salary	20,000	
	John's salary	21,000	
	Jack's interest on capital	6,000	
	John's interest on capital	7,000	154,000
	Profit for the year		**46,000**

Disallowable expenses included in general overheads amount to €26,000.
The profit sharing ratios were as follows (after salaries and interest on capital)

Y/e 30/4/2012: 50/50

Requirement
Prepare the Case II computation and allocate the profits to the partners.

4.7 Anthony and Sandrine Kelly (Investment Income)

Anthony and Sandrine Kelly are married and have four children, one of whom is incapacitated. They are both resident and domiciled in Ireland. Details of their income for the tax year 2012 is set out hereunder:

Anthony Kelly:	€
Salary	50,000
(PAYE deducted)	(5,800)
AIB ordinary deposit interest (gross) 31/12/2012	130
Credit Union interest (gross) - deposit account	80
- medium term share account	100
Vodafone (UK) dividend received (net of UK tax 10%)	900
Sandrine Kelly:	
Salary	28,000
(PAYE deducted)	(4,000)
Dresdner Bank (Germany) deposit interest gross	2,000
Independent Newspapers plc (Irish) dividend received net	2,500

Requirement
Calculate their liability to income tax for 2012 on the assumption that a valid election for joint assessment is in force. Their personal tax credits are €9,900.

4.8 David Lee

David Lee, who is a single person aged 44, works for a travel agency. He lives with his daughter Judy, aged 14, whom he maintains. He had the following income and outgoings:

	Notes:	**Tax Year 2012** €
Income:		
Salary (gross)		42,000
Ordinary bank interest (net)		500
Interest on government loans (gross)		1,130
Ordinary building society interest (net)		140
Income from Credit Union regular share account		29
Outgoings:		
PAYE deducted		4,900
Post Office	**1.**	1,200

Notes:
1. David buys €100 worth of Post Office Savings Certificates every month.

Requirement
You are required to calculate David Lee's income tax liability for 2012, stating clearly the amount payable by, or refundable to, him. His personal tax credits are €4,950.

4.9 Mr O' Reilly

Mr O' Reilly owns several properties which he lets. Details of his income from these properties and the letting terms are as follows:

Property A (Residential Property)
Acquired in November 2008 and let on a five-year lease expiring in November 2013 at a monthly rent of €500 payable monthly in advance. The rent due on 1 December 2012 was not received until 10 January 2013. Interest of €5,500 was incurred evenly during the year on a bank loan taken out to acquire the property.

Property B (Commercial Property)
Acquired on 1 April 2012 and let for the first time on 1 August 2012 on a 21-year lease at a full annual rent of €12,000 payable monthly in advance A bank loan was raised to help purchase the property and interest of €1,800 was paid on 30 June 2012 and €3,600 on 31 December 2012. A premium of €10,000 was also received under the terms of the new lease.

Property C (Residential Property)
Let at a full annual rent of €6,000 under a seven-year lease which expired on 30 April 2012. The property was vacant until 1 November 2012, when it was let again on a five-year lease at a full rent of €9,000 per annum.

Property D (Residential Property)
Let to Mr O' Reilly's aunt on a 21-year lease from 1 May 2000, at a annual rent of €52 (not a full rent).

Mr O' Reilly is responsible for repairs on all properties, except for Property A, in respect of which there is a "tenants repairing" lease.

During the tax year 2012, the following additional expenses were incurred:

Property B

		€
30 April	Dry rot repairs	950
30 June	Window broken by vandals	80
31 December	Storm damage	1,400

Property C

20 May	Blocked drains	90
31 July	Painting	700
31 October	Advertising for tenant	130

Property D

28 September	Roof repairs	160

Requirement

You are required to compute Mr O' Reilly's rental income assessable under Schedule D Case V for the tax year 2012.

4.10 Sonya

Sonya, a widow, has recently brought you details of her rental income which will be needed to prepare schedules supporting her tax return. All properties are non-residential. Relevant information is as follows:

Property

1. This property is let on a 10-year lease. The lease was granted in December 2006 at an annual rent of €16,000 payable monthly in arrears subject to review every three years.
2. This property is let at a rent of €8,000 per annum payable monthly in advance.
3. This property is let at a rent of €9,600 per annum payable monthly in advance. The instalment of rent due on 1 December 2012 was not received until 10 January 2013. This property was first let some years ago.
4. This property was first let on a 15-year lease on 30 June 2012 and a rent of €9,000 per annum payable quarterly in arrears on 30 September, 31 December, 31 March and 30 June subject to review every three years.
5. This property is let on a 15-year lease expiring in June 2013 at a nominal rent of €10 per month payable annually in advance on 30 June. The tenant is Sonya's sister.

The expenses (all allowable) paid in 2012 by Sonya for each property were:

Property	€
1.	4,300
2.	1,200
3.	800
4.	NIL
5.	900

In addition, mortgage interest of €1,400 gross was paid on a loan to finance the purchase of property 3. Her property portfolio is entirely commercial.

Requirements
(a) Prepare a schedule summarising Sonya's property income assessable in 2012.
(b) Sonya is contemplating an investment in:
    (i) National Instalment Savings Scheme
    (ii) Government Securities

Prepare notes briefly summarising the tax effects of each of these investments.

4.11 Ray Houghton

Mr Houghton, a single person aged 60, retired from Liver Ltd on 30 June 2012 after 18 years' service. As a token of its appreciation, the board of directors of Liver Ltd voted him a lump sum of €65,000.

Mr Houghton's remuneration for the three years prior to retirement was as follows and it **accrued evenly throughout the year**.

	€
Year to 30 June 2010	52,000
Year to 30 June 2011	55,000
Year to 30 June 2012	57,000

On 30 June 2012 Mr Houghton also commuted part of his pension to a tax-free lump sum of €3,000 and received an annual pension thereafter of €18,000. His total PAYE deducted for the tax year 2012 was €7,000.

Mr Houghton's tax position for the previous three tax years was as follows:

Chargeable	**Taxable Income** €	**Tax Charge** €
2009	50,000	12,700
2010	50,000	14,200
2011	60,000	15,200
	160,000	42,100

Requirement
Calculate Mr Houghton's income tax liability for the tax year 2012. His personal tax credits are €3,300.

4.12 Mr Moran

Mr Moran, who is 57 years old, retired on 30 September 2012 after 18 years and three months of service with his employer. He received a lump sum of €30,000 from his employer and a tax-free lump sum of €19,000 from his employer's pension scheme. His remuneration for the last three years to the date of retirement was:

	€
Year ended 30/9/2012	37,250
Year ended 30/9/2011	34,500
Year ended 30/9/2010	32,625

He had the following taxable incomes and tax payable

Tax year	€	€
2011	35,000	2,900
2010	33,000	2,800
2009	31,500	2,100
Total	99,500	7,800

His only other income, apart from the lump sum, in 2012 was a salary of €28,500. Mr Moran is married with no dependent children. His wife has no income of her own. His total PAYE deducted for 2012 was €2,200.

Requirement
Calculate his tax liability for the tax year 2012. His personal tax credits were €4,950.

4.13 Mr Lynch

Mr Lynch was made redundant by his employer, Tree Ltd., on 31 December, 2012. He received a lump sum payment of €30,000 (excluding statutory redundancy).

He also received a refund of his pension contributions of €5,600 from which income tax of €1,120 was deducted. He had been employed by the company for 10 complete years and had not received a termination lump sum payment from any previous employer. Mr Lynch's remuneration for the three years prior to his redundancy was:

	€
Year to 31 December 2012	43,000
Year to 31 December 2011	35,000
Year to 31 December 2010	30,000

His income tax position for the previous three tax years was as follows:

	Taxable Income	Tax liability
	€	€
2011	32,000	4,400
2010	29,000	3,400
2009	22,000	1,900
	83,000	9,700

Total PAYE deducted from salary and lump sum payment in the tax year 2012 was €6,000.

Requirement

You are required to calculate the balance of income tax payable *(or repayable)* in respect of Mr Lynch for the tax year 2012, assuming he is a widower with no dependent children and qualifies for a €3,840 tax credit.

4.14 Terence Flynn – Termination Payment

Terence Flynn, who is married, had been manager of a garage in Co. Monaghan until 30 September 2012. At that date, due to falling petrol sales and high taxes, the garage was closed and Mr Flynn was made redundant. His wife has no income.

You are given the following additional information regarding Mr Flynn.

He received an ex gratia lump sum of €57,000 from his employer as compensation for loss of office. This was in addition to his statutory redundancy payments of €7,800. He also received holiday pay of €2,000 to which he was entitled. He has no entitlement to a tax free pension lump sum payment.

He had worked in the garage for 15 complete years. He received pay related unemployment benefit of €134 a week for eight weeks in the period October/November 2012.

On 1 December 2012, he moved to Dublin to take up a new job with a multinational oil company at a salary of €2,500 per month, together with a BIK projected at €2,000 per annum.

His earnings for the last four years to 30 September were:

	€
Year ended 30/09/2012	47,000
Year ended 30/09/2011	54,000
Year ended 30/09/2010	52,000
Year ended 30/09/2009	50,000

His pay accrued evenly from month to month.

The total PAYE deducted from both employments for the tax year 2012 was €4,800. His agreed balancing statements show the following pay and tax deducted for the last three tax years.

	Taxable Income	Income Tax
	€	€
2011	54,000	13,900
2010	52,000	13,300
2009	50,000	12,600
	156,000	39,800

Requirement

(a) calculate the amount of the lump sum that is liable to tax
(b) calculate the tax year 2012 income tax liability with personal tax credit of €4,950

4.15 Dermot O'Donnell

Dermot O'Donnell, a single parent with one five-year-old son, was an employee of Super McBurgers, a fast food restaurant chain. He has been employed by the company for 15 years and 8 months. He was made redundant on 30 September 2012. You have the following information:

1. As part of the redundancy package he received:

Statutory redundancy	€8,000
Holiday pay	€1,200
Company car worth	€22,500
Compensation payment	€40,500

2. In the period from 1 January 2012 to 30 September 2012, Dermot earned a salary including BIK on his company car of €37,000. PAYE deducted was €9,500.
3. He commenced new employment in Burger Palace on 1 November 2012 and his earnings in the period to 31 December 2012 was €4,200 (PAYE deducted was €900).
4. Dermot's salary was pensionable and, as part of the termination package, Super McBurgers made a special contribution of €11,700 into the Revenue approved pension scheme. Dermot is entitled to a tax-free lump sum payment under the terms of the pension scheme. The actuarial value of the lump sum entitlement on 1 October 2012 was €22,000.
5. His salary and BIK for the prior tax years were follows:

y/e 30/9/12 Salary	€46,000
BIK	€2,900
y/e 30/9/11 Salary	€36,000
BIK	€2,000
y/e 30/9/10 Salary	€39,000
BIK	€3,100

6. His taxable income for the previous tax years were as follows:

Year	Taxable income	Tax payable
2011	€33,000	€2,940
2010	€37,000	€3,740
2009	€31,000	€2,500
	€101,000	€9,180

Requirement
(a) To calculate the tax-free termination payment that can be made to Dermot O'Donnell.
(b) Compute Dermot's final liability to income tax for the year 2012 with tax credits of €4,950.

4.16 Sid Harvey

Sid Harvey is an employee of General Services Limited.
His gross basic salary for 2011 amounted to €38,000 and for 2012 amounted to €40,000.

His employer also gives him €100 every month by way of round sum expense allowance to meet incidental outlay. He is not obliged to provide his employer with receipts to account for this expenditure.

Sid is supplied with a company car which was bought second hand by General Services Ltd, in July 2010 for €15,000. The car is a 2006 model and originally cost €35,000 (after 10% cash discount) when first registered. General Services Ltd pay all the outgoings in respect of the running of the car. However Sid is required to reimburse the company for private fuel and the cost of insurance. The amount reimbursed by Sid for fuel and insurance during 2012 amounted to €1,300. In recognition of the fact that he has the car available to him during leisure hours, Sid is also obliged to make a monthly contribution of €100 to his employer. This is deducted from his salary. Sid's total travel by car in the tax year 2012 amounted to 40,000 km of which 26,400 km were in the course of the performance of his duties. Sid spends approximately 50% of his working time away from the premises of General Services Ltd.

General Services Ltd also provide a free apartment to Sid. The market value of the apartment is estimated at €110,000.

General Services Ltd pay the annual management charge and light and heating costs of the apartment which, for 2012, amounted to €890. The apartment was purchased for €55,000 in 1997.

Sid receives free meals in the staff canteen on the days in which he is located at his Head Office. The cost of providing these meals to his employer amounted to approximately €300. The staff canteen is available to all staff and all meals are provided free.

On 1 November 2008, General Services Ltd provided Sid with a €1,000 interest-free loan to enable him to go on his annual holidays. On 1 February 2012, the Board of Directors of General Services Ltd decided to waive repayment of the loan, together with 2012 interest outstanding at that date.

Sid is not married and paid €13,900 PAYE in the tax year 2012.

Requirement
(a) Calculate the amount of BIK to be included with Sid's gross pay for PAYE purposes for 2012.
(b) Compute Sid's income tax liability for the tax year 2012, clearly showing all workings. His personal tax credits for 2012 are €3,300.

4.17 Terry

Terry is reviewing an offer from a new employer, Rich Bank plc, to start on 1 January 2012. In addition to an attractive salary of €70,000, Rich Bank plc have offered to take over his mortgage loan of €125,000, which he used to purchase his first main residence in January 2004. The rate of interest payable on the loan is 2%.

His employer will also provide an interest free loan of €10,000 to pay Terry's affiliation fees at the "Posh Golf and Country Club". The bank will pay annual membership of €3,500 on his behalf.

He will also be provided with a new VW Passat car in CO_2 emissions category C, which has an original market value of €30,000. The Bank will pay all expenses. Terry estimates that he will drive 46,400 km in the tax year 2012, of which 10,400 km will be private, which he must reimburse to the Bank at a rate of 15c per km.

Terry is married and will earn €75,000 with no benefits if he stays in his current job in 2012. He pays 5% on his mortgage and estimates that his car costs €10,500 per annum. He is not a member of any golf club and has no business mileage in his current job. His wife does not work.

Requirement

Calculate the taxable benefits assessable for 2012 from his new employer. Assume he has tax credits of €4,950.

Prepare income tax computations for both jobs and advise which leaves him better off.

You may ignore tax relief on the mortgage loan for the purposes of this question.

4.18 Philip Stodge

Philip Stodge is employed as a commercial representative by his employer. Details of his income are as follows:

	2012	2011
	€	€
Gross salary	41,600	28,200
Sales commission	6,000	9,000

The following additional information is available:

1. PAYE deducted amounted to €4,900 for 2012 and €2,500 for 2011.

2. The sales commission of €6,000 earned during 2012 was paid to him on 1 June 2013 and the commission earned for 2011 was paid in July 2012.

3. He receives a monthly lump sum expense allowance of €100 to meet routine incidental expenses such as telephone calls, tips, etc. In addition, his employer pays his hotel accommodation costs directly. He is obliged to provide his own car, pay all operating expenses and non hotel meal costs personally.

4. Philip runs an Audi A4 car which he first leased on 6th April 2009 for €27,000 on taking up his present employment. His car operating costs were as follows:

	2012	2011
	€	€
Lease charges	5,700	5,700
Car tax	500	480
Car insurance	850	750
Petrol	3,200	2,800
Tyres	–	150
Maintenance	400	230
Crash repairs	1,500	0
	6,450	4,410

He maintains receipts for all his motor expenses. 90% of his total mileage is undertaken in the performance of the duties of his employment. The emissions rating of his car is Category B.

5. In addition to car expenses, Philip has made the following expense claims (vouched with receipts) in his tax returns in respect of expenses not reimbursed by his employer:

	2012	2011
	€	€
Work related telephone charges	180	120
Cost of new suit	450	340
Cost of advanced commercial correspondence course	150	–
Taxi/Train fares while on business	<u>130</u>	<u>100</u>
	910	560

6. Philip is married and his wife earned €5,500 (PAYE €230) in 2012.

Requirement

Compute Philip Stodge's tax liability for the tax year 2012, claiming the maximum reliefs available. His personal tax credits are €6,600.

4.19 Frank

Frank, a sales representative who is single (tax credits €3,300), received a salary of €50,000 and sales commission of €8,000 from his employer during 2012. To visit his customers, Frank used a car costing €51,000, which he had leased new on 1 July 2010 (Emissions rating Category F). Lease charges paid in the tax year 2012 were €6,600. During the tax year 2012, he incurred the following motor expenses:

	€
Petrol	4,300
Insurance	1,500
Motor tax	1,480
Repairs and service	1,400

Frank travelled 44,800 km in 2012, of which 8,960 were for private purposes.

Frank's employer has suggested that they enter into a new arrangement whereby the employer would provide Frank with a category C motor car costing €31,000 and pay all the expenses. In return, Frank would receive his normal salary and 2/3rds of his usual commission.

Requirement

(a) You are required to calculate Frank's gross income tax liability (before credit for PAYE deducted) for the tax year 2012.

(b) You are required to re-calculate Frank's income tax liability for the tax year 2012, assuming that the new arrangement had been in force during the entire year and that the car was first provided in 2011. Advise Frank which arrangement is financially more advantageous.

Capital Allowances and Loss Relief

5.1 Capital Allowances – Plant and Machinery

5.1.1 Introduction

In arriving at the tax-adjusted trading profits of a business, depreciation for accounting purposes is specifically disallowed. The computation of adjusted profits **does not** include any capital allowances either. Capital allowances are a **separate calculation** and are included in the income tax computation as a **deduction** from taxable Case I and II profits, or Schedule E income, by reference to the **tax year,** i.e. capital allowances for the 2012 tax year are deducted from the tax-adjusted trading profits for 2012.

The basic objective of the system of tax capital allowances is to allow the business a **deduction** against assessable business profits for the **net cost of certain capital assets employed** for the purpose of the business.

5.1.2 Meaning of "Plant"

The basic test applied is to determine whether the specific capital asset in question is **functional** to the operation of the business, as distinct from representing the **setting** in which the business is carried out.

There is no statutory definition of plant and machinery for the purposes of capital allowances. Accordingly, one must have recourse to case law to determine various tests which must be satisfied if an item of expenditure is to qualify as "plant" for the purposes of capital allowances. The question of whether an item is plant is a **matter of fact**, which will be decided according to the circumstances of each particular case. The question of whether an item is **machinery** can, in certain circumstances, be an easier test to satisfy as it is usually an **either/or** test. However where there is any doubt, as for plant, the question is a **matter of fact** which will be decided by the circumstances of **each** case.

The most quoted definition of the word "plant" arose under a case in connection with the Employer's Liability Act 1880, **Yarmouth v. France (1887)**, in which Lord Justice Lynley said:
"There is no definition of plant in the Act, but in its ordinary sense, it includes whatever apparatus is used by a businessman for carrying on his business – not his stock-in-trade, which he buys or makes for sale but all goods and chattels, fixed or moveable, live or dead, which he keeps for permanent employment in the business".

To determine whether an item would qualify as plant, relevant case law has indicated that the following tests are applied:

- Is the item functional or merely a setting in which the business is carried on?
- Is the expenditure incurred directly on the provision of plant and not, for instance, on the provision of finance which is used to acquire plant?
- Does the expenditure replace an item previously regarded as plant?
- Is the expenditure related to an entire unit or is it merely expenditure on part of a larger non-functional unit?

As the practice in relation to plant has resulted mainly from a study of case law, brief details of some of the more important cases on the subject are outlined below:

Jarrold v. Good (40 TC)
In this case, reference was made to the case of *J. Lyons & Co. v. Attorney General (1944)* in which it was stated as a principle that *"the term (plant) does not include stock-in-trade, nor does it include the place where the business is carried on"*. It was held in this case that purpose-built partitioning, although forming part of the setting of the business, was an essential part of the equipment necessary for the operation of the business and should, therefore, be regarded as plant. The partitions in this case were moveable and it was contended that they were specifically designed to enable employees to carry out their duties according to the state of the company's business and were and could be moved as required by the volume of the company's activities.

Barclay Curle & Co. Ltd. v. CIR (45 TC)
This case, concerning expenditure on a dry dock, was heard by the House of Lords in 1979. The main facts of the case were as follows:

Shipbuilders constructed a dry dock that involved the excavation of some 200,000 tons of earth and rock, which was then lined throughout with 100,000 tons of concrete. The installations included a dock gate, pump and valves, piping, electrical machinery, etc. The dock acted like a hydraulic chamber in which a volume of water, variable at will, could be used to lower a ship so that it could be exposed for inspection and repair, and to raise it again to high tide level. The taxpayer contended that the dock was a single and indivisible entity, performing the function of a large hydraulic lift cum vice, and that the expenditure on both the excavation and concrete work was incurred on the provision of machinery and plant.

The House of Lords found in favour of the taxpayer and the following quote from Lord Reid is important in considering the tests to be applied: *". . . It seems to me that every part of the dry dock plays an essential part in getting vessels into a position where work on the outside hull can begin and that it is wrong to regard either the concrete or any part of the dock as a mere setting or part of the premises in which the operation takes place. The whole dock is, I think, the means by which, or plant with which, the operation is performed."*

This decision stressed the **functional** test as opposed to the **setting** test.

Schofield (HMIT) v. R & H Hall (1974)

In this case, the company claimed capital allowances on expenditure it incurred on the construction of two silos which were used to take grain from ships and to dispense it to customers. The silos consisted of large concrete structures into which were built concrete bins, a small structure, the workhouse containing machinery and plant, and machinery consisting of gantries, conveyor belts, mobile chutes, etc. The taxpayer claimed that all of the expenditure qualified for capital allowances as plant and machinery. It was held that, considering the function of the silos in relation to the company's trade, they seemed an essential part of the overall trade activity. Their function was to hold grain in a position from which it could be conveniently discharged in varying amounts. Accordingly, they found that the silos were plant, qualifying for wear and tear allowances.

An important aspect of the case was the **detailed description of the plant** given by the company by way of documentation and evidence.

S. O'Culachain (Inspector of Taxes) v. McMullan Brothers (1995)

In this case, it was claimed that forecourt canopies at petrol filling stations constituted plant for capital allowances purposes on the grounds that the canopies were essential to provide advertising, brand image and attractive surroundings, and therefore created an ambience and had a function in carrying on the business.

The Revenue Commissioners argued that the canopies provided no more than shelter from the rain and wind and played no part in the trade of selling petrol.

It was held that the canopies performed a function in the actual **carrying out** of the trade and therefore qualified for capital allowances as an item of plant.

Hampton (HMIT) v. Fortes Auto Grill Ltd. (1979)

It was held that a false ceiling is not plant on the basis that it simply provided a covering, which was not functional to the actual carrying on of the catering business by the taxpayer.

5.1.3 Wear and Tear Allowance

Plant and Machinery

This is an annual allowance for the wear and tear of plant and machinery (new or second-hand) in use for the purpose of a trade, profession or employment at the end of an accounting period.

The qualifying asset must be **owned** by the taxpayer and **in use**, wholly and exclusively for the purposes of the taxpayer's trade, profession or employment, **at the end** of the relevant basis period for the year of assessment. (The basis period is the accounts year from which the tax year is calculated.)

The allowance is calculated on the **cost price** of the plant **less** any grants received. The **wear and tear rate is 12.5%** on expenditure incurred from 4 December 2002 on a straight line basis.

The wear and tear allowance is an **annual** allowance. The only circumstance in which a full 12.5% will not be granted is where the **basis period** for the particular tax year, for which the allowance is being claimed, **is less than 12 months**.

This would only occur in the **year of commencement** of trade. (The year of cessation of trade may also be less than 12 months but no annual allowance would be due for that year as the asset would not be in use at the end of the basis period.)

It is important to emphasise that it is the **length of the basis period** that determines whether or not a full annual allowance is available and **not the period from the date of purchase** of an asset to the end of the particular basis period.

In the year of acquisition, a full year's wear and tear allowance is granted (provided the basis period is at least 12 months long). In the year of disposal or cessation of use, no wear and tear allowance is granted, as the asset is not in use at the end of the basis period.

	Plant & Machinery @ 12.5%	Vehicles @ 12.5%	Total
	€	€	€
Opening Qualifying Cost of Assets purchased on 1 Jan 2008	50,000	0	50,000
Add:			
Additions at Qualifying Cost	25,000	20,000	45,000
Deduct:			
Disposals at Qualifying Cost	(7,000)	0	(7,000)
Cost of Assets Qualifying for Wear and Tear Allowance (A)	**68,000**	**20,000**	**88,000**
Opening Tax Written Down Value (TWDV) at 1 Jan 2012	**25,000**	0	25,000
Add:			
Additions at Qualifying Cost during the basis period, i.e. y/e 30/9/2012	25,000	20,000	45,000
Deduct:			
Tax written down value of assets sold during the basis period, i.e. y/e 30/9/2012	(3,500)	0	(3,500)
	46,500	20,000	66,500
Wear and Tear for 2012 (Line A × qualifying rate)	(8,500)	(2,500)	(11,000)
Tax WDV @ 31/12/2012	**38,000**	**17,500**	**55,500**

Motor Vehicles

The wear and tear rate for motor vehicles, other than that used in a taxi or car hire business, is 12.5% on expenditure incurred from 4 December 2002 on a straight line basis.

For income tax basis periods ending on or after 1 January 2007, the allowable cost of new and second-hand cars (for wear and tear allowance purposes) is restricted to a **maximum limit of €24,000**.

Section 380L TCA 1997 introduced certain additional restrictions on capital allowances available on cars which are based on CO_2 emissions levels for vehicles bought on or after 1 July 2008. There are three categories:

Category A/B/C Vehicles	Category D/E Vehicles	Category F/G Vehicles
121–155g/km	156–190g/km	191g/km

Category A – C	Use the specified amount regardless of cost
Category D – E	Two steps to calculate limit
	1. Take the lower of the specified limit or cost
	2. Limit is 50% of the above amount
Category F – G	no allowance available

No restrictions apply to:

- Commercial vehicles, e.g. lorries, vans etc.,
- Cars used for the purposes of a taxi business.
- Cars used for the purpose of a car hire business.

The wear and tear allowance for cars used in a **taxi or car hire** business is **40%** on a **reducing balance** basis. The "specified amount" reduction, i.e. the maximum cost limit of €24,000 does not apply to such cars.

Where a business asset is partly used for private purposes, the wear and tear allowance is calculated as normal and is then reduced by the private element. However, the full annual allowance is deducted when arriving at the tax written down value at the end of each tax year.

Example:

Joe, who is self-employed **and** prepares annual accounts to 31 December, purchased a new car on 1 August 2012 which cost €35,000 (Emissions category D). His annual travel is 32,000 kilometres of which 8,000 are private. Joe's Sales Director Sarah also has a company car which was purchased on 30 September 2009 (Emissions category C) for €25,000. Sarah's travel is 56,000 kilometres of which 44,800 are business related.

Wear and Tear Calculation Motor Vehicles 12.5%	Notes:	Sarah's Car €	Joe's Car €
Written Down Value (WDV) 1/1/2009		–	
Additions y/e 31/12/2009	1.	24,000	
Wear and tear allowance 2009		(3,000)	
WDV 31/12/2009		21,000	
Wear and tear allowance 2010		(3,000)	
WDV 31/12/2010		18,000	
Wear and tear allowance 2011		(3,000)	
WDV 31/12/11		15,000	

(continued overleaf)

		2.		12,000
Additions 2012				12,000
Wear and tear allowance 2012			(3,000)	*(1,500)
WDV 31/12/2012			12,000	10,500

Note 1: Sarah's car cost is restricted to €24,000 for 2009. As Sarah is an employee, there is no private motoring restriction.

Note 2: Joe's car is restricted to 50% of €24,000 for 2012 as a Category D car.

*The wear and tear allowance on Joe's car will be further restricted to the business use only, i.e.

$$1,500 \times \frac{(32,000-8,000)}{32,000} = 1,125$$

5.1.4 Balancing Allowances and Charges

Profits and losses on the disposal of fixed assets are **not included** in the tax-adjusted profits of a business. In order to adequately capture these profits and losses, the capital allowances systems use balancing charges and balancing allowances to reflect any profit or loss on the disposal of an asset.

A **balancing allowance arises when the sales proceeds of an asset are less than its tax written down value (loss on disposal).**

A **balancing charge arises when the sales proceeds of an asset are greater than its tax written down value (profit on disposal).**

Note that the "tax" profit or loss will not be the same as the profit/loss on disposal in the accounts due to the differing rates and rules between depreciation and tax capital allowances.

Balancing allowances and charges may arise when one of the following occurs:

- The trade or profession ceases => the assets are no longer "in use".
- An asset, on which wear and tear allowances were claimed, is sold/scrapped.
- An asset permanently ceases to be used for the purposes of the trade, profession or employment.

In computing the balancing allowance/charge, market value is imposed where the sale proceeds are **not** at arm's length or there are no sale proceeds (e.g. takeover/gift of a business asset for personal use).

Limitation of Balancing Charges

- The balancing charge **cannot exceed** the aggregate of the wear and tear allowances **already claimed** on the asset.
- With effect from **1 January 2002**, a balancing charge will not arise in respect of plant and machinery where the **disposal proceeds are less than €2,000**. This does not apply if the disposal is to a connected person.

Example:
Damien Jones is self employed and prepares annual accounts to 30 June. Damien disposed of the following assets:

	Counting Machine	Binding Machine	Printer
Date of Disposal	23/1/2012	10/6/2012	28/4/2012
Proceeds	€6,250	€220	€1,750
Original Cost	€5,000	€900	€4,000
WDV 1 Jan 2012	€4,000	€425	€1,250

(continued overleaf)

Balancing Allowance/Charge Calculation	Counting Machine €	Binding Machine €	Printer €
WDV 1 Jan 2012	4,000	425	1,250
Less:			
Sale proceeds	(6,250)	(220)	(1,750)
Balancing allowance/(charge)	(2,250)	205	(500)
Restricted to:			
Balancing allowance/(charge)	*(1,000)	205	**NIL

*The balancing charge on the counting machine is restricted to the amount of wear and tear allowances already claimed (Cost €5,000 less WDV €4,000 = €1,000).

**No balancing charge will apply in respect of the printer as the sales proceeds are less than €2,000. *Year end 30th June 2011 formed the last basis period (i.e. 2011) for which wear and tear allowances were claimed. The assets were disposed in yle 30 June 2012, which is the basis period for 2012. No wear and tear allowance is claimable in the year of disposal.*

Replacement Option

If plant and machinery (including motor vehicles) is replaced with **similar** equipment, any balancing charge arising on the old equipment may be **deferred**. If such a claim is made, the cost of the new equipment is **reduced by the balancing charge** deferred. This claim is referred to as the "replacement option". This option may only be claimed to avoid a balancing charge if a similar item replaces the item of plant sold.

Example:

Damien Jones sold printing equipment and a balancing charge of €1,000 arose. He bought replacement equipment on 10 January 2012 for €6,000. This equipment was in turn sold on 29 March 2013 for €6,050.

Balancing Allowance/Charge Calculation	Printing Equipment €
2012:	
Cost of new printing equipment	6,000
Less:	
Balancing charge on original asset	(1,000)
Qualifying cost of replacement asset for capital allowances	5,000
Wear and tear allowance 2012 **12.5%**	(625)
WDV 31/12/2012	4,375
2013:	
WDV 1/1/2013	4,375
Less:	
Sales proceeds	(6,050)
Balancing charge	(1,675)
Restricted to:	
Actual allowances granted (including deferred balancing charge) (€625 + €1,000)	(1,625)

Motor Cars

As the qualifying cost of a motor car for wear and tear allowance is capped at **€24,000** (from 2007), any balancing allowance/charge on disposal must too be restricted in the same proportion as the **original restriction** to the actual cost of the vehicle. The deemed sales proceeds are calculated as follows:

$$\text{Total Sales Proceeds} \times \frac{\text{Restricted Value of car}}{\text{Original Cost of car}}$$

Where there is private use, any balancing allowance/charge is further restricted to the proportion of business use.

Example:
Damien Jones purchased a new car on 15 January 2010 for €25,000 (emissions category A). He sold the car on 15 April 2012 for €15,500. Business usage was agreed at 75%. Damien prepares accounts to 30 June each year.

	Motor Vehicle **12.5% S.L.**	**Allowable** **75%**
Wear and Tear Allowance	**€**	**€**
WDV 1/1/2010	–	
Additions y/e 30/6/2010 (restricted to €24,000)	24,000	
Wear and tear allowance 2010	(3,000)	(2,250)
WDV 31/12/2010	21,000	
Wear and tear allowance 2011	(3,000)	(2,250)
WDV 31/12/2011	18,000	
Disposal:		
WDV 1/1/2012	18,000	
Deemed proceeds: €15,500 × 24,000/25,000	(14,880)	
Balancing charge	(3,120)	
Restricted to business use of 75%		(2,340)

5.1.5 Treatment of Capital Grants, Hire Purchase, Lessors, Lessees and VAT

Capital Grants

- *Expenditure incurred prior to 29/1/86.*
  The qualifying cost is the total cost **before** government grants.

- *Expenditure incurred from 29/1/86.*
  The qualifying cost is the **net cost,** i.e. total cost minus grant receivable.

Hire Purchase

- A full wear and tear allowance is allowed in respect of the first tax year in the basis period for which the asset is put into use and every year thereafter, subject to the qualifying conditions continuing to be met.

- The qualifying cost for the purposes of computing the wear and tear allowance is limited to the cost of the asset, **exclusive** of hire purchase charges (i.e. interest). The interest charge is allowable against taxable profits.
- The timing of the actual hire purchase instalments is not relevant provided the agreement is **executed** during the relevant basis period.

Treatment of Lessors

A person who **leases** plant or equipment **to** other individuals carrying on qualifying trades or professions will be entitled to a wear and tear allowance in respect of the cost of the plant and equipment leased, provided it can be shown that the **lessor** bears the burden of wear and tear.

Treatment of Lessees

Section 299 TCA 1997 states that where plant and machinery is leased to a person (lessee) who is carrying on a trade and the **lessee** bears the burden of wear and tear, then the lessee is **deemed** to have incurred the capital expenditure on the assets and is therefore entitled to claim capital allowances on the assets. The lessee was also able to claim a deduction for the full lease payments payable to the lessor which, in some cases, allowed a double deduction for the cost of the asset.

FA 2010 amended section 299 TCA 1997 to ensure that an entitlement to capital allowances only exists where:

1. a joint election is made by both lessor and lessee, **and**

2. the lessor has made a claim under section 80A TCA 1997 to be taxed on the income of the lease in accordance with its accounts, **and**

3. the amount of the lease payments deducted by the lessee does not exceed the amount included by the lessor as income in his accounts, **and**

4. in computing his profits, the lessee is not entitled to deduct an amount equivalent to the cost of the asset to the lessor.

The effect of the FA 2010 amendment is that the lessee will no longer be entitled to a deduction for both the "capital" element of the lease payments AND capital allowances on the equipment, but will continue to get a deduction against taxable profits for the interest.

Qualifying Cost and VAT

The qualifying cost of plant and equipment for wear and tear purposes is the **actual expenditure incurred** on the plant or equipment **exclusive** of VAT which is recoverable. If, however, an **unregistered** business is involved, then the VAT element of the purchase price obviously represents a cost and the **total cost, including VAT**, would be allowable.

5.1.6 Unutilised Capital Allowances

Where the capital allowance claim for a particular year of assessment exceeds the assessable profits from the trade or profession concerned, the excess may be used in the following two ways:

- the excess capital allowances may be **carried forward** indefinitely against assessable profits in future years from the **same** trade or profession until such time as they have been utilised; or

- the capital allowances may be used to **create** or **augment** a **loss claim** that can be used to reduce the individual's total income liable to income tax in that year.

It should be noted that there is **no right** to carry forward unutilised capital allowances in the case of an **employment**. This is probably not important in practice, as it is difficult to envisage a situation where Schedule E income of an employee would be insufficient to offset any capital allowance claim made.

5.2 Capital Allowances – Industrial Buildings

5.2.1 Introduction

Capital allowances are available in respect of expenditure incurred on **certain types** of buildings. Such buildings are referred to as "industrial buildings". **If a building is not an industrial building, then no capital allowances are available**.

5.2.2 Meaning of "Industrial Buildings"

Unlike the term "plant", TCA 1997 contains a clear definition of what is meant by an "industrial building". It is defined as a **building or structure in use**:

- For the purposes of a trade carried on in a mill, factory, or other similar premises.
- For the purposes of a dock undertaking.
- For the purposes of growing fruit, vegetables or other produce in the course of a trade of market gardening.
- For the intensive production of cattle, sheep, pigs, poultry or eggs in the course of a trade other than farming.
- For the purpose of a trade of **hotel-keeping**, which includes:
  - holiday camps registered with Fáilte Ireland;
  - a guest house or holiday hostel registered in the register of guest houses/holiday hostels kept under the Tourist Traffic Acts; *or*
  - buildings as part of a caravan/camping site registered under the Tourist Traffic Acts. These include laundry rooms, toilets and showers, café/canteen, etc.
- As a laboratory used wholly or mainly for mineral analysis in connection with the exploration for, or the extraction of, oil, gas and minerals.
- For the purposes of a trade which consists of the operation or management of an airport and which is an airport runway or an airport apron used solely or mainly by aircraft carrying passengers or cargo for hire or reward.
- For the purpose of operating or managing a private nursing home. (The nursing home must be registered with the HSE under the Health (Nursing Homes) Act 1990).
- For the purpose of the recreation of employees by an employer who carries on any of the above trades.
- For the purpose of operating a convalescent facility (approved by the HSE and subject to the Health (Nursing Homes) Act 1990).
- For the purpose of operating a private hospital.
- For the purpose of operating a qualifying mental health centre.
- For the purpose of operating a qualifying specialist palliative care unit.
- For the purpose of the operation or management of a qualifying sports injuries clinic.

The following types of building or structure are specifically **excluded** from the definitions of "industrial buildings" above:

Buildings or Structures Used

■ As a dwelling house;
■ As a retail shop;
■ As a showroom or office; or
■ For a purpose ancillary to any of the foregoing.

The **site cost** is specifically disallowed for the purposes of industrial buildings allowances. However, expenditure incurred on the **development** of such a site would be allowable. This would include the cost of preparing, cutting, tunnelling, leveling land and the installation of services on the site.

In relation to the items excluded above, TCA 1997 provides an **exception** if the following conditions can be satisfied:

■ The retail shop, showroom, etc., must be physically **part of a larger structure** which qualifies, *and*
■ The cost of expenditure on such retail shops, showrooms, etc., must **not exceed 10%** of the total expenditure on the building or structure, inclusive of any grant-aided expenditure, but **exclusive** of the site cost.

It should be noted that the exclusion for offices refers to **administrative offices**, and would **not include**, for instance, **a drawing office**, as under case law it is held to be an industrial building, as it is used for **purposes ancillary to the industrial operations** carried out in the rest of the factory.

Example: €

Site cost   5,000
Cost of factory portion of building   55,000
Cost of administration portion of building and factory shop   5,000

The €55,000 expenditure on the factory portion of the building qualifies for a 20% government capital grant.

The appropriate fraction to work out the 10% test is as follows:

$$\frac{\text{Cost of administrative offices}}{\text{Total cost of factory and offices exclusive of site cost}} = \frac{5,000}{60,000} = 8.33\%$$

In this case, therefore, the administrative offices and shop will qualify in full for capital allowances. If, however, the computation worked out at say, 12%, no part of the expenditure on the offices and shop would qualify.

5.2.3 Industrial Buildings Annual Allowance

To qualify for industrial buildings annual allowance, the building or structure must be **in use** on the **last day of the chargeable period** (basis period in the case of income tax) for the purpose of a **qualifying trade**.

Industrial buildings annual allowance rate is normally **4% per year**. This is on a **straight line rate** and is calculated as a **percentage of the qualifying cost** of the industrial building (exclusive of grants).

Annual allowance is also known as **writing down allowance**.

5.2.4 "Tax Life" of Industrial Buildings

The "tax life" of an industrial building is an important and unusual feature of industrial buildings allowances. Generally, the **length of the tax life** is determined by the **rate of annual allowance applicable** to the industrial building in question. The following table summarises the annual allowance rates.

Type of Expenditure	Date Incurred	Writing Down Allowance Rate	Time Limit on Balancing Charge "Tax Life"
Factories, mills and docks		4%	25 years
Buildings for growing fruit and vegetables by market gardener		10%	10 years
Production of cattle, sheep, pigs, poultry and eggs by non farmer		10%	10 years
Hotels *(Note 2)*	Up to 26/01/94	10%	10 years
	27/1/94 – 3/12/02	15% first 6 years 10% year 7	7 years
	4/12/02 to date	4%	25 years
Guest houses and holiday hostels *(Note 2)*	27/1/94 – 3/12/02	15% first 6 years 10% year 7	7 years
	4/12/02 to date	4%	25 years
Holiday cottages *(Notes 1 and 2)*	Up to 3/12/02	10%	10 years
Nursing home *(Note 3)*	3/12/97 to 31/12/09	15% first 6 years 10% year 7	10/15/20 years
Convalescent facility *(Note 3)*	2/12/98 to 31/12/09	15% first 6 years 10% year 7	10/15/20 years
Childcare facilities *(Note 4)*	2/12/98 to 30/09/10	15% first 6 years 10% year 7	10/15 years
Private hospital *(Note 3)*	15/05/02 to 31/12/09	15% first 6 years 10% year 7	10/15 years
Sports injury clinic *(Notes 2 and 5)*	15/05/02–31/12/06	15% first 6 years 10% year 7	10/15 years

Note 1: Capital allowances do not apply to holiday cottages where the expenditure is incurred on or after 4 December 2002, subject to the transitional provisions set out at Note 2 below.

Note 2: The 15%/10% rate and 7/10 year life continues to apply to eligible expenditure up to **31 July 2008** where:

- A planning application has been made before 31 December 2004 (confirmed by the planning authority),
- The Local Authority certifies that at least 15% of the construction expenditure was incurred before 31 December 2006, and
- A binding contract was in place by 31 July 2006.

After that date, a 4% annual allowance applies for hotels, and holiday cottages no longer qualify for annual allowances.

Note 3: For buildings first used **prior** to **1 February 2007**, the tax life is **10 years** and allowances will be clawed back if the building ceases to be used as a qualifying facility. For buildings first used **after** 1 February 2007, the tax life is **15 years**. For capital expenditure incurred under contracts or agreements, which are entered into on or after **1 May 2007**, the tax life **is 25 years**. **FA 2007** also capped the qualifying expenditure on the latter at 50% for individuals and **75%** for companies.

FA 2009 provided for the **termination** of capital allowance schemes for registered nursing homes, convalescent facilities, private hospitals and mental health facilities (but not palliative care centres) on qualifying expenditure incurred **after 31 December 2009**, subject to some transitional arrangements for projects already underway:

- Where planning permission was not required and 30% of the qualifying work had been incurred before 31 December 2009, the qualifying period was extended to **30 June 2010**.
- Where planning permission was required and the application was submitted and acknowledged by the Local Authority on or before 31 December 2009, the qualifying period was extended to **30 June 2011** for nursing homes, convalescent homes and mental health centres, and to **30 June 2013** for qualifying hospitals.

Note 4: Accelerated capital allowances by way of initial allowance and free depreciation are available in respect of expenditure incurred on newly constructed childcare facilities on or after **1 December 1999**.

FA 2010 provided for the termination of this scheme from 30 September 2010, though some transitional arrangements will apply to extend the termination dates to 31 March 2011 and 31 March 2012 (section 843A TCA 1997).

Note 5: The allowances in respect of qualifying expenditure in 2007 and 2008 are restricted to **75%** and **50%** respectively.

*These reliefs are all "specified reliefs" under Chapter 2A TCA 1997. As a result there is a restriction on the use of tax relief by certain high-income individuals for the tax year 2007 et seq., to the extent that the "specified reliefs" used in any one year are restricted to such an amount that the effective tax rate on the individual's "adjusted income" rises to 30% from 1 January 2010 (20% 2009). This restriction only applies to individuals with adjusted income over €125,000 from

1 January 2010 (€250,000 2009) with tapering relief applying for incomes between €125,000 and €400,000 from 1 January 2010 (€250,000 and €500,000 2009).

Changes to treatment of Property Based Capital Allowances

FA 2011 sought to introduce substantial restrictions to property-based capital allowances claimed by **passive investors**. However, these restrictions were subject to a commencement order following an economic impact assessment of the proposed changes.

Section 17 FA 2012 has repealed all the FA 2011 measures. Section 17 states that passive investors will no longer be able to claim accelerated capital allowances beyond the original tax life of the scheme where the tax-life ends after 1 January 2015. If the tax life ends before 1 January 2015, the passive investor will not be able to carry forward any unused allowances into 2015 or beyond.

Section 3 FA 2012 also introduced a new 5% property relief surcharge on investors (both passive and active) with gross income greater than €100,000. The surcharge will be collected as an additional Universal Social Charge (USC) of 5% on the amount of income sheltered by property reliefs in a given year from 2012. (See **Section 8.10.3** for more detail on the USC.)

5.2.5 Balancing Allowances and Charges

If the building is sold, and the **"tax life"** of the relevant qualifying expenditure has **elapsed**, then the vendor **does not** suffer a **balancing charge** and the purchaser is **not entitled** to capital allowances in respect of that expenditure (see exception below).

If, on the other hand, any industrial building is sold **before** its tax life has elapsed, the vendor must compute a balancing allowance/charge in the normal way, and the purchaser is **entitled to annual allowances** in respect of all or part of the cost of the building or structure. The allowances available to the purchaser of a second-hand industrial building are only available provided it is **used** as an industrial building. If this condition is satisfied, the annual allowance, based on the **lower** of the price paid for the second-hand building and the original cost of the building, is granted. The annual allowance available is spread **equally** (i.e. on a straight line basis) over the **balance of the tax life** of the building.

No balancing allowance arises on the sale of an industrial building where the vendor and the purchaser are connected with each other.

Exception

However, with the following property-based tax schemes, the tax life is seven years, but a balancing charge can be triggered if the building is sold **within 10 years** of its first use prior to 1 February 2007. The schemes in question are:

- private hospitals;
- nursing homes, nursing home residential units and convalescent facilities;
- childcare facilities; and
- sports injury clinics.

Section 16 FA 2012 states that if a building is sold **after** its tax life has expired (i.e. after seven years) but **before** the 10-year period, then the balancing charge due may be reduced by the unused capital allowances which would, but for the introduction of the 2015 cut-off point, have been carried forward. Note that these allowances will not be allowable against any other income or gain, merely the balancing charge on the building in question.

5.2.6 Qualifying Cost; Foreign Properties; Lessors

Qualifying Cost

The qualifying cost for the purposes of industrial buildings allowance depends on whether or not the **vendor is a builder**.

If the **vendor is a builder**, the qualifying cost for allowance purposes is equal to:

$$\text{Total Purchase Price} \times \frac{\text{Construction Expenditure}}{\text{Site Cost} + \text{Construction Expenditure}}$$

If the vendor is a **non-builder**, the qualifying cost is deemed to be the **lower of**:

(i) the actual construction expenditure; or
(ii) the net price paid which is calculated using the above formula.

Foreign Properties

Expenditure incurred on or after 23 April 1996 on industrial buildings situated outside the State does not qualify for any allowances.

Lessors

The landlord will qualify for industrial buildings allowance where the lessee is carrying on a qualifying trade in the building.

The allowance can also be claimed if the building is leased to the IDA, SFADCO, or Udaras na Gaeltachta, who in turn sub-lease the building to a tenant who carries on a qualifying trade.

5.2.7 Unutilised Industrial Buildings Allowance

General

The balance of any unused Case V capital allowances can be carried forward against **future** rental profits **in priority** to Case V losses brought forward (**section 384 TCA 1997**). Allowances carried forward from an earlier year are first deducted from Case V income, before allowances for the current year are deducted.

Industrial buildings allowance can be set off against **all** rental income. Where capital allowances exceed rental income, the excess can be offset against other income, subject to a **maximum offset of €31,750**, where the capital expenditure was incurred **after 3 December 1997**. There is no restriction on expenditure **prior** to 3 December 1997.

Hotels

Capital allowances on hotels in excess of rental income **cannot** be offset against non-rental income, **except** where the expenditure was incurred **prior** to 3 December 1997.

Acquisition from a Company

Where, on or after 1 January 2003, an individual acquires an industrial building from a company, the excess of the capital allowances over the rental income of that building may only be carried forward against future rental income of **that** building, i.e. the excess may **not be offset** against rental income from **other** properties or against any other income.

Example:

Jack Brown acquired a second-hand industrial building on 1 December 2009. He is entitled to annual capital allowances of €70,000 in respect of the new property and in 2012 he received rental income of €20,000 for that property. Jack had other rental income of €10,000 and non-rental income of €50,000 for 2012.

Tax Computation 2012	€	€
A. Property acquired from an individual:		
Case V income	30,000	
Less: capital allowances	(70,000)	
Excess capital allowances	(40,000)	
Restricted to: Maximum offset		(31,750)
Other income		50,000
Taxable Income 2012		**18,250**
Capital allowances carried forward		
against rental income:		
Excess allowances	40,000	
Less: utilised against non-trading income	(31,750)	
Allowances carried forward	8,250	
B. Property is a hotel and acquired from an individual:		
Case V income	30,000	
Less: capital allowances	70,000	
Restricted to: Total Case V income		(30,000)
Net Case V income		–
Other Income		50,000
Taxable Income 2012		**50,000**
Capital allowances carried forward against		
all rental income:		
Capital allowances	70,000	
Less: Utilised 2012	(30,000)	
Allowances carried forward	40,000	
C. Property acquired from a company:		
Case V income	30,000	
Less: capital allowances	70,000	
Restricted to: Amount of rent from new building		(20,000)
Net Case V income		10,000
Other income		50,000
Taxable Income 2012		**60,000**
Capital allowances carried forward against		
rental income from new building only:		
Capital allowances	70,000	
Less: Utilised 2012	(20,000)	
Allowances carried forward	50,000	

5.3   Loss Relief

5.3.1   Introduction

Section 381 TCA 1997 provides relief for a loss sustained, in a trade, profession, employment or farming, by way of deduction from **any other income** chargeable to tax in that year. The loss is deducted from **gross income** before deduction of charges on income or personal allowances/reliefs.

Any loss not relieved under section 381 can be **carried forward** and set-off against the profits of the **same** trade or profession in subsequent years (section 382 relief). The loss must be set-off against the **first** subsequent year's trading profits, and so on. Losses may be carried forward indefinitely provided the trade that incurred the loss **continues** to be carried on.

Terminal loss relief can be claimed in respect of a loss incurred in the **final** year of a trade or profession. This loss can be **carried back** against profits from the same trade or profession for the last **three years** of assessment preceding that year in which the cessation occurs.

5.3.2   "Legal Basis" and "Conventional Basis"

The strict legal interpretation of section 381 relief indicates that it is the **actual** loss for a particular tax year that may be relieved ("legal basis"). In practice, however, relief will be granted against the total income of the taxpayer for the **year of assessment** in which the accounting period ends ("conventional basis"), e.g. a section 381 claim for a €10,000 loss for the accounts year ended 30 September 2012 is available for 2012. Note, however, the following **exceptions** where the **legal basis** is applied:

- In the first, second and third year of a **commencing** business.
- For any year of assessment immediately **following** a year of assessment where section 381 relief was allowed on the legal basis.
- Where the claimant formally **claims** the legal basis.
- In the year of **cessation** of a business, any relief under section 381 is allowed in respect of the loss applicable to the period from the beginning of the tax year to the date of cessation, e.g. cease on 30 June 2012: loss period 1 January 2012 to 30 June 2012 = section 381 claim for 2012.

5.3.3   Effect of Capital Allowances

Capital allowances for a year of assessment may be used to create or augment a loss, provided that such allowances are **first** set-off against any **balancing charge** arising in the year of assessment to which they relate, which are not covered by capital allowances forward.

Example:

Mary White has been in business for many years and prepares annual accounts to 30 June. Her details are as follows:

Tax-adjusted profit for the y/e 30 June 2012	€9,000
Capital allowances 2012:	
– Wear and tear allowance	€7,000
– Balancing allowances	€500
– Balancing charge	€3,000
Unutilised capital allowances forward from 2011	€9,600

Section 381 Claim 2012	€
Tax-adjusted Case I profit y/e 30/6/12	9,000
Deduct: Capital allowances forward (€9,600; limited to actual profit)	(9,000)
Net Case I	**Nil**
Balancing charge 2012	3,000
Deduct: Balance of capital allowances forward (€9,600 − €9,000)	(600)
Net balancing charge	2,400
Deduct: Wear and tear allowance 2012	(7,000)
Balancing allowances 2012	(500)
Section 381 loss (available to reduce total income for 2012)	**(5,100)**

5.3.4 Order of Relief

A section 381 loss is deemed to first reduce the earned income of the individual, then the unearned income, next the earned income of the spouse/civil partner and finally the unearned income of the spouse/civil partner. This is relevant in calculating the allowance for retirement annuities.

5.3.5 Amount of Relief Taken

A section 381 loss must be used up to the **full amount** of the loss available, or the amount of the **gross income** for the year of assessment, whichever is less. A section 381 loss **cannot** be **partially** used, so as to leave sufficient income to cover charges and use up tax credits, or to avoid the taxpayer being taxed at higher rates only.

5.3.6 Section 381 Relief Claim

Any claim for relief under section 381 must be made, in writing, to the Inspector of Taxes not later than two years after the end of the year of assessment in which the loss is incurred. In practice, the claim is normally made as part of filing the income tax return.

Section 381 relief is not compulsory and is only applied if a claim is made.

5.3.7   Section 382 Loss Relief

Method of Relief
This relief is available where a person incurs a loss in any trade or profession and it entitles him to carry it **forward** for set-off against the assessable profits (after deduction of capital allowances) of **the same trade or profession**.

The loss must be used, as far as possible, against the first subsequent year's trading profits, and so on.

Loss relief is only available under section 382 to the extent that it has not already been effectively relieved under section 381 or via time apportionment in commencement and change of accounting date situations. Losses may be carried forward indefinitely provided the trade which incurred the loss continues to be carried on.

Limitation on Section 382 Loss Relief
A loss can only be carried forward under section 382 provided it has not already been effectively relieved by any one or more of the following:

- section 381 relief; and
- relief by way of apportionment or aggregation of profits and losses.

This is a common problem on commencements.

Example:
A trader commenced business on 1 February 2012 and makes up accounts to 30 September each year. His results were as follows:

	Profit/(Loss)
	€
7 Months to 30 September 2012	(7,000)
Year to 30 September 2013	7,200
Year to 30 September 2014	6,000

His assessable profits for first three years of assessment are calculated as follows:

Year of Assessment	Basis Period		Assessment
2012	1/2/2012 − 31/12/2012		
	(7,000) + (3/12 × 7,200) = (5,200)		Nil
2013	Year ended 30/9/2013 = 7,200		
	less: loss forward = (5,200) (note)		2,000
2014	Year ended 30/9/2014:		
	Profits:		6,000
	Note: LOSS		(7,000)
	Less: Utilised		
	2012	(1,800)	
	2013	(5,200)	(7,000)
			(Nil)

5.3.8 Section 382 Relief Arising due to the Third Year Adjustment

As you are aware, the profits assessable in the third year of assessment are based on the basis period of 12 months ending during the year of assessment, but this figure can be reduced by:

Profits assessable in the second tax year
Less: Actual profits of the second year of assessment.

Where this deduction is greater than the amount of the original profits assessable for the third year, then the excess is treated as if it were a loss forward under section 382.

The claim for this deduction must be in writing and must be included in the self assessment tax return for the third year of assessment.

Loss relief in respect of the excess **cannot be claimed under section 381**.

Example:
Derek commenced to trade as a furniture manufacturer on 1 July 2012.
His first year results were as follows:

	Profit
	€
Period 1 July 2012 to 30 June 2013	28,000
Year ended 30 June 2014	7,000
Year ended 30 June 2015	60,000

Computation of assessable profits

Year of assessment	Basis Period	Amount assessable
		€
2012	1/7/2012 − 31/12/2012	14,000 (28,000 × 6/12)
2013	y/e 30/6/2013	28,000
2014	y/e 30/6/2014 (note)	Nil

Note:

Amount assessable for second year, i.e. 2013:	28,000

Less: Actual profits for 2013: (28,000 × 6/12) + (7,000 × 6/12)
	14,000 + 3,500	=	17,500
	Excess		10,500

Final 2014 assessment: 7,000 − 10,500 =	(3,500)
	i.e nil

The excess of €3,500 is carried forward under section 382 against future trading profits for 2015 onwards.

Questions (Chapter 5)

(See Solutions to Questions at the end of this text.)

5 Capital Allowances and Loss Relief

5.1 Regina Briers

Regina Briers, a sole trader, in business for many years, makes up accounts to 30 April each year. During the year ended 30 April 2012, she bought the following secondhand assets.

		€
10/5/2011	Office equipment	€1,000
20/4/2012	Printer	€3,500

The tax written down value of her other assets at 1/1/2012 were as follows:

Motor Vehicle (Cat D) (purchased 1/12/11 for €35,000)	€10,500
Plant and machinery (purchased 10/6/10 for €2,500)	€1,875

Requirement
Prepare the wear and tear computation for 2012.

5.2 Lillian Hanney

Lillian Hanney has practiced as a self-employed dentist for many years and makes up accounts to 30 June each year. During the year ended 30 June 2012, she purchased the following assets.

		€
10/7/2011	Chairs for waiting room	1,000
22/2/2012	X-Ray machine	4,100

The details of her other assets are as follows:

Year of Acquisition:	Tax Year	Cost €	WDV at 1/1/2012 €
Bought y/e 30/6/2009	2009	15,000 (12.5%)	9,375
Bought y/e 30/6/2010	2010	9,000 (12.5%)	6,750

Requirement
Prepare the plant wear and tear computation for 2012.

5.3 Barney Connor

Barney Connor is a self-employed accountant, who has been in business for many years and prepares accounts to 30 September each year. During the year ended 30 September 2012, he purchased the following assets:

		€
29/12/2011	Computer	8,000
1/3/2012	Desktop calculator	120
8/6/2012	Desks	1,800
5/8/2012	Printer ink cartidges	750
20/9/2012	Filing cabinets	2,300
		12,970

The filing cabinets were not delivered until 15 October 2012.
The details of his other assets are as follows:
   Plant and machinery bought during the y/e 30 September 2008 for €10,000 had a WDV at 1 January 2012 of €5,000.

Requirement
Prepare the plant wear and tear computation for 2012.

5.4 Commencement Situation

Facts – Business commenced 1 October 2012

   – First accounts prepared to 30 September 2013

   – Office equipment purchased on 12 December 2012 at a cost
     of €1,000 and immediately put into use.

Requirement
Prepare the wear and tear computation for the tax years for which the first accounts to 30 September 2013 relate.

5.5 Sean – Commencement Situation

Facts – Sean's business commenced 1 June 2012

   – First accounts prepared to 31 May 2013

   – Machinery purchased on 8 December 2012 for €10,000
     and immediately put into use.

Requirement
Prepare the wear and tear computation for the tax years for which the first accounts to 31 May 2013 relate.

5.6 Joan O'Reilly Commencement Situation

Joan O'Reilly is a bookbinder who commenced business as a sole trader on 1 May 2012. In the year ended 30 April 2013, she purchased the following second-hand assets:

		€
21/5/2012	Bookbinding machine	9,000
10/4/2013	Computer	1,700

Requirement
Prepare the wear and tear computation for the tax years for which the first accounts to 30 April 2013 relate.

5.7 Cormac Molloy – Annual Allowances Motor Vehicles

Cormac Molloy is a self-employed farmer, who has been in business for many years and prepares accounts to 31 December each year. Here are his motor vehicle details:

Motor car cost 1/8/2012	€21,000	Emissions category D
Total estimated annual km	20,000 kms	(i.e. 75% of total
Total estimated private km	5,000 kms	kms is business)

Requirement
Calculate wear and tear on the car for 2012.

5.8 Joseph Ryan – Wear and Tear Computation

Joseph Ryan is a shopkeeper who is in business many years and prepares accounts to 30 June each year. On 10 November 2011 he bought a second hand car for €27,000 (Emissions category C). The private use is 1/3.

Requirement
Calculate the wear and tear allowances and tax written down value of the car for 2012.

5.9 Dan Bell – Claim in a Continuing Business

Dan Bell is a doctor who prepares his accounts up to 31 December each year. In the year ended 31 December 2012 he purchased a second hand car for €25,000 on 20 May 2012 and new office equipment for €1,000 on 1 February 2012. (Assume 70% business use for motor car emissions category A).

Dan Bell also sold equipment on 28 January 2012 for €3,500. The tax written down value of the equipment at 1 January 2012 was €7,500. (Cost €15,000).

He has been in practice for many years.

Requirement
Calculate capital allowance claim and written down value of the assets for 2012.

5.10 Joe Bracken – Balancing Charge

Joe Bracken is a butcher who prepares annual accounts to 30 September. He has traded for many years. His car is used 70% for business purposes. The cost of his second hand car (purchased in October 2009) was €27,000. He sold his car in January 2012 for €20,000.

Requirement
Calculate the balancing charge or allowance due on the car.

5.11 Fitzroy

Fitzroy carries on a manufacturing business in Dublin. He has been in business for many years and prepares annual accounts to 30 April. During the year ended 30 April 2012 the following transactions took place:

1. Second hand plant costing €17,000 on 1 May 2003 was sold in February 2012 for €2,200. (Tax written down value at 1/1/2012 was nil)
2. Plant that was acquired new for €25,000 in November 2005 was sold for €1,500 in January 2012. (Tax written down value at 1/1/2012 was nil). New plant was acquired for €50,000 on 15 April 2012.
3. On 20 December 2010 he purchased second hand plant costing €10,000. (Tax written down value @ 1/1/2012 was €8,750.)
4. Fitzroy has two lorries. One cost €20,000 on 5 January 2012 and the other €26,000 on 1 December 2006 (Tax written down value @ 1/1/2012 was nil).
5. Fitzroy owns a car that he bought on 16 July 2008 for €25,000 (emissions category C). One-third of his travel relates to business use.

Fitzroy has no other assets in respect of which capital allowances were claimed.

Requirement
Compute maximum capital allowances for 2012 and 2013, assuming no further additions or disposals are made.

5.12 Sarah

Sarah commenced to trade as a hairdresser on 1 June 2009. She made the following tax-adjusted profits:

12 months ended 31 May 2010	–	€59,000
12 months to 31 May 2011	–	€46,000
12 months to 31 May 2012	–	€120,000
12 months to 31 May 2013	–	€160,000

During the above periods she bought and put the following assets into use:

1 June 2009	–	General equipment €26,000 second hand
1 September 2009	–	Additional hairdryers €800 second hand
10 April 2010	–	Chairs €1,400 second hand
23 April 2010	–	Car (60% business use) €14,000 second hand

Requirement
Compute assessable profits and associated capital allowances for first four years of assessment.

5.13 Joe Bloggs Case I and Capital Allowances

Joe Bloggs has operated a newsagent/tobacconist/confectionery shop for many years. He has previously dealt with his own income tax affairs and supplies the following details relating to his business for the year ended 31 December 2012:

	€	€
Gross profit	26,880	
Sale proceeds of old equipment	1,500	
Building society interest received	<u>210</u>	28,590
Less: Overhead costs:		
Wages to self	5,200	
Motor expenses	1,750	
Light and heat	1,200	
Wages to wife as book-keeper and assistant	1,500	
Wages to other employees	7,600	
Advertising	270	
Christmas gifts to customers (bottles of whiskey)	300	
Depreciation:		
Motor car	500	
Fixtures and equipment	400	
Rates	800	
Covenant to church (net) paid on 31 December 2012	105	
Repairs to yard wall	200	
Painting of shop	450	
New cash register (purchased 1 February 2012)	380	
Deposit on new shelving (paid 10 February 2012)	1,000	
New display freezer (purchased 1 March 2012)	600	
Insurance	375	
Insurance on contents of flat	100	
Hire purchase instalments on new shelving 8 @ €240	1,920	
Payment to self in lieu of rent	2,000	
Sundry expenses	<u>2,250</u>	
		<u>(28,900)</u>
Loss for year		<u>(310)</u>

Mr Bloggs owns the property which consists of the shop and the flat above the shop where he and his wife live. He estimates that 25% of the heat and light relate to the living accommodation.

The motor car cost €14,000 on 1 January 2007. Mr Bloggs has advised you that business travel accounts for 75% of his annual motoring.

The new shelving costing €5,633, excluding VAT, was purchased under a hire purchase agreement and you have calculated that interest charges of €376 have arisen before 31 December 2012.

At 1 January 2012, the following were the written down tax values for income tax purposes of the equipment and shelving, and the motor car:

	€
Equipment and shelving (Cost €2,500 in January 2008	1,250
Sold for €1,500 in 2012).	
Motor car	5,250

Requirement

You are required to compute:

(a) Joe Bloggs taxable Case I income for 2012; and
(b) His capital allowances claim for 2012.

5.14 Mr Goa and Mrs Statham Industrial Buildings

Mr Goa, a long established manufacturer, acquired a new industrial building on 30 April 2008 for €160,000 (including land costing €20,000). On 1 May 2009 he sold the building for €190,000 (land being valued at €25,000) to Mrs Statham who immediately commenced trading from it at that date, also as a manufacturer. Mr Goa's accounts are made up to 30 June each year. Mrs Statham made up her first set of accounts to 30 April 2010 and thereafter on a yearly basis.

Requirement

You are required to calculate the capital allowance position of both Mr Goa and Mrs Statham in respect of the building for the years of assessment 2008–2012.

5.15 James – IBAA Qualifying Items

James built and occupied a factory for the purpose of his trade during the year ended 30 June 2012.

His costs were as follows:	€
Site purchase cost	10,000
Site development costs	5,000
Construction of factory	95,000
Construction of adjoining administrative office	10,000
Construction of adjoining showroom	15,000
Total cost	135,000

Requirement

Compute James' industrial buildings annual allowance (IBAA) for 2012.

5.16   Mr Plant

Mr Plant carries on a manufacturing trade in Ireland. He prepares his annual accounts to 31 December. During the year ended 31 December 2012, he incurred the following capital expenditure:

1.   He purchased new office furniture and equipment on 30 March 2012 for €10,000. The items involved were brought into use immediately.
2.   He purchased a new truck on 30 September 2012 for €25,000 for the purposes of the trade.
3.   On 30 November 2012, he placed deposits on two items of machinery:
     (a)   €5,000 on a used milling machine for delivery on 31 January 2013; and
     (b)   €4,000 on a new pump for delivery on 15 February 2013.
4.   He purchased a new car on 1 April 2012 for €26,000, which is Emissions Category D. The agreed portion of business usage is 75%. He sold his existing car on the same date for €7,500 in a straight cash deal. The car originally cost €26,000 in December 2007. The allowable cost for wear and tear purposes had been restricted to €24,000.
5.   On 15 April 2012, he purchased new machinery for €24,000, which was brought into use immediately. He received a grant of €4,000 on the purchase of the machinery.
6.   On 31 July 2012, he purchased a second-hand factory premises for €120,000. The original qualifying cost of the factory premises for capital allowances purposes was €75,000, and the building has a remaining "tax life" of 15 years. The factory premises were brought into use within three months of the date of purchase.
7.   In October 2012, he commenced building an extension to his original factory premises. The expenditure incurred to 31 December 2012 was €60,000 on actual building work and €8,000 on architect's fees. The extension is due to be completed in March 2013. A grant of €10,000 had been received on the expenditure incurred to 31 December 2012.

The situation regarding assets acquired prior to 1 January 2012 is as follows:

	Date of Purchase	Cost €	Written Down Value at 1/1/2012 €
Fixtures and fittings 12.5%	2009	12,000	7,500
Plant and machinery 12.5%	2009	13,500	8,437
Motor car 12.5%	10/12/2007	24,000	9,000
Trucks 12.5%	June 2010	18,750	14,062

Requirement
You are required to compute Mr Plant's capital allowances for 2012.

5.17   Janet

Janet has been in business for many years as a manufacturer. She prepares accounts to 31 May each year.

During the year ended 31 May 2012, she engaged in an expansion programme. She incurred capital expenditure and received capital sums as follows:

2 June 2011	Sold machinery for €14,000. This machinery had cost €35,000 when purchased. The written down value at the date of sale was Nil.
15 June 2011	Purchased new replacement machinery costing €49,000 on which roll-over relief was claimed. This machinery qualified for a grant of €10,000.
30 June 2011	Purchased a second-hand industrial building for €220,000. The building had cost the original owner €120,000 to construct in June 2000.
1 August 2011	She sold her office building which had been located some distance away from the industrial buildings. The office building had cost €20,000 in May 1991. Proceeds received from the sale amounted to €60,000.
31 October 2011	Completed an extension to the industrial building purchased on 30 June.

Details of the expenditure are as follows:	€
Levelling of site	2,000
Architect's fees	3,000
Offices	6,000
Factory	59,000
	70,000

1 November 2011	Purchased two new cars for sales representatives at a cost of €26,000 each which are Emissions Category C. She partly funded the purchases by trading in a car used by one of the sales representatives for €12,500. That car had cost €24,000 when purchased in June 2007 and had a tax written down value of €12,000 at the date of disposal.
30 May 2012	Purchased a second-hand photocopier at a cost of €2,000. The copier was not put into use until June 2012.

The situation regarding assets bought prior to 1 June 2011 is as follows:

	Date of Purchase	Cost €	Written Down Value at 1/1/2012 €
Plant and machinery (12.5%)	July 2007	10,000	5,000
Delivery truck (12.5%)	November 2004	17,000	2,125
Motor vehicles (12.5%)	June 2007	24,000	12,000

Requirement

Compute the capital allowances due for the tax year 2012.

5.18   Linda – Loss Relief

Linda's income is as follows:

	€
Trading loss for year ended 30 September 2012	(60,000)
Salary for 2012	80,000

Requirement
Compute her assessable income for 2012.

5.19   Mr Jones – Loss Relief

Tax Year 2012

	€
Mr Jones' income is as follows	
Trading profit (loss) y/e 30 June 2012	(30,000)
Salary	50,000
Interest on Government Securities	25,000

Mr Jones possessed the above sources of income for many years. He is single.

Requirement
Compute his assessable income for 2012.

5.20   Mr Fool – Loss Relief

Mr Fool, who has traded for many years, has the following profits and capital allowances:

Profit y/e	31/12/2012	€20,000
Capital allowances	2012	€(37,000)

He also had a balancing charge of €10,000 for 2012.

Requirement
What is Mr Fool's taxable income for 2012?

5.21   John – Loss Relief

John has been in business for many years and prepares annual accounts to 30 September. He has a tax-adjusted profit for year ended 30 September 2012 of €9,000. The capital allowances position for 2012 is:

	€
Wear and tear allowance	7,000
Balancing allowances	500
Balancing charge	(3,000)

Unutilised capital allowances forward from 2011 amount to €9,600.

Requirement

Calculate the capital allowances available to John in 2012.

5.22   Jim – Loss Relief

Jim's only source of income is his travel agency business which he has carried on for many years. He prepares annual accounts to 30 June. Recent tax-adjusted results are as follows:

	€
Y/e 30/6/2010 Tax-adjusted loss	(18,000)
Y/e 30/6/2011 Tax-adjusted profit	17,000
Y/e 30/6/2012 Tax-adjusted profit	50,000

Jim is single.

Requirement

Calculate Jim's assessments for all years, claiming relief in the earliest possible year.

5.23   Basil Bond – Loss Relief

Basil Bond has the following income:

Tax Year	2010	2011	2012
	€	€	€
Rents	20,000	30,000	25,000
Irish taxed interest (gross)	1,000	1,200	1,200
Trading profit (loss) for year ended 30 September in tax year.	80,000	(37,000)	45,000

The above sources of income have existed for many years.

Requirement

Calculate the assessable income for 2010 to 2012 inclusive, claiming optimum relief for losses.

Tax Credits and Reliefs and Charges on Income

Learning Objectives

In this chapter you will learn:

■ the main income tax credits available to individual taxpayers;
■ the manner of granting tax relief at the standard rate and at the marginal rate;
■ expenditures which attract tax relief – mortgage interest payments, fees to third level institutions, etc.;
■ the operation of tax relief at source;
■ the concept of charges on income and the granting of tax relief for the payment of charges; and
■ special tax incentive based reliefs.

6.1 Introduction

Prior to 6 April 1999, an individual was entitled to personal allowances, which were deductions allowable against **income** when calculating taxable income. FA 1999 commenced the process of giving these allowances as **credits** against **income tax liabilities** instead of **deductions** against **income**. A full tax credit system was introduced with effect from 6 April 2001 where every €1,000 of a personal tax allowance is now equivalent to a **tax credit** of €200, i.e. the tax allowance at the standard rate of 20%.

However, it must be noted that some reliefs are still given as a **deduction from income** and, therefore, obtain tax relief at the marginal rate.

There are three methods of granting tax relief for reliefs relating to personal status, expenses incurred or source of income:

1. Non-refundable tax credit – related to personal circumstances, e.g. married tax credit *or* related to expenses incurred, e.g. rent paid.

2. Refundable tax credit.
3. Deduction from income source (e.g. pension) *or* deduction from total income (e.g. employment of carer for an incapacitated person).

As a general rule, the taxpayer must be **tax resident** in Ireland before tax credits are given. **Non-refundable** tax credits **cannot** reduce the tax due **below zero**, **nor** can they **reduce** the tax payable on **charges on income** (e.g. covenants).

Refundable/Non-refundable Tax Credits

Generally, credits for tax withheld from income are refundable (e.g. PAYE, DWT), whereas all other tax credits (e.g. basic personal tax credits, incapacitated child, home-carer, etc.) are not refundable. However, DIRT is only repayable in certain circumstances – where the individual is not liable or fully liable to income tax **and** is aged 65 years or over in the tax year **or** became permanently incapacitated, by reason of mental or physical infirmity, from maintaining himself.

6.2 Personal Tax Credits

6.2.1 Introduction

Personal tax credits are credits to which an individual is entitled depending on his personal circumstances, e.g. married, civil partners, single, widowed, employed, etc. The amount of the qualifying credit is the same for each individual.

6.2.2 Chart of Personal Tax Credits

Description	Tax Year 2011 €	Tax Year 2012 €
Single person	1,650	1,650
Married couple/civil partners	3,300	3,300
Widowed person/surviving civil partner		
– With dependent children*	1,650	1,650
– Without dependent children	2,190	2,190
– In the year of bereavement	3,300	3,300
Single-parent family (additional)		
– Widowed person/surviving civil partner	1,650	1,650
– Other	1,650	1,650
Widowed/surviving civil partner-parent (additional)		
– First year after bereavement	3,600	3,600
– Second year after bereavement	3,150	3,150
– Third year after bereavement	2,700	2,700
– Fourth year after bereavement	2,250	2,250
– Fifth year after bereavement	1,800	1,800
Employee (PAYE) tax credit	1,650	1,650
Blind person	1,650	1,650
Both spouses/civil partners blind	3,300	3,300
Guide dog allowance	825	825
	(continued overleaf)	

	@ Standard Rate 20%	@ Standard Rate 20%
Age credit (65 years and over)		
– Single/widowed person/surviving civil partner	245	245
– Married/civil partners	490	490
Incapacitated child	3,300	3,300
Dependent relative	70	70
Income limit	13,837	13,837
Home carer	810	810
– Income limit lower	5,080	5,080
– Income limit upper	6,880	6,700

Also entitled to single-parent family allowance

6.2.3 Basic Personal Tax Credits

The basic personal tax credits are determined by the marital status of the taxpayer.

Married/Civil Partners Tax Credit
This is available for a year of assessment where:

- a husband and wife or civil partners are jointly assessed, *or*
- where the couple are living apart and one party, in the year of assessment, is wholly or mainly maintained by the other, and that person is not entitled to deduct any legally enforceable maintenance payments to the other when computing his or her total income for the year of assessment.

Widowed/Surviving Civil Partner Tax Credit
This is available to a widowed person/surviving civil partner. The widowed person's or surviving civil partner's "year of bereavement" credit is given in the year of bereavement **only**. This credit is not available to a surviving spouse/civil partner who is the subject of a joint assessment for that year.
   A widowed person/surviving civil partner **with dependent children** is **also** entitled to:

- The *One-Parent Family* tax credit, *and*
- The *Widowed or Surviving Civil Partner's Parent's* tax credit of:
  - €3,600 in the first year after bereavement
  - €3,150 in the second year after bereavement
  - €2,700 in the third year after bereavement
  - €2,250 in the fourth year after bereavement
  - €1,800 in the fifth year after bereavement

A "qualifying" child for the purpose of this allowance is a child who:

- is born in the year of assessment, *or*
- is **under 18 years** at the start of the year of assessment, *or*
- if **over 18 years** at the start of the year of assessment:
  - is receiving full-time education at an educational establishment or is in full-time training with an employer for a trade or profession, *or*

- is permanently incapacitated by reason of mental or physical infirmity from maintaining himself, and, if he has reached 21 years of age, was so incapacitated before reaching that age, *or*
- is a child of the claimant, or a child in the custody of the claimant, who is maintained by the claimant at the claimant's own expense for the whole or part of the year of assessment.

"Child" includes a stepchild, a child whose parents have not married, and an adopted child.

Single Tax Credit
This credit is available to individuals, other than married/civil partners or widowed.

Single-Parent Family Tax Credit
In addition to the single tax credit, a widowed parent, surviving civil partner or other single parent, who has a "qualifying" child (as defined above) resident with him for the whole or part of the tax year, is entitled to a "single-parent family tax credit". This credit is **not available** to an unmarried couple that are **living together**, but is available to both single parents where they are not living with anyone else as man and wife or civil partners and who jointly maintain a "qualifying" child. The tax credit is the same for all single parents irrespective of the number of qualifying children.

Example:
Mary is a widow since 2007 with one dependent child. She has not remarried and lives alone with her child. What are her non refundable tax credits (NRTC) for 2012?

	€
Widowed person - with dependent children	1,650
Single-parent family (additional)	1,650
Widowed parent 5th year	<u>1,800</u>
Total NRTC 2012	<u>5,100</u>

6.2.4 *Employee (PAYE) Tax Credit*

An individual who is in **receipt of emoluments** chargeable under Schedule E and subject to the PAYE system is entitled to this tax credit. In the case of joint assessment and where **each** spouse/civil partner is in employment, the credit is available to each spouse/civil partner.

The employee tax credit **cannot exceed** the individual's Schedule E income at the standard rate of tax, i.e. if the individual's salary for 2012 is €1,000, the employee tax credit would be limited to €200 (€1,000 @ 20%).

An individual may also receive the employee tax credit where he received income from an employment held **outside the State** and where the income has been subject to a tax deduction system similar to the Irish PAYE system, e.g. an Irish individual, living in Dundalk and working in Newry for a UK employer, receives his salary after deduction of UK PAYE. The individual will be entitled to the employee tax credit.

The employee tax credit is **not applicable** to emoluments paid by a company to a **proprietary director** or his spouse/civil partner. A "proprietary director" means a director of a company who is the beneficial owner of or able to control, either directly or indirectly, more than **15%** of the ordinary share capital of the company.

Children of proprietary directors or of the self-employed, who are employees in the business, will only get the employee tax credit where:

- the child is required to devote, throughout the tax year, substantially the whole of his time to the duties of the employment, *and*
- the child's gross salary from the employment is at least €4,572, *and*
- the child is in insurable employment for PRSI, *and*
- PAYE is operated on the child's salary.

6.2.5   Blind Persons' Tax Credit

A blind person is entitled to a "blind person's tax credit". If a husband and wife or civil partners are both blind, they are entitled to double the tax credit.

An individual does not have to be completely blind to obtain the credit. A medical certificate showing the degree of blindness is required before the credit will be granted.

An additional allowance (deductible from total income) is available if an individual or the individual's spouse/civil partner has a guide dog and is a registered owner with the Irish Guide Dog Association. The amount of the additional credit is €825 at the standard rate.

6.2.6   Age Tax Credit

In addition to a basic personal tax credit, an individual may claim the "age tax credit" where he, or his spouse/civil partner, is at least 65 years of age during the year of assessment. The married couple's/civil partner's age tax credit may be claimed where only one of the couple is aged 65 or more.

6.2.7   Incapacitated Child Tax Credit

Where an individual has a "qualifying child" living with him at any time during the year, he is entitled to an "incapacitated child tax credit".

In this context a "qualifying child" is one who:

- is **under** the age of 18 and is permanently incapacitated by reason of mental or physical infirmity; *or*
- **if over** the age of 18, is permanently incapacitated by reason of mental or physical infirmity from maintaining himself, and was so before he reached 21 years, *or* was in full-time education/training with an employer when he became so incapacitated; *and*
- is a child of the claimant or, if he is not such a child, is in the custody of the claimant, and is maintained by the claimant at the claimant's own expense for the whole or part of the year in question.

"Child" includes a stepchild, an adopted child, a child whose parents have not been married or an informally adopted child or any child of whom a person has custody. The credit is available for **each qualifying** child.

Where two or more persons are entitled to relief in respect of the same child, i.e. where both parents maintain the child jointly, the tax credit is **allocated among** those persons by reference to the amount which each spends in maintaining the child.

Qualifying Incapacities
The incapacity of the child must be such that it permanently prevents the child from being able in the long term (i.e. when over 18 years of age) to maintain himself/herself independently. If the incapacity can be corrected or relieved by the use of any treatment, device, medication or therapy (e.g. coeliac disease, diabetes, hearing impairment which can be corrected by a hearing aid, etc.) the child will not be regarded as permanently incapacitated for the purposes of this relief.

The following are examples of disabilities which are regarded as permanently incapacitating: cystic fibrosis, spina bifida, blindness, deafness, Down's syndrome, spastic paralysis, certain forms of schizophrenia, acute autism. (Note: this list is not exhaustive.)

Note that a person who is entitled to an incapacitated child tax credit is not entitled to a dependent relative tax credit (see below) in respect of the same child.

6.2.8 Dependent Relative Tax Credit

An individual who proves that he maintains at his own expense a "dependent relative" is entitled to a "dependent relative tax credit".

A "dependent relative" is defined as:

- a relative of the claimant or of his/her spouse/civil partner who is incapacitated by old age or infirmity from maintaining himself, *or*
- the widowed father or widowed mother of the claimant or the claimant's spouse/civil partner, whether incapacitated or not, *or*
- the son or daughter of the claimant who lives with the claimant and upon whom he is dependent, by reason of old age or infirmity.

If the income of the dependent relative exceeds the specified limit (€13,837: 2012), the dependent relative tax credit is not available.

Where two or more persons jointly maintain a dependent relative, the tax credit is allocated between them in proportion to the amount which each spends in maintaining the relative.

6.2.9 Home Carer Tax Credit

This is claimable by a married couple or civil partners that are jointly assessed where one spouse/ civil partner (i.e. the home carer) works in the home caring for one or more dependent persons. The tax credit will be granted where:

- the couple must be married or civil partners and must be **jointly assessed**;
- one or more qualifying persons normally **reside** with the claimant and his/her spouse/civil partner (or, in the case of an aged or incapacitated person, resides nearby within 2 km); and
- the home carer's **income** is not in **excess of €5,080**. A reduced tax credit applies where the income is between **€5,080 and €6,700**. In calculating total income, no account is taken of the carer's allowance payable by the Department of Social, Community and Family Affairs.

A "dependent" person is defined as:

- a child for whom Social Welfare Child Benefit is payable i.e. children under 16 and children up to age 19 in full-time education, *or*
- a person aged 65 years or more in the year, *or*
- an individual who is permanently incapacitated by reason of mental or physical infirmity.

Note: A spouse/civil partner cannot be a "dependent" person.

Only **one** tax credit is given **regardless** of the number of dependent persons being cared for.

For **2012**, if the home carer has total income of €5,080 or less, the full tax credit is given. If the income of the home carer is in excess of €5,080, the tax credit is reduced by **one-half of the**

excess over the limit. For example, if the home carer has income of €5,500 a tax credit of €600 (€810 – ((€5,500 – €5,080) × ½)), may be claimed. Where a home carer has income of €6,700 i.e. (€810 – ((€6,700 – €5,080) × ½)), no tax credit is due.

Where the income of the home carer exceeds the permitted limit, the credit **will be granted** for that year if the home carer qualified for the credit in the **immediately preceding** tax year. However, in these circumstances, the tax credit granted is **restricted to the tax credit** granted in the previous tax year.

Note that married couples/civil partners **cannot claim** both the home carer's tax credit and the increased standard rate band for dual-income couples, but they can claim whichever of the two is more beneficial.

Example:
Jim and Katie Bloom are jointly assessed and they have two children under the age of 16 years. Jim has a salary of €47,000 and Katie has investment income of €6,000.

Option One:

Claim Increased Standard Rate Tax Band 2012	€	€
Taxable Income:		
Jim	47,000	
Katie	6,000	53,000
Taxation:		
€47,800 @ 20% (Jim max €41,800 + Katie €6,000)	9,560	
€5,200 @ 41%	2,132	11,692
Tax Credits		
Married credit	3,300	
Employee credit (Jim)	1,650	(4,950)
Tax Liability		**6,742**

Option Two:

Claim Home Carer Tax Credit 2012		
Taxable Income:		
Jim	47,000	
Katie	6,000	53,000
Taxation:		
€41,800 @ 20% (Jim max €41,800 only)	8,360	
€11,200 @ 41%	4,592	12,952
Tax Credits		
Married credit	3,300	
Home carer (€810 – (6,000 – 5,080) × 50%)	350	
Employee credit (Jim)	1,650	(5,300)
Tax Liability		**7,652**

As their tax liability is lower if the increased standard rate tax band is claimed, Jim and Katie should claim this instead of the home carer tax credit.

A married couple or civil partners, **where both persons have income**, are entitled to a standard rate tax band of up to €65,600. A married couple or civil partners cannot claim **both** the increased standard rate tax band **and** the home carer tax credit. However, they can claim whichever of the two gives them a lower tax liability.

In practice, when calculating tax credits and standard rate cut-off point applicable, the Inspector will grant whichever option is more beneficial.

6.3 Tax Reliefs at the Standard Rate

6.3.1 Introduction

These reliefs are available in the same manner as the personal tax credits at **Section 6.2** above, but the amounts of the relief **vary** depending on the expenditure involved. These reliefs are granted at the standard rate of tax and are given as a credit against the income tax liability.

6.3.2 Medical Insurance

Relief is available for premiums, paid to an authorised insurer or society, in respect of insurance to provide for the payment of actual medical expenses of the individual, his/her spouse/civil partner and dependants.

With effect from **1 January 2004**, relief is also available in respect of premiums paid on **dental insurance** policies for non-routine dental treatment provided by those insurers who only provide dental insurance.

Since 6 April 2001, the relief is granted **"at source"** i.e. the amount of the gross premium is **reduced** by the **tax credit** available (20%). The medical insurance company **reclaims the 20% tax** from the Revenue and the taxpayer **does not** need to make a separate claim for relief.

However, where an employer pays medical insurance premiums for an employee, the employee is treated as if he had received additional salary equal to the **gross** medical insurance premium payable. In these circumstances, the employer pays the premium to the medical insurer **net of tax at 20%** (however, see the age related tax credit below.) The employer pays the tax deducted to the Revenue Commissioners. The employee must then **claim** a tax credit for this tax deducted.

(See example overleaf.)

Example:

Monica is is an employee of Scalp Ltd and earned €20,000 (PAYE paid €800) in 2012. Scalp Ltd also paid her medical insurance of €1,200 net to VHI.

	€	€
Schedule E salary		20,000
BIK medical insurance – (€1,200/0.8)		<u>1,500</u>
Net Income		<u>21,500</u>
Income tax @ 20%		4,300
Less NRTC:		
Single	(1,650)	
Medical insurance - 1,500*20%	(300)	
Employee tax credit	<u>(1,650)</u>	(3,600)
Less PAYE paid		<u>(800)</u>
Tax refund due		(100)

Age Related Tax Credit

The Health Insurance (Miscellaneous Provisions) Act 2009 amended section 470B TCA 1997 to provide for an additional age related tax credit for medical insurance premiums. These credits, as detailed below, are granted at source (TRS).

Age of Insured Person	TRS 2011	TRS 2012
	€	€
Greater or equal to 60 years but less than 65 years	625	600
Greater or equal to 65 years but less than 70 years	625	975
Greater or equal to 70 years but less than 75 years	1,275	1,400
Greater or equal to 75 years but less than 80 years	1,275	2,025
Greater or equal to 80 years but less than 85 years	1,725	2,400
Greater or equal to 85 years	1,725	2,700

Employers who pay medical insurance premiums for employees over 60 years of age need to take account of these credits when calculating the tax payable to the Revenue Commissioners.

6.3.3 Rent Paid by Certain Tenants

Tax relief may be claimed by tenants for rent paid in respect of rented residential accommodation, which is their sole or main residence, except where the tenant is a child of the landlord. However, **section 14 FA 2011** announced the phasing out of this relief, over the period **2011 to 2017**, for tenancies in existence at **7 December 2010** and the **abolition** of relief to new claimants or those claimants that were not tenants at 7 December 2010.

The tax credit is equal to the **lower** of the **actual rent paid** at the standard rate of tax **OR** the **specified limit** at the standard rate of tax.

The "specified limits" for **2012** are as follows:

	Rent Limit 2012	Max. Tax Credit 2012
	€	€
Person **under** 55 years:		
▦ Married/Widowed/Civil Partners	2,400	480
▦ Single	1,200	240
Person **over** 55 years:		
▦ Married/Widowed/Civil Partners	4,800	960
▦ Single	2,400	480

For years **2013 to 2017** the "specified limits" will be as follows:

Year	Married/Widowed/Civil Partners under 55 years	Single under 55 years	Married/Widowed/Civil Partners over 55 years	Single over 55 years
	€	€	€	€
2013	2,000	1,000	4,000	2,000
2014	1,600	800	3,200	1,600
2015	1,200	600	2,400	1,200
2016	800	400	1,600	800
2017	400	200	800	400
2018	Nil	Nil	Nil	Nil

Any claim to relief for rent paid must be supported by:

1. A Revenue form (*Form Rent 1*) completed by the tenant which sets out:
    (a) tenant's name, address and income tax reference number;
    (b) the name, address and tax reference number of the landlord;
    (c) the address of the rented premises; and
    (d) full details of the tenancy concerned; *and*

2. A receipt from the landlord showing:
    (a) the tenant's name and address;
    (b) the name, address and tax reference number of the landlord;
    (c) the amount of rent paid in the year of assessment;
    (d) the period in respect of which the rent was paid; and
    (e) the amount of rent payable each month.

"**Rent**" which qualifies for the relief is limited to the amount paid in return for the **use** of the premises and adjoining garden or grounds. It **does not** include the following amounts:

▦ amounts paid for repairs or maintenance.
▦ amounts paid for the provision of goods and services, e.g. furniture in a furnished accommodation letting; or
▦ any payment made which has a right of reimbursement, e.g. a deposit.

6.3.4 Fees Paid for Third-level Education and Training Courses

Third-level Education
Relief is available for "qualifying fees" paid in the tax year, in respect of an "approved course" to an "approved college" on behalf of the individual or any other person. (FA 2007 **abolished** the previous requirement that there had to be a defined relationship between the taxpayer and the subject of the tax relief claim.)

"Qualifying fees" are fees in respect of un-reimbursed tuition only of an "approved course".

"Approved college," means a college/university in the State or in the EU or in a non-EU Member State which is maintained/assisted by public funds of that country. (See Revenue website **www.revenue.ie** for a full list of colleges).

An "approved course" is:

- a full-time or part-time undergraduate course which is of at least two academic years duration; *or*
- a postgraduate course of at least one year's duration, but not exceeding four years. This course must lead to a postgraduate award based on exam and/or thesis.

Relief is available on qualifying fees, per course, per academic year, e.g. if an individual pays qualifying fees for two students attending college in an academic year, he is entitled to relief up to the maximum limit for **each** of these students.

The maximum level on qualifying fees for academic years 2011/2012 is **€7,000**.

Section 473A TCA 1997 restricts this relief by disallowing the tax credit on the **first €2,250** of qualifying fees for each **full-time course** and the **first €1,125** of qualifying fees for each **part-time course**, effective for years of assessment **2012 onwards**.

Training Courses
Relief is given for tuition fees paid for certain approved training courses, of less than two years duration, in the areas of **information technology** and **foreign languages**. For 2012, relief applies to fees ranging from €315 to €1,270. The relief is given as an additional tax credit equal to the fees paid, subject to the €1,270 maximum, at the standard rate of tax.

The course must result in the awarding of a certificate of competence, not just a certificate of attendance.

6.3.5 Energy-efficient Works

Section 13 FA 2011 introduced a new tax relief for expenditure incurred on certain energy-efficient works on residential premises situated in the State. The relief is not available to landlords or anyone in receipt of rent (other than rent received under the *Rent-A-Room* scheme) but is available to tenants and to those who do not own the property (e.g. a son renovating his mother's house).

In order for the expenditure to qualify for the relief the works must be:

- **"energy-efficient works"**, which means that the purpose of such work is to reduce the cost of **heating** the residential premises; and
- carried out by an **"approved contractor"**, who is a contractor registered with the Sustainable Energy Authority of Ireland (SEAI) **and** who has a tax clearance **or** a C2 certificate.

Relief will be available at the standard rate of tax for qualifying expenditure, per year of assessment, of up to **€10,000** for a single individual and up to **€15,000** for **married couples**, with an **overall** annual **cap** of **€15,000** per qualifying residence. Relief is given by way of **repayment** in the tax year **following** the year in which the expenditure is incurred.

Note that, at the time of printing, the introduction of this relief is subject to a Commencement Order by the Minister for Finance.

6.3.6 Home Loan Interest Payments

Since 1 January 2002, tax relief for home mortgage interest is granted **at source** by the mortgage lender (**Tax Relief at Source – TRS**). Prior to this, the relief was only given through the tax credit system. Tax credits are **still available** for qualifying loans from **non-TRS** sources. Under TRS, the mortgage lender gives the relief either in the form of a reduced monthly mortgage payment or a credit to the borrowers funding account.

All individuals who have a "qualifying mortgage" on their main residence are entitled to apply to Revenue to have the relief on the interest charged/paid on their qualifying mortgage **applied at source** by the lender.

A "qualifying mortgage" is a secured loan, used to purchase, repair, develop or improve an individual's **sole or main** residence, which must be situated in the State. An individual can also claim relief in respect of a mortgage paid in respect of a separated/divorced spouse/civil partner and/or a dependent relative for whom a dependent relative tax credit is claimed. Mortgage interest relief **cannot** be claimed in respect of an investment property.

Mortgage Interest Relief Ceilings

- Mortgages taken out **prior to 1 January 2004** are no longer eligible for mortgage interest relief. However, top-up loans/equity release loans taken out since 1 January 2004 on these pre-2004 loans may be eligible for mortgage interest relief, provided they adhere to the "qualifying mortgage" criteria above.
- Mortgages taken out **from 1 January 2004 to 31 December 2012**, subject to qualifying mortgage criteria, are eligible for mortgage interest relief until **31 December 2017**.
- Mortgages taken out **after 31 December 2012** will **not qualify** for mortgage interest relief.

A distinction is made between **First-time buyers (FTB)** and **Non-first-time buyers (NFTB)** for mortgage interest relief. It is also important to note that the upper limits relief apply for the tax year in which the mortgage was taken out (not when the taxpayer first claimed the relief), plus six subsequent qualifying tax years. Note that after year seven, the rates are those that apply to non-first-time buyers.

Table 1. Interest Ceilings or Upper Limits for First Time Buyers (FTB)							
Status	Ceiling	Rate of Relief Year 1 & 2	Max. relief available	Rate of Relief Year 3, 4 & 5	Max. relief available	Rate of Relief Year 6 & 7	Max. relief available
Single	€10,000	@ 25%	€2,500	@ 22.5%	€2,250	@ 20%	€2,000
Married/Widowed/ Civil Partnership	€20,000	@ 25%	€5,000	@ 22.5%	€4,500	@ 20%	€4,000

Table 2. Interest Ceilings or Upper Limits for Non First-Time Buyers (NFTB)			
Status	Ceiling	Rate of Relief	Max. relief available
Single	€3,000	@ 15%	€450
Married/Widowed/Civil Partnership	€6,000	@ 15%	€900

FA 2012 Amendments

Exemption: Notwithstanding the rates of tax relief mentioned above, for individuals who purchased their first principal private residence on or **after 1 January 2004 and on or before 31 December 2008**, the rate of tax relief will be **30%** of the interest paid for the tax years **2012 to 2017**.

Table 3. Interest Ceilings for First-Time Buyers for Tax Years 2012 to 2017						
Year FTB loan taken out	2012 Ceiling @ Rate Single or Married / Widowed/Civil Partnership	2013 Ceiling @ Rate	2014 Ceiling @ Rate	2015 Ceiling @ Rate	2016 Ceiling @ Rate	2017 Ceiling @ Rate
2012	S: €10K @ 25% M/W/CP: €20K @ 25%	S: €10K @ 25% M/W/CP: €20K @ 25%	S: €10K @ 22.5% M/W/ CP: €20K @ 22.5%	S: €10K @ 22.5% M/W/ CP: €20K @ 22.5%	S: €10K @ 22.5% M/W/ CP: €20K @ 22.5%	S: €10K @ 20% M/W/CP: €20K @ 20%
2011	S: €10K @ 25% M/W/CP: €20K @ 25%	S: €10K @ 22.5% M/W/ CP: €20K @ 22.5%	S: €10K @ 22.5% M/W/ CP: €20K @ 22.5%	S: €10K @ 22.5% M/W/ CP: €20K @ 22.5%	S: €10K @ 20% M/W/ CP: €20K @ 20%	S: €10K @ 20% M/W/CP: €20K @ 20%
2010	S: €10K @ 22.5% M/W/CP: €20K @ 22.5%	S: €10K @ 22.5% M/W/ CP: €20K @ 22.5%	S: €10K @ 22.5% M/W/ CP: €20K @ 22.5%	S: €10K @ 20% M/W/CP: €20K @ 20%	S: €10K @ 20% M/W/ CP: €20K @ 20%	S: €3K @ 15% M/W/CP: €6K @ 15%
2009	S: €10K @ 22.5% M/W/CP: €20K @ 22.5%	S: €10K @ 22.5% M/W/ CP: €20K @ 22.5%	S: €10K @ 20% M/W/CP: €20K @ 20%	S: €10K @ 20% M/W/CP: €20K @ 20%	S: €3K @ 15% M/W/CP: €6K @ 15%	S: €3K @ 15% M/W/CP: €6K @ 15%
2008	S: €10K @ 30% M/W/CP: €20K @ 30%	S: €10K @ 30% M/W/CP: €20K @ 30%	S: €10K @ 30% M/W/CP: €20K @ 30%	S: €3K @ 30% M/W/CP: €6K @ 30%	S: €3K @ 30% M/W/CP: €6K @ 30%	S: €3K @ 30% M/W/CP: €6K @ 30%
2007	S: €10K @ 30% M/W/CP: €20K @ 30%	S: €10K @ 30% M/W/CP: €20K @ 30%	S: €3K @ 30% M/W/CP: €6K @ 30%	S: €3K @ 30% M/W/CP: €6K @ 30%	S: €3K @ 30% M/W/CP: €6K @ 30%	S: €3K @ 30% M/W/CP: €6K @ 30%
2006	S: €10K @ 30% M/W/CP: €20K @ 30%	S: €3K @ 30% M/W/CP: €6K @ 30%	S: €3K @ 30% M/W/CP: €6K @ 30%	S: €3K @ 30% M/W/CP: €6K @ 30%	S: €3K @ 30% M/W/CP: €6K @ 30%	S: €3K @ 30% M/W/CP: €6K @ 30%
2005	S: €3K @ 30% M/W/CP: €6K @ 30%	S: €3K @ 30% M/W/CP: €6K @ 30%	S: €3K @ 30% M/W/CP: €6K @ 30%	S: €3K @ 30% M/W/CP: €6K @ 30%	S: €3K @ 30% M/W/CP: €6K @ 30%	S: €3K @ 30% M/W/CP: €6K @ 30%
2004	S: €3K @ 30% M/W/CP: €6K @ 30%	S: €3K @ 30% M/W/CP: €6K @ 30%	S: €3K @ 30% M/W/CP: €6K @ 30%	S: €3K @ 30% M/W/CP: €6K @ 30%	S: €3K @ 30% M/W/CP: €6K @ 30%	S: €3K @ 30% M/W/CP: €6K @ 30%

Year NFTB loan taken out	2012 Ceiling @ Rate Single or Married / Widowed/Civil Partnership	2013 Ceiling @ Rate	2014 Ceiling @ Rate	2015 Ceiling @ Rate	2016 Ceiling @ Rate	2017 Ceiling @ Rate
2012	S: €3K @ 15% M/W/CP: €6K @ 15%	S: €3K @ 15% M/W/CP: €6K @ 15%	S: €3K @ 15% M/W/CP: €6K @ 15%	S: €3K @ 15% M/W/CP: €6K @ 15%	S: €3K @ 15% M/W/CP: €6K @ 15%	S: €3K @ 15% M/W/CP: €6K @ 15%
2011	S: €3K @ 15% M/W/CP: €6K @ 15%	S: €3K @ 15% M/W/CP: €6K @ 15%	S: €3K @ 15% M/W/CP: €6K @ 15%	S: €3K @ 15% M/W/CP: €6K @ 15%	S: €3K @ 15% M/W/CP: €6K @ 15%	S: €3K @ 15% M/W/CP: €6K @ 15%
2010	S: €3K @ 15% M/W/CP: €6K @ 15%	S: €3K @ 15% M/W/CP: €6K @ 15%	S: €3K @ 15% M/W/CP: €6K @ 15%	S: €3K @ 15% M/W/CP: €6K @ 15%	S: €3K @ 15% M/W/CP: €6K @ 15%	S: €3K @ 15% M/W/CP: €6K @ 15%
2009	S: €3K @ 15% M/W/CP: €6K @ 15%	S: €3K @ 15% M/W/CP: €6K @ 15%	S: €3K @ 15% M/W/CP: €6K @ 15%	S: €3K @ 15% M/W/CP: €6K @ 15%	S: €3K @ 15% M/W/CP: €6K @ 15%	S: €3K @ 15% M/W/CP: €6K @ 15%
2008	S: €3K @ 15% M/W/CP: €6K @ 15%	S: €3K @ 15% M/W/CP: €6K @ 15%	S: €3K @ 15% M/W/CP: €6K @ 15%	S: €3K @ 15% M/W/CP: €6K @ 15%	S: €3K @ 15% M/W/CP: €6K @ 15%	S: €3K @ 15% M/W/CP: €6K @ 15%
2007	S: €3K @ 15% M/W/CP: €6K @ 15%	S: €3K @ 15% M/W/CP: €6K @ 15%	S: €3K @ 15% M/W/CP: €6K @ 15%	S: €3K @ 15% M/W/CP: €6K @ 15%	S: €3K @ 15% M/W/CP: €6K @ 15%	S: €3K @ 15% M/W/CP: €6K @ 15%
2006	S: €3K @ 15% M/W/CP: €6K @ 15%	S: €3K @ 15% M/W/CP: €6K @ 15%	S: €3K @ 15% M/W/CP: €6K @ 15%	S: €3K @ 15% M/W/CP: €6K @ 15%	S: €3K @ 15% M/W/CP: €6K @ 15%	S: €3K @ 15% M/W/CP: €6K @ 15%
2005	S: €3K @ 15% M/W/CP: €6K @ 15%	S: €3K @ 15% M/W/CP: €6K @ 15%	S: €3K @ 15% M/W/CP: €6K @ 15%	S: €3K @ 15% M/W/CP: €6K @ 15%	S: €3K @ 15% M/W/CP: €6K @ 15%	S: €3K @ 15% M/W/CP: €6K @ 15%
2004	S: €3K @ 15% M/W/CP: €6K @ 15%	S: €3K @ 15% M/W/CP: €6K @ 15%	S: €3K @ 15% M/W/CP: €6K @ 15%	S: €3K @ 15% M/W/CP: €6K @ 15%	S: €3K @ 15% M/W/CP: €6K @ 15%	S: €3K @ 15% M/W/CP: €6K @ 15%

Table 4. Interest Ceilings for Non First-Time Buyers for Tax Years 2012 to 2017

An individual who sells his only or main residence and acquires another is entitled to claim additional interest on the **bridging loan** up to the **maximum** of his marital status threshold.

Although TRS is **not available** for the following loans, a non-refundable tax credit is available on the interest payable at the standard tax rate (subject to the same interest limits as TRS):

- loans to acquire a residence that qualifies for mortgage interest relief in Northern Ireland or the UK;
- non-mortgage loans, e.g. term loans for home improvements; and
- loans from non TRS lenders, e.g. employers or foreign banks.

Example:

Sean Smith, a single man, received a loan from his employer (not a bank) to assist with the purchase in 2012 of his first residence. He paid interest of €10,500 in 2012.

His non-refundable tax credit for 2012 is limited to the **lower** of the actual interest paid @ 25% **or** the €10,000 limit for a first time buyer, in 2012.

Interest paid: €10,500 @ 25%	=	€2,625
Mortgage allowance restricted to	=	€2,500 (€10,000*25%)

6.3.7 Medical Expenses

Relief may be claimed by way of tax credit at the standard rate (with the exception of nursing home expenses which may be claimed at marginal rate – see **Section 6.4.3**), in respect of **un-reimbursed** medical expenses incurred by the individual on his **own behalf**, or **on behalf of others**.

FA 2007 abolished the previous requirement that there had to be a defined relationship between the taxpayer and the subject of the tax relief claim.

"**Medical expenses**" include expenses incurred on:

- Cost of doctors and consultants fees.
- Items/treatments prescribed by a doctor/consultant (see below).
- Maintenance or treatment in a hospital or other location where such expenses were **necessarily** incurred in connection with the services of a medical practitioner or diagnostic procedures carried out on the advice of a medical practitioner. **FA 2010** removed the requirement for the location to be an Irish hospital.
- Costs of speech and language therapy carried out by a speech and language therapist for a qualifying child.
- Transport by ambulance.
- Costs of educational psychological assessments carried out by an educational psychologist for a qualifying child.
- Certain items of expenditure in respect of a child suffering from a serious life threatening illness (including relief for mileage to/from hospital at €0.17 per km, relief for some telephone costs, overnight accommodation costs for parents, hygiene products and special clothing).
- Kidney patients' expenses (including relief for mileage to/from hospital at €0.17 per km, and, depending on whether the patient uses hospital dialysis, home dialysis or CAPD, relief for electricity, telephone and laundry costs up to a maximum amount).
- Specialised dental treatment – (see below).
- Routine maternity care.
- In-vitro fertilisation.

FA 2010 specifically excludes **cosmetic surgery**, unless such surgery is necessary to ameliorate a physical deformity arising from or directly related to:

- a congenital abnormality; *or*
- a personal injury; *or*
- a disfiguring disease.

The emphasis on medical expenses relief appears to be relief for **unavoidable** health costs as opposed to those that are **discretionary**.

The following, where **prescribed by a doctor**, qualify for medical expenses relief:

- Drugs and medicines.
- Diagnostic procedures.
- Orthoptic or similar treatment.
- Hearing aids.
- Orthopaedic bed/chair.
- Wheelchair/wheelchair lift (no relief is due for alteration to the building to facilitate a lift).
- Glucometer machine for a diabetic.
- Engaging a qualified nurse in the case of a serious illness.
- Physiotherapy or similar treatment.

■ Cost of a computer where it is necessary to alleviate communication problems of a severely handicapped person.

■ Cost of gluten-free food for coeliacs. As this condition is generally ongoing, a letter (instead of prescriptions) from a doctor stating that the individual is a coeliac sufferer is acceptable. Receipts from supermarkets in addition to receipts from chemists are acceptable.

Where qualifying health care is only available outside Ireland, reasonable travelling and accommodation expenses can also be claimed. In such cases the expenses of one person accompanying the patient may also be allowed where the condition of the patient requires it.

The following **dental treatments** qualify for relief, provided the **dentist** supplies a Form MED2:

■ Bridgework
■ Crowns (including post and core buildups made from materials other than gold)
■ Tip replacing
■ Veneers/Rembrandt type etched fillings
■ Endodontics – root canal treatment
■ Orthodontic treatment (including provision of braces)
■ Periodontal treatment.
■ Surgical extraction of impacted wisdom teeth.

Tax relief is not available for routine dental care, i.e. the cost of scaling, extraction and filling of teeth, and the provision and repair of artificial teeth and dentures.

Tax relief is also **not available** for **routine ophthalmic care**, i.e. the cost of sight testing, provision and maintenance of spectacles and contact lenses.

To claim the relief at the end of the year of assessment (i.e. 2012 medical expenses may be claimed for tax year 2012), the individual must complete **Form MED 1** for medical expenses paid or incurred during the tax year. Receipts **do not** have to be submitted for the claims but only **receipted expenditure** can be claimed.

6.4 Tax Reliefs at the Marginal Rate

6.4.1 Introduction

Tax reliefs at the marginal rate are given as a deduction against taxable income.

6.4.2 Employment of Carer for Incapacitated Person

Where an individual employs a person to take care of a **family member** who is totally incapacitated by reason of old age or physical or mental infirmity, the individual is entitled to a deduction from his **total income** in calculating his taxable income. For 2012, this deduction is the lesser of the amount actually borne by the individual in employing the carer and **€50,000**.

Where two or more persons employ the carer, the allowance will be apportioned between them in proportion to the amount borne by each. A separate carer's allowance is available for each totally incapacitated person for whom the individual incurs expense. Carers may be employed on an individual basis or through an agency.

The **incapacitated child tax credit** (see **Section 6.2.7**) and/or the **dependent relative tax credit** (see **Section 6.2.8**) **cannot** be claimed for the incapacitated relative where the carer's allowance is being claimed in respect of the same individual.

The deduction for the first year of claim will be limited to the lower of the actual cost incurred or the maximum deduction of €50,000, **apportioned** by reference to the number of months during the year in which the individual was permanently incapacitated.

6.4.3 Nursing Home Expenses

Relief is available for expenses paid to a nursing home for health care, maintenance or treatment. **FA 2010** states that the expenses will only qualify if the nursing home provides **24-hour nursing care on-site. FA 2010** also states that even if the individual has received State support under the *Fair Deal* scheme (NHSSA 2009), any contribution to nursing home fees by the individual over and above the *Fair Deal* scheme will be allowable at the marginal rate.

6.4.4 Permanent Health Benefit Schemes

Relief is given for premiums payable under Revenue-approved permanent health benefit schemes, which provide for periodic payments to an individual in the event of loss of income in consequence of ill health.

Relief is given by way of **deduction** from the individual's total income.

Allowable premiums are **restricted** to a **maximum of 10% of total income**. (Total income is income from all sources before deducting reliefs allowable as deductions in calculating taxable income, e.g. medical expenses, allowance for employed person taking care of incapacitated person etc.)

Any **benefits** payable under such schemes are **chargeable to tax** under PAYE.

6.4.5 Revenue Job Assist (Long Term Unemployed)

Where an individual, who has been unemployed for at least 12 months and has been in receipt of **jobseeker's benefit or assistance**, takes up employment of at least **30 hours** duration per week which is capable of lasting **at least 12 months**, he will be entitled to a **deduction** from his emoluments from that employment in calculating taxable income as follows:

	Deduction for Self	Deduction for each Qualifying Child
Year 1	€3,810	€1,270
Year 2	€2,540	€850
Year 3	€1,270	€425

"Qualifying child" has the same definition as **Section 6.2.3** above.

Participation in activities such as the FAS administered *Community Employment Scheme* or *Job Initiative* are treated as being periods of unemployment for the purposes of qualifying under this section, provided the individual was in receipt of jobseeker's benefit or assistance immediately before commencing the activity.

This allowance is also available to those who have been in receipt of either **disability allowance** or **blind person's pension** for 12 months or more.

6.4.6 *Charitable Donations and Gifts*

Relief may be claimed for donations to "**eligible charities**", "**approved bodies**" and certain **educational institutions** where the **minimum aggregate donation** to any one of these bodies, in any year, is **€250**.

The legislation differentiates between donations made by a PAYE taxpayer and an individual who pays tax under the self-assessment system.

PAYE taxpayer
No relief is available to the taxpayer. Relief is granted on a "grossed up" basis to the approved body, rather than by way of a separate claim by the donor. For example, if an individual, who pays tax at the higher tax rate (41%), gives a donation of €500 to an approved body, the body will be deemed to have received €847 (€500 ÷ (100% − 41%)) less tax of €347 (€847 @ 41%). The **approved body will then be able to claim a tax refund** of €347 from Revenue.

Self-employed taxpayer
The claim for relief is made when the taxpayer files his tax return and there is no "grossing up" arrangement. For example, a self-employed person, who makes a donation of €500 in 2012 to an eligible charity, is entitled to deduct this €500 is calculating his taxable income for 2012.

In order for a donation to qualify for relief, it must satisfy the following conditions:

- The donation must be a minimum amount of at least €250 in the tax year, to any one charity/ approved body/educational institution/sporting body.
- The donation must be in the form of money or quoted securities.
- It must not be repayable.
- It must not confer any benefit on the donor or any person connected with the donor.
- It must not be conditional on, or associated with, any arrangement involving the acquisition of property by the recipient from the donor or a person connected with the donor.
- The donor must be resident in the State.
- In the case of PAYE donors, a certificate must be given by the donor to the charity/approved body/educational institution/sporting body confirming that the donation satisfies the conditions necessary to qualify for relief, the amount of tax that will be paid in respect of the donation at the donor's marginal tax rate and giving his PPS number.

Note that this tax relief may be restricted in the case of certain high-income individuals.

With effect from 6 February 2003, where an individual makes a donation **in excess** of **10% of his total income** to an approved body with which he is "associated", only an **amount equal to 10%** of his total income will qualify for tax relief. An individual is regarded as associated with an approved body if he is an employee or member of the approved body or of a body associated with the approved body.

In order to qualify for relief, donations to certain sporting bodies must **additionally** satisfy the following conditions:

- The donation is made to the approved sporting body for the sole purpose of funding an approved project.
- The sporting body applies it for that purpose.
- Neither the donor nor any person connected with him obtains membership of the sports body or a right to use its facilities as a result of making the donation.

An **eligible charity** is a charity which has been approved by the Revenue Commissioners.

An **approved body** means a body or institution approved by the Minister for Finance, which teaches approved subjects, i.e. architecture, art and design, music, film arts or other similar subjects. (Following representations from the EU Commission, FA 2007 removed the requirement that the body or institution has to be "in the State")

Educational institutions that qualify for relief include primary, secondary and third-level educational institutions (provided their programmes are approved by the Minister for Education and Science or validated by the Higher Education Training and Awards Council), bodies that promote the Universal Declaration of Human Rights and certain bodies approved for research.

An **approved sports body** is a body which is in possession of a certificate from the Minister for Tourism, Sport and Recreation confirming that its income is exempt from tax because it is a body which was established for and exists for the sole purpose of promoting athletic or amateur games or sports and whose income is applied solely for those purposes. In addition, the sporting body must have a tax clearance certificate.

6.4.7 Pension Contributions

There are two categories of persons making pension contributions:
1. employees in company schemes; and
2. self-employed or employees with no company pension scheme.

1. Contributions to an approved Superannuation Pension Fund, i.e. employees in company pension schemes

Contributions paid by an employee to a superannuation scheme, approved by the Revenue Commissioners, are allowed as a deduction against gross assessable Schedule E income from the employment. For the tax years 2002 *et seq.*, the maximum allowable deduction varies depending on the age of the employee. For tax years commencing on/after 1 January 2006, the maximum allowable deductions for pension contributions are as follows:

Age	% of Remuneration
Under 30 years of age	15%
30 to 39 years of age	20%
40 to 49 years of age	25%
50 to 54 years of age	30%
55 to 59 years of age	35%
60 years and over	40%

The **age** of the person is taken at any time during the tax year, e.g. if a person is age 30 at any time in the tax year, he will qualify for the 20% rate.

Remuneration for this purpose includes fees, bonuses and benefits in kind.

The pension contribution paid is deducted directly from Schedule E income to arrive at the assessable Schedule E income, e.g:

	€
Gross salary of employee aged 45	35,000
Deduct: Superannuation paid (<25% of €35,000)	(2,000)
Assessable Schedule E income	33,000

There is an **earnings cap of €115,000** on remuneration. Remuneration **in excess** of this amount will not be taken into account when calculating the allowable contribution.

Where the full amount of the premium paid does not qualify for relief due to an insufficiency of remuneration, the amount not qualifying **is carried forward** and treated as a premium paid in the **next** year. With effect from 6 February 2003, where an employee pays a retirement contribution before 31 October which is not an ordinary annual contribution, he may elect that the premium should be treated as a premium paid in the **previous tax year**. For example, an individual makes a non-ordinary annual contribution to his company pension scheme on 1 July 2012. The individual may elect to treat the contribution **as if it had been paid** in 2011 and claim relief for the contribution against his 2011 remuneration.

However, FA 2011 amended section 790A TCA 1997 and stipulated that, effective from 1 January 2011, the **earnings cap of €115,000** applies to **all contributions** paid in the year of assessment, **irrespective** of the fact that the contribution relates to the previous year.

Note also that the exemption from PRSI and USC on employee pension contributions has been abolished effective from 1 January 2011.

2. **Contributions to a Retirement Annuity Contract (RAC), i.e. self-employed or employees with no company pension scheme:**

The maximum amounts on which tax relief may be claimed in respect of qualifying premiums, for the tax years 2006 *et seq.*, are as follows:

Age	% of Net Relevant Earnings
Under 30 years of age	15%
30 to 39 years of age	20%
40 to 49 years of age	25%
50 to 54 years of age	30%
55 to 59 years of age	35%
60 years and over	40%

The **30% limit** also applies to individuals who are engaged in specified occupations and professions, **primarily sports professionals**, irrespective of age.

Relevant earnings is defined to mean the following types of income:

- Non pensionable salaries, wages, fees, benefits, etc., taxable under Schedule E and
- Case I/Case II profits from trades or professions (including profits arising to a partner).

Net relevant earnings is defined to mean the "relevant earnings" assessable for a particular year of assessment **as reduced** by:

- Loss relief available for the particular year of assessment in respect of losses, which if they had been profits, would constitute "relevant" income.
- Relief for capital allowances claimed in respect of the "relevant" source of income for the particular year of assessment.
- Charges paid (see **Section 6.5**) during the particular year of assessment to the extent that they cannot be set against other non-relevant income (i.e. income under Case III, IV, V or Schedule F) of the taxpayer. Broadly, this means any earned income that is not already subject to a pension scheme.

Non-relevant income represents any income of the taxpayer for the particular year of assessment **other than** relevant income. For example, a self-employed solicitor would be assessed under Case II, Schedule D on his practice profits and this would be regarded as relevant earnings. However, the solicitor may have other sources of income assessed on him e.g. bank deposit interest, dividend income, rents, etc., and these would **not** be taken into account in computing net relevant earnings, except and to the extent that they are used to offset charges paid during the particular year of assessment.

It is specifically provided that **remuneration from an investment company** is **not included** in computing net relevant earnings.

Example:

Joe Green is a chartered accountant, aged 50, who has been in practice for many years. His Case II tax-adjusted profits assessable for 2012 are €37,000. He is entitled to Case II capital allowances of €14,000 for 2012 and he has an allowable Case II loss forward from 2011 of €10,000. His only other income is €1,500 interest from Government Securities received annually. He pays an allowable covenant to his widowed mother of €2,000 (gross) per annum and he pays €4,000 per annum under a Revenue approved Retirement Annuity Contract.

Net Relevant Earnings	€	€
Case II (relevant earnings)		37,000
Less:		
Loss relief	(10,000)	
Capital allowances	(14,000)	(24,000)
Charges paid in 2012 to extent not covered by non-relevant income:		
Gross covenant	2,000	
Less: Non relevant income (Government Securities)	(1,500)	(500)
Net Relevant Earnings ("NRE")		**12,500**
Amount of retirement premium paid		4,000
Relief restricted to a max. of 30% of NRE	12,500 @ 30%	(3,750)
Unrelieved portion of premium		250

In cases where the full amount of the premium paid does not qualify for relief in a particular year of assessment (e.g. as in the above example), any **unrelieved portion** of the premium may be **carried forward** to the following and subsequent years and treated as a **premium paid** in those years until such time as relief has been granted. For instance, in the above example Joe did not receive relief in respect of €250 of the total €4,000 premium paid during 2012. He would, therefore, be entitled to treat the €250 unrelieved payment as a premium paid in 2013. It would be added to his annual premium of €4,000 to give a total premium paid of €4,250. Provided this amount was less than 30% of his net relevant earnings for 2013, he would be entitled to a full deduction for the €4,250 in that year.

The relief for qualifying contracts is **normally** based on the amount of the premium paid **in the actual tax year**, i.e. a premium paid on 1 December 2012 would qualify for relief in the taxpayer's computation for 2012.

To enable taxpayers to fully benefit from the relief available, a provision exists which effectively enables relief for retirement annuity premiums to be **backdated**. If a taxpayer pays a qualifying premium after the end of the tax year but **before** the due date for the **filing of his tax return** for that tax year, he may elect for the premium to be deducted in the **earlier** tax year. For example, currently an individual subject to self-assessment must file his tax return for 2012 **before 31 October 2013**. Such an individual may elect that a qualifying retirement annuity premium paid in the period 1 January 2013 to 31 October 2013 may be deducted from his relevant income for 2012.

This provision clearly enables the taxpayer to know with certainty what his net relevant earnings are for a particular year, thereby permitting him to effectively top-up the premiums paid to ensure that they are equal to the net relevant earnings limits.

There is also an **earnings cap of €115,000** on net relevant earnings. Earnings **in excess** of this amount will **not** be taken into account when calculating the allowable contribution.

6.4.8 Relief for Investment in Corporate Trades – Employment and Investment Incentive (EII)

The Employment Investment Incentive (EII) is a tax relief incentive scheme that provides tax relief for investment in certain corporate trades. The scheme replaced the Business Expansion Scheme (BES), which was in operation until 25 November 2011.

The scheme allows an investor to obtain income tax relief on investments up to a maximum of **€150,000 per annum** in each tax year up to **31 December 2013**. Relief is initially available to the individual at **30%**, with **a further 11% tax relief** available where it has been **proven** that **employment levels** have **increased** at the company at the end of the **holding period (three years)**, or where evidence is provided that the company used the capital raised for increased expenditure on **research and development**.

The **maximum investment** which will qualify for relief in any one tax year is **€150,000**. This limit applies to **individuals**. A married couple/civil partnership can **each** obtain individual relief on an investment of €150,000, **provided** each spouse/civil partner has sufficient taxable income to absorb the amount of his/her investment.

Where relief cannot be obtained, either because the investment exceeds the maximum of €150,000 or due to an insufficiency of income, the unrelieved amount can be carried forward and claimed as a deduction in future years **up to** and including **2013**, subject to the overall annual limit of €150,000. There is **no limit** to the **number of companies** an investor can invest in, but tax relief is subject to the **overall investment limit** of **€150,000** per annum.

In order for the investment to qualify for relief, there are **three main "qualifying" headings**:

1. Qualifying Individual/Investor
2. Qualifying Company and its Trade
3. Qualifying Shares

1. Qualifying Individual/Investor
A qualifying investor is an individual who is:

- resident in the Republic of Ireland for the tax year in respect of which he/she makes the claim;
- subscribes on his/her own behalf for eligible shares in a qualifying company; *and*
- is not, for the relevant period, connected with the company.

2. Qualifying Company and its Trade
A qualifying company is one that:

- is a **Micro, Small or Medium-Sized Enterprise** within the European Commission definition in force for the relevant period, as follows:

- A **micro** enterprise has **less** than **10 employees** and has an annual turnover and/or annual balance sheet total not exceeding **€2 million**.
- A **small** enterprise has **less** than **50 employees** and has an annual turnover and/or annual balance sheet total not exceeding **€10 million**;
- A **medium-sized** enterprise has **less** than **250 employees** and has an annual turnover not exceeding **€50 million** or an annual balance sheet total not exceeding €43 million. The medium-sized enterprise must also be located in **"assisted areas"**, which are all areas of Ireland, **excluding** Dublin, Meath, Kildare, Wicklow and Cork City and County, but including Cork Docklands. Under EU State Aid rules, medium-sized enterprises operating in the **"non-assisted areas"** are limited to their **seed/start-up phase** of development for the purpose of raising EII investments.

- is incorporated in the State or the EEA (EU, Norway, Liechtenstein, Iceland);
- is resident in the State or is resident in another EEA State and carries on business in the State through a branch or agency;
- is not regarded as a firm in difficulty for the purposes of the EU *"Guidelines on State Aid for rescuing and restructuring firms in difficulty"*;
- throughout the three-year holding period:
  - carries on relevant trading activities from a **fixed place of business** in the State, *or*
  - is a company whose business consists wholly of:
    - the holding of shares or securities of, or the making of loans to, one or more qualifying subsidiaries of the company, *or*
    - both the holding of such shares or securities, or the making of such loans and the carrying on of relevant trading activities, where relevant trading are carried on from **a fixed place of business in the State**;
- is an unquoted company (except in the case of companies listed on the Irish Enterprise Securities Market);
- has its issued share capital fully paid up; *and*
- is not intending to wind up within three years of receiving EII investment (unless for bona fide commercial reasons).

The Trade

This scheme is available to the majority of small and medium-sized trading companies. However, the following trading activities are *not eligible* for the scheme:

- adventures or concerns in the nature of trade;
- dealing in commodities or futures in shares, securities or other financial assets;
- financing activities;
- professional service companies;
- dealing in or developing land;
- forestry;
- operating or managing hotels, guest houses, self-catering accommodation or comparable establishments or managing property used as a hotel, guest house, self-catering accommodation or comparable establishment;
- operating or managing nursing homes or residential care homes or managing property used as a nursing home or residential care home;
- operations carried on in the coal industry or in the steel and shipbuilding sectors; and
- the production of a film (within the meaning of section 481 TCA 1997).

Approval from other State Agencies

Under BES rules, companies were required to obtain prior approval of their trading activities from the various certifying agencies or authorities. This requirement has been removed for EII in respect of all trading activities, **except Tourist Traffic Undertakings**. A company carrying on these undertakings must have **prior** approval, from Fáilte Ireland, **before** making any application to the Revenue Commissioners.

3. Qualifying Shares

The qualifying investor must subscribe on his/her own behalf for shares which must:

- be new ordinary share capital in a qualifying company; *and*
- carry no preferential rights as to dividends or redemption.

The whole of the company's issued share capital must be fully paid up.

The **minimum investment** in any one company **is €250**, and the maximum investment in any one company or its associated companies is **€10,000,000**, subject to a maximum of **€2,500,000** in any one twelve-month period.

Holding Period for Share Capital

Shares must be held by the investor for a period of **three years**.

Requirements under EU Rules

As the scheme is a form of State Aid, any changes to the scheme require the **approval** of the European Commission (EC), to ensure that it remains compatible with EU law. A further **condition** of approval is that Ireland must implement the EU rules on **cumulation of State Aids**. With effect from 1 January 2007, a company that raises capital under EII/BES will have to **reduce** other State Aids. This means that the maximum eligible amounts available from a State Agency will be reduced by **50%** and **20%** in "non-assisted" and "assisted" areas, respectively. Also, full details of a company that has been a beneficiary of State Aid in the form of EII/BES must be notified to the EC, and these details will be published on the EC website and also on the Irish Revenue website.

*For further details see Revenue leaflet **IT55** at www.revenue.ie.*

6.4.9 Relief for Investment in Films

Section 481 TCA 1997 allows for individual investors to claim tax relief, at their marginal rate, on their investment in a **qualifying film company** up to **€50,000** in any one tax year. Where relief cannot be obtained, either because the investment exceeds the maximum of €50,000 or due to an insufficiency of income, the unrelieved amount can be **carried forward** and claimed in **future years**, subject to the overall annual limit of €50,000. **Section 32 FA 2011** states that no unrelieved amount can be carried forward **beyond** the year of assessment **2015**.

Note that this relief is a "specified relief" and may be restricted in the case of certain high-income individuals.

Relief may be claimed on investments made up to **31 December 2015**. In order for the investment to qualify for relief there are four main "qualifying" headings:

1. Qualifying Company
2. Qualifying Film
3. Qualifying Investors
4. Qualifying Shares

Qualifying Company

A qualifying company is an Irish incorporated and resident company, or a company that is carrying on a trade in the State through a branch or agency. The company must exist solely for the production and distribution of **one and only one qualifying film**.

Qualifying Film

A qualifying film is a film in respect of which the Revenue Commissioners has given a **certificate**. Certification takes into account the contribution that the film will make to the development of the film industry in Ireland, and the promotion and expression of Irish culture.

Qualifying Investors

A qualifying investor is an individual investor who is **not connected** with the film production company. An individual is connected if he, or an associate, controls the company.

Qualifying Shares

The investment must be made in **new** ordinary shares, i.e. shares that do not have a right to a dividend at a fixed rate and which have no existing or future preferential right to a dividend or to redemption or to the film company's assets in a winding up.

6.5   Relief for Charges on Income

Charges on income are payments made which are **deductible** from the **gross income** of the taxpayer, to arrive at total income or net statutory income. In order for relief to be claimed, the amount must be **actually paid** during the tax year in question and not simply incurred.

6.5.1   Payments made under a Deed of Covenant

A deed of covenant is a legally binding written agreement, made by an individual, to pay an agreed amount to another individual without receiving **any** benefit in return. To be legally effective, it must be properly drawn up, signed, witnessed, sealed and delivered to the individual receiving the payments. Any amount can be paid under a deed of convenant but only covenants in favour of **certain individuals** qualify for tax relief.

The person who makes the payment is called a **covenantor**. The person who receives the payment is called a **covenantee** or beneficiary.

To qualify for tax relief, a deed must be capable of **exceeding** a period of **six years**. Therefore, the period provided should be for a minimum of **seven years**.

Covenants allowable for tax relief

Unrestricted tax relief is available for covenants payable to the following:

■ a permanently incapacitated minor child (i.e. under 18 years) where the covenant is paid by a person **other** than the parent; and
■ a permanently incapacitated person.

Tax relief is **restricted** to **5%** of the covenantor's **total income** (gross income minus all other charges) on covenants payable to persons aged 65 years or older.

Example:
Marie Murphy is single and earned €42,000 from her job in 2012. She paid the following covenants during 2012:

– Her permanently incapacitated sister Mary received €3,200 (net)
– Her 66 year old widowed mother €2,400 (net).

Marie's allowable charges for 2012 were:

Incapacitated sister €3,200 (net) × 100/80	=	€4,000 gross (no restriction)

Widowed mother: restricted to the **lower** of gross amount paid **or** 5% of gross income less charges:

Amount paid €2,400 (net) × 100/80	=	€3,000 gross
Gross Income less charges:		
€42,000 – €4,000 = € 38,000 @ 5%	=	€1,900
Total allowable covenants €4,000 + €1,900	**=**	**€5,900**

The covenantor must deduct tax at the **standard rate** from the gross payment and **account** for it to Revenue. The covenantor must also give a **Form R185**, detailing the payment and the tax deducted, to the covenantee **each time** a payment is made.

To **claim the tax relief** in the first year, the covenantor must send the original deed of covenant together with a copy of Form R185 to the Revenue. For subsequent years, only a copy of Form R185 needs to be included with the claim for tax relief.

Relief is allowed in the covenantor's income tax computation for the **gross amount paid** and he must pay over to the Revenue Commissioners the income tax which he has deducted. In practice, this liability is simply added to the covenantor's tax liability in respect of his income in the tax computation. **Tax credits**, other than credits for tax paid, **cannot reduce the tax due** on the charges. The individual always remains liable to pay the full amount of income tax on any charges.

Example:
Peter Byrne is a single individual and is employed as a marketing manager. He has a salary of €43,000 for the tax year 2012 and paid PAYE of €6,500 in respect of this salary. Peter has executed an **annual** covenant of €5,000 in favour of his widowed mother aged 66, who is incapacitated, for seven years. His mother's only other source of income is €6,000 per annum.

Peter Byrne – Income Tax Computation 2012

	€	€
Schedule E salary	43,000	
Less: Gross amount of covenant paid*	(5,000)	
Total/Taxable Income		**38,000**
Tax Calculation:		
€32,800 @ 20%	6,560	
€5,200 @ 41%	2,132	8,692
Less:		
Single person tax credit	1,650	
Employee tax credit	1,650	(3,300)
Plus:		5,392
Tax deducted on payment of covenant which must be returned to		
Revenue (€5,000 @ 20%)		1,000
Net tax liability		6,392
Deduct: PAYE paid		(6,500)
Tax refund due		**(108)**

*If Peter's mother was not incapacitated, the allowable covenant would be restricted to 5% of Peter's income, i.e. €43,000 @ 5% = €2,150. However, the tax deducted and due on payment of the covenant would be based on the actual payment made, not on the amount that qualifies for tax relief.

Mrs Byrne – Income Tax Computation 2012		
Income:	€	€
Case IV Schedule D (gross covenant income)	5,000	
Other income	6,000	
Total/Taxable Income		**11,000**
Covered by exemption limit – no tax liability		
Tax calculation:		
Tax liability		NIL
Less: Tax deducted by Peter on payment of covenant		(1,000)
Tax refund due		**(1,000)**

6.5.2   Interest on Loans to Invest in Partnerships

Section 253 TCA 1997 provides for unrestricted interest relief to an individual in respect of a loan taken out to:

■ purchase a share in partnership; *or*
■ lend money to a partnership, **provided** the money is used wholly and exclusively for the purposes of the trade or profession carried on by the partnership.

The individual must have personally acted as a partner in the conduct of the trade or profession carried out by the partnership and he must not have "recovered" any capital from the partnership unless such capital is first used to repay the loan in question. An individual is treated as "recovering capital" from a partnership if:

■ he sells his partnership interest;
■ if the partnership returns any capital or repays any loan to the partner; *or*
■ the partner receives any money for the assignment of a debt due to him by the partnership.

Note that this relief is a "specified relief" and may be restricted in the case of certain high-income individuals.

6.5.3   Interest on Loans to Acquire Shares or Lend Money to a Company

Relief is given to individuals under section 248 TCA 1997 for interest on loans taken out to acquire shares in, or to lend money to, a "qualifying company".
   A "qualifying company" is a company:

(a) which exists, wholly or mainly, for the purpose of carrying on a trade or trades, *or*
(b) whose business consists wholly or mainly of the holding of stocks, shares or securities of a company referred to in (i) above.

Relief is **not available** on loans taken out on or after **7 December 2005** to acquire shares in, or to lend money to, a company or holding company, whose income consists wholly or mainly of **Case V (rental) income**.

Relief is available to individuals who:

- work for the greater part of their time in the actual management or conduct of the business of the company or of a connected company **AND** who have a **"material interest"** (more than 5% of the equity) in the company. The relief for these individuals is **unrestricted (section 248 TCA 1997)**; *or*
- are full-time or part-time directors or employees of the company, even if the "material interest" test is not satisfied, or are full-time directors and employees of a connected company.

The relief available can be summarised as follows:

Loans taken out on or after 7 December 2005

	Unquoted Trading Company	Unquoted Holding Company of a Trading Company
Full-time employee or director	Unrestricted relief	Unrestricted relief
Part-time employee or director	Unrestricted relief	No relief available

Restriction of Relief

Section 11 FA 2011 removed any entitlement to relief for interest on loans taken out **after 7 December 2010**. For loans taken out prior to this date, the interest relief is being **restricted** and phased out as follows:

Year	Restricted to
2011	75% of interest paid
2012	50% of interest paid
2013	20% of interest paid
2014 *et seq.*	No deduction

Example 1:

Joe took out a loan of €90,000 in June 2010 to buy 5% of the share capital in Harford Ltd, a private trading company. He is a full-time employee of the company and the interest paid in the tax year 2012 was €12,000.

Relief due as a charge: €12,000 @ 50% = €6,000

Example 2:

Mary took out a loan of €100,000 in April 2009 to buy a 10% interest in Mills Ltd, a private manufacturing company. The interest paid in the tax year 2012 was €10,000. She is not an employee or director of the company.

No relief due as she is not an employee or director.

Example 3:

Liam is a full-time director of FED plc, an unquoted trading company. In October 2011, Liam took out a loan of €50,000 to acquire a 1% interest in FED plc. Liam had not previously held shares in FED plc. Interest paid by Liam in 2012 in respect of this loan amounted to €5,000.

No relief due as loan was taken out after 7 December 2010.

Example 4:

Jill is a full-time employee of PEC plc an unquoted trading company. Jill took out a loan of €70,000 in October 2010 to buy shares in PEC and paid interest of €7,000 in respect of this loan in 2012.

Relief due as a charge: €7,000 @ 50% = €3,500

Relief is not available where the company, or anyone connected with it, makes a loan to the employee/director or anyone connected with them, unless the loan is made as part of the normal business of the company (e.g. a bank).

Relief **may not** be claimed in respect of interest paid on a loan to acquire shares for which **BES/film relief** has been claimed.

Where the investment in the company is by way of a loan, relief is **only** available if the money lent is used **wholly or exclusively** for the trade or business of the company or a connected company.

Note that this relief may be restricted in the case of certain high income individuals.

6.5.4   Patent Royalties

Where an individual pays patent royalties, a deduction is not allowed for the royalties under any of the Schedules. Instead the **royalties** paid in the particular tax year are allowed as a **charge**.

6.6   Other Reliefs

6.6.1   Relief on the Retirement of Certain Sports Persons

Schedule 23A TCA 1997 introduced a specific relief for the tax years 2002 *et seq.* for certain **retiring** sports persons who are **resident** in the State. The sports persons to whom the relief applies include the following:

- Athletes
- Badminton players
- Boxers
- Cyclists
- Footballers
- Golfers
- Jockeys
- Motor racing drivers
- Rugby players
- Squash players
- Swimmers
- Tennis players
- Cricketers (effective from 1 January 2012)

The features of this relief are as follows:

(a) The relief is applied by allowing a **deduction of 40%** against gross earnings, before deducting expenses, for **up to any ten tax years** back to and including the tax year 1990/91, for which the sports person was resident in the State.

(b) The earnings to which the relief applies are those received from **actual participation** in the sport concerned including match and performance fees, prize money and appearance fees, but **does not include** sponsorship fees, advertising income or endorsement fees, income from newspaper or magazine articles and interviews.

(c) The relief **cannot** create or augment a **Case I or II loss**.

(d) The relief will be given by way of a **tax repayment** (which will not carry interest) and is to be claimed in the year in which the sports person **permanently ceases** to be engaged in that sport.

(e) Where the sports person recommences to be engaged in that sport, the relief will be **clawed back** and taxable under **Case IV**. However, this does not prevent a subsequent claim for relief if and when the sports person finally does retire.

(f) The sports person must be resident in the State in the **year of retirement**.

(g) This relief will not affect the calculation of net **relevant earnings** for the purpose of relief for pension contributions.

6.6.2 Age Exemption

Exemptions from income tax are available to individuals aged 65 years and over, and with low incomes.

Age Exemption
Where total income does not exceed the following amounts, there is a **total exemption** from income tax for 2012 for an individual aged **65 years and over**.

Marital Status	Income Limit 2012
Single/Widowed/Surviving Civil Partner	€18,000
Married Couple/Civil Partners	€36,000

Increase in Exemption Limits for Qualifying Children
The age exemption limits are **increased** where a claimant proves that a qualifying child (children) has lived with them at any time during the tax year. The income limits are increased for **each** qualifying child as follows:

	Increase for each child
First and second child	€575
Third and subsequent children	€830

Example:
Peter Blake, aged 66, is a self-employed carpenter and is married with four children. His wife, Sheila, aged 42 works full time in the home and does not have any income. Peter had a total income of €38,000 for 2012.

Calculation of Specified Income Limit	€	€
Income limit – married couple over 65		36,000
Plus: Increase for qualifying children:		
1st and 2nd child (€575 × 2)	1,150	
3rd and 4th child (€830 × 2)	1,660	2,810
Specified Income Limit		**38,810**
Actual Income		38,000
Income Tax Liability		**NIL**

For CAP 1, marginal relief as applied to age exemption is not examinable.

6.6.3 Provision of Childcare Services

Section 216C TCA 1997 introduced tax relief for income received from the provision of childcare services from the individual's **own home**. The exemption applies where the income in a tax year does **not exceed €15,000** (from 1 January 2007) and no more than **three children** at any time are cared for in the individual's own home. No deductions are allowable when calculating the income limit for this relief and notification of the service being provided must be given to the HSE. Where the income exceeds €15,000, the **entire amount** becomes taxable under self-assessment.

6.6.4 Rent-a-Room Relief

Where an individual rents out a room (or rooms) in a "qualifying residence" and the gross income received (including sums arising for food, laundry or similar goods and services), **does not exceed €10,000**, this income will be exempt from income tax **(section 216A TCA 1997)**. It is also not liable to PRSI or USC but it must be **included** in an individual's income tax return. In determining whether the limit has been exceeded for the tax year, no deductions for expenses incurred are made.

Where the income exceeds €10,000, the entire amount is taxable.

A "qualifying residence" is a residential premises situated in the State which is occupied by the individual as his or her sole or main residence during the year of assessment.

Room rentals under this scheme will not affect:

- mortgage interest relief available to the individual who qualifies for relief; or
- Principal Private Residence (PPR) relief for CGT purposes on the disposal of the house.

Where the room or rooms are rented out by more than one individual, the €10,000 limit is divided between the individuals.

Exclusions:
Rent-a-room relief will not apply where:

(1) The room is rented to a child of the individual renting the rooms (**FA 2007**) *or*

(2) Where the individual receiving the rent (or a person connected to them) is an office holder or employee of the person making the payment (or someone connected to them) (**FA 2010**).

6.6.5 Artists' Exemption

This exemption is available to individuals who are deemed by the Revenue Commissioners to have produced an original and creative "work" which is generally recognised as having cultural or artistic merit **(section 195 TCA 1997).**

The first **€40,000 per annum (FA 2011)** of profits or gains earned by writers, composers, visual artists and sculptors from the sale of their work is **exempt from income tax** in Ireland in certain circumstances.

A "work" must be original and creative, and fall into one of the following categories:

- A book or other writing
- A play

- A musical composition
- A painting or other like picture
- A sculpture

Claimants must be individuals and resident, or ordinarily resident and domiciled, in the State and not resident elsewhere. The artists' exemption only provides an exemption from **income tax**. All exempt income is subject to USC and PRSI at the appropriate annual rates.

Note: This relief is a "specified relief" and may be restricted in the case of certain high-income individuals.

Questions (Chapter 6)

(See Solutions to Questions at the end of this text.)

6 Tax Credits and Reliefs

6.1 Joyces – Home Carer

The Joyces are a married couple jointly assessed with two children under 16. Only one spouse has income of €46,000 for 2012.

Requirement
(a) Calculate their income tax liability for 2012.
(b) What would the liability be if the home carer had income of say €7,000 in 2013 (the following tax year).

6.2 Roches – Home Carer

The Roches are a married couple jointly assessed with two children under 16. One spouse has a salary of €46,000 and the other has investment income, i.e. Schedule F of €6,000.

Requirement
Calculate their income tax liability for 2012.

6.3 Mr Murray – Medical Expenses

Mr Murray is married with two children, Michael and David.
Michael was formally adopted in 2002. He is 12 years old and in receipt of €2,500 per annum from a trust set up by his aunt.
David is 14 years of age and is not in receipt of any income.
During 2012 the following medical expenses were paid:

	€
Mr Murray	80
Michael Murray	200
David Murray	210
Sean Ryan	650

Sean Ryan, his friend, was involved in a motor accident and Mr Murray paid €650 for medical treatment for him.

He also pays €100 per month towards nursing home care for his elderly mother. The nursing home provides 24-hour nursing care on-site.

Requirement
Compute Mr Murphy's allowable medical expenses for 2012 and advise how tax relief may be obtained.

6.4 Rachel

Rachel is an active partner in firm of solicitors, aged 45. Her tax-adjusted profits assessable for 2012 are €320,000. Capital allowances for 2012 are €10,000. She pays €75,000 per annum under a Revenue approved Retirement Annuity Contract.

On 1 January 2012 Rachel took out a loan of €100,000 which she lent to the partnership. On 1 July 2012 the partnership repaid €25,000 of the loan to Rachel. Rachel used the €25,000 repaid to buy a new car. Interest paid by Rachel during 2012 in respect of the €100,000 loan amounted to €10,000. Assume interest accrued evenly throughout the year.

Requirement
Calculate:
(a) Rachel's entitlement to interest relief for 2012.
(b) Rachel's net relevant earnings for 2012.

6.5 Mr Frost – Medical Insurance Premiums

Mr Frost is an employee of ABC Ltd. ABC Ltd paid €960 net, i.e. €1,200 less 20%, for Mr Frost to the VHI in November 2012 for Mr Frost.

Mr Frost is single and had a salary of €46,000 for 2012.

Requirement
Calculate Mr Frost's income tax liability for 2012.

6.6 Charitable Donations

Compare and contrast the tax relief available on charitable donations between self-employed and PAYE taxpayers who make a €300 donation to an approved charity.

6.7 John – Loan Interest

John, a separated man with no children, had a salary of €75,000 for 2012 from which PAYE of €20,500 was deducted. During 2012 John paid mortgage interest of €11,000 in respect of a house in Belfast occupied by his wife as her main residence. The mortgage in respect of this house was taken out in June 2007. John is assessed as a single person and is not a first-time buyer.

Requirement
Calculate John's income tax liability for 2012.

6.8 June

June is a widow aged 56 whose husband died in March 2009. For 2012, she had a salary of €43,000 (PAYE deducted €5,000) and a social welfare widow's pension of €5,900. June's employment is non-pensionable. During 2012, June paid a retirement annuity premium of €2,000. June has three children whose circumstances are as follows:

(a) John is 21 years of age. He works part-time and is taking an evening degree course in computer science in UCD. During 2012 he earned €8,000 from his part-time work. Total fees payable in respect of his degree course came to €4,800, of which €3,000 was paid by June and €1,800 by John. June spent €350 on an eye test and new spectacles for John during 2012.

(b) Mary, who has been incapacitated since birth, receives a covenant net of tax at the standard rate of €3,200 per annum from her elderly aunt.

(c) David, who is 19 years of age, studies full-time at Bolton Street College. He has assessable income of €500 gross per annum. David is also incapacitated since birth. June paid €500 in respect of doctors fees and prescription medicines for David during 2012.

June and her family live in rented accommodation. June paid rent of €12,600 and a premium to the VHI of €1,400 during 2012. The premium paid to the VHI was after deduction of tax at 20%.

Requirement
Calculate June's income tax liability for 2012.

6.9 John Fitzpatrick – Tax Credits

John Fitzpatrick became 65 years of age on 1 May 2012. He is widowed for many years with no dependent children and lives alone.

He is retired and his only source of income is his pension of €29,400 gross per annum.

During 2012, €1,900 of PAYE was deducted from his gross pension. He paid VHI €750 during 2012.

The amount paid in respect of VHI was net of tax at the standard rate tax. John contributed €300 to an eligible charity during 2012.

John has no other source of income or allowances.

Requirement
Compute John Fitzpatrick's income tax liability for 2012 claiming all reliefs due to him.

6.10 Jason and Damien – income exemption

Jason and Damien are aged 61 and 66 respectively and are in a civil partnership. Their only income for 2012 was a pension of €35,000 from Jason's previous employer, from which PAYE of €2,000 was deducted. (They are not entitled to a home carer tax credit.)

Requirement
Calculate Jason and Damien's income tax liability for 2012.

6.11 Bob

Bob, aged 55 in 2012, pays retirement annuity premiums to Irish Life annually to provide for a pension on his retirement as his employer does not operate a superannuation scheme.

The amount of the premiums paid were as follows:

	€
2011	6,000
2012	4,000

Bob's salary for 2011 was €20,980 and for 2012 was €24,480.

He is married and paid allowable charges of €3,000 in 2011 and in 2012. His only other source of income is deposit interest of €1,160 gross for 2011 and €1,195 gross for 2012.

Requirement
Calculate his retirement annuity relief for the tax year 2011 and 2012.

6.12 Maria – Covenant

Maria's salary for the tax year 2012 is €35,000. (PAYE deducted €4,400). She has no other income and is single.

She made a seven-year covenant in 2007 to her incapacitated widowed father (aged 60). The total covenant payments made in the tax year 2012 were €4,000 net.
Her father's only other income is rental income of €8,000 per annum.

Requirement
Calculate the 2012 income tax liability of Maria and her father.

6.13 Robert O Sullivan – Pension and Charges

Robert O Sullivan, a 36 year old single man, is employed as an electrician by Midland Electrical Services Ltd. His P60 for 2012 showed gross pay of €84,000 and tax deducted of €13,780.

He made pension contributions of €22,800 in that year directly into his PRSA and he made a covenant payment of €4,500 (gross) to his father Jack, who is 69 and in good health. He also made a covenant payment of €3,200 (net) to his permanently incapacitated brother Anthony. He receives bank interest of €1,600 (net after DIRT) annually on 31 December each year.

He owns an apartment, which is let. In 2012, rents received were €1,200 per month and he paid mortgage interest on the property of €3,200 and also paid €2,250 for new furniture, management fee of €3,100 and allowable expenses of €2,600. He had a tax rental loss forward from the previous year of €3,000.

He also invested €20,000 to buy shares in a qualifying Employment and Investment Incentive (EII) company.

John received a cheque from Independent Newspapers plc of €5,200 (net) in respect of dividends on shares which he owns in this quoted Irish company. He also owns shares in Chemcorp, an unquoted Irish resident pharmaceutical company. He is offered the option of receiving one share for every €5 due in cash. John would be entitled to €800 gross cash dividend from Chemcorp. He takes up the offer and received 160 shares during the tax year 2012.

He also paid €45 for a doctors visit, non-routine dental fees of €800 for his brother Dermot (who lives with him full time) and €125 for a new pair of reading glasses.

Requirement
Calculate Robert's income tax liability for 2012.

Computation of Income Tax

Learning Objectives

In this chapter you will learn:

- how income tax is calculated once taxable income, under all tax heads, has been established;
- how single individuals, married couples and civil partners are assessed using single, joint and separate assessments;
- who is accountable in the case of married couples/civil partners;
- the special rules which apply in the year of marriage and the year of death of a spouse/ civil partner; and
- the tax consequences of divorce, separation or dissolution of a civil partnership.

7.1 Introduction

Income tax is calculated on taxable income, and the tax due is then reduced by personal tax credits and refundable tax credits, resulting in net tax due or net tax refundable.

- **Gross Income** is income from all sources net of relevant deductions (e.g. Schedules D, E and F).
- **Total Income** or **Net Statutory Income** is gross income reduced by charges on income (e.g. covenant payments, qualifying interest etc.).
- **Taxable Income** is total income/net statutory income reduced by personal reliefs at the marginal rate.
- **Income Tax Liability** is the tax calculated on the taxable income (by reference to the marital status of the taxpayer); the tax so calculated is then reduced by non-refundable tax credits (i.e. personal tax credits at the standard rate).
- **Tax Due/Repayable** is the income tax liability reduced by refundable tax credits (i.e. tax already paid, e.g. PAYE/DWT) and increased by income tax deducted from payments made (e.g. covenants).

```
┌─────────────────────────────────────┐
│     Gross Income under Schedules     │
│              D, E and F              │
└─────────────────────────────────────┘
                 LESS
┌─────────────────────────────────────┐
│         Relief for Charges Paid      │
└─────────────────────────────────────┘
                EQUALS
┌─────────────────────────────────────┐
│        TOTAL INCOME/NET              │
│        STATUTORY INCOME              │
└─────────────────────────────────────┘
                 LESS
┌─────────────────────────────────────┐
│    Personal reliefs @ Marginal Rate  │
└─────────────────────────────────────┘
                EQUALS
┌─────────────────────────────────────┐
│           TAXABLE INCOME             │
└─────────────────────────────────────┘

┌─────────────────────────────────────┐
│     Tax Payable on Taxable Income    │
└─────────────────────────────────────┘
                 LESS
┌─────────────────────────────────────┐
│     Tax Credits @ Standard Rate      │
└─────────────────────────────────────┘
                EQUALS
┌─────────────────────────────────────┐
│            Tax Liability             │
└─────────────────────────────────────┘
                 LESS
┌─────────────────────────────────────┐
│   Refundable Tax Credits (PAYE/DWT)  │
└─────────────────────────────────────┘
                 ADD
┌─────────────────────────────────────┐
│    Tax Deducted from Payments Made   │
└─────────────────────────────────────┘
                EQUALS
┌─────────────────────────────────────┐
│         TAX DUE/REPAYABLE            │
└─────────────────────────────────────┘
```

7.2   Pro-forma Income Tax Computation

7.2.1   Employment Income Only

Joe Taxpayer			
Income Tax Computation for 2012			
Income:		€	€
Schedule E:	Income from employments/offices:		
	– Salary/wages/directors' fee/pensions	X	
	– Bonus/commissions	X	
	– Benefits-in-kind	X	
	– Taxable lump sum	X	
	– Share options	<u>X</u>	X
	Less: Allowable expenses	(X)	
	Employee's contribution to a Revenue		
	approved superannuation fund	<u>(X)</u>	<u>(X)</u>
			(continued overleaf)

Gross Income				X
Deduct:	Relief for charges paid during the tax year:			
	– Qualifying covenants paid		(X)	
	– Qualifying interest paid		<u>(X)</u>	<u>(X)</u>
Total Income/Net Statutory Income				X
Deduct:	**Personal reliefs** (i.e. reliefs @ marginal rate)			<u>(X)</u>
TAXABLE INCOME				<u>X</u>
Tax	€32,800 @ 20%		X	
Payable:	Balance @ 41%		<u>X</u>	X
	(Single Person)			
Deduct:	**Non-refundable tax credits**			
	(i.e. Reliefs @ standard rate)			<u>(X)</u>
INCOME TAX LIABILITY				X
Deduct:	Refundable tax credits:			
	– PAYE paid in tax year		(X)	
	– Dividend Withholding Tax		<u>(X)</u>	(X)
Add:	**Income Tax deducted from payments made:**			
	Tax deducted from covenant payments			<u>X</u>
NET TAX DUE/REFUNDABLE				<u>X</u>

7.2.2 Income from All Sources

		€	€
Joe Taxpayer			
Income Tax Computation for 2012			
Income:			
Schedule D:	**Case I** (Self-employed traders):		
	Adjusted Case I profit in basis period	X	
	Less: Trading loss carried forward S382	(X)	
	Less: Case I capital allowances	(X)	
	Less: Allowable retirement annuity premium	<u>(X)</u>	X
	Case II (Self-employed professionals):		
	Adjusted Case II profit in basis period	X	
	Less: Loss in profession carried forward	(X)	
	Less: Case II capital allowances	(X)	
	Less: Allowable retirement annuity premium	<u>(X)</u>	X
	Case III (Interest and income from abroad received without deduction of income tax)		X
	Case IV (Interest and income received under deduction of tax; miscellaneous income)		X

(continued overleaf)

	Case V (rental income from property in the State after deduction of allowable expenses)	X	
	Less: Case V loss carried forward	(X)	
	Less: Case V capital allowances	<u>(X)</u>	X
Schedule E:	Income from employments/offices:		
	– Salary/wages/directors' fee/pensions	X	
	– Bonus/commissions	X	
	– Benefits-in-kind	X	
	– Taxable lump sum	X	
	– Share options	<u>X</u>	
		X	
	Less: Allowable expenses	(X)	
	Less: Employee's contribution to a Revenue approved superannuation fund	<u>(X)</u>	X
Schedule F:	Distributions/dividends from Irish resident companies		<u>X</u>
Gross Income			X
Deduct:	Relief for EII/films paid during the tax year:	(X)	
Deduct:	Relief for charges paid during the tax year:		
	– Qualifying covenants paid	(X)	
	– Qualifying interest paid	(X)	
	– Patent royalties paid	<u>(X)</u>	<u>(X)</u>
Total Income/Net Statutory Income			X
Deduct:	**Personal reliefs** (i.e. reliefs @ marginal rate)		<u>(X)</u>
Taxable Income			X
Tax Payable:	€32,800 @ 20%	X	
(Single Person)	Balance @ 41%	<u>X</u>	X
Deduct:	Non-refundable tax credits		
	(i.e. Reliefs @ standard rate)		<u>(X)</u>
Income Tax Liability			X
Deduct:	**Refundable tax credits:**		
	– PAYE paid in tax year	(X)	
	– Dividend Withholding Tax	<u>(X)</u>	(X)
Add:	**Income Tax deducted from payments made:**		
	– Tax deducted from covenants payments	X	
	– Tax deducted from patent royalties	X	<u>X</u>
Net Tax Due/Refundable			X

7.3 Tax Treatment of Married Couples or Civil Partners

The Civil Partnership and Certain Rights and Obligations of Cohabitants Act 2010 was enacted on 19 July 2010. The Act established a civil partnership registration scheme for **same-sex** couples, which confers a range of rights, obligations and protections **consequent on registration**. It also set out the manner in which civil partnerships may be dissolved and with what conditions. Additionally, it set out a redress scheme for long-term opposite-sex and same-sex cohabiting couples who are not married or registered in a civil partnership.

Legislative changes required to give effect to the taxation changes arising from the Act were included in the **Finance (No. 3) Act 2011**. In short, on the registration of a civil partnership, civil partners are treated **in the same way** as spouses under tax law. **FA (No. 3) 2011** does not give opposite-sex cohabiting couples or same-sex cohabiting couples the same tax treatment as married couples or civil partners. Cohabiting couples are treated as single persons under tax law.

Married couples and civil partners can be assessed for tax in three different ways as follows:

- **Joint Assessment**, where all income is taxed as if it were the income of one of the spouses/civil partners, but with higher tax bands at the standard rate of tax.
- **Single Assessment**, where each spouse/civil partner is assessed to tax as if they were not married or in a civil partnership, with no transferability of unutilised credits or tax bands.
- **Separate Assessment**, where a married couple/civil partners, who are assessable on a joint assessment basis, can claim for separate assessment of their joint tax liability.

7.3.1 Joint Assessment

Under joint assessment the income of **each** spouse/civil partner is taxed as if it was the income of the assessable spouse or nominated civil partner. The couple themselves elect which one of them is to be the **assessable spouse** or **nominated civil partner** and the nomination can be done by writing or verbally to the Revenue. In the absence of such a nomination, the spouse/civil partner with the highest income becomes the assessable spouse or nominated civil partner.

Joint assessment is automatic, i.e. it is provided in the legislation that a husband and wife or civil partners will be deemed to have elected for joint assessment **unless**, before the end of the year of assessment, **either** spouse/civil partner writes to the Revenue indicating that they would prefer to be assessed as **single** individuals.

Under joint assessment, the tax credits and standard rate tax band can be allocated between spouses or civil partners in a way that suits their circumstances. For example, where one spouse/civil partner has no taxable income, all the tax credits and standard rate tax band will be given to the other spouse/civil partner. However, the PAYE tax credit, employment expenses and the basic standard rate band of €23,800 are non-transferrable.

The **income bands** chargeable at the standard rate of tax are increased, depending on whether the married couple/civil partners have one or two incomes.

Tax Year 2012	Tax Rate	Single/ Widowed/Surviving Civil Partner	Joint Assessment (One Income)	Joint Assessment (Two Incomes)
Taxable Income	20%	€32,800	€41,800	€65,600*
	41%	Balance	Balance	Balance

Transferable between spouses/civil partners up to a maximum of €41,800 for any one spouse/civil partner.

7.3.2 Single Assessment

If a married couple/civil partners wish to be assessed on the single assessment basis, then either spouse/civil partner must give notice to this effect to Revenue before the end of the year of assessment for which they wish to be assessed as single persons. If such a notice is given for any year of assessment, it will then apply for that year and all future years **unless** withdrawn by the spouse/civil partner who gave the notice of election.

If an election for single assessment is made, then each spouse/civil partner will be assessed to income tax as if they were not married or in a civil partnership, i.e. they are effectively treated as single persons, and tax credits and reliefs are granted accordingly. In such cases, if either spouse/civil partner has tax credits or reliefs in excess of his or her assessable income, there is **no right to transfer** unutilised credits to the other spouse/civil partner. From a tax point of view, in most cases, it will probably be undesirable for married couples/civil partners to elect for single assessment.

7.3.3 Separate Assessment

A married couple/civil partners that are assessable on a joint basis may claim for separate assessment of their joint income tax liability. Either spouse/civil partner can make an election for separate assessment not later than 1 April in the year of assessment.

Such an application applies for the year of claim and all subsequent years and may only be withdrawn by the spouse/civil partner who made the application. An election for separate assessment will result in the **same total income tax liability** as if the spouses/civil partners were jointly assessed, with each spouse paying their portion of the total tax liability.

The amount of income tax payable by each spouse/civil partner is calculated by reference to their total income and the proportions of tax credits or reliefs to which they are is entitled. Separate assessment **does not diminish** or **increase** the total liability that would have arisen under normal joint assessment.

A couple would opt for separate assessment so that they could each deal with their own tax affairs while not losing out financially.

Calculation of Separate Liabilities:

1. Ascertain the gross income assessable for each spouse/civil partner and the overall reliefs and allowances due for the year.
2. Any deductions from total income, e.g. permanent health insurance, are deducted from the income of the person who incurred the expenditure.
3. Each spouse/civil partner is given a standard rate tax band equal to that applicable to a single person, i.e. €32,800. However, to the extent that one spouse/civil partner does not fully utilise the standard rate band, i.e. their income is less than €32,800, the part of the tax band not utilised may be transferred to the other spouse/civil partner, subject to the proviso that the spouse/civil partner with the higher income may not have a standard rate tax band in excess of €41,800.
4. Apportion tax credits as follows:

Basic personal tax credit	} **Half each**
Blind person's tax credit	} **Half each**
Age tax credit	} **Half each**
Incapacitated child tax credit	} **Half each**

Employee tax credit	}	**Granted to each spouse/ civil partner**
	}	**to the extent that each**
	}	**has Schedule E income to**
	}	**utilise the allowance.**
Medical insurance relief, long-term care	}	**Allowed to the person**
policies, college fees, employment of a carer,	}	**who bears the**
dependant relative,	}	**expenditure**
health Insurance, etc.	}	

5. If any tax credits or reliefs are not fully utilised in calculating the tax liability of one of the spouses, then the unutilised balance is available in calculating the other spouse's/civil partner's tax liability.

Comparison of treatment under Joint, Single and Separate Assessment

Example:
James Cotter is married to Claire and they have one child, who is incapacitated. Their income for 2012 is as follows:

	James	Claire
Salary	€52,000	€25,500
PAYE paid	€9,500	€1,300

Income Tax Calculation for 2012 – Joint Assessment	Notes:	€	€
Income:			
Schedule E			
– James		52,000	
– Claire		25,500	77,500
Tax Calculation:			
(€41,800 + €23,800) = €65,600 @ 20%	**1.**	13,120	
(€77,500 – €65,600) = €11,900 @ 41%		4,879	17,999
Deduct:			
Basic personal tax credit (married)		3,300	
Employee tax credit	**2.**	3,300	
Incapacitated child credit		3,300	(9,900)
Income tax liability			8,099
Deduct:			
PAYE paid			(10,800)
Tax refund due			(2,701)

Note 1:
The standard rate band is increased by €23,800, being the lower of the income of the lower income spouse (Claire €25,500) or €23,800, i.e. to an overall maximum of €65,600 at the standard rate.
Note 2:
As both are employed, both spouses are entitled to the employee tax credit.

Income Tax Calculation for 2012 – Single Assessment	€	€	€	€
	James		**Claire**	
Income:				
Schedule E		52,000		25,500
Tax Calculation:				
€32,800 @ 20%	32,800	6,560	25,500	5,100
Balance @ 41%	19,200	7,872	0	0
		14,432		5,100
Deduct:				
Basic personal tax credit	1,650		1,650	
Employee tax credit	1,650		1,650	
Incapacitated child credit	1,650	(4,950)	1,650	(4,950)
Income tax liability		9,482		150
Deduct:				
PAYE paid		(9,500)		(1,300)
Tax refund due		**(18)**		**(1,150)**

Income Tax Calculation for 2012 – Separate Assessment	€	€	€	€
	James		**Claire**	
Income:				
Schedule E		52,000		25,500
Tax Calculation:				
@ 20% (65,600 – 25,500)	40,100	8,020	25,500	5,100
@ 41% (52,000 – 40,100)	11,900	4,879	0	0
		12,899		5,100
Deduct:				
Basic personal tax credit	1,650		1,650	
Employee tax credit	1,650		1,650	
Incapacitated child credit	1,650	(4,950)	1,650	(4,950)
Income tax liability		7,949		150
Deduct:				
PAYE paid		(9,500)		(1,300)
Tax refund due		**(1,551)**		**(1,150)**

Comparison of liability under each type of assessment:			
	James	Claire	Total
	€	€	€
Tax refundable 2012:			
Joint			**2,701**
Single	18	1,150	**1,168**
Separate	1,551	1,150	**2,701**

The total amount refundable is the same under joint and separate assessment. Single assessment would result in an extra amount of tax payable of €1,533.

7.3.4   Individualisation

Minister Charlie McCreevy introduced tax individualisation in Budget 2000, which was designed to move away from the system at the time, whereby the single person's tax band was doubled for married couples to one which would involve **each** person having their **own** standard rate tax band. This process has yet to be completed with the difference of €9,000 between the single person's tax band and the married couple/civil partners (one income) tax band remaining static since 2002.

7.3.5   Tax Treatment in Year of Marriage/Civil Partnership

Each party to the marriage/civil partnership is initially taxed as a **single** person for the complete year.

The legislation permits them to elect, after the end of the year of assessment, to have their tax liability computed on a joint assessment basis as if they had been married/were civil partners for the **whole** of the tax year in which the marriage/civil partnership took place. If this election is made, the tax saving, if any, *vis-à-vis* the amount of their combined liabilities on a single assessment basis, is scaled down in the proportion that the period of marriage/civil partnership during the tax year bears to the full tax year, i.e.:

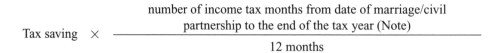

$$\text{Tax saving} \quad \times \quad \frac{\text{number of income tax months from date of marriage/civil partnership to the end of the tax year (Note)}}{12 \text{ months}}$$

Note: An income tax month is a calendar month, with part of a month being treated as a full month in the formula.

Example:

John married Mary on 15 July 2012.

John earned a gross salary of €44,000 in 2012 and paid PAYE on it of €7,500.

Mary earned a salary of €23,000 in 2012 on which she paid PAYE of €1,300.

(continued overleaf)

Assessment of John and Mary as Single Individuals for 2012

	John		Mary	
	€	€	€	€
Income:				
Schedule E		44,000		23,000
Tax Calculation:				
32,800 @ 20%	32,800	6,560	23,000	4,600
Balance @ 41%	11,200	4,592	0	0
		11,152		4,600
Deduct:				
Basic personal tax credit	1,650		1,650	
Employee tax credit	1,650	(3,300)	1,650	(3,300)
Initial income tax liability		**7,852**		**1,300**
Deduct:				
Year of marriage relief (Note)		(811)		(134)
PAYE paid		(7,500)		(1,300)
Tax refund due		(459)		(134)

Note: Notional Liability under Joint Assessment for 2012	€	€
Income:		
Schedule E		67,000
Tax Calculation:		
64,800 @ 20% (€41,800+€23,000)	64,800	12,960
Balance @ 41%	2,200	902
		13,862
Deduct:		
Basic personal tax credit	3,300	
Employee tax credit	3,300	(6,600)
Total liability under joint assessment		7,262
Total combined liability under single assessment		9,152
Saving under joint assessment		1,890

Saving restricted to:

$$\frac{\text{6 months (period of marriage in tax year)}}{\text{12 months}} \times €1,890 = €945$$

SPLIT: John

$$\frac{€7,852}{€7,852 + €1,300} \times €945 = €811$$

SPLIT: Mary

$$\frac{€1,300}{€7,852 + €1,300} \times €1,029 = €134$$

$$€945$$

7.3.6 Tax Treatment in Year of Death

The tax treatment of the surviving spouse/civil partner in the year of bereavement depends on how the surviving spouse/civil partner and the deceased were taxed **before** the bereavement.

7.3.7 Joint Assessment and Death of Assessable Spouse/Nominated Civil Partner

If the couple were assessed under joint assessment and if the **deceased** was the "assessable spouse" or "nominated civil partner", i.e. the person responsible for making a joint tax return, the **surviving spouse/civil partner** will be taxable in their **own right from the date of death** of the deceased. The surviving spouse/civil partner is entitled to the widowed person/surviving civil partner in the year of bereavement tax credit and the widowed person's/surviving civil partner's (without dependent children) tax band for this period. Any income (of the surviving spouse/civil partner and the deceased) **prior** to the death of the deceased is treated as the **income of the deceased** to the date of death.

Example:

Mr Andrews, who was the assessable spouse under joint assessment, died on 1 November 2012. His salary from 1 January 2012 to the date of death was €46,000 from which PAYE of €5,900 was deducted.

Mrs Andrews was employed by a local wholesale company and earned €16,000 from 1 January to 1 November 2012, (PAYE deducted €2,200) and €3,500 from 2 November to 31 December 2012 (PAYE deducted €480).

Mr Andrews Deceased – Income Tax liability			
Period 1/1/2012 to 1/11/2012		€	€
Schedule E salary self			46,000
Schedule E salary wife			16,000
Gross income			62,000
Tax:			
(€41,800 + 16,000) @ 20%	€57,800	11,560	
€4,200 @ 41%		1,722	
			13,282
Less: Basic personal tax credit		3,300	
Employee tax credits €1,650 × 2		3,300	(6,600)
Tax liability			6,682
Less: PAYE - self		5,900	
PAYE - wife		2,200	(8,100)
Refund due			(1,418)

Mrs Andrews Income Tax Liability Period 2/11/2012 to 31/12/2012	€	€
Schedule E salary		3,500
Tax: €3,500 × 20%		700
Less: Basic personal tax credit (year of bereavement)	(3,300)	
Employee tax credit (restricted to)	(700)	
	(4,000)	

(continued overleaf)

Tax credits limited to the amount which reduces tax liability to nil	(700)
Tax Liability	Nil
PAYE	(480)
Refund due	(480)

7.3.8 Joint Assessment and Death of the Non-assessable Spouse or Non-nominated Civil Partner

If the couple were assessed under joint assessment and if the surviving spouse/civil partner was the "assessable spouse" or "nominated civil partner", i.e. the person responsible for making a joint tax return, the surviving spouse/civil partner will continue to receive the married person's/civil partner's tax credits and income tax bands for the remainder of the tax year. The surviving spouse/civil partner will be taxable on their own income for the full year of bereavement plus the deceased's income from the start of the tax year to the date of death.

Example:

Jane Murphy died on 1 November 2012. Her salary from 1 January 2012 to the date of death was €36,000 from which PAYE of €5,900 was deducted.

Her civil partner, Ann Ward is employed by a local wholesale company and earned €46,000 from 1 January to 1 November 2012 (PAYE deducted €9,200) and €13,500 from 2 November to 31 December 2012 (PAYE deducted €4,900). Ann is the nominated civil partner under joint assessment.

Ann Ward – Income Tax Calculation 2012		€	€
Income:			
Schedule E			
– Ann Ward (Total 2012)		59,500	
– Jane Murphy (To 01/11/2012)		36,000	95,500
Tax Calculation:			
(€41,800 + €23,800) @ 20%	65,600	13,120	
Balance @ 41%	29,900	12,259	25,379
	95,500		
Deduct:			
Basic personal tax credit		3,300	
Employee tax credit (x 2)		3,300	(6,600)
Income Tax liability			**18,779**
Deduct:			
PAYE paid:			
– Ann Ward (€9,200 + €4,900)		14,100	
– Jane Murphy		5,900	(20,000)
Tax refund due			**(1,221)**

7.3.9 Single Assessment and Death of a Spouse/Civil Partner

If the couple have been assessed as single persons, the deceased is taxed as a single person up to the date of death. The surviving spouse/civil partner is also taxed as a single person but is **entitled** to the widowed person/surviving civil partner in the year of bereavement tax credit (€3,300 for 2012) instead of the single person's basic personal tax credit. The single person's mortgage interest ceiling will apply to the deceased, and the widowed person's/surviving civil partner's ceiling will apply to the surviving spouse/civil partner.

As can be seen from the above examples, where a couple have been jointly assessed and the **assessable spouse/nominated civil partner dies, extra tax credits** are given in the year of bereavement (i.e. widowed person/surviving civil partner in the year of bereavement personal tax credit to the surviving spouse/civil partner, the married/civil partner's personal tax credit to the deceased, an extra employee tax credit and an **additional** mortgage interest relief ceiling) and the couple, in effect, get an additional standard rate tax band.

Accordingly, a couple who have been assessed as single persons should consider electing for joint assessment in the year of death. An **election** can be made by the surviving spouse and the personal representative of the deceased and must be made **before the end** of the tax year in which the death occurs.

Tax Treatment of Surviving Spouse/Civil Partner for Subsequent Years
In the years following the year of bereavement, the surviving spouse/civil partner is entitled to the widowed person's/surviving civil partner's tax credit. If the surviving spouse/civil partner has dependent children, he/she will also be entitled to the single parent family tax credit and the widowed/surviving civil partner parent tax credit (for five years after the date of bereavement). The widowed person's/surviving civil partner's (without dependent children) income tax band or the one-parent family (with dependent children) tax band will also apply, depending on whether the surviving spouse/civil partner has dependent children.

7.3.10 Tax Treatment of Separated Spouses/Civil Partners

The general rule is that separated spouses/civil partners are assessed to income tax as **single individuals**. The following rules apply:

- **Legally enforceable** maintenance payments are **deductible as a charge** in arriving at the tax liability of the payer and are chargeable to income tax under Case IV of Schedule D in the hands of the receiving spouse/civil partner. **Voluntary** payments (i.e. payments which are not legally enforceable) are **not** taken into account when calculating either spouse's/civil partner's tax.

- Income tax is **not deducted** at source from legally enforceable maintenance payment arrangements by one party to the other party.

- **Legally enforceable** maintenance payments made for the use or **benefit of a child are disregarded** for tax purposes, i.e. the payer does not get a tax deduction for the payment and the child is not assessed on the payment. Generally, **one-parent family tax credit** and **one parent family tax bands** can be due to both spouses/civil partners if the child resides with each one for part of the tax year.

Example 1:

Mr and Mrs Pearce are separated. Under a legal deed drawn up in 2008, Mr Pearce pays Mrs Pearce €900 per month, of which €500 is specifically for their only child, Stuart, aged 8. Mr Pearce is employed by an insurance company and Mrs Pearce is employed by a local wholesale company. His salary for the tax year 2012 was €59,000 (PAYE deducted €11,000) and her salary for the tax year 2012 was €28,000 (PAYE deducted €570)

The child resides with Mrs Pearce during the week and with Mr Pearce at weekends.

Mr Pearce: Income Tax Liability 2012		€
	Schedule E	59,000
Less Charges:	Maintenance payments (€400 × 12)	(4,800)
	Net income	54,200
Tax	€36,800 × 20% =	7,360
	€17,400 × 41% =	7,134
		14,494
Less:	Basic personal tax credit	(1,650)
	Employee tax credit	(1,650)
	One-parent family tax credit	(1,650)
Tax Liability		9,544
Less:	PAYE deducted	(11,000)
	Tax refund due	(1,456)

Mrs Pearce: Income Tax Liability 2012		€
Case IV	Schedule D	4,800
	Schedule E	28,000
		32,800
Tax:	€32,800 × 20% =	6,560
Less:	Basic personal tax credit	(1,650)
	Employee tax credit	(1,650)
	One-parent family tax credit	(1,650)
Tax Liability		1,610
Less:	PAYE deducted	(570)
	Tax due	1,040

7.3.11 Option for Joint Assessment on Divorce/Dissolution of Civil Partnership

If the marriage/civil partnership has not been **dissolved or annulled**, and the couple obtain an Irish divorce/civil partner dissolution, then the same rules apply for income tax purposes as apply to separated spouses/civil partners, i.e.:

- they are treated as **single individuals;**
- **legally enforceable maintenance payments** are deducted as a **charge** in arriving at the income tax liability of the payer, and are chargeable to income tax under Schedule D Case IV for the receiving spouse/civil partner;

- each spouse/civil partner will be entitled to the **single person tax credits** and **rate bands**; and
- each spouse/civil partner will be entitled to the **one-parent family tax credit** and **one-parent family tax band** provided that they satisfy the conditions outlined in **Section 6.2.3** and that the child resides with each spouse/civil partner for part of the tax year.

The couple may elect for **joint assessment** only if:

- both individuals are **resident in Ireland** for tax purposes for the year of assessment;
- **legally enforceable maintenance payments** are made by one spouse/civil partner to the other; and
- **neither has re-married or registered a new civil partnership.**

If this election is made under Section 1026 TCA 1997, the following rules apply:

- the payer **cannot deduct maintenance payments** made to the divorced spouse/civil partner in arriving at his total income and the **divorced spouse/civil partner is not assessed** on the maintenance payments;
- the **married person's/civil partner's tax credits** and rate bands are granted; and
- if the divorced spouse/civil partner has income in his/her own right, apart from maintenance payments received by her/him, the income tax liability applicable to each spouse's/civil partner's separate income is calculated using the separate assessment procedures.

Example 2:
Same circumstances as Example 1 with joint assessment option.

Mrs Pearce – Income Tax Calculation 2012

Income:			€
Schedule E			28,000
Tax Calculation:			
€28,000	@ 20%	5,600	
€ –	@ 41%	0	5,600
€28,000			
Less: Non Refundable Tax Credits:			
Basic personal tax credit		1,650	
Employee tax credit		1,650	(3,300)
Tax liability			2,300
Deduct:	PAYE paid		(570)
Net tax due			**1,730**

(continued overleaf)

Mr Pearce – Income Tax Calculation 2012

Income:

			€
Schedule E			<u>59,000</u>

Tax Calculation:

€32,800	@20%	6,560	
€4,800	@20% (Note)	960	
<u>€21,400</u>	@41%	<u>8,774</u>	16,294
€59,000			

Less: Non Refundable Tax Credits:

Basic personal tax credit		1,650	
Employee tax credit		<u>1,650</u>	(3,300)
Tax liability			12,994
Deduct:	PAYE paid		(11,000)
Net tax due			<u>**1,994**</u>

Note: Part of standard rate tax band not used by Mrs Pearce = €4,800 (€32,800 – €28,000) can increase the standard rate tax band of Mr. Pearce.

In this case, it is more beneficial for Mr and Mrs Pearce not to opt for joint assessment as not only will they lose both one-parent family tax credits but their combined income taxed at 20% is reduced by €4,000.

7.3.12 Tax Treatment in Year of Separation

In the year of separation, where **joint assessment** had been elected for under section 1026 TCA 1997, the tax treatment of the couple is similar to the tax treatment that applies in the year of death of the assessable spouse/nominated civil partner.

Treatment of Assessable Spouse/Nominated Civil Partner

1. He/she is assessable on his/her entire personal income for the year of separation and his/her spouses's/civil partner's income (applying appropriate basis of apportionment) for the proportion of the year up to the date of separation.
2. He/she is entitled to a **married person's basic personal tax credit**, €3,300 for the tax year 2012, and the benefit of the **married person's tax bands**.

Treatment of Non-assessable Spouse/Nominated Civil Partner

1. He/she is assessable as a single person on his/her own sources of income for the period of the year after the date of separation.
2. He/she is entitled only to a single person's basic personal tax credit and to the benefit of the rate bands applicable to a single person. If there are dependent children, he/she is entitled to a **full one-parent family tax credit** and **one parent family tax band**, assuming he/she satisfies the conditions as set out in **Section 6.2.3**.
3. Other allowances/reliefs, etc. available to him/her are given by reference to single person limitations.

Separated Persons Election for Joint Assessment

Clearly the above rules do not apply where the separated spouses/civil partners elect for joint assessment as previously discussed.

Example:

Mr and Mrs Doyle had been married for 10 years when they separated on 30 September 2012. Under the terms of the deed of separation drawn up on that day, Mr Doyle pays Mrs Doyle €300 per month, from 1 October 2012, which specifically includes €100 for the maintenance of their only child Ruth, who lives with her mother.

Mr. Doyle earned €49,000 in 2012, from which PAYE of €5,600 was deducted. Mrs Doyle earned €22,000 in 2012, from which PAYE of €3,900 was deducted. Mrs Doyle earned €16,500 (PAYE paid €2,900) for the period 1 January 2012 to 30 September 2012.

Mr Doyle – Income Tax Computation 2012

Income:

		€	€
Schedule E - self		49,000	
Schedule E – wife (1/1/2012 – 30/9/2012)		16,500	65,500
Less: Charges			
Maintenance payments (€300 – €100 × 3)			(600)
Total Income			**64,900**
Tax Calculation:			
€41,800	@ 20%	8,360	
€16,500	@ 20%	3,300	
€6,600	@ 41%	2,706	
€64,900			14,366
Less: Non Refundable Tax Credits:			
Basic personal tax credit (married)		3,300	
Employee tax credits (x 2)		3,300	(6,600)
Tax liability			**7,766**
Deduct:			
PAYE paid - self		5,600	
PAYE paid - wife (1/1/2012 – 30/9/2012)		2,900	(8,500)
Net Tax Refund			(734)

Mrs Doyle – Income Tax Computation 2012

Income:

		€	€
Schedule D Case IV		600	
Schedule E (1/10/2012 – 31/12/2012)		5,500	6,100
Tax Calculation:			
€6,100	@ 20%		1,220
Less: Non Refundable Tax Credits:			
Basic personal tax credit		1,650	
One parent family tax credit		1,650	
Employee tax credit		1,650	
		4,950	
Restrict to amount which gives a NIL tax liability			(1,220)
Tax liability			**NIL**
Deduct:			
PAYE paid (1/10/2012 – 31/12/2012)			(1,000)
Net tax refundable			**(1,000)**

Questions (Chapter 7)

(See Solutions to Questions at the end of this text.)

7 Computation of Income Tax

7.1 Patrick and Helen

Patrick and Helen have been married for a number of years. They have the following income and outgoings for the tax year 2012.

	Patrick	Helen
	€	€
Income		
Salary	10,500	50,000
Benefit in kind	–	2,100
Outgoings		
Mortgage Interest – loan taken out in 1992 (Note)	4,200	–
VHI premiums (joined June 2011) (Note)	–	150
Permanent Health Insurance	–	600
PAYE	830	9,000
Notes:		
Mortgage interest is paid to a qualifying lender.		
VHI – tax relief is given at source.		

Requirement
Compute the income tax liability on the basis that the following options had been claimed for 2012:
1. Joint assessment
2. Separate assessment
3. Single assessment

7.2 Peter and Paul

Peter and Paul entered into a civil partnership on 20 June 2011. The couple elected for joint assessment with Peter as the nominated civil partner.

Peter is employed by a firm of auctioneers. His gross salary for 2012 was €50,000 (PAYE deducted €10,300).

Paul is employed by a firm of stockbrokers. He earned €26,000 gross (PAYE deducted €2,050) during 2012.

Requirement
Compute Peter and Paul's tax liability for 2012 on the basis that they wish to minimise their total liability.

7.3 Mr and Mrs Thorne

Mr and Mrs Thorne separated in 1990. Under the terms of the deed of separation which was drawn up at that time, Mr Thorne pays Mrs Thorne €800 per month, of which €600 is specifically for their two children. The children reside with Mrs Thorne from Monday to Saturday, and with Mr Thorne on Sundays. Joint assessment does not apply.

Mr Thorne's projected salary for the tax year 2012 is €50,000 and Mrs Thorne's projected salary is €35,000.

The terms of the deed are being reviewed at present and Mr Thorne has suggested increasing the maintenance payments to €1,000 per month, on condition that only €100 per month is specifically for their two children, and that the deed is reviewed every year.

Mrs Thorne, who has little knowledge of income tax, has contacted you confirming that she seems satisfied with this, as long as there are no tax disadvantages arising.

Requirement:
1. Calculate Mrs Thorne's income tax liability for the tax year 2012 if:

   (a) The deed is not reviewed
   (b) The deed is reviewed with effect from 1 January 2012.

2. Indicate under which situation she is better off financially and by how much.

7.4 Mr and Mrs Lynch

Mr and Mrs Lynch separated on 30 June 2012. Under the terms of the deed of separation which was drawn up on that date, Mr Lynch pays Mrs Lynch €700 per month, of which €100 is specifically for their only child Mary, who resides with her mother. The first monthly payment is made on 1 July 2012. He also pays the mortgage on the family home where Mrs Lynch continues to reside.

Mr Lynch's salary for 2012 was €48,000 and Mrs Lynch's salary was €15,000. Mrs Lynch's payslip for the month ended 30 June 2012 showed cumulative gross salary of €7,000 for the period 1 January 2012 to 30 June 2012. Mr Lynch had the following outgoings:

	Tax Year	
	2011	2012
	€	€
Gross mortgage interest		
Payable to Bank of Ireland – loan taken out in 2002	3,900	4,100
VHI payments (net of tax @ 20%)	412	458

Mr and Mrs Lynch had been jointly assessed for all years up to the year of their separation.

Requirement:

Calculate Mr and Mrs Lynch's tax liability for 2012 on the basis that:

1. Joint assessment was claimed for the year of assessment in accordance with section 1026 TCA 1997.
2. No election was made under section 1026 TCA 1997.

If Mr and Mrs Lynch had separated during 2011, calculate their tax liability for 2012 assuming that:

3. An election was made for joint assessment under section 1026 TCA 1997.
4. The election under section 1026 TCA 1997 was not made.

The PAYE System

8.1 Introduction

The PAYE (Pay As You Earn) system is the method used by the Revenue Commissioners to collect income tax on most **Schedule E** income.

Broadly speaking, it obliges an employer to deduct income tax from wages, salaries and other income assessable to tax under Schedule E **when the remuneration is actually paid**. The primary objective of the system is to collect the income tax due in respect of the relevant Schedule E payments so as to avoid a deferral of liability by the employees concerned.

The PAYE system is a good example of the principle of deduction of **tax at source** in operation, whereby the **payer** rather than the **recipient** of the income is liable to account for the income tax to the Revenue Commissioners. Under this system, it is the **employer** who is **obliged** to deduct the tax on making payments of emoluments to his employees and to account for the tax so deducted to the Collector-General. Payments made under Schedule E are **deemed** to have been paid **net of tax**. Where refunds of tax are due to the employee, the system provides, in certain circumstances, that these are made by the employer.

Under this system, much of the administration cost involved in collecting income tax due by people assessable under Schedule E is effectively put on to the employer.

8.2 Scope of Application of the PAYE System

The PAYE system applies to all income from offices or employments (including directorships and occupational pensions). The system therefore applies to:

- Salaries, wages, directors' fees, back pay, pensions, bonuses, overtime, sales commissions, holiday pay, tea money, etc.
- **Round sum expenses** must be paid under the PAYE system. Such round sum expenses would include, for example, a fixed sum (whether paid weekly, monthly or yearly) to cover expenses to be met by the employee, or an amount put at the disposal of the employee for which he or she does not have to account to the employer with receipts, vouchers, etc.
- Commencement/inducement payments and termination payments.
- With effect from 1 January 2004, Benefits in Kind ("BIK") and perquisites ("perks") must be paid under the PAYE system. Examples of BIK are the private use of a company car, loans at a preferential rate of interest, free or subsidised accommodation. Examples of perks are medical insurance premiums, payment of club subscriptions and vouchers. The calculation of the taxable value of BIK and perks is included in **Chapter 4**.
- Payments by employees to employer superannuation schemes may be deducted from their gross pay for PAYE purposes. From 1 January 2011, employee contributions to pension schemes are liable to employee PRSI and Universal Social Charge (USC) and are not deductible from gross pay for PRSI and USC purposes.

From 1 January 2011, share-based remuneration is included as notional pay for the calculation of PAYE/PRSI and USC at the time the shares are given to the employee.

Reimbursements of expenses actually incurred by employees/directors in the performance of their duties of employment are not treated as "pay" for PAYE purposes.

8.3 Employer's Responsibilities

8.3.1 Registration

An employer is obliged **by law** to register for PAYE purposes if he has any person in his employment whose earnings, if employed full time, exceed €8 per week (or €36 per month) **or**, if employed part-time, exceed €2 per week (or €9 per month). A company **must register** as an employer and operate PAYE/PRSI/USC on the pay of directors even if there are no other employees. However a "qualifying domestic employer" does not have to register and operate PAYE on emoluments paid to a domestic employee. A qualifying domestic employer is an individual who has only one domestic employee to whom he pays **less than €40** a week. A domestic employee is an individual employed to carry out domestic duties, including child minding, in the private residence of the employer.

To register for PAYE, one of the following forms must be completed:

- Form **TR1** – employer is an individual *or* partnership.
- Form **TR2** – employer is trading as a company.

- Form **PREM Reg** – employer who is **already registered** for income tax (either as an employee or self-employed) or for corporation tax.

8.3.2 Commencement of Tax Year

Before the beginning of a new tax year, the employer should ensure that he has notification of the tax credits and standard rate cut-off point for **every** employee for the new tax year. Revenue should be notified immediately of the name and address and PPS number of any employee for which the notification has not been received.

If, on the first pay day of the new tax year, the employer has not received a tax credit certificate for the new tax year for an employee, the following options apply:

- Where the **cumulative basis** of tax deduction is in operation, the employer should use the previous year's certificate, **provided** it has the **employer's name** on it.
- Where the **non-cumulative basis** (week1/month1 basis) is in operation, the employer should use the tax credits and standard rate cut-off point, as advised in the **previous year's** non-cumulative tax credit certificate.
- Where the **temporary basis** of tax deduction is in operation, the employer can continue to use, on a temporary basis, the tax credits and standard rate cut-off point as advised on the **P45**, provided the P45 relates to the **current year or previous year**. Otherwise, the **emergency basis** of tax deduction will apply from 1 January until a notification is received.
- Where the **emergency basis** of tax deduction is in operation, the employer should continue to use the emergency basis on a cumulative basis.

Note: An employer is legally obliged to deduct tax and pay it over to the Collector-General whether or not a tax credit certificate has been received.

8.3.3 Cessation of Employment

Where an employee leaves the employment, takes a career break, or dies while in employment, the employer should complete a **Form P45**. This is a form certifying the employee's pay, tax, PRSI and USC contributions from the **start of the tax year** to the **date of cessation**.

The Form P45 is a four-part form – Part 1 should be sent to Revenue and Parts 2, 3 and 4 given to the employee on his cessation date or with his final wages payment. It is an important form, **which cannot be duplicated**, and is required by the employee for the following:

- **to give to their next employer** – Parts 2 and 3 should be given by an employee to his new employer who would retain Part 2 and send Part 3 to Revenue, as a request for a tax credit certificate for the employee in question;
- **any claim for a refund of tax during unemployment; and**
- **claiming Social Welfare Benefits** (Part 4).

The Revenue On-Line Service (ROS) provides a facility for the submission of Form P45 (Part 1) on-line and the printing of Parts 2, 3 and 4 onto computer stationery.

In the case of a deceased employee, Parts 1 to 4 together with the employee's tax credit certificate should be sent to Revenue.

To prevent fraud, an employer is **prohibited**, in any circumstances, from supplying **duplicates** of forms P45 to an employee who has left the employment and claims to have lost the original.

8.3.4 Commencement of Employment

Procedure where Employer Receives Parts 2 and 3 of Form P45

The new employer should follow the instructions given on Part 2 and should immediately send Part 3 to Revenue. Part 3 is effectively a request by the new employer for a tax credit certificate in respect of the employee. Until he receives such a tax credit certificate, he should operate PAYE on the temporary basis (week 1/month 1/basis) or on the emergency basis if the letter "E" appears on the P45.

If the temporary basis is used, the weekly or monthly tax credits and SRCOP on Form P45 should be applied on a **non-cumulative** basis.

A refund of tax should not be made to an employee on the week 1/month 1 basis.

If the P45 is for a **previous** tax year the employer is obliged to operate the **emergency basis** pending receipt of a current tax credit certificate from Revenue as a result of the submission of the Form P45.

Procedure Where New Employer is given a Certificate of Tax Credits and Standard Rate Cut-Off Point

An employer who has been given a certificate of tax credits and SRCOP showing the name and registered number of **another employer** should notify Revenue on **Form P46**. If the certificate is for the current tax year, PAYE should be operated on the **temporary basis** by reference to the tax credits and SRCOP printed on the notice. If the certificate does not cover the current tax year, the employer is obliged to operate the **emergency basis** pending receipt of a current tax credit certificate and SRCOP or a tax deduction card from Revenue, as a result of the submission of a Form P46.

New Employee Taking up Employment for the First Time

The new employee should be requested to obtain a tax credit certificate and SRCOP. He can secure such a certificate by completing income tax Form 12A and submitting it to Revenue. Until the employer receives a PPS number for the new employee, tax at the **marginal** rate (with no credits or SRCOP) must be deducted from all payments.

8.3.5 Duties at the End of the Tax Year

At the end of each tax year the employer must complete Revenue's **"end of year return"** Form **P35** and prepare and distribute a **Form P60** for every employee in their employment at the **end** of the tax year.

Once proper records have been maintained during the year, completion of the end of year returns is relatively straightforward. It essentially involves transferring details from the employee records to the Form P35 and Form(s) P60. The Form P35 must be returned electronically through ROS **before 23 February** to avoid penalties.

In summary, the employer must:

- Total and complete the bottom of each payroll record for each employee. The final figures of pay, tax, PRSI and USC entered in the coded boxes at the bottom of the payroll records should be the totals for that employee for all periods of employment with the employer during that tax year.
- Complete forms P35, P35L and P35L/T (see below). All entries for PAYE, PRSI and USC on the P35L and P35L/T should be added together and the totals transferred to the P35 Declaration.

■ Calculate any PAYE, PRSI or USC outstanding and send the payment with the completed P35 form to the Collector-General.

■ Give a Form P60 to each employee who is employed at the end of the tax year (i.e. on 31 December). The employer will already have given a Form P45 to those employees who left employment during the year. The P60 form for 2011 onwards is revised to cater for the USC.

Form P35 is a declaration that the details being returned are correct. It is issued to all employers on record irrespective of the type of payroll system they use. This is the form on which the employer declares the overall amount of PAYE/PRSI/USC deducted from his/her employees during the tax year.

Form P35L is pre-printed with the name and PPS number of each employee. The details from the employee records are transferred to the corresponding boxes on this form. If any employee's name and PPS number are omitted from the list provided they should be added to the list.

Form P35L/T must be completed for any employee for whom the PPS number is not known. The employee's private address, date of birth and mother's birth surname must be shown on this form. This is to ensure that the correct PPS number is traced by Revenue.

Form P35 on diskette: most computer payroll systems can now produce the P35 details in soft copy for upload into Revenue's online system (ROS).

Every person who was employed at any time during the tax year, even if no tax was deducted, must be returned on the P35. All documents relating to pay, tax, PRSI and USC must be retained by an employer for six years after the end of a tax year.

Form P60 is a form issued by an employer to an employee certifying details of the employee's pay, tax, PRSI and USC contributions for the tax year. Form P60 must be given to each employee, who is in employment at 31 December, before 15 February in the following year. The figures on the Form P60 should be copied from the employee records. Blank forms P60, either manual or computer format, are issued by Revenue to the employers each year.

8.3.6 *Payment of PAYE/PRSI/Universal Social Charge (USC)*

PAYE deducted, USC deductions and total PRSI contributions (the amount deducted from pay plus the amount payable by the employer) must be **remitted to the Collector-General electronically via Revenue On-line Service (ROS) by the 23rd of the calendar month** following the month in which the deductions were made, except for the month of December where they are due on **15 February**.

Each month a **Form P30** bank giro/payslip is issued by the Collector-General on which the employer's name, address, registration number and the relevant month are computer printed and taxpayer specific. Only forms **showing the correct details** should be used as otherwise payments made may not be correctly credited. The figures for total PAYE (including USC) and total PRSI contributions should be entered on the form and totalled, which will equal the amount of the payment. USC amounts are to be included with the figure for PAYE on Form P30. Where there is no PAYE/PRSI/USC liability for a particular month, the Form P30 must be returned marked Nil.

The completed Form P30 together with any payment must be filled electronically via ROS.

Where an employer pays PAYE/PRSI/USC by monthly **direct debit,** he is only required to file an annual P35 – the monthly P30 need not be filed.

In certain circumstances, PAYE, PRSI and USC can be returned and paid on an annual or quarterly basis. Authorisation to do so is at the discretion of the Collector-General and this authorisation may be terminated at any time.

Late payments of PAYE/PRSI/USC are charged at a rate of **0.0274% for each day or part thereof** for which the payment is overdue from 1 July 2009 (previously 0.0322%).

8.3.7 Unpaid Remuneration

Where remuneration, which is deductible as an expense in calculating Case I or II profits for a particular tax year, is **unpaid** at the end of the accounting period and is not paid **within six months** of that date, such remuneration is deemed to have been paid on the **last day of the accounting period** for PAYE purposes. For example, a trader's accounts for the year ended 31 December 2012 include an accrual of €10,000 for bonuses due to employees. Normally, PAYE is only due in respect of the bonuses when they are actually paid. If, however, the bonuses remain unpaid at 1 July 2013, for PAYE purposes the bonuses are deemed to have been paid on 31 December 2012, and the PAYE deductible therefrom is due for payment on 14 February 2013.

8.3.8 Credit for PAYE Paid by Certain Employees

With effect from 1 January 2006, employees who have a "material" interest in a company **will not** be entitled to a **credit** against their income tax liability for PAYE deducted from emoluments paid to them by the company **unless** there is documentary evidence to show that the PAYE **has been paid** to the Collector-General.

An employee is deemed to have a material interest in a company if he (either on his own or with one or more connected persons) or a person, with whom he is connected, is the beneficial owner of, or is able to control directly or indirectly, more than **15%** of the ordinary share capital of the company.

Any PAYE remitted to the Collector-General is treated as being paid firstly in respect of other employees of the company.

Section 997A TCA 1997 provides that PAYE remitted on behalf of proprietary directors is treated as paid in respect of each proprietary director in the **same proportion** as the emoluments paid bears to the total directors' emoluments, **provided** that the tax split does not result in a **credit exceeding** the amount of the tax actually deducted from the individual director (FA 2010).

8.4 Employee Tax Credits and Standard Rate Cut-Off Point

8.4.1 Introduction

Before the beginning of the new tax year, every employee is sent a **Tax Credit Certificate** giving him details of his tax credits and standard rate cut-off point (SRCOP) for the new tax year. This notice gives a detailed breakdown of how the total tax credits due have been calculated. At the same time, his employer is sent a tax credit certificate **and SRCOP** which gives the same information. The employer is not given details of how the employee's total tax credit or SRCOP has been determined so as to preserve the confidentiality of the personal circumstances of the employee.

The employer is **obliged** to use the **latest** official tax credit certificate that he holds, even if the employee claims that he has disputed the amount of the tax credits or SRCOP granted to him.

Under the tax credit based PAYE system, tax is calculated at the 20% and/or 41% rates, as appropriate, on **gross pay**. Tax thus calculated is "gross tax", which is reduced by tax credits to arrive at net tax payable.

8.4.2   Tax Credits

As outlined in **Chapter 6**, an individual is entitled to certain tax credits depending on his personal circumstances, e.g. basic personal tax credit for a single person, married/civil partners, widowed person/surviving civil partner, employee tax credit, one-parent family tax credit etc. In addition, certain reliefs are given as a tax credit at the standard rate of tax, e.g. relief for college fees, etc.

8.4.3   Standard Rate Cut-Off Point (SRCOP)

The SRCOP is the amount of the individual's **standard rate tax band** for the year. Tax is paid at the standard rate, currently 20%, up to the SRCOP. Any income in excess of the SRCOP is taxed at the higher rate, currently 41%.

Example:

Liam Cotter is married with two children and his wife works full-time in the home. Liam's salary for 2012 is €48,000.

Tax credits due for 2012:	€
Basic personal tax credit (married)	3,300
Home carer tax credit	810
Employee tax credit	1,650
Total	5,760

The notice of determination of tax credits and SRCOP sent to Liam will show total tax credits due to him of €5,760 for 2012. These will be expressed as a monthly tax credit amount of €480 (€5,760/12) and a weekly tax credit amount of €110.77 (€5,760/52).

The notice of determination of tax credits and SRCOP sent to Liam will also show a SRCOP of €41,800 (married, one income) for 2012. This will also be expressed as a monthly cut-off amount of €3,483.33 (€41,800/12) and a weekly cut-off amount of €803.84 (€41,800/52).

8.4.4   Non-PAYE Income

If an individual has small amounts of non-PAYE income, the total tax credits due to him may be reduced by the non-PAYE income at the standard rate of tax and his SRCOP is reduced by the amount of the non-PAYE income. This will avoid any under-payment of tax on the non-PAYE income.

Example:
If, in the above example, Liam Cotter has UK dividend income of €1,000 for 2012, his total tax credits due to him for 2012 will be reduced by €1,000 @ 20% (i.e. €200) to €5,560. His SRCOP will also be reduced by €1,000 to €40,800. This ensures that the 41% income tax due on the dividend is collected.

Tax due by Liam Cotter for 2012		€	€
Income:			
Salary		48,000	
Dividend received		1,000	
Taxable Income			49,000
Tax Calculation:			
€41,800	@ 20%	8,360	
€7,200	@ 41%	2,952	
€49,000			11,312
Less: Non Refundable Tax Credits:			
Basic personal tax credit		3,300	
Home carer tax credit		810	
Employee tax credit		1,650	(5,760)
Tax liability			**5,552**
Tax collected under the PAYE system:			
Salary			48,000
Tax Calculation:			
SRCOP (reduced)			
€40,800	@ 20%	8,160	
€ 7,200	@ 41%	2,952	
€48,000			11,112
Less:			
Tax credits due (reduced)			(5,560)
PAYE deducted			**5,552**

Note: The onus is on the individual to inform Revenue of any non-PAYE income that is taxable, most notably any social welfare benefits being received (e.g. State pension or widowed/surviving civil partner) that are taxable.

8.4.5 Reliefs Given as a Deduction from Gross Income

Certain reliefs are given as a deduction from income rather than as a tax credit, for example, permanent health insurance. Where an employee is entitled to such a relief, which is given as a deduction from income, the total tax credits due to him are **increased** by the amount of the relief at the standard rate of tax and his SRCOP is **increased** by the amount of the relief.

As in the example above, if in 2012, Liam Cotter is entitled to deduct Schedule E expenses relating to his employment of €500, his tax credits will be increased by €100 (€500 × 20%), and his SRCOP will be increased by €500.

8.5 Computation of Liability under the PAYE System

The PAYE system obliges the employer to calculate and deduct the income tax due (if any) from the pay of every employee. This tax is then paid over monthly to the Collector-General.

8.5.1 Tax Deduction Card

Revenue discontinued the issue of paper tax deduction cards (TDCs) with effect from 1 January 2009 as being no longer the most practical method of recording PAYE/PRSI information.

As an alternative to the paper TDC, an electronic TDC is available at *www.revenue.ie* to assist employers who wish to record payroll information in this manner. The electronic TDC allows employers to:

- complete the employee's record on screen;
- save the record electronically on the employer's computer;
- print the record; and
- print a blank TDC and complete it by hand.

Alternative System to Electronic Tax Deduction Card
For administrative purposes, an employer may wish to use a different system to the electronic TDC as follows:

- A PAYE/PRSI record system of the employer's own design; *or*
- A computerised system; *or*
- A computer bureau system.

If an employer wishes to use any of these alternative tax deduction methods, he must advise his local Inspector of Taxes.

Basis of calculation of PAYE to be deducted from employees
The purpose of the PAYE system is to ensure that an employee's tax liability is spread out **evenly** over the year, thus allowing the correct tax liability to be paid in full without causing hardship to the employee.

PAYE tax deductions are calculated using one of the following methods:

1. **Cumulative Basis**
2. **Non-Cumulative Basis (Week 1/Month 1 Basis)**
3. **Temporary Basis**
4. **Emergency Basis with PPS No**
5. **Emergency Basis where PPS No is not available**

8.5.2 Cumulative Basis

The cumulative basis is used ONLY when Revenue provides a tax credit certificate and SRCOP effective from 1 January in the tax year, in the name of the employer.

To ensure that that an employee's tax liability is spread out **evenly** over the year, PAYE is normally calculated on a **cumulative basis**. This means that when employers calculate the tax liability of an employee, they actually calculate the **total tax due** from 1 **January** to the date on which the payment is being made. The tax deducted in a particular week is the cumulative tax due from 1 January to that date, **reduced** by the amount of tax previously deducted. Any tax credits and/or SRCOP which are not used in a pay period can be carried forward to the next pay period within the tax year.

The cumulative basis also ensures that refunds can be made to an employee where the employee's tax credits and SRCOP have been increased.

The cumulative basis is used ONLY when Revenue provides a tax credit certificate and SRCOP effective from 1 January in the tax year. If the employee is paid weekly, this figure is divided into weekly amounts; if monthly, this figure is divided into monthly amounts.

These are printed on the card on a cumulative basis as in the following example:

Example:
Joe Long's tax credits for 2012 are €3,300 (€63.46 per week) and his SRCOP is €32,800 (€630.77 per week). He is paid weekly. Joe was paid €620 for weeks 1 to 3 and was paid €850 for week 4. His TDC (for the first 8 weeks) will show the following:

Week No	Gross Pay	Cum. Gross Pay	Cum. Standard Rate Cut-Off Point	Cum. Tax due at Standard Rate	Cum. Tax due at Higher Rate	Cum. Gross Tax	Cum. Tax Credit	Cum. Tax	Tax deducted this period	Tax refund this period
1	620.00	620.00	630.77	124.00	0.00	124.00	63.46	60.54	60.54	
2	620.00	1,240.00	1,261.54	248.00	0.00	248.00	126.92	121.08	60.54	
3	620.00	1,860.00	1,892.31	372.00	0.00	372.00	190.38	181.62	60.54	
4	850.00	2,710.00	2,523.08	*504.62	*76.64	581.25	253.84	327.41	145.79	
5			3,153.85				317.30			
6			3,784.62				380.76			
7			4,415.39				444.22			
8			5,046.16				507.68			

* *Week 4 cumulative tax: SRCOP week 4 @ 20% = €2,523.08 @ 20% = €504.62*

Cum Gross Pay less SRCOP week 4 @ 41% = (€2,710.00 − €2,523.08) @ 41% = €76.64

8.5.3 Non-cumulative Basis (Week 1/Month 1 Basis)

In certain circumstances, Revenue may **direct an employer** to deduct tax on a **week 1 or month 1 basis**. This instruction will be printed on the employer's copy of the tax credit certificate and SRCOP.

Under the week 1/month 1 basis, **neither** the pay, the tax credits **nor** the SRCOP are **accumulated**. The pay for each income tax week or month is dealt with **separately**. The tax credits and SRCOP for week 1, or month 1, are used in the calculation of tax due each week, or each month. In such cases, the employer **may not make any refunds of tax**.

8.5.4   Temporary Tax Deduction System

The temporary tax deduction form (P13/P14) must be used in the following **commencement of employment** circumstances:

1.   when the employer has been given parts 2 and 3 of a **Form P45** stating:
     - the employee's PPS number, *and*
     - the employee was not on the emergency basis, *and*
     - the employer has sent Part 3 of the Form P45 to Revenue and is awaiting the issue by Revenue of a tax credit certificate and SRCOP; *or*

2.   when the employee has given the employer a tax credit certificate and SRCOP in the name of **another employer** and the employer has sent Form P46 to Revenue.

The entries on the temporary TDC are made on a **non-cumulative** basis and the calculation of tax due each week or month is done on the same basis as in the **week 1/month 1** procedure. This temporary procedure continues until Revenue issues the ordinary cumulative tax credit certificate to the employer.

Example:
Joe Long's tax credits for 2012 are €3,300 (€63.46 per week) and his SRCOP is €32,800 (€630.77 per week). He is paid weekly. Joe was paid €620 for weeks 1 to 3 and was paid €850 for week 4. His TDC (for the first 8 weeks) will show the following:

Week 1 Basis

Week No	Gross Pay	Standard Rate Cut-Off Point	Tax due at Standard Rate	Tax due at Higher Rate	Gross Tax	Tax Credit	Tax deducted this period	Tax refund this period
1	620.00	630.77	124.00	0.00	124.00	63.46	60.54	
2	620.00	630.77	124.00	0.00	124.00	63.46	60.54	
3	620.00	630.77	124.00	0.00	124.00	63.46	60.54	
4	850.00	630.77	126.15	89.88	216.03	63.46	152.75	
5		630.77				63.46		
6		630.77				63.46		
7		630.77				63.46		
8		630.77				63.46		

8.5.5   Emergency Basis

Revenue provides a single form for use either as an emergency TDC or as a temporary TDC (P13/P14).

The emergency TDC must be used in one of the following circumstances:

1.   if the employer **has not** received a tax credit certificate and SRCOP or a Form P45 for the current tax year;

2.   if the employer has not received a tax credit certificate for a **previous year** which states that the certificate is valid for **subsequent or following years;**

3. the employee gives the employer a P45 with the letter "**E**" in the Tax Table box indicating that the emergency basis applies; *or*
4. the employee has given the employer a completed P45 **without** a PPS number and not indicating that the emergency basis applies.

In such cases the employee's tax is calculated as follows:

The Employee does not provide a PPS Number

In this case, tax is deducted at **41%** from gross pay (less pension contributions and permanent health contributions where relevant). No tax credit is due.

The Employee provides a PPS Number

In this case tax is applied to gross pay (less pension contributions and permanent health contributions where relevant) as follows:

1. **Weeks 1–4 or Month 1 if paid monthly**
    Gross tax is calculated on taxable pay, at the **standard rate** of tax, up to an amount equal to **1/52nd** of the SRCOP for a single individual (2012: €32,800) if weekly paid, or **1/12th** if monthly paid. Any **balance** is taxed at the **higher rate**. The gross tax, as calculated, is **reduced** by a **tax credit**, which is equivalent to **1/52nd** of the personal tax credit for a single person (2012: €1,650) if weekly paid, or **1/12th** if monthly paid.
2. **Weeks 5–8 or Month 2 if monthly paid**
    Gross tax is calculated on the taxable pay as above. However, **no tax credit** is due.
3. **Each subsequent Week or Month if monthly paid**
    Gross tax is calculated on the taxable pay at the **higher rate of tax** and **no tax credit** is due.

Example:
Alice Casey commenced work with a new employer. She provides her new employer with a valid PPS number but she has not received a P45 from her previous employer. Alice is paid €2,550 monthly with overtime of €250 in month 2 and €500 in month 3.

Emergency Basis

Month No	Gross Pay	Standard Rate Cut-Off Point	Tax due at Standard Rate	Tax due at Higher Rate	Gross Tax	Tax Credit	Tax deducted this period	Tax refund this period
1	2,550.00	2,733.33	510.00	0.00	510.00	137.50	372.50	
2	2,800.00	2,733.33	546.67	27.33	574.00	0.00	574.00	
3	3,050.00	0.00	0.00	1,250.50	1,250.50	0.00	1,250.50	
4		0.00					0.00	
5		0.00					0.00	

Where an employee has two separate periods of employment with one employer in 2012 and the emergency basis applies in **each** period of employment, the employment is deemed to be **continuous** from the start of the first period of employment to the end of the last period of employment or to 31 December 2012, whichever is earlier.

It will be readily appreciated from the foregoing that the operation of the emergency basis on any employee is extremely onerous. However, the **employer is legally obliged** to operate the emergency basis and the onus is on the employee to remove himself from the emergency basis by securing a tax credit certificate and SRCOP. Generally, completing and submitting either tax return **Form 12** or **12A** or **Form P46** can achieve this.

If an employer, who is obliged by circumstances to operate the emergency system, **fails** to do so, then he is **legally liable** for the tax that **should** have been deducted from the employee's wages and the Revenue will seek to collect it from him.

8.6   Refunds of Tax under the PAYE System

Employee Taxed on Cumulative Basis

The most likely situation where an employee will receive a refund in these circumstances is where Revenue issues a **revised** tax credit certificate and SRCOP showing increased tax credits and, if applicable, increased SRCOP. In such cases, the tax paid to date may **exceed** the cumulative tax due to date and a refund may need to be made. However tax credits are non-refundable and, if tax credits to date **exceed cumulative gross tax**, the excess may not be refunded.

Employee Taxed under Week 1/Month 1/Emergency/Temporary

Example:

Alice Casey has been on the emergency tax basis for months 1–3 (as above). In month 4, a tax credit certificate on a cumulative basis is issued to her employer. This certificate shows cumulative tax credits of €3,300 and cumulative SRCOP of €32,800 for 2012. Alice is paid €2,550 monthly with no overtime payment for month 4.

Emergency Basis

Month No	Gross Pay	Standard Rate Cut-Off Point	Tax due at Standard Rate	Tax due at Higher Rate	Gross Tax	Tax Credit	Tax deducted this period	Tax refund this period
1	2,550.00	2,733.33	510.00	0.00	510.00	137.50	372.50	
2	2,800.00	2,733.33	546.67	27.33	574.00	0.00	574.00	
3	3,050.00	0.00	0.00	1,250.50	1,250.50	0.00	1,250.50	
Total	8,400.00	0.00				0.00	2,197.00	
5		0.00				0.00		

New "Cumulative" TDC

Month No	Gross Pay	Cum. Gross Pay	Com. Standard Rate Cut-Off Point	Cum. Tax due at Standard Rate	Cum. Tax due at Higher Rate	Cum. Gross Tax	Cum. Tax Credit	Cum. Tax	Tax deducted this period	Tax refund this period
1	0.00	0.00	2,733.33	0.00	0.00	0.00	275.00	0.00	0.00	
2	0.00	0.00	5,466.67	0.00	0.00	0.00	550.00	0.00	0.00	
3	0.00	*8,400.00	8,200.00	0.00	0.00	0.00	825.00	*2,197.00	0.00	
4	2,550.00	10,950.00	10,933.33	2,186.67	6.83	2,193.50	1,100.00	1,093.50	0.00	1,103.50
5			13,666.67				1,375.00			
6			16,400.00				1,650.00			
7			19,133.33				1,925.00			

* Transferred from Emergency TDC

8.7   Taxation of Social Welfare Benefits

8.7.1   Illness Benefit

With effect from 6 April 1993, illness benefits (and occupational injury benefits) are taxable. Prior to 1 January 2012, illness benefit payable for the first 36 days in the tax year was exempt from tax. **From 1 January 2012, illness benefit is taxable from the first day of payment.**

The following outlines what employers must do where one of their employees is in receipt of illness benefit:

1.   If the employee is paid a top-up amount while out sick and keeps his illness benefit:
The employer has three options as follows:

(a)   add the amount of the benefit received to pay and calculate tax due accordingly; *or*
(b)   reduce the weekly/monthly tax credit by the weekly/monthly amount of the benefit × 20% and reduce the weekly/monthly SRCOP by the weekly/monthly amount of the benefit; *or*
(c)   put the employee on a week 1/month 1 basis for the rest of the year on their wages from the employer.

2.   If the employer pays the employee while out sick and recoups the illness benefit from them:
The employer taxes the gross amount of wages by opting for one of the options outlined in 1. above.

However, PRSI and USC are operated on the net salary arrived at after deducting illness benefit, because **illness benefit is not liable for PRSI and USC.**

3.   If the employer does not pay the employee while out sick:
When the employee resumes work, the employer should prepare a TDC on a week 1/month 1 basis, granting the normal weekly or monthly tax credits and SRCOP.

8.7.2   Maternity Benefit

Maternity benefit is not regarded as income for the purposes of TCA 1997 and should be disregarded for all tax purposes.

Whether the payment must be taken into account by the payroll office will depend on the particular circumstances or arrangements between employers and employees while employees are on maternity leave and in receipt of maternity benefit from the Department of Social and Family Affairs.

The treatment in specific situations is outlined below:

1.   Employers who pay wages, salary etc. to employees while out on maternity leave and recover the maternity benefit from the employees or directly from the Department of Social and Family Affairs.
In such circumstances, only the difference between the wages, salary, etc. paid and the maternity benefit recovered is subject to tax, PRSI and USC in the pay period.
2.   Employers who pay wages, salary, etc. to employees while out on maternity leave (top-up etc.) and the employees retain the maternity benefit.
Where an employer pays an employee full or partial wages or salary while out on maternity leave and the employee retains the maternity benefit, tax, PRSI and USC should be charged only on the full amount of wages or salary actually paid.

3. **Employers who do NOT pay wages, salary, etc, to employees while out on maternity leave and the employee retains the maternity benefit.**

    If owing to the absence from work through maternity leave, the employee is not entitled to receive emoluments on the usual payday, the employer shall, on application being made in person by the employee or his or her authorised representative, make such repayment of tax to the employee as may be appropriate, having regard to his or her cumulative emoluments at the date of the pay day in question and the corresponding cumulative tax.

    Alternatively, on the employee's return to work after a period of maternity leave, any refund of tax, which may be due to the employee, can be calculated having regard to his or her cumulative emoluments at the date of the pay day in question and the corresponding cumulative tax. In this situation, the employer should contact the employee's regional Revenue office to confirm that it is in order to make such a refund.

    An employer should not make a refund unless he is in possession of a current year cumulative tax credit certificate and SRCOP in respect of the employee in question.

8.7.3   Jobseekers' Benefit

Jobseekers' benefit is a taxable source of income. However the child dependant element and the **first €13** per week of benefit are exempt from tax. When an employee resumes employment having claimed jobseekers' benefit, Revenue will notify the new employer of the employee's earnings and net tax deducted up to the date of the resumption of employment. The employee's tax credits and SRCOP will be reduced by the amount of the taxable jobseekers' benefit.

8.8   Computation of Liability under Pay Related Social Insurance (PRSI)

In addition to PAYE, employers are obliged to calculate and deduct employee PRSI and USC from the pay of every employee. They are also obliged to calculate employer PRSI. The PRSI and USC are then paid over monthly to the Collector-General.

8.8.1   PRSI Contributions

Pay Related Social Insurance (PRSI) contributions are payable in respect of full-time employees and part-time employees. PRSI is deducted at source by the employer and remitted to the Collector-General. **USC** was introduced in **2011** and replaced the **health contribution** and **income levies** which were in operation up to 31 December 2010. USC will be dealt with later in this chapter.

PRSI is payable on most sources of income e.g

- Salaries and pensions
- Tax-adjusted profits of a trade or profession (less capital allowances)
- Dividends received
- Rental income
- Investment income, including ordinary bank deposit interest but not interest on special savings accounts or special savings incentive accounts
- With effect from **1 January 2004** PRSI applies to **benefits in kind** (e.g. company cars, vans) and **perquisites** (e.g. preferential loans) provided by an employer to an employee.

- With effect from **1 January 2011** PRSI now applies to any benefits arising out of **employee share schemes** (e.g. approved share option schemes, approved profit sharing schemes, approved SAYE share option schemes)

PRSI on Employee Pension Contributions
Prior to 1 January 2011, employee contributions to pension schemes were exempt from employee and employer PRSI. From **1 January 2011**, employee contributions to occupational pension schemes and other pension arrangements will **no longer be exempt from employee PRSI**. Such contributions will also be subject to the USC.

Public Service Pension-Related Deduction (PRD)
From 1 January 2011, employee PRSI will apply to the pension-related deduction ("pension levy") which is charged to earnings in the **public service**. This deduction will also be subject to the USC.

PRSI is **not** charged on:

- social welfare payments (e.g. illness or maternity benefit);
- redundancy payments (USC is payable on the **taxable** element of a redundancy lump sum payment).

8.8.2 PRSI Contribution Classes

In general, PRSI contribution classes are decided by the **nature** of the employment and the **amount** of the employee's gross reckonable earnings in any week. Most workers pay PRSI contributions at Class A and are covered for all social welfare benefits and pensions. However, people who earn less than €38 per week (from all employments) are covered for occupational injuries benefits only – **Class J.** Some workers in the public sector do not have cover for all benefits and pensions and they pay a modified PRSI contribution – **Class B, C, D or H.**

Others, such as people who are retired but receiving pensions from their former job, are recorded under different classes of PRSI – **Class K or M.** These classes do not give cover for social welfare benefits and pensions.

Self-employed people and company directors are covered for certain pensions; maternity and adoptive benefit, orphan's contributory allowance and bereavement grant; and pay **Class S.**

The PRSI contribution classes are further divided into **subclasses, 0 and 1. A8** is a subclass of **A9**, which is used for community employment participants only. These subclasses represent different bands of weekly earnings and categories of people within each earnings band as outlined below.

Deciding the Correct PRSI Class
If there is any doubt as to whether PRSI should be paid or which class of PRSI should apply, the Department of Social Protection **Scope Section** may be asked to decide the issue. Before a decision is made, the employment details are investigated thoroughly by a social welfare inspector who will interview the people concerned.

8.8.3 Rates of Contribution

Employee contributions and employer contributions are calculated separately and then added together to get **Total PRSI**.

An extract of SW 19 *Rates of Payment 2012* is reproduced below. The full leaflet is available on www.welfare.ie.

PRIVATE AND PUBLIC SECTOR EMPLOYMENTS
Rates of contribution from 1 January 2012

Class A: This covers employees in industrial, commercial and service-type employment who have reckonable pay of €38 or more per week from all employments and public servants recruited from 6 April 1995.

Weekly pay is the employee's monetary pay plus notional pay (if applicable).

Subclass	Weekly Pay Band	How much of Weekly Pay	All Income EE	All Income ER
AO	€38 – €352 inclusive	ALL	Nil	4.25%
AX	€352.01 – €356 inclusive	First €127	Nil	4.25%
		Balance	4%	4.25%
AL	€356.01 – €500 inclusive	First €127	Nil	10.75%
		Balance	4%	10.75%
A1	More than €500	First €127	Nil	10.75%
		Balance	4%	10.75%

SELF EMPLOYED
Rates of contribution from 1 January 2012
Class S: This covers self-employed people, including certain company directors.

Subclass	Weekly Pay Bands	How much of Weekly Pay	All Income EE
S0	Up to €500	ALL	4%
S1	More than €500	ALL	4%

8.9 Income Levy

The income levy, which was in effect from 1 January 2009 to 31 December 2010, was a levy payable on **gross income**, including notional pay, before any relief for any capital allowances, losses or pension contributions.

All individuals were liable to pay the income levy if their gross income exceeded the threshold of **€15,028 p.a. (€289 per week)** or if they exceeded the income exemption limit of €20,000 p.a. for an individual aged 65 or over.

8.10 Universal Social Charge (USC)

The USC, which came into effect on **1 January 2011**, is a tax payable on **gross income**, including notional pay, **after** any relief for certain trading losses and capital allowances, but **before** pension contributions.

All individuals are liable to pay USC if their gross income is greater than **€10,036** (€4,004 2011) **per annum** (€193 per week).

Note that once the total income goes above the relevant limit, all the income is subject to USC and not just the excess over the limit.

Persons who are **not domiciled** in Ireland are liable for USC on Irish source income in the same way as they are liable to pay income tax on it.

Directors' fees paid by an Irish company to a non-resident director are also subject to USC.

Income exempt from USC

- Where an individual's total income for the year does not exceed **€10,036** (€4,004 2011).
- All Department of Social Protection payments including social welfare payments received from abroad.
- Payments that are made in lieu of Department of Social Protection payments such as community employment schemes paid by the Department of Enterprise, Trade and Innovation or back to education allowance paid by the Department of Education and Science.
- Income subjected to DIRT.
- Termination payments – USC is only charged on the balance after granting the statutory exemptions, e.g.
  - Statutory redundancy payments – i.e. two weeks pay per year plus a bonus week, subject to a maximum payment of €600 per week are exempt;
  - Ex-gratia redundancy payments in excess of the statutory redundancy amount up to certain limits (i.e. €10,160 plus €765 for each year of service, plus up to €10,000 if the person is not a member of an occupational pension scheme – see **Section 4.5.2**), and after granting any additional deduction for Standard Capital Superannuation Benefit (SCSB).

Special Treatments for Medical Card Holders and Individuals over 70 years.
Medical card holders (irrespective of age) and individuals over 70 years will only pay USC at a maximum rate of 4% on income over €10,036 per annum.

Surcharge on Self-Employment Income and Bank Bonuses
There is a **surcharge of 3%** on individuals who have income from **self-employment** that **exceeds €100,000** in a year, regardless of age. Thus, where such individuals are under 70 years and do not hold a full medical card, a rate of 10% applies to such income and where such individuals are aged over 70 years or hold a full medical card, a rate of 7% applies.

A special USC rate of **45%** applies to certain **bank bonuses** paid to employees of **financial institutions** that have received financial support from the State. Performance-related bonus payments paid to employees of Bank of Ireland, AIB, Anglo Irish Bank, EBS and Irish Nationwide Building Society are chargeable to USC at 45% where the cumulative amount of any bonus payments **exceeds €20,000** in a single tax year. Where this threshold is exceeded the full amount is charged to USC at 45% and not just the excess over €20,000.

8.10.1 Rates and Income Thresholds 2012 – Employees

Persons Under 70 and Not in Receipt of a Medical Card			
THRESHOLDS			RATE OF USC
Per Year	Per Month	Per Week	Rate %
Up to €10,036	Up to €837	Up to €193	2%
From €10,037 to €16,016	From €837 to €1,335	From €193 to €308	4%
In excess of €16,016	In excess of €1,335	In excess of €308	7%

Persons in Receipt of a Medical Card or Over 70 Years			
THRESHOLDS			RATE OF USC
Per Year	Per Month	Per Week	Rate %
Up to €10,036	Up to €837	Up to €193	2%
In excess of €10,036	In excess of €837	In excess of €193	4%

Employers must pay the USC to the Collector-General at the same time and in the same manner as the deductions under the PAYE system. The USC amount is included with the PAYE figure on the form P30.

From 1 January 2012, employers are to operate USC on a cumulative basis. Employer tax credit certificates will now also feature USC rates and cut-off points.

Cumulative, Temporary and Emergency Basis for USC

- Where an employee is on the cumulative basis for PAYE, they will be on the cumulative basis for USC, and vice versa.
- Where an employee is on a week 1 basis for PAYE, they will also be on a week 1 basis for USC, and vice versa.
- Where an employee is on the emergency basis for PAYE, they will also be on the emergency basis for USC, and vice versa.

USC under the emergency basis is calculated at 7% with no cut-off point.

8.10.2 USC – Rates and Income Thresholds 2012 – Self-Employed

Self-assessed Persons Under 70 and Not in Receipt of a Medical Card	
THRESHOLDS	RATE OF USC
The first €10,036	2%
The next €5,980	4%
The next €83,984	7%
The remainder (>€100,000)	10%

Self-assessed Persons in Receipt of a Medical Card <u>or</u> Over 70 Years	
THRESHOLDS	RATE OF USC
The first €10,036	2%
The next €89,964	4%
The remainder (>€100,000)	7%

Self-employed individuals will make a payment of USC along with their preliminary tax payment by 31 October with any balance payable by 31 October in the following year.

8.10.3 USC – Surcharge on use of Property Incentives

Section 3 FA 2012 introduced a new **property relief surcharge** on investors (both passive and active) with **gross income** greater than **€100,000**. The surcharge will be collected as **additional** USC of **5%** on the **amount of income sheltered** by the use of certain property and area-based capital allowances as well as section 23-type reliefs in a given year **from 1 January 2012**. The surcharge does not apply to income sheltered by non-property tax reliefs, such as EII/BES or investment in film relief.

Where specified reliefs are restricted under the **high earners restriction** in any year, that relief can be carried forward to be used in subsequent years, subject to the high earners restriction applying in that year. Any income in that **subsequent year** which is sheltered by relief of this kind **will not** be subject to the surcharge, on the grounds that it already has been surcharged in an earlier year.

Example 1:

Joe Long's income and allowances/reliefs for 2012 are as follows:

	€	€
Gross income		210,000
Less: Property reliefs	80,000	
EII/BES relief	7,000	
Film relief	3,000	(90,000)
Taxable income		120,000
USC surcharge: Property relief €80,000 @5%		**4,000**

Example 2:

Sheila Short's income and allowances/reliefs for 2012 are as follows:

	€	€
Employment income	90,000	
Rental income (gross)	12,000	102,000
Less: Case V rental expenses	2,500	
Section 23 relief	10,000	(12,500)
Taxable income		89,500

(continued overleaf)

USC surcharge calculation:	
Rental income (gross)	12,000
Less: Case V expenses	(2,500)
Net Case V income	9,500
Less: Section 23 relief (€500 c/fwd)	(9,500)
USC surcharge – €9,500 @ 5%	€475

Note: Where the additional 5% USC applies to a taxpayer in 2012, his preliminary tax for 2012 must be calculated as if this additional surcharge applied in 2011.

8.11 Calculation of PRSI and USC for Employees

PRSI

The entries on the tax deduction card are made on a **non-cumulative** basis, and the calculation of PRSI due each week or month is done on the same basis as in the **week 1/month 1** procedure.

Example:
Joe Long is a private sector worker. Using Joe Long's TDC, calculate the PRSI payable for week 1–4 of 2012, assuming that Joe pays PRSI at Class A.

Week No.	Gross Pay PRSI Purposes	Social Insurance Weekly Record		PRSI Employee's Share	Total PRSI
	€	Insurable Employment	PRSI Class	€	€
1	650.00	√	A1	20.92	90.80
2	650.00	√	A1	20.92	90.80
3	650.00	√	A1	20.92	90.80
4	875.00	√	A1	29.92	123.98
5					

			€
Employee PRSI: Weeks 1 to 3	Pay €650 > €500 A1 rate applies	First €127 @ 0%	0.00
		Balance €523 @ 4%	20.92
		Total EE PRSI	20.92
Employer:		€650 @ 10.75%	69.88
		Total PRSI	90.80

			€
Employee PRSI: Week 4	Pay €875 > €500 A1 rate applies	First €127 @ 0%	0.00
		Balance €748 @ 4%	29.92
		Total EE PRSI	29.92
Employer:		€875 @ 10.75%	94.06
		Total PRSI	123.98

USC

From **1 January 2012**, the deduction of USC has changed from a week 1 basis to a **cumulative basis** similar to the way PAYE is deducted. As with PAYE tax credits and rate bands, Revenue will notify employers (on employers' tax credit certificates) of the USC rates and thresholds to be applied for each employee. The USC information will be shown in the section below the PAYE section. USC rates and cut-off points, along with previous USC pay and USC deducted, where applicable, will be shown.

The following is an extract from a tax credit certificate showing USC rates and cut-off point:

Universal Social Charge (USC)				

Rates of USC			Exemption Case	N		
				Yearly COP	**Monthly COP**	**Weekly COP**
USC Rate 1	2%	**USC Rate 1 Cut-Off Point**		10,036.00	836.34	193.00
USC Rate 2	4%	**USC Rate 2 Cut-Off Point**		16,016.00	1,334.67	308.00
USC Rate 3	7%					

The following details of gross pay for USC purposes and USC deducted, from 1 January 2012, to date of commencement of your employment, should be taken into account when calculating current USC deductions.

Total Gross Pay
for USC purposes: 0.00   **Total USC deducted:**   0.00

Example:
Using the example of Joe Long again, calculate the USC payable for week 1 – 4 of 2012, assuming that Joe is not exempt from USC.

Date of payment	Week No	Gross Pay for USC this period	Cum. Gross Pay for USC to date	Cum. USC Cut-Off Point 1	Cum. USC due at USC Rate 1	Cum. USC Cut-Off Point 2	Cum. USC due at USC Rate 2	Cum. USC due at USC Rate 3	Cum. USC	USC deducted this period	USC refunded this period
		€	€	€	€	€	€	€	€	€	€
	1	650	650	193	3.86	115	4.60	23.94	32.40	32.40	0.00
	2	650	1,300	386	7.72	230	9.20	47.88	64.80	32.40	0.00
	3	650	1,950	579	11.58	345	13.80	71.82	97.20	32.40	0.00
	4	875	2,825	772	15.44	460	18.40	111.51	145.35	48.15	0.00
	5			965		575					

			€
USC:	First €193 @ 2%		3.86
Week 1	Next €115 @ 4%		4.60
	Balance: €650 − (€193 + €115) @ 7%		23.94
	Total USC this week		32.40

			€
USC:	First €386 @ 2%		7.72
Week 2	Next €230 @ 4%		9.20
	Balance: €1,300 − (€386 + €230) @ 7%		47.88
	Cumulative USC		64.80
	Less: Cumulative USC from previous week 1		(32.40)
	Total USC this week		32.40

(continued overleaf)

USC: Week 3		€
	First €579 @ 2%	11.58
	Next €345 @ 4%	13.80
	Balance: €1,950 − (€579 + €345) @ 7%	71.82
	Cumulative USC	97.20
	Less: Cumulative USC from previous week 2	(64.80)
	Total USC this week	32.40

USC: Week 4		€
	First €772 @ 2%	15.44
	Next €460 @ 4%	18.40
	Balance: €2,825 − (€772 + €460) @ 7%	111.51
	Cumulative USC	145.35
	Less: Cumulative USC from previous week 3	(97.20)
	Total USC this week	48.15

8.12 Calculation of PRSI and USC for Self Employed

PRSI

PRSI is generally charged on the gross income of the taxpayer before contributions to retirement annuities/PRSAs are deducted. Capital allowances and trading losses forward may be deducted.

No PRSI is payable on income below €5,000 p.a (€3,174 2010) and a minimum €253 PRSI is due on all income above this amount.

The PRSI rate for class S is 4% for 2012 (3% 2010).

Universal Social Charge

USC is charged on **all income** (except deposit interest subject to DIRT) **before** contributions to retirement annuities or PRSAs are deducted, but **after** deducting capital allowances. Only standard rate capital allowances are allowable and must be actually used in a tax year to be deductible. Capital allowances due to persons that do not actively carry on a trade are not deductible (e.g. lessors and passive investors). USC applies to all persons whose income **exceeds €10,036 per annum** (€4,004 2011) and the rates are listed in **Section 8.10** above.

Example:

John Healy is a married man who owns and operates an equestrian centre in Cork. His accounts for the year ended 31 October 2012 show a tax-adjusted profit of €48,000. He has capital allowances due for 2012 of €7,000. He received gross interest of €420 on his Credit Union share account. His wife Mary is employed by the local doctor and her gross salary for 2012 was €32,000 (PAYE deducted €3,100). She received net bank deposit interest of €700 in 2012. The Healys are jointly assessed.

Calculate the income tax, PRSI and USC payable by John Healy in 2012.

(continued overleaf)

Mr Healy Income Tax Computation 2012		€	€
Income:			
Schedule D Case I		48,000	
Less: Capital Allowances		(7,000)	41,000
Schedule D Case III - John			420
Schedule D Case IV - Mary (gross)			1,000
Schedule E - Mary			32,000
Taxable Income			74,420
Tax Calculation:			
€65,600	@ 20%	13,120	
€1,000	@ 30%	300	
€7,820	@ 41%	3,206	
€74,420			16,626
Less: Non Refundable Tax Credits:			
Basic personal tax credit (married)		3,300	
Employee tax credit (Mary)		1,650	(4,950)
Tax Liability			**11,676**
Less: Tax Paid			
PAYE deducted (Mary)		3,100	
DIRT (Mary)		300	(3,400)
Net tax liability			**8,276**
Universal Social Charge:			
John:			
€10,036	@ 2%	201	
€5,980	@ 4%	239	
€25,404	@ 7%	1,778	
€41,420			2,218
PRSI:			
John:			
€41,420	@ 4%		1,657
Total Liability			**12,151**

Both PRSI and USC were collected from Mary through the PAYE system.

8.13 Domicile Levy

Section 531AA TCA 1997 introduced a new levy in 2010 to ensure that individuals who are domiciled in and citizens of Ireland would make a contribution to the Exchequer irrespective of their residence status. The domicile levy applies to an individual:

1. who is domiciled in Ireland in that tax year; *and*
2. whose worldwide income for the tax year is greater than €1 million; *and*
3. whose final Irish income tax liability is less than €200,000; **and**
4. who has Irish property with a market value exceeding €5 million at 31 December.

Section 119 FA 2012 removed the requirement that the individual had to be an Irish citizen.

The amount of the levy is **€200,000**. Irish income tax paid by an individual will be allowed as a credit against the domicile levy. However, taxes paid overseas on the worldwide income are not allowed as a credit. Irish property does not include shares in a company (or a holding company) **carrying on a trade**, but includes all property **situate in Ireland** to which the individual is beneficially entitled in possession at 31 December. The market value is the price at which the property would sell on the open market and does not take into account any charges or mortgages taken out against the property.

The levy operates on an individual basis, i.e. if jointly-assessed spouses both meet the conditions above, the levy is payable by both spouses. The tax is payable on a self-assessment basis on or before 31 October in the year following the valuation date, i.e. 31 December each year.

Questions (Chapter 8)

(See Solutions to Questions at the end of this text.)

8   The PAYE System

8.1   Mary and Andrew

(a)   An employee, Mary, commenced work in 1 August 2012 under a contract with normal terms and conditions. The agreed monthly salary was €2,200. Mary's Form P45 from her previous employment showed the following amounts for the period 1 January 2012 to 31 July 2012:

Gross Salary	€16,310
Tax deducted	€1,208
Monthly tax credit	€275
Monthly SRCOP	€2,733
Month Number	7
Gross salary for USC purposes	€16,310
Total USC deducted	€744.17
Monthly USC cut-off point 1	€837
Monthly USC cut-off point 2	€498

Requirement

Calculate the net pay receivable by Mary for August 2012, after deduction of PAYE, PRSI and USC assuming that Revenue have issued a certificate of tax credits and SRCOP.

(b)   An employee, Andrew, who is paid €4,167 gross monthly, is provided with a company car by his employer for the first time from 1 June 2012. The original market value of the car is €28,000 (after allowing a 10% cash discount). Andrew's total annual travel is estimated at 51,200 km, of which 8,000 km are personal.

Andrew is required to pay €1,500 per annum to his employer for the private use of the car. This will be deducted monthly from Andrew's salary.

Requirement

Calculate Andrew's total gross taxable pay for June 2012.

8.2   Sean – NEW Ltd BIK on Van and Emergency Basis

Sean, a married man, is employed by NEW Ltd from 1 July 2012. He is allowed unrestricted private use of a company van in respect of which he will incur business travel of 26,000 km per annum. NEW bears all the costs of running the van except diesel, which Sean pays for himself. Sean contributes €10 per month to NEW Ltd towards the running costs of the van. NEW bought the van second hand for €10,000 on 30th June 2012. The van had a market value of €17,500 when first registered on 30th April 2008.

Requirement

(a) Calculate Sean's taxable benefit for 2012 in respect of his use of the company van.
(b) Sean's gross weekly wages are €500 inclusive of the BIK on the van. Assuming the emergency basis of tax applies, calculate the PAYE/PRSI and USC to be deducted from Sean's first week's wages:

    (1) If NEW Ltd is provided with Sean's PPS No
    (2) If NEW Ltd is not provided with Sean's PPS No

8.3 Paul

Paul commenced work on 12 October 2012 under a contract with normal terms and conditions, at a rate of €21 per hour, with overtime accruing at time and a half after 39 hours.

Paul's P45 from his previous employment showed the following details for the period 1 January 2012 to 10 October 2012:

Gross salary to date	€43,540.00	Gross salary for USC	€43,540.00
Tax deducted to date	€5,995.50	Total USC deducted	€2,458.30
Weekly Tax Credit	€95.19	USC cut-off point 1	€193.00
Week Number	45	USC cut-off point 2	€115.00
Weekly SRCOP	€803.85		

Paul's hours for his first week ending 17 October 2012 were 39 plus 11 hours overtime.

Requirement

Calculate the net pay receivable by Paul for his first week after deducting PAYE/PRSI/USC using each of the following scenarios:

(a) Revenue have NOT issued a notice of determination of tax credits and SRCOP
(b) Revenue HAVE issued a notice of determination of tax credits and SRCOP in accordance with the P45

Administration and Procedures

9.1   Self-Assessment

9.1.1   "Chargeable Persons"

Self-assessment is a system whereby "chargeable persons" **calculate** and **return** taxes due within the timeframes and deadlines specified by tax law.

Self-assessment applies to people, chargeable to income tax, who are in receipt of income from sources which are **not chargeable** to tax **under the PAYE** system, or where some, but **not all**, of the tax on these sources of income is paid under PAYE.

For income tax purposes, self-assessment applies to the following chargeable persons:

- self-employed persons (i.e. people carrying on their own business including farming, professions or vocations);
- proprietary company directors (i.e. holds or controls more than 15% of the ordinary share capital of the company) **regardless** of whether they have non-PAYE income or not; and

- individuals with gross non-PAYE income of €50,000 **or more** from all sources, even if there is **no net taxable income** from that source, for example:
  - income from rental property and investment income;
  - foreign income and foreign pensions; and
  - trading or professional income.

An individual becoming a chargeable person under this rule continues to be a chargeable person for future years, as long as the source(s) of the non-PAYE income continues to exist, **irrespective** of the amount of the annual gross income.

- Individuals with **assessable** non-PAYE income of **€3,174 or more, irrespective** of the amount of gross non-PAYE income.
- Individuals with profits arising on exercising various share options/share incentives.
- Where an Irish resident opens a foreign bank account of which he is the beneficial owner, he is to be regarded as a chargeable person for the years of assessment during which the account is open.
- Where a person acquires certain foreign life policies, he will be deemed to be a chargeable person.
- Where a person acquires a material interest in an offshore fund, he is deemed to be a chargeable persons.
- Individuals in receipt of legally enforceable maintenance payments.

The following are not chargeable persons for the purposes of self-assessment:

- Individuals whose **only source** of income consists of income chargeable to tax under the PAYE system.
- An individual who is in receipt of income chargeable to tax under the PAYE system but who is **also** in receipt of income from other non-PAYE sources will not be regarded as a chargeable person if the total gross income from all non-PAYE sources is **less than €50,000 AND** the net assessable income is **less than €3,174 AND** the income is coded against PAYE tax credits (i.e collected through the PAYE system).
- Non-proprietary directors **provided** they are not otherwise a chargeable person and **all** of their income is subject to PAYE.
- Directors of dormant and shelf companies.
- An individual who has received a notice from an Inspector of Taxes excluding him from the requirement to make a return (i.e. an exempt person).
- An individual who is only liable to income tax in respect of tax withheld from annual payments.

9.1.2 Obligations under Self-assessment

An individual who is a chargeable person for the purposes of self-assessment income tax must:

- complete a "pay and file" income tax return Form 11 or Form 11E (short version) which return must be filed on or before **31 October** and, **at the same time**, the balance of tax outstanding for the previous year must be paid; and
- pay preliminary tax for the current tax year on or before 31 October each year (i.e. preliminary tax for the year of assessment 2012 is payable by 31 October 2012).

From 1 **January 2013** a chargeable taxpayer will have to submit a **self-computation** of the tax due at the time of filing the tax return (**section 959R TCA 1997**).

9.1.3 Preliminary Tax

Preliminary tax is the taxpayer's **estimate** of their income tax payable for the year and must be paid by **31 October** in the tax year. Preliminary tax **includes** PRSI and USC as well as income tax. To avoid interest charges the amount of preliminary tax paid is not less than the **lower** of:

- **90%** of the final tax liability for the current tax year, i.e. 2011; *or*
- **100%** of the final tax liability for the immediately previous year (see note), i.e. 2011; *or*
- **105%** of the final tax liability for the year preceding the immediately previous year, i.e. 2010; This option is **only available** where the Collector-General is authorised to collect tax by **direct debit**. The 105% rule does not apply where the tax payable for the pre-preceding year is NIL.

Universal Social Charge – Surcharge on use of Property Incentives
Where the new **5% property relief surcharge** applies to a taxpayer in 2012, his/her preliminary tax for 2012 must be calculated **as if** this additional surcharge applied in 2011.

Note: any relief claimed under EII/BES or under film investment must be ignored when calculating the previous year's final tax liability.

Example:
Paul Gasbag is a self employed confectioner and his accounts for the year ended 31 December 2012 show a tax-adjusted profit of €44,000. The capital allowances due for 2012 total €7,000. He received €450 gross interest on his AIB ordinary deposit account which he has held for a number of years. His wife Sharon is employed by an insurance company and her gross salary for 2012 was €52,000 (PAYE deducted €9,962). She received €400 gross interest on her medium term savings account.

Paul's final tax liability for 2011 was as follows:

Case I income	€40,000	Income tax due	€6,520
Capital allowances	€6,000	USC	€1,699
Case IV interest (gross)	€350	PRSI	€1,031
		Total Liability 2011	€9,250

Paul's tax liability for 2010 was €8,400 (including PRSI and levies)

Income Tax Computation 2012	€	€
Income:		
Case I	44,000	
Less: Capital Allowances	(7,000)	37,000
Case IV – Paul (gross)		450
Taxable Income Paul		37,450
Schedule E – Sharon		52,000
Taxable income		89,450
Tax Calculation:		
€65,600 @ 20%	13,120	
€450 @ 30%	135	
$\frac{€23,400}{€89,450}$ @ 41%	9,594	
		22,849
Less: Non Refundable Tax Credits:		
Basic personal tax credit (married)	3,300	
Employee tax credit (Sharon)	1,650	(4,950)
Tax Liability		**17,899**

(continued overleaf)

Less: Tax Paid		
PAYE deducted (Sharon)	9,962	
DIRT (Paul)	135	(10,097)
Net Tax Liability		**7,802**
Universal Social Charge:		
Paul:		
€10,036 @ 2%	201	
€5,980 @ 4%	239	
€20,984 @ 7%	1,469	
€37,000		1,909
PRSI:		
Paul:		
€37,450 @ 4%		1,498
TOTAL LIABILITY 2012		**11,209**

Note: The medium term saving account interest is disregarded. The ordinary deposit interest has no further income tax liability but is subject to PRSI though not USC.

Preliminary tax payment for 2012 will be:

Lower of: Year 2011 @ 100%		=	€9,250 **OR**
Year 2012 @ 90%		=	€10,088

Preliminary tax for 2012 will be €9,250 and is payable by 31 October 2012. The balance of the tax due (€11,209 − €9,250 = €1,959) is payable by 31 October 2013.

If Paul pays his preliminary tax by way of direct debit, his preliminary tax for 2012 will be as follows:

Lower of: Year 2010 @ 105%	= €8,820	**OR**
Year 2011 @ 100%	= €9,250	**OR**
Year 2012 @ 90%	= €10,088	

Therefore, Paul's preliminary tax for 2012 will be €8,820 and is payable by 31 October 2012. The balance of the tax due (€11,209 − €8,820 = €2,389) is payable by 31 October 2013.

Underpayment of Preliminary Tax

Where preliminary tax paid is based on 90% of the **estimated** liability for the current year and the final tax liability is greater than the estimate, interest will be chargeable on the difference between the preliminary tax amount paid and the final tax liability at a rate of 0.0219% per day (from 30 June 2009).

9.1.4   Notice of Assessment

Generally, the Inspector of Taxes issues a notice of assessment once a return has been made by the taxpayer. The assessment will be based on the amounts included in the return. The taxpayer may submit his own calculation of his tax liability, but it is not compulsory to do so for 2012 (it will become mandatory to do so from 1 January 2013).

There are two types of notices of assessment:

(1) Short notice

This is issued where the taxpayer submits his return of income (Form 11/11E) and the Inspector of Taxes agrees with his computation.

(2) Long notice

This is issued if either the taxpayer does not submit a return of income (Form 11/11E) or if he does but the Inspector of Taxes does not agree his computation (e.g. incorrect calculation of an allowance or relief due).

From **1 January 2013** a changeable taxpayer will have to submit a **self-computation** of the tax due at the time of filing the tax return (**section 959R TCA 1997**).

9.1.5 Interest Payable and Late Filing Surcharges

Interest on Overdue Tax

From 1 July 2009, the rate of interest on overdue tax is 0.0219% per day or part thereof (approx. 8% p.a.).

Late Filing Penalties

If a return of income is **not submitted** by the "specified date", i.e. 31 October, in the year following the year of assessment, the tax liability for that year is **increased** by a **surcharge** on the amount of tax assessed. The surcharge is calculated on the **full tax payable for the year** and does not take account of any tax payments already made (e.g. PAYE). The surcharge is calculated as follows:

(a) Return submitted within two months of the specified return date, i.e. by 31 December. The surcharge is 5% of the full tax payable for the year subject to a maximum surcharge of €12,695.

(b) Return submitted more than two months from the specified return date, i.e. after 31 December. The surcharge is 10% of the full tax payable for the year subject to a maximum surcharge of €63,485.

From 1 January 2004, where an individual files a return and fails to include on the return details relating to any exemption, allowance, deduction, credit or other relief the person is claiming (referred to as "specified details") and the return states that the details required are specified details, the individual may be liable to a 5% surcharge (subject to the usual maximum of €12,695) **even if** he has filed the return **on time**. However, this surcharge may only be applied where, after the return has been filed, it has come to the person's notice (or has been brought to his attention) that the specified details were not included in the return and the person **failed to remedy** the matter without reasonable delay.

9.1.6 Interest on Overpayments of Tax

From 1 November 2003, interest is paid by the Revenue at **0.011% per day** or part thereof (4.015% p.a.) on overpaid tax.

FA 2003 amended the basis on which interest is to be paid by the Revenue on overpayments of tax. Under **section 865A TCA 1997**, the **date** from which interest runs will **depend** on whether the overpayment is as a result of **Revenue's mistake** or the **taxpayer's**. Where the overpayment arises because of a mistaken assumption by the Revenue in the application of tax law, and a claim for repayment is made within the requisite time limit, interest is paid from the day after the end of the tax year to which the repayment relates or, if later, the date of payment, until the date the repayment is made.

Where the overpayment **does not arise** because of a mistaken application of the law by the Revenue, the overpayment will only carry interest for the period beginning on the day which is **93 days (FA 2007)** after the day on which a "valid claim" for repayment has been filed with Revenue. A "valid claim" is one where all the information, which the Revenue might reasonably require to enable them to determine if and to what extent a repayment is due, has been provided to them.

Interest on the overpayment of tax is **not subject** to withholding tax and is **exempt** from income tax. Interest will not be paid where the overall amount due is less than €10.

9.2   Relevant Contracts Tax

Relevant Contracts Tax (RCT) was introduced with the main objective of reducing the perceived level of tax evasion by sub-contractors in the construction, forestry and meat-processing industries. A new electronic RCT system has been introduced effective **from 1 January 2012 (sections 530A–530V TCA 1997)**.

9.2.1   General Scheme

The general rule is that a **"principal contractor"** is required to deduct RCT from payments made to subcontractors under a **"relevant contract"** at one of three rates **to be advised by Revenue**, as follows:

- **rate of 0%** will apply where a subcontractor is in possession of a **C2 card**;
- **rate of 20%** will apply where a subcontractor is registered for tax and has a record of tax compliance; and
- **rate of 35%** will apply to subcontractors who are not registered with Revenue or where there are serious compliance issues to be addressed.

9.2.2   Operation of the RCT Scheme

1. Contract Notification
When a principal contractor enters into a "relevant contract" with a subcontractor, he will be obliged to provide Revenue, online, details of the subcontractor and the contract, including a declaration that the contract is **not a contract of employment**. The **contract notification** will include the following:

- *Where tax reference number of subcontractor is provided:*
  - subcontractor's name and tax reference number;
  - details of the contract (i.e. sector, nature and location of work, start/end date, value of contract);
  - details of the subcontractor's fixed place of business;
  - details if the subcontractor will supply materials, plant and machinery;
  - details if the subcontractor will provide his own insurance; and
  - details if the subcontractor will engage other people to work on the contract at the subcontractor's own expense.

■ ***Where the tax number of the subcontractor is not provided or is unknown,*** the following details must be provided in addition to the information above:
- the subcontractor's address, date of birth, country, e-mail address, mobile and telephone numbers;
- if registered for tax outside Ireland, state the country and tax registration number in that country; and
- details regarding the type of contractor, e.g. individual, company or partnership.

2. Payment Notification

Prior to making any payment under the contract, the principal contractor must notify Revenue, **online**, of his intention to make the payment and provide details of the gross amount to be paid.

3. Deduction Authorisation

On receipt of a payment notification Revenue will issue a deduction authorisation, which will detail the **rate of tax** and the **total amount of tax** to be deducted from the payment. The principal contractor can only pay the subcontractor in accordance with this notification and must provide a copy of the deduction authorisation to the subcontractor.

4. Deduction Summary

The deduction summary is created by Revenue from the payment notifications received from the principal contractor during the return period. Depending on the principal contractor's filing frequency, the summary will be available online to the principal contractor shortly after the end of the return period.

5. Payment of RCT deducted.

The principal contractor should check the deduction summary and make any amendments necessary and arrange for the RCT to be paid on or before the due date which, as electronic filers, will be the **23rd of the month** following the end of the return period. If the deduction summary is amended after the due date, the return will be late and a surcharge will apply.

Subcontractors will no longer be able to apply for interim refunds of RCT deducted during the tax year. Instead, any tax deducted will be credited against other tax liabilities which the subcontractor may have. Any excess will only be refunded after the tax return for the chargeable period has been filed and paid.

9.2.3   Definitions

Principal Contractor

A principal contractor in the construction, forestry and meat processing industry is a person who takes on a subcontractor and who:

■ carries on a business that includes the erection of buildings or the development of land, or the manufacture, treatment or extraction of materials for use in construction operations;

■ carries on a business of meat processing operations in an establishment approved and inspected in accordance with the EU meat and poultry regulations;

■ carries on a business of forestry operations that includes the processing (including cutting and preserving) of wood from thinned or felled trees, in sawmills or other like premises, or the supply of thinned or felled trees for such processing;

- is connected with a company which carries on any of the above businesses;
- is a local authority or a public utility society, or a body referred to the Housing Act 1966;
- is a Minister of the Government;
- is a Board established by or under Statute or Royal Charter and funded wholly or mainly out of moneys provided by the Oireachtas;
- carries on any gas, water, electricity, hydraulic power, dock, canal or railway undertaking; or
- is a subcontractor who subcontracts all or part of the contract to a subcontractor.

Note: A principal contractor in the provision of construction services is subject to the VAT reverse charge rules effective since 1 September 2008 (see Chapter 10).

Relevant Contract
This is defined as a contract (not being a contract of employment) whereby a person is liable to another person:

1. to carry out relevant operations;
2. to be responsible for the carrying out of such operations by others; or
3. to furnish his own labour or the labour of others in the carrying out of such operations, or to arrange for the labour of others to be furnished for the carrying out of such operations.

Where a principal contractor engages the same subcontractor on various or multiple contracts, they will be required to notify each contract separately, unless the contracts can be considered to be part of one on going relevant contract with the subcontractor.

Relevant Operations
The main relevant operations are:

1. The construction, alteration, repair, extension, demolition or dismantling of buildings, including site preparation and haulage.
2. Meat processing operations.
3. Forestry operations.

Relevant Operations Carried on Abroad
Strictly, a principal contractor is required to deduct RCT in respect of relevant operations carried out by a sub-contractor whether or not the sub-contractor is carrying on business in the State and whether or not the relevant operations are carried out abroad. In practice, however, the Revenue accept that RCT does not apply where the relevant operations are performed wholly abroad. Where a contract is performed partly in the State and partly abroad, RCT will only apply to payments in respect of work carried out in the State.

9.2.4 End of Year Return

The principal contractor is required to complete a **Form RCT 35/35L** (annual return of payments to sub-contractors). This return is **due by 15th February**. This end of year return consists of a two-part form that is a declaration of gross payments made and tax deducted for the year together with a list of all subcontractors to whom payments were made, irrespective of whether tax was deducted or not.

9.3 Payments in respect of Professional Services

9.3.1 Introduction

Chapter 1, Part 18 TCA 1997 provides for a **withholding tax of 20%** to be **deducted at source** from payments made by certain bodies in respect of professional services. The tax is known as Professional Services Withholding Tax (PSWT).

PSWT is deducted by **Accountable Persons** from **Relevant Payments** made by them to **Specified Persons** in respect of **Professional Services**.

Accountable Persons
For the purposes of PSWT, the following public bodies are accountable persons:

- Government departments and offices;
- local authorities;
- the Health Service Executive; and
- commercial and non-commercial semi-State bodies and their subsidiaries.

A list of accountable persons is set out in Schedule 13 TCA 1997.

Relevant Payments
Relevant payments are payments made by accountable persons in respect of **professional services**. The payments need not be in respect of services provided to the accountable person. PSWT applies to the **entire payment** including any element which is in respect of the reimbursement of expenses incurred by the specified person **except for** stamp duties, Land Registry and Deed of Registration Fees, Companies Office and Court fees. **VAT charged by the specified person should be excluded when calculating PSWT**.

Excluded Payments
PSWT should **not be** deducted from the following payments:

- payments which are subject to PAYE;
- payments which come within the RCT scheme;
- payments to other accountable persons:
  - in reimbursement of payments for professional services, *or*
  - where the income of the accountable person receiving the payment is exempt from income tax or corporation tax;
- payments to charities which have been granted an exemption from tax by the Revenue Commissioners; and
- where the payment is made by a foreign-based branch or agency of an accountable person to a person resident abroad.

Specified Persons
Specified persons are persons who provide professional services in respect of which relevant payments are made to them by accountable persons. Specified persons can be individuals, companies or partnerships and includes non-residents. PSWT deducted is available for **offset** against the specified person's final **income tax/corporation tax liability** for the period in which the relevant payment is charged to tax.

Tax Clearance Certificate

Suppliers of goods or services who enter into a public sector contract with a value of €10,000 (including VAT) or more must produce a tax clearance certificate to the public body with whom the contract is being entered into.

PSWT **must be deducted** from relevant payments made by an accountable person to a specified person **irrespective** of the fact that the specified person produces a tax clearance certificate.

Professional Services

Section 520 TCA 1997 provides that professional services that are subject to PSWT include:

- services of a medical, dental, pharmaceutical, optical, aural or veterinary nature;
- services of an architectural, engineering, quantity surveying or surveying nature, and related services;
- services of accountancy, auditing or finance and services of financial, economic, marketing, advertising or other consultancies;
- services of a solicitor or barrister or other legal services;
- geological services; and
- training services provided on behalf of FÁS.

The above is not an exhaustive list. In some cases, a service may not of itself attract PSWT, but where a service forms **part of a wider consultancy service,** it would then come within the scope of PSWT, e.g. where printing a brochure forms part of an overall professional service provided to an accountable person, it is an expense incurred in the **provision** of that service. The **full amount** of the payment (including the printing costs) in respect of the overall service is subject to PSWT.

Services that are not regarded as professional services for the purposes of PSWT include:

- teaching, training or lecturing services (**other than** training services provided on behalf of FÁS);
- translation services, including the services of an interpreter;
- proof-reading services;
- services of stenographers;
- setting and assessing oral, aural or written examinations;
- contract cleaning services; and
- maintenance and repair work.

9.3.2 Administration

Where a person provides professional services to an accountable person, he must supply the following to the accountable person:

1. his income (PPS number) or corporation tax number; and
2. if the payment includes VAT, his VAT reference number.

If the specified person does not reside in the State or have a permanent establishment in the State, he must supply details of his country of residence and his tax reference number in that country.

When the specified person has supplied the above information, the accountable person must, when making a payment, complete a **Form F45** which contains the following information:

1. the name and address of the specified person;
2. the person's tax reference number;
3. the amount of the relevant payment;
4. the amount of PSWT deducted from the payment;
5. the date on which payment is made; and
6. the amount of VAT charged.

The specified person also gets a copy of this form (Form F45).

A **Form F45** must be issued in respect of **each relevant payment** made, including a relevant payment to a specified person who has not supplied their tax reference number. Only one form F45 should ever be issued in respect of each relevant payment. If a Form F45 issued to a specified person is lost or destroyed or where the details entered require amendment, a **Form F43** can be issued by the accountable person.

The accountable person must make a monthly return **Form F30** to the Revenue, declaring the total amount of PSWT deducted in that month. The form must be returned to the Collector General together with payment of the PSWT within 14 days from the end of each income tax month. Where no PSWT is deducted by an accountable person in a month, a "NIL" return should be made. An **annual return Form F35** declaring the PSWT liability for a tax year must be returned by 15 February following the end of the tax year.

9.3.3 Credit for Professional Services Withholding Tax (PSWT)

Credit will be given to the specified person for PSWT deducted (as confirmed in Forms F45) against their income tax or corporation tax liabilities.

Income Tax
PSWT deducted in the basis period may be set against the income tax liability for that year of assessment. Any excess PSWT over and above the income tax liability will be refunded.

Where the basis period for two tax years overlap, the overlapping period is deemed to form part of the second tax year only.

Example:
An individual commences to trade on 1 July 2012 and makes up accounts for the year ended 30 June 2013. The period 1 July to 31 December 2012 will form part of the basis period for the tax year 2012 and 2012. For PSWT purposes this period will be deemed to form part of the 2012 basis period only. Accordingly credit for PSWT deducted from payments included in the period 1 July to 31 December 2013 will be given against the individual's tax liability for 2013.

Where a period falls into a gap between two basis periods, it is deemed to fall into the **later basis period**.

Example:
An individual makes up accounts annually to 30 September. The individual ceases to trade on 30 June 2012. Actual profits for 2011 were less than those originally assessed; therefore, there is no revision of 2011 profits to actual. The period 1 October 2011 to 31 December 2011 does not form part of the basis period for 2011 or 2012. Credit will be given for PSWT deducted from payments relating to the period 1 October 2011 to 31 December 2011 against the individual's tax liability for 2012.

Where the PSWT deducted refers to two or more persons, for example in the case of a partnership, the PSWT suffered is apportioned in the partner profit sharing ratios.

The taxpayer must submit the form (Form F45) which is given to him by the accountable person when making a claim for an interim refund of PSWT (see below). Forms F45 no longer need to be submitted with the taxpayer's annual tax return but they should be retained as they may be requested by Revenue for verification purposes at a later date.

Preliminary Tax

A taxpayer who has had PSWT deducted can take this into account when paying preliminary tax. For example, if a taxpayer estimates his preliminary tax liability for a tax year to be €15,000 and has PSWT credits of €10,000 available, these can be used as part payment of the preliminary tax liability, leaving the balance of €5,000 to be paid directly to the Collector-General under the pay and file rules of the self-assessment system.

9.3.4   Refunds of Professional Services Withholding Tax (PSWT)

Where a taxpayer considers that the amount of PSWT deducted from payments is in excess of likely final liability to tax, an application may be made to the taxpayer's Revenue office for an interim refund of any excess, instead of waiting to have it credited against final liability. The application is made on **Form F50.**

Ongoing Business

An interim refund of PSWT may be given to a person who satisfies the following requirements:

(a) the profits of the basis period for the tax year immediately preceding the tax year in question must have been finally determined;

(b) the amount of tax due in respect of the tax year immediately preceding the tax year in question must have been paid; and

(c) the individual must provide Forms F45 in respect of the withholding tax reclaimed.

The amount of the interim refund which will be made to the person will be:

Tax withheld according to Forms F45

Less Tax liability for previous tax year

Less any outstanding VAT, PAYE or PRSI due by the individual.

> *Example:*
> An individual makes up accounts to 30 September each year. In order for the individual to be able to claim a refund of tax withheld from receipts included in his accounts for the year ended 30 September 2012, the individual must have filed a return for 2011 and paid his tax liability for 2011. The individual files his return for 2011 on 31 October 2012 and pays the balance of tax due for 2011 on the same day. An assessment issues on 1 December 2012 showing a total liability for 2011 of €26,500 which has been paid in full. During the year ended 30 September 2012, the individual received €128,000 after deduction of PSWT of €32,000 in respect of services provided during the year ended 30 September 2012. Provided the individual has no arrears of VAT, PAYE or PRSI and has Forms F45 in respect of the PSWT paid of €32,000, he may submit a claim for an interim refund of PSWT of €5,500, i.e. €32,000 − €26,500.

Commencing Businesses

Where an individual wishes to make a claim for an interim refund of PSWT in the year in which he commenced business he does not have to satisfy requirements (a) and (b) above. Instead the Inspector may make an interim refund to the individual of 20% of an amount calculated using the following formula:

$$E \times \left(\frac{A}{B} \times \frac{C}{D} \right)$$

A = The estimated amount of payments from which PSWT will be deducted to be included as income in the basis period for the tax year.

B = The estimated total receipts to be included in income in the basis period for the tax year.

C = The estimated number of months or fractions of months in the period in respect of which the claim is being made

D = The estimated number of months or fractions of months in the basis period for the tax year.

E = The estimated expenses to be incurred by the individual in the basis period for the tax year.

Example:

John commences to trade on 1 June 2012. He intends to make up accounts annually to 31 December. His first set of accounts will be made up for the 7 months to 31 December 2012. Up to 30 September 2012, he has received payments of €16,000 from which PSWT of €4,000 was deducted. It is estimated that his accounts for the 7 months to 31 December 2012 will include income of €100,000 and expenses of €45,000. €40,000 of his total income will be paid under deduction of PSWT. In October 2012, he makes a claim for an interim refund of €2,057 calculated as follows:

$$20\% \times \left(\text{€45,000} \times \frac{\text{€40,000}}{\text{€100,000}} \times \frac{4}{7} \right)$$

If the actual PSWT suffered was less than €2,057, his refund would be restricted to the amount of tax withheld.

Cases of Particular Hardship

Where an individual claims and proves particular hardship, Revenue may waive all or some of the conditions outlined above which govern the payment of interim refunds. In such circumstances, the amount of the refund to be made to the individual is at the discretion of the Inspector.

9.4 Appeal Procedures

9.4.1 Introduction

If a taxpayer **disagrees** with a notice of assessment or with a determination of the Revenue Commissioners in relation to income tax, he has the **right to appeal** against such an assessment or determination. If the matter is not subsequently settled by agreement between the Inspector and the taxpayer, an Appeal Commissioner will eventually hear the appeal.

The taxpayer **can only** appeal if:

1. he has submitted his return of income form; *and*
2. he has paid the correct tax he believes is due, together with any interest or penalties payable.

The appeal must be made within **30 days** of the issue of the notice of assessment. A taxpayer cannot appeal against a notice of assessment that is in accordance with the information contained in the return of income form or agreed between the Inspector of Taxes and the taxpayer.

Conditions for a Valid Appeal

For an appeal to be valid:

1. it must be in writing;
2. the precise item in the assessment which the taxpayer disputes must be specified; and
3. the grounds for disputing the item must be detailed.

9.4.2 Taxpayer's/Revenue's Right of Appeal – Hearing before Appeal Commissioner

If an assessment that has been appealed cannot be settled by correspondence or negotiation between the taxpayer and the Inspector, the Inspector will list the case for hearing before the Appeal Commissioner. At the hearing, the Appeal Commissioner will consider the facts of the case and reach a decision, either in favour of the taxpayer or the Inspector. The taxpayer must be given at least **10 days notice** by the Inspector of the date for the hearing of the appeal.

The most common reasons resulting in a case being listed for hearing before the Appeal Commissioners would include:

- Disputes between the Inspector and taxpayer or his agent over the validity of items contained in the accounts/tax returns.
- Disputes as to the interpretation of tax law or case law in relation to a particular item included in the accounts/tax return of the taxpayer.

Where the taxpayer or his agent fails to persuade the Inspector to remove his case from the appeal list, the taxpayer must arrange to be **represented** at the hearing to prevent the original assessment automatically becoming final and conclusive (and therefore legally payable) by default.

Request for an Adjournment

If the matter at issue is not a question of argument as between the Inspector and the taxpayer but rather a failure by the taxpayer to submit certain information to the Inspector, then a **request for an adjournment** may be made to the Appeal Commissioners to allow additional time to enable the taxpayer to submit the necessary information. If reasonable cause is given to the Commissioner and the Inspector does not object too forcibly then, normally, the adjournment request is granted for a specified period of time e.g. four weeks, six weeks, etc., depending on the circumstances. The Inspector's reaction to a request for an adjournment is normally determined by his experience in dealing with the particular taxpayer's case in the past.

Refusal of Request for Adjournment

A request for adjournment **may not** be refused if it is made **within nine months** from the earlier of the end of the tax year to which the notice of assessment applies or the date on which the notice of assessment is issued.

Dismissing/Determining an Appeal

Where the Commissioner has refused an application for adjournment and the taxpayer has furnished a return, but the information contained therein or in the accompanying statements is inadequate, the Commissioner is **required** to make an order **dismissing** the appeal, unless the Commissioner is satisfied that sufficient information has been furnished to enable him to **determine** the appeal (i.e. increase or reduce the original assessment).

If an assessment is **dismissed** as opposed to **determined,** there are serious implications for the taxpayer. In the case of the **dismissal** of the appeal, the original tax, as assessed by the Inspector, is **confirmed** and becomes **immediately payable** to the Collector-General, as if no appeal had been lodged against the assessment. In addition, the taxpayer automatically loses **his right** to appeal to the Circuit Court. The taxpayer retains his rights, under general law, to appeal to the High Court and the Supreme Court if a **point of law** is involved.

If the assessment is **determined** by the Commissioner, the right of a rehearing to the Circuit Court is **retained** by the taxpayer. **FA 2007** stipulates that where a determination of the Appeal Commissioners is to be reheard by the **Circuit Court**, or a case is to be stated for the opinion of the **High Court**, **tax will be neither collected nor repaid** by the Revenue on the basis of the Appeal Commissioner's determination. Also the Inspector of Taxes will not be obliged to amend the assessment under appeal until the appeal process has been **fully completed**. This reverses the previous rule that, pending an appeal to the Circuit Court, the amount of tax due under determination of the Appeal Commissioner became immediately payable to the Collector-General.

9.4.3 Taxpayer's/Revenue's Rights to Appeal – Hearing before Circuit Court/High Court/Supreme Court

If a taxpayer's appeal has been **determined** before the Appeal Commissioners he may apply, **within ten days**, to have the case re-heard before the Circuit Court. This right is not available to the taxpayer if his case has been **dismissed** before the Appeal Commissioners.

If the Appeal Commissioner has decided in favour of the taxpayer, as opposed to the Revenue, the **Inspector is given no right of appeal** to the Circuit Court. If the Inspector wishes to pursue the matter further, he must go directly to the High Court. Such a right to go to the High Court is only available where the matter under dispute is a **point of law rather than a question of fact**.

If the taxpayer fails at the Circuit Court stage, he may pursue his appeal to the High Court, **provided** the matter under dispute is a **point of law**. The taxpayer must lodge an application to have the case stated for hearing before the High Court **within 21 days** of the Circuit Court hearing. The taxpayer may also proceed **directly** to the High Court after the Appeal Commissioners hearing, presuming that the question at issue is a **point of law**.

Any party aggrieved by the decision of the High Court has a **right of appeal** to the **Supreme Court**.

9.4.4 Settlement of Appeal

An appeal may be settled where:

- Agreement has been reached between the individual and the Inspector of Taxes.
- The individual withdraws his appeal.
- There is a determination of the appeal by the Appeal Commissioner, Circuit Court Judge, High Court or Supreme Court.
- The default provisions apply i.e. failure to be represented at the Appeal hearing before the Appeal Commissioner.

9.5 Revenue Audits and Investigations

9.5.1 Introduction

The Irish tax system is primarily a **self-assessment system** where the taxpayer calculates the amount of tax due and pays it over to the Revenue within the stipulated time frame. (The exception is PAYE taxpayers who are not generally self-assessed.) For the Revenue Commissioners, it is a fundamental principle of self-assessment tax systems that returns filed by **compliant** taxpayers are **accepted** as the basis for computing tax liabilities. Revenue police the self-assessment system through the use of Revenue audits, assurance checks and Revenue investigations.

9.5.2 Definition of a Revenue Audit

Revenue's October 2010 "**Code of Practice for Revenue Audit**" (www.revenue.ie) states that the primary objective of a Revenue audit is to promote "*voluntary compliance with tax and duty obligations*" and that the audit programme is mainly concerned with "*detecting and deterring non-compliance*".

A Revenue audit is an **examination** of:

- a tax return (e.g. income tax (including DIRT and other fiduciary taxes), corporation tax, CGT or CAT (either in whole or in part));
- a declaration of liability, or a repayment claim, (e.g. VAT, PAYE/PRSI or RCT);
- a statement of liability to stamp duties; and
- the compliance of a business with tax and duty legislation.

Location of Audit

The audit is normally carried out at the taxpayer's place of business, or the principal place of business in the case of multiple businesses or locations. The length of such visits depends on the number and complexity of the points at issue. Advance notice of between fourteen days and twenty days is generally given in such cases to both the taxpayer and his agent. In certain exceptional circumstances (e.g. where it is suspected that records are likely to be removed or altered), a visit may take place unannounced.

Assurance Checks

An assurance check is **not** an audit but is usually an enquiry, by letter or telephone, about a specific issue. An example would be a request for further documentation to support a claim for a particular tax relief. Revenue can raise an assurance check on any kind of taxpayer including those not liable to self-assessment (e.g. PAYE taxpayers).

9.5.3 Definition of a Revenue Investigation

An investigation is an examination of a customer's affairs where Revenue has evidence or concerns of **serious tax evasion**. Some investigation cases may lead to criminal prosecution. During the course of a Revenue audit, an auditor may also notify the taxpayer that the audit is ceasing and an investigation commencing.

Where a Revenue investigation is being notified, the letter issued will include the wording: "*Notification of a Revenue Investigation*". Revenue auditors engaged in the investigation of serious tax evasion, may visit a taxpayer's place of business without advance notice.

Note: Once an investigation is initiated, the taxpayer will not have any opportunity to make any type of qualifying disclosure.

9.5.4 Audit Notification

Twenty-one days' notice is generally given, in writing, to both the taxpayer and his agent. The notice will clearly state that it is a "Notification of a Revenue Audit". Revenue will specify a date at which they wish to visit the taxpayer's premises to examine the books and records of the business. Almost all audits are carried out for a reason, i.e. Revenue will have information or indications that the taxpayer may be at fault, though some audits are carried out on a random basis.

The audit notification will specify the tax head (income tax, VAT, etc) and the year of assessment or period in question. The Revenue Inspector is confined to examining the issues **as notified** and cannot extend the audit without good reason at the time of the visit.

9.5.5   Tax, Interest and Penalties

Tax
Any tax due as a result of the Revenue audit must be paid.

Interest
Interest is always charged if a failure to pay is identified. Interest **cannot** be mitigated. Interest is charged on a daily basis by reference to the date the tax was originally due and payable.

Application of Penalties
Penalties will apply if, in the course of the audit, tax defaults are identified. Penalties are "tax-geared" which means that the penalty is expressed as a **percentage of the tax** (but not the interest) due.

Penalties will apply in circumstances where there has been:

- careless behaviour without significant consequences;
- careless behaviour with significant consequences; or
- deliberate behaviour.

(1)   Careless Behaviour without Significant Consequences
The penalty for this category is **20% of the tax**. This will arise if a taxpayer of ordinary skill and knowledge, properly advised, would have foreseen as a reasonable probability or likelihood the prospect that an act (or omission) would cause a tax underpayment, having regard to all the circumstances, but nevertheless, the act or omission occurred. The tax shortfall must be **less than 15%** of the tax liability ultimately due in respect of the particular tax for that period.

(2)   Careless Behaviour with Significant Consequences
The penalty here is **40% of the tax**. This category is the lack of **due care** with the result that tax liabilities or repayment claims are **substantially incorrect** and do not pass the 15% test described above. Careless behaviour with significant consequences is distinguished from "deliberate behaviour" by the **absence** of indicators consistent with **intent** on the part of the taxpayer.

(3)   Deliberate Behaviour
The penalty for deliberate behaviour is **100% of the tax**. Deliberate behaviour has indicators consistent with **intent** and includes tax evasion and the non-operation of fiduciary taxes such as PAYE.

Self-correction
This category arises outside of the audit or enquiry process. A return may be self-corrected **without** penalty where:

- Revenue is notified in writing of the adjustments to be made, and the circumstances under which the errors arose; and

■ a computation of the correct tax and statutory interest payable is provided, along with a cheque in settlement.

Time Limits for Self-correction

Income Tax	Within 12 months of the due date for filing the return.
Corporation Tax	Within 12 months of the due date for filing the return.
Capital Gains Tax	Within 12 months of the due date for filing the return.
VAT	Before the due date of the income tax or corporation tax return for the period in which the VAT period ends. A self correction of the Jan/Feb 2012 VAT Return for a company with a 31 December 2012 year end must occur before 21 September 2013.
PAYE/PRSI/USC	Within 12 months of the due date for filing the annual return.
Relevant Contracts Tax	Within 12 months of the due date for filing the annual return.
Capital Acquisitions Tax	Within 12 weeks of the due date for filing the return.

Innocent Error

A penalty will not be payable in instances where the Revenue auditor is satisfied that:

■ the amount of tax is less than €6,000;
■ the mistake was not intentional;
■ good books and records were kept; *and*
■ the taxpayer has a good compliance record.

Statutory interest is payable upon settlement of the tax due as a result of "innocent errors".

Technical Adjustments

Technical adjustments are adjustments to liability that arise from differences in the interpretation or the application of legislation. For a technical adjustment not to attract a penalty, the Revenue auditor must be satisfied that:

■ due care has been taken by the taxpayer; *and*
■ the treatment concerned was based on an interpretation of the law, which could reasonably have been considered to be correct.

A taxpayer who takes a position on a matter that has significant tax consequences is expected to take **due care**. Matters that are well established in case law and precedent will not be entertained as technical adjustments.

No Loss of Revenue

The expression "no loss of revenue" is used to describe a situation whereby there is no cost to the State even though tax was not properly charged. Take the example of where a sale was made between two VAT registered businesses without the addition of VAT. This resulted in no VAT being paid on the sale but, correspondingly, no input VAT credit being claimed by the other party. In this case, there was no loss of revenue to the State. However, in the event of an audit, Revenue is entitled to seek the VAT and interest and penalties due for the non-operation or incorrect operation of the VAT system. Taxpayers may, however, make a "no loss of revenue claim" if:

■ the tax involved is either VAT or RCT;
■ the taxpayer can provide conclusive evidence to demonstrate, to the satisfaction of Revenue, that there was "no loss of revenue"; and

■ the taxpayer's compliance record is good and the default in question wasn't as a result of deliberate behaviour.

Where Revenue accepts no loss of revenue claims, statutory interest may be payable but limited to any period where there was a temporary loss of revenue. Reduced penalties are payable as set out in **Section 9.5.6** below.

Revenue will not accept no loss of revenue claims in the following circumstances:

■ where there is a general failure to operate the tax system (and not just a once off);
■ where the default was as a consequence of deliberate behaviour;
■ where no loss of revenue has not been proven to the satisfaction of Revenue;
■ where the taxpayer has not co-operated; or
■ where the default is in the careless behaviour category and there is neither a qualifying disclosure nor co-operation.

9.5.6 Mitigation of Penalties

Under TCA 1997 Revenue has the power to mitigate the penalties in the following circumstances:

■ co-operation by the taxpayer; and
■ "qualifying disclosures" made by the taxpayer.

Co-operation
Co-operation includes the following:

■ having all books, records, and linking papers available for the auditor at the commencement of the audit;
■ having appropriate personnel available at the time of audit;
■ responding promptly to all requests for information and explanations;
■ responding promptly to all correspondence; and
■ prompt payment of the audit settlement liability.

Qualifying Disclosures
The taxpayer may elect to carry out a review of his own tax affairs and identify where mistakes were made **prior** to their discovery by the Revenue auditor. This type of review is called a "qualifying disclosure", and Revenue has in place special incentives for taxpayers who wish to make qualifying disclosures. A qualifying disclosure results in the following:

■ non-publication under section 1086 TCA 1997;
■ no prosecution – a Revenue assurance that, in certain circumstances, an investigation with a view to prosecution will not be initiated; and
■ further mitigation of penalties.

Qualifying disclosures can be either "**unprompted**" or "**prompted**":

■ An "unprompted" disclosure is a disclosure that is made **before** the taxpayer is notified of an audit, *or* contacted by Revenue regarding an enquiry or investigation relating to his or her tax affairs.
■ A "prompted" disclosure is a disclosure made **after** an audit notice has issued but **before** an examination of the books and records or other documentation has begun.

Format of a Qualifying Disclosure

A qualifying disclosure is a disclosure of the full particulars of all matters occasioning a liability to tax that give rise to a penalty. It must be made **in writing and signed by, or on behalf of, the taxpayer**. It must be accompanied by:

- A **declaration**, to the best of that person's knowledge, information and belief, that all matters contained in the disclosure are correct and complete.
- A **payment** of the tax or duty and interest on late payment of that tax or duty. Penalties due do not need to be stated – these are subsequently agreed and paid.

In addition:

- All qualifying disclosures (prompted and unprompted) in the *Deliberate Behaviour* category must state the amounts of all liabilities to tax and interest, in respect of **all taxheads and periods,** where liabilities arise as a result of deliberate behaviour, that were previously undisclosed.
- In the case of a **prompted** qualifying disclosure in the *Careless Behaviour* category, the qualifying disclosure must state the amounts of **all** liabilities to tax and interest in respect of the **relevant taxheads and periods** within the scope of the **proposed audit**.
- In the case of an **unprompted** qualifying disclosure in the *Careless Behaviour* category, the qualifying disclosure must state the amounts of **all** liabilities to tax and interest in respect of the taxheads and periods that are the subject of the unprompted qualifying disclosure.

Preparation of a Qualifying Disclosure

In order for the taxpayer to secure an agreed period of time in which to prepare and make a qualifying disclosure, **notice of the intention** to make a disclosure must be given to the Revenue.

In the case of an **unprompted disclosure**, the notice of the intention to make a disclosure must be given **before** a notice of audit is issued *or* the taxpayer has been contacted by Revenue regarding an enquiry or investigation relating to his tax affairs.

In the case of a **prompted disclosure**, the notice of intention to make a disclosure must be given **within 14 days** of the day of issue of the notification of audit.

A person who has given notice within the time allowed of his intention to make a **qualifying disclosure** will be given **60 days** in which to quantify the shortfall and to make the relevant payment. This period of 60 days will begin from the day on which the notice of intention to make a disclosure was given and will be communicated to the taxpayer in writing by Revenue.

Mitigation of Penalties on First Qualifying Disclosure (for defaults occurring on/after 24 December 2008):

Category of Tax Default	Penalty as a % of Tax Underpaid	Net Penalty after Mitigation where there is:		
		Co-operation Only	Co-operation AND a Prompted Qualifying Disclosure	Co-operation AND an Unprompted Qualifying Disclosure
Deliberate Behaviour	100%	75%	50%	10%
Careless Behaviour *with* Significant Consequences	40%	30%	20%	5%
Careless Behaviour *without* Significant Consequences	20%	15%	10%	3%

A separate table of penalties applies to a second and subsequent qualifying disclosure made within a five year period.

Mitigation of Penalties on "No Loss of Revenue" (NLOR) defaults:

Category of Tax Default	Penalty as a % of Tax Underpaid	Net Penalty after Mitigation where there is:		
		Co-operation Only	Co-operation AND a Prompted Qualifying Disclosure	Co-operation AND an Unprompted Qualifying Disclosure
Careless Behaviour	100%	Lesser of 9% or €100,000	Lesser of 6% or €15,000	Lesser of 3% or €5,000

A separate table of penalties applies to second and subsequent NLOR qualifying disclosures made within a five-year period.

9.5.7 Conduct of a Revenue Audit

At the commencement of any **field audit**, the auditor identifies himself, shows his authorisation and explains to the taxpayer the purpose of the audit. He will draw the **Customer Service Charter** to the attention of the taxpayer and outline the authority that is vested in him under the various Finance Acts in relation to the inspection of records, documents, etc. The taxpayer is **informed** about the Revenue practice on charging interest and penalties and is offered the opportunity to make a prompted qualifying disclosure. In addition, the auditor advises the taxpayer of the **effects** of a **disclosure** regarding penalties and publication.

Having explained his authority, the auditor will normally proceed to point out that in the event of any irregularities being found which have led to an apparent underpayment in tax, he will request a **final meeting** with the taxpayer and his agent to:

- discuss and present a report on the results of his audit;
- ask for comments and responses from the taxpayer and his agent;
- if possible, reach agreement on the undercharges (if any) under each tax heading, i.e. income tax, USC, VAT, PAYE, PRSI, surcharges, interest and penalties; and
- invite the taxpayer/agent to make a formal settlement offer in writing in the event of discrepancies not being fully explained.

Following the final interview, a **written report** will be sent to the taxpayer or his agent setting out the main points arising from the audit.

The auditor will also normally indicate at the interview the **approximate duration** of the audit, where it will be carried out, and will invite questions from the taxpayer and his agent in relation to the audit.

A **written record** of all requests, replies and other requirements, whether raised at the initial interview or subsequently, should be kept by the taxpayer to ensure that the audit is conducted in an orderly way. If some questions raised by the audit are complex, it may be preferable to request the auditor to submit them **in writing**.

In the case of a **desk audit**, the auditor will request records to be submitted to him for examination and, other than in exceptional circumstances, an auditor will **not retain** records for **longer than 30 days**. If more time is required the Inspector will negotiate this with the taxpayer or his agent. The 30-day period can commence only **from the date** on which the auditor has received **all** of the records requested. If items are omitted then, clearly, the auditor cannot commence his audit until he has all relevant documentation.

Revenue **does not**, as a matter of normal practice, **issue assessments** where a settlement is reached and agreed with the taxpayer and/or his agent. An assessment is normally only issued where it is **requested** by the taxpayer to enable him to take the matter before the Appeal Commissioners.

9.5.8 Review Procedures

The taxpayer has the right to request a **review** in relation to the conduct of an audit, in particular in relation to the following:

- proposed adjustments to receipts or profits figures, claims for reliefs or allowances, other adjustments to tax computations;
- penalties to be imposed;
- publication of the settlement; and
- the issue of a notice of opinion regarding penalties.

The request for a second opinion should be submitted in writing to the **Internal Review Unit in the Office of the Revenue Commissioners, Dublin Castle, Dublin 2.**

The request should state the reasons why a review is requested and whether the taxpayer wishes the review to be carried out solely by the Inspector of Taxes in charge of the Review Unit or jointly with an external reviewer.

The entitlement of the taxpayer to request a review is **separate** from his right to **appeal** any assessment raised as a result of the audit. Accordingly, if the taxpayer is not happy with the findings of the reviewer, he still has a **statutory right** to appeal any assessment raised. A review will not be granted once notification of the time and place for the hearing of an appeal has been issued to the taxpayer.

9.6 Revenue On-line Service (ROS)

9.6.1 Introduction

The Revenue On-line Service (ROS) is an Internet facility that allows taxpayers or their agents to file tax returns, pay tax liabilities and access their tax details on-line.
The main features of ROS include facilities to:

- file returns and declarations on-line;
- make payments by laser card, debit instruction or on-line banking (on-line banking applies to income tax only);
- calculate tax liabilities, and
- claim repayments.

ROS also provides taxpayers (including PAYE taxpayers) with access to their tax account information, including the facility to view details of returns filed and due, payments made, view and amend tax credits, etc.

9.6.2 Mandatory e-Filing

Since **1 June 2011,** the following categories of taxpayer are **required** to pay and file returns electronically:

- all companies;
- all trusts;
- all partnerships;
- self-employed individuals filing a return of payments to third parties (Form 46G);
- self-employed individuals subject to the high earners restriction (Form RR1, Form 11);
- self-employed individuals benefiting from or acquiring foreign life policies, offshore funds or other offshore products; and
- self-employed individuals claiming a range of property based incentives (residential property and industrial buildings allowances).

In addition, **all stamp duty returns** and payments due on or after 1 June 2011 must be filed electronically.

Employers with **10 or more employees**, not already covered above, are required to pay and file returns electronically from **1 October 2011**.

From **1 June 2012**, the following categories of taxpayer will be required to pay and file returns **online**:

- all taxpayers who are registered for VAT; and
- individuals who avail of the following reliefs and exemptions:
  - retirement annuity contract payments,
  - PRSA contributions,
  - overseas pension plans: migrant member relief,
  - retirement relief for sportspersons,
  - relief for AVCs,
  - artists exemption,
  - woodlands exemption,
  - patent income exemption,
  - income on which trans-border relief is claimed,
  - EII/BES relief,
  - seed capital scheme relief,
  - film relief,
  - significant buildings/gardens relief, and
  - interest relief: loan to acquire share in company or partnership.

9.6.3 On-line Returns

The following is a list of returns and specified tax liabilities that must be paid and filed on ROS (mandatory e-filing):

Taxhead	Specified Return	Specified Tax Liability
Corporation Tax	Form CT1	Preliminary Tax and Balance Due
Partnership	Form 1 (Firms)	-

(continued overleaf)

Taxhead	Specified Return	Specified Tax Liability
Trusts	Form 1	Preliminary Tax and Balance Due
Income Tax	Form 11	Preliminary Tax and Balance Due
High Earner Restriction	Form RR1	-
Employer PAYE/PRSI/USC	Form P30 Form P35 Forms P45 and P46	All PAYE/PRSI/USC due
Value Added Tax	Form VAT 3 Annual Return of Trading Details (RTD) VAT on e-services Quarterly Return	VAT due Quarterly VAT due on e-services
Capital Acquisitions Tax	Annual Return	Annual Payment
VIES	Monthly/Quarterly/Annual Statement of intra-Community Supplies	
Relevant Contracts Tax	Form RCT30 Form RCT35	All RCT due
Vehicle Registration Tax	Form VRT40 Vehicle Registration Form Vehicle Birth Certificate	Monthly VRT due (current payment method remains unchanged)
Betting Duty	Quarterly Return	Quarterly Payment
Dividend Withholding Tax (DWT)	Monthly Return	Payment of DWT deducted from relevant distributions in previous month
Deposit Interest Retention Tax (DIRT)	Annual Return	Interim payment and Balance Due
Life Assurance Exit Tax (LAET)	Biannual Return	Biannual payment
Investment Undertaking Exit Tax (IUT)	Biannual Return	Biannual payment
EU Savings Directive	Annual Return	–
Environmental Levy	Quarterly/Annual Return	All Payments due
Gift and Inheritance Tax	Annual Return	Annual Payment
Transit declaration and notifications	Monthly Return	–
3rd Party Payments Return (46G/46G company)	Annual Return	–
INTRASTAT	Monthly Return	–
CAP Export Trader Refunds	Monthly Return	–
Air Travel Tax	Annual Return	Monthly Payment

The following facilities are also available through ROS:

■ A facility is available for ROS business customers and agents to check if a tax clearance certificate is valid.

■ A facility where employers can download tax credit certificates (Form P2C) via ROS. This data can be exported to the customer's payroll system. Payroll agents can also download the P2C via ROS on behalf of their clients. For this, the employer must be registered for ROS and have elected to receive P2Cs electronically.

■ A facility for customers and agents to make CGT payments for income tax-registered customers who are not yet registered for CGT.

9.6.4 Off-line Returns

All returns are also available to **upload** to ROS. These have to be created **off-line** via the **ROS Off-line Application**, which has to be downloaded from ROS. Some of the returns can be created off-line using compatible third party software. Once created and saved, these files can be **uploaded** to ROS.

9.6.5 Registration

In order to use ROS, the taxpayer must first **register** with the service.

Self-employed individuals, business and practitioners
This is a three-step process, which is completed on-line on the ROS Home Page.

■ **Step 1: Apply for a ROS Access Number (RAN)**
The taxpayer enters one of his tax registration numbers. If an agent is applying for a RAN, he should enter his Tax Advisor Identification Number (TAIN). Revenue will post the ROS Access Number to the taxpayer at his registered address.

■ **Step 2: Apply for a Digital Certificate**
The taxpayer enters his RAN and his registration number together with an e-mail address. When this step of the application has been processed by Revenue, a password will be generated and posted to the taxpayer who will use this password to retrieve his Digital Certificate.

■ **Step 3: Retrieve Digital Certificate**
The taxpayer will enter his ROS system password (from step 2 above) and will install his Digital Certificate on his computer in a password-protected file. The taxpayer becomes a ROS customer once the Digital Certificate is installed.

Correspondence from ROS
A ROS customer will be provided with a secure ROS Inbox. Correspondence posted to this inbox includes reminders to file returns, copies of returns, statements of account and payment receipts. Customers are notified upon accessing ROS if there are any new items of correspondence that have not been viewed. Approaching the due date for filing relevant returns, ROS issues notification to file to customers and/or tax agents acting on behalf of customers. This notification is issued in the form of an e-mail to the designated e-mail address provided by the customer and/or tax agent.

Registering for PAYE Services

In order to avail of the full range of PAYE services in ROS, the taxpayer will need to register and have his personal details verified by **PAYE Anytime**, which is a two-step process.

- **Step 1: Enter personal details on screen and submit these on-line for verification.**
  Following the successful Revenue verification of his personal details, the taxpayer will be issued with a Revenue PIN by post.
- **Step 2: Enter activation code**
  Once his activation code is entered correctly, the taxpayer will be fully registered and able to log in to the **PAYE Anytime** service.

Registering with **PAYE Anytime** will provide the taxpayer with the means to access the range of PAYE services in ROS. However, if the taxpayer is already registered for other business taxes with Revenue (e.g. VAT or self-employed income tax), he will not be able to access these with the **PAYE Anytime** registration. Instead he will require a ROS digital certificate. Note that the digital certificate will allow the taxpayer to access services for all taxes in ROS (including PAYE) for which he is registered.

9.6.6 Payments to Revenue using ROS

ROS users may pay their taxes using **laser** or **ROS debit instruction** (RDI). Users that are registered for income tax also have an option to make a payment using the **on-line banking** facility.

Taxes may also be paid by credit card (VISA or Master card only), but this is subject to a transaction charge of 1.49% of the value of the payment.

A ROS Debit Instruction (RDI) is not a direct debit instruction. Unlike direct debit, RDI is not a fixed monthly payment amount. With RDI, the taxpayer determines the amount of the payment and when the payment is made. RDI does not confer on Revenue **any right** to take money from a taxpayer's bank account.

To set up a RDI using the ROS system, the taxpayer will be asked to enter the details of the bank account from which the payments will be debited i.e. account name, sort code and account number. He will be asked to indicate which tax type he wishes to pay from this account. It will be possible to pay **more than one tax type** from the same account. The taxpayer will be asked to sign the RDI with his Digital Certificate and send the form to ROS. Once the taxpayer has submitted these details on-line, he will be permitted to file returns immediately for the relevant taxes.

An existing direct debit customer can continue to have deductions made under the standard direct debit scheme every month.

If a taxpayer files his tax return early, Revenue **will not** debit the payment amount from his bank account **before** the due date for payment provided the taxpayer specifies that date as their payment date.

9.6.7 Incentives for using ROS

ROS taxpayers, who are obliged to meet "pay and file" obligations for self-assessed income tax on 31 October 2012, will be entitled to have the due date extended to 15 November 2012 when they **file their 2011 income tax return** (Form 11) **AND submit their payment on-line** using ROS for both the income tax balance due for 2011 and preliminary tax 2012.

If the payment is specified on-line at any date before 15 November 2012, the taxpayer's bank account will not be debited until 15 November 2012, **provided** the taxpayer **specifies that date** as the payment date.

Note: The extended deadline for return and payment will only apply where the taxpayer both files the Form 11 and makes the payment online, i.e. it is necessary to do both transactions on-line. Where only one of these actions is completed through ROS, the extension will not apply.

Taxpayers who pay or file by means **other** than ROS are required to submit both payments and returns on or before 31 October 2012.

Extended date for customers who pay and file electronically

With effect from 1 January 2009, a **general extension** to existing deadlines for filing returns and paying tax where the customers both **pay and file** electronically is available to anyone who makes the relevant returns and associated tax payments via ROS, whether voluntarily or under the new mandatory regime.

The existing time limits have been extended to the **23rd of the month** for the following returns and payments:

Corporation Tax

Preliminary tax, annual CT1 return and balancing payment.

Relevant Contracts Tax

Monthly RCT 30 return, annual Form RCT 35 and RCT due.

Value Added Tax

VAT 3 return, annual return of trading details (RTD) and VAT due.

Employer PAYE/PRSI

Monthly Form P30, annual Form P35 and PAYE/PRSI due.

Where a return **and** associated payment are not made electronically by the new extended deadlines, the extended time limits will be **disregarded** so that, for example, any interest imposed for late payment will run from the former due dates and not the extended dates.

Questions (Chapter 9)

(See Solutions to Questions at the end of this text.)

9   Administration and Procedures

9.1 Mr Murphy

The senior partner of your firm has come to you with a letter from one of the firm's clients, John Murphy, who was previously an employee and has set up his own business on 1 July 2011. Mr Murphy will prepare accounts annually to 31 December. Mr Murphy is very worried about the self-assessment system.

Requirement
You are required to write a brief letter to Mr Murphy describing the self-assessment system, paying attention to the procedure for each of the following:
(a) Income tax returns and surcharges
(b) Preliminary tax

9.2 Self Assessment

Requirement
Give a brief outline of the income tax self-assessment system, with particular reference to the requirements regarding:

(a) returns of income
(b) payment of tax
(c) assessments
(d) appeals against assessments

Value Added Tax (VAT)

Learning Objectives

In this chapter you will learn:

- the general principles of VAT;
- the importance and distinction between the supply of goods and the supply of services;
- how to compute the value of the goods or services on which VAT was chargeable;
- the special rules for supplies cross-border within the European Community;
- the rules for the supplies of goods and services outside of the European Community; and
- the administration of VAT – books and records to be kept and tax payment dates.

The Chartered Accountants Ireland *Code of Ethics* applies to all aspects of a Chartered Accountant's professional life, including dealing with VAT issues. As outlined at the beginning of this book, further information regarding the principles in the *Code of Ethics* is set out in **Appendix 4**.

10.1 General Principles of VAT

10.1.1 Introduction

VAT is a tax on consumer spending. It is chargeable on:

- the supply of goods and services within the State by a **taxable person** in the course of any business carried on by him;
- goods imported into the State from outside the EU (VAT at the point of entry);
- intra-Community acquisition of goods by VAT registered persons; and
- intra-Community acquisition of new means of transport, e.g. motor vehicles, boats, etc. by either a registered or unregistered person.

Registered traders collect VAT on the **supply of goods and services** to their customers. Each such trader in the chain of supply, from manufacturer through to retailer, **charges VAT on his sales** and he is entitled to **deduct** from this amount the **VAT paid on his purchases** (input credit). The effect of offsetting purchases against sales is to impose the tax on the **value added** at each stage of production – hence Value Added Tax. The final consumer, who is usually not registered for VAT, absorbs VAT as part of the purchase price.

10.1.2 Legislation and Directives

The main Irish legislation governing the VAT system are:

- Value Added Tax Consolidation Act 2010 (VATCA 2010); and
- Value Added Tax Regulations.

European Union Directives and Case Law

The EU issues VAT directives to Member States and they, in turn, **must modify** their VAT legislation accordingly. In the event of any inconsistency, **EU law takes precedence.** Any judgement from the European Court of Justice takes precedence over Irish case law on VAT, including determinations by Appeal Commissioners.

10.1.3 Taxable Persons/Accountable Persons

A **taxable person** is one who independently (i.e. other than as an employee) carries on a business in the EU or elsewhere.

An **accountable person** is a taxable person who engages in the supply, within the State, of taxable goods or services. An accountable person may also be someone who is in receipt of certain services or goods **in the State** from a supplier established **outside of the State** and the recipient has to **self-account** for VAT as if they were the supplier, i.e. **reverse charge**.

With effect from 1 July 2010, the State and public bodies are regarded as accountable persons for certain activities.

Note: Accountability is a key concept in VAT, as persons who are accountable must register for the tax, submit tax returns and payments, keep records and comply with the provisions of the VATCA 2010.

10.1.4 Charge to VAT

VAT is chargeable on the following:

- The supply of goods or services within the State by a taxable person;
- The importation of goods into the State from **outside** the EU (VAT is usually charged at the point of entry by Customs);
- The intra-Community acquisition by an accountable person of goods (other than new means of transport) when the acquisition is made within the State;
- The intra-Community acquisition of new means of transport by either an accountable or non-accountable person.

10.1.5 Registration

"Taxable persons" are obliged to register for VAT if any of the VAT thresholds outlined below are exceeded, or are likely to be exceeded, in a **twelve-month** period.

- **€37,500** for persons supplying **services.**
- **€75,000** for persons supplying **goods**, including persons supplying both goods and services, where **90% or more** of sales is derived from supplies of goods.
- **€37,500** for persons supplying goods liable at the 13.5% or 23% (21% 2011) rates which they have manufactured or produced from **zero rated** materials.
- **€35,000** for persons making mail order or distance sales into the State.

- **€41,000** for persons making intra-Community acquisitions.
- A **non-established** person supplying taxable goods or services in the State is **obliged** to register and account for VAT, **irrespective** of the level of turnover (i.e. **NIL thershold**).

For the purposes only of deciding if a person is obliged to register for VAT, the **actual turnover** may be **reduced** by an amount equivalent to the **VAT borne** on purchases of stock for resale. Therefore a trader, whose annual purchases of stock for resale are €61,000 (€49,593 plus €11,407 VAT at 23%) and whose actual turnover is €75,000 inclusive of VAT is not obliged to register. This is because the traders turnover, after deduction of the €11,407 VAT charged to him on purchases of stock, is below the registration limit of €75,000.

No threshold applies in the case of taxable services received from abroad and in the case of cultural, artistic, sporting, scientific, and educational or entertainment services received from a person **not established** in the State. All such services are liable to VAT on a reverse charge basis.

Suppliers of goods and services that are exempt from VAT and non-taxable entities, such as State bodies, charities, etc., are **obliged to register** for VAT where it is **likely** that they will acquire **more than** €41,000 of intra-Community acquisitions in any twelve-month period.

A taxable person established in the State is not required to register for VAT if his turnover does not reach the appropriate threshold above. However, he may **opt to register** for VAT.

Registration Procedure

Every applicant for VAT registration must complete either a **Form TR1** or **TR2**. Registration is effective from the date on which the application for registration is **processed**, or from such earlier date as may be agreed between Revenue and the applicant. In the case of a person not obliged to register but who is opting to do so, the effective date **will be not earlier** than the beginning of the taxable period during which the application is made.

A person who is setting up a business, but who has **not yet commenced** supplying taxable goods or services, **may** register for VAT as soon as it is clear that he will become a taxable person. This will enable him to obtain credit for VAT on purchases made before trading actually commences.

10.1.6   Group Registration

When a **group of persons**, such as a number of inter-linked companies, are registered for VAT, they may apply for group registration. This means that they are treated as a **single** taxable person. In these circumstances, only one member of the group will submit VAT returns for the taxable period and that return will include **all activities** of all members of the group.

All parties to the group are **jointly and severally liable** for all the VAT obligations of the other group members. The issue of tax invoices in respect of inter-group transactions is not required.

To qualify for group registration, the Revenue Commissioners must be satisfied that:

- no loss of VAT would be involved;
- the persons seeking the group registration are all established in the State;
- they are closely bound by financial, economic and organisational links; and
- it would be expedient, in the interest of efficient administration of VAT, to grant the group registration.

The granting of group registration is at the discretion of the Revenue Commissioners, and there is no right of appeal.

10.1.7 Returns and Payment of VAT

A VAT-registered person normally accounts for VAT on a two-monthly basis (January/February, March/April, etc.). The return is made on Form **VAT 3,** and this form, together with a payment for any VAT due, should be furnished electronically (through ROS) to the Collector General on or before the **23rd day** of the month following the **end** of the taxable period (e.g. a return for the VAT period January/February 2012 is due by 23 March 2012). The VAT return shows the **gross amount** of the tax due by the taxpayer, the amount of **input tax deductible** and the **net VAT due** to Revenue or **VAT refund** due to the trader.

In addition, traders are required to submit an **annual** "VAT Return of Trading Details" (Form RTD EUR) which gives details of purchases and sales for the year, broken down by VAT rates.

Payment of VAT

VAT is payable through ROS on or before the **23rd day** of the month following the **end** of the taxable period.

A trader may pay VAT by **direct debit** in monthly instalments. If a business is seasonal, a trader can vary the amounts paid each month to reflect cash flow. Where a trader pays his VAT liability by direct debit he is only required to make an **annual VAT3** return, together with the annual VAT Return of Trading Details. At the end of the year, if a shortfall arises, the balance must be included when submitting the annual return of trading (RTD EUR). Where insufficient amounts are paid by direct debit and, as a result, the **balance of tax payable** with the annual return is **more than 20% of the annual liability for VAT**, then a trader will be liable to an **interest charge** backdated to the mid point of the year.

VAT Returns on an Annual Basis

There is a provision whereby VAT can be returned and paid on an annual basis. Authorisation to do so is at the discretion of the Collector-General, and this authorisation may be terminated at any time. The VAT returns and payment must be submitted electronically to the Collector-General between the 10th and 23rd days of the month following the end of the year.

Interest on Late Payments of VAT

If VAT is not paid within the proper period, interest is chargeable (as a fiduciary tax) for each day at the rate of 0.0274% per day. This interest also applies where a refund of VAT has been made on the basis of an incorrect return, and where all or part of the tax refunded was not properly refundable. Where a person fails to make returns, Revenue are entitled to make estimates of tax payable and to recover the amount so estimated subject to the usual appeal procedures.

10.1.8 VAT Rates

Standard rate of VAT – 23%

This applies to all goods and services that are not exempt or liable at the zero or reduced rates. (effective 1 January 2012 – 21% 2011)

Reduced rate of VAT – 13.5%

Goods and services which attract VAT at 13.5% include bakery products (excluding bread), certain fuels, building services, newspapers, magazines and periodicals, repair, cleaning and maintenance services generally, holiday accommodation, certain photographic supplies, restaurant services, and provision of commercial sporting facilities, etc.

Reduced rate of VAT – 9%

A new temporary reduced rate of **VAT at 9%** was introduced in 2011 on the following services, with effect from **1 July 2011 until the end of December 2013:**

- Catering and restaurant supplies, including vending machines and take-away food (excluding alcohol and soft drinks sold as part of the meal).
- Hotel lettings, including guesthouses, caravan parks, camping sites etc.
- Cinemas, theatres, certain musical performances, museums, art gallery exhibitions, fairgrounds or amusement park services.
- Facilities for taking part in sporting activities, including green fees charged for golf and subscriptions charged by non-member-owned golf clubs.
- Printed matter, e.g. newspapers, brochures, leaflets, programmes, maps, catalogues, printed music (excluding books).
- Hairdressing services.

Reduced rate of VAT – 4.8%

This applies to livestock, live greyhounds and the hire of horses.

Farmer Flat Rate Addition – 5.2%

This applies to the sale of agricultural produce and services by non-registered farmers to VAT-registered persons.

Zero-rated goods and services

These include exports, certain food and drink, oral medicine, certain books, nursing home services, etc.

Exempted goods and services

These include financial, medical and educational activities.

A full list of applicable VAT rates is available at www.revenue.ie – *VAT Rate Subject Index.*

Difference between Exempt and Zero-rated

These terms appear to have the same meaning, but only to the extent that both exempt and zero rated supplies do not attract what is referred to as a positive rate of VAT. They are different, however, to the extent that a VAT-registered trader making zero-rated supplies (e.g. a book shop or food store) is entitled to a refund of VAT on the taxable business purchases (e.g. shop fittings, wrapping materials, cash registers, etc.) while normally a VAT exempt trader is **not entitled** to any refund of VAT on purchases in respect of the business. It is a crucial difference.

10.2 Supply of Goods/Services and Place of Supply

VAT becomes due, or a liability for VAT arises, at the time when a supply of goods or services takes place, or on receipt of payment, if an earlier date.

10.2.1 Supply of Goods

A taxable supply of goods means the **normal transfer of ownership** of goods (including developed property) by one person to another and includes the supply of goods liable to VAT at the zero rate. This includes:

- The transfer of ownership of goods by agreement.
- The sale of movable goods on a commission basis by an auctioneer or agent acting in his own name but on the instructions of another person.

■ The handing over of goods under a hire-purchase contract.

■ The handing over by a person to another person of immovable goods (property) which have been developed.

■ The seizure of goods by a sheriff or other person acting under statutory authority.

■ The application or appropriation **(self-supply)** by the taxable person of materials or goods to some private or exempt use, e.g. if a builder uses building materials to build or repair his private house this is a self-supply.

■ The provision of electricity, gas and any form of power, heat, refrigeration or ventilation.

■ With some exceptions, the transfer of goods from a business in the State by a taxable person to the territory of another Member State for the purposes of the business.

■ The transfer of ownership of immovable goods by way of very long leases is a supply of goods.

■ Gifts of taxable goods made in the course or furtherance of business are liable to VAT where the cost to the donor, excluding VAT, is €20 or **more**.

■ Where vouchers and tokens having a face value are supplied at a discount to an intermediary with a view to their ultimate re-sale to private consumers, such tokens or vouchers become liable to VAT at the standard rate of 23% at the time the consideration is received. VAT is also chargeable on the re-sale of the vouchers by the intermediary to the private customer.

A taxable supply is **not effected** where:

■ Gifts of taxable goods are made in the course or furtherance of business where the cost to the donor, excluding VAT, is €20 or **less**.

■ Advertising goods and industrial samples are given free to customers in reasonable quantities, in a form **not ordinarily available for sale** to the public, even where the €20 limit is exceeded.

■ Replacement goods are supplied free of charge in accordance with **warranties** or **guarantees** on the original goods.

■ Goods change ownership as **security** for a loan or debt.

■ A business is transferred from one taxable person to another.

■ Gift vouchers, etc. (other than vouchers sold to and by intermediaries) are sold **except** where the amount charged **exceed**s the value shown on the voucher. The supply of goods or services in exchange for such vouchers, tokens, etc. is liable at the rate appropriate to the goods or services supplied.

10.2.2 Supply of Services

For VAT purposes, a "service" is any commercial activity **other than** a supply of goods. Typical services include:

■ The services of caterers, mechanics, plumbers, accountants, solicitors, consultants, etc.

■ The hiring or leasing of goods.

■ The supply of digitised goods delivered on-line as well as the physical supply of customised software.

■ **Refraining** from doing something and the granting or surrendering of a right.

■ Contract work, i.e. the handing over by a contractor, to a customer, of movable goods made or assembled by him from goods entrusted to him by the customer.

■ A self-supply of a catering or canteen service (e.g. a vending machine).

Insurance agents, banking agents and certain related agents are **exempt** from VAT.

Services Taxable as Supplies of Goods (the "Two-thirds" Rule)

A transaction which may **appear** to be a **supply of a service** is nevertheless taxable as a **supply of goods** if the value of the goods (i.e. cost excluding VAT) used in carrying out the work **exceeds two-thirds** of the total charge, exclusive of VAT. For example, where the VAT exclusive cost of materials used by a plumber in the repair of a washing machine is €120, and the total charge for the repair work is €150, the 23% rate applicable to the materials applies, rather than the 13.5% rate which normally applies to repair services. The repair and maintenance of motor vehicles and agricultural machinery is **not subject** to the "two-thirds" rule.

The two-thirds rule does not apply where principal contractors operate the **reverse-charge** rule with sub-contractors (see **Section 10.8**) or, from **1 May 2012**, to supplies of construction services between **connected persons** to whom the reverse-charge rule for VAT applies from **1 May 2012 (section 74 FA 2012)**.

10.2.3 Place of Supply

Goods and services are liable to VAT **in the place where they are supplied** or deemed to be supplied. If the place of supply is outside or is deemed to be outside the State, then Irish VAT **does not** arise.

Place of Supply of Goods

The place of supply of goods is deemed to be as follows:

- If the supply requires their transportation, the place where the transportation **begins** is deemed to be the place of supply.
- Where goods are installed or assembled by or on behalf of the supplier, the place of supply is the place where the goods **are installed or assembled**. For example, a French-based company supplies and installs a machine in an Irish company's factory in the State. The place of supply is Ireland and the recipient Irish company self-accounts for the VAT on the supply and can claim a simultaneous input credit if the goods are used for the taxable business.
- Where goods are supplied on board **sea vessels, aircraft and trains** (during intra-Community transport) the place of supply is the place where the **transport begins** (e.g. a person buys goods on board the Dublin-Holyhead ferry which leaves from Dublin; the place of supply is the State and Irish VAT arises.
- In all other cases, the **location** of the goods at the time of supply determines the place of supply.

Distance Sales Rules

Distance sales into Ireland covers mail order and other distance sales to Irish **non-registered** customers, where the supplier is responsible for delivering the goods. Where the value of distance sales into the State **exceeds €35,000** in a calendar year, the **supplier** must **register** for VAT in the State.

Similar rules apply to Irish mail order businesses and other distance sellers supplying to non-registered individuals in other Member States. The Irish business must register in **each Member State** in which the sales threshold is **exceeded**. The threshold is €100,000 for Germany, France, Luxembourg, Netherlands, Austria and the United Kingdom and €35,000 for the other Member States.

Suppliers may opt to register in any State even if the annual thresholds are not exceeded.

Intra-community Acquisition of Goods

The basic rule is that the place where an intra-Community acquisition occurs is the Member State where the dispatch or transportation **ends** (see **Section 10.5**).

Place of Supply of Services

From 1 January 2010, there are two general "place of supply" rules, depending on whether the recipient is a **business** or a **consumer**:

- For supplies of **Business to Business** (B2B) services, the place of supply is the place where the **recipient is established** (reverse charge).
- For supplies of **Business to Consumer** (B2C) services, the place of supply is where the **supplier is established**.

Unless covered by an exception, the position is as follows:

- Service suppliers in the State must **not charge** VAT when supplying services to a **business** customer established **outside** Ireland.
- Service suppliers in the State must **charge** VAT to **non-business** customers **outside** Ireland. However, many services supplied from Ireland to non-business customers **outside** the EU will not be subject to Irish VAT.
- Businesses that **receive** services from a supplier **outside** Ireland will not be charged VAT by the supplier of those services but the recipient will be required to **account** for Irish VAT unless the services concerned are exempt in Ireland (and the business has notified its supplier that such services are exempt from Irish VAT).

For services received from abroad by a **Department of State, a local authority or a body established by statute in the State**, such entities will **not be liable** for Irish VAT in respect of the receipt of the foreign services such as consultancy services, legal services, etc., **except** where they act as **taxable persons**. The services should be taxed in the country from where they are supplied.

Summary of place of supply rules for services (unless subject to exceptions or effective use and enjoyment provisions)

Country of establishment of supplier	Country in which customer established	Place of supply	Person liable to account for Irish VAT
B2B			
Ireland	Other EU State	Other EU State	No Irish VAT
Ireland	Outside EU	Outside EU	No Irish VAT
Other EU State	Ireland	Ireland	Customer
Outside EU	Ireland	Ireland	Customer
B2C			
Ireland	Other EU State	Ireland	Supplier
Ireland	Outside EU	Depends on service	Supplier (if VAT occurs)
Other EU State	Ireland	Other EU State	No Irish VAT
Outside EU	Ireland	Depends on service	Supplier (if taxable in the State)

It should be noted that financial services supplied by a supplier in the State to a private individual from outside the EU who avails of them **here** are deemed to be supplied in the State.

Exceptions to the General Rules

There are a number of exceptions to the general rules that more closely **link** the place of supply to **where** the service is performed. Unless covered by a reverse charge arrangement, the supplier will be **required** to register and account for VAT in the **Member State of supply**.

The following table summarises the exceptions and sets out the current place of supply rule that applies from 1 January 2010 onwards.

Exceptions to VAT place of supply of services rules effective from 1 January 2010

Supply	Place of Supply
Supply of services connected with immovable goods (property) (B2B and B2C)	Place of supply is where the goods are located. *(When the service provider is outside Ireland and the work is carried out in Ireland, VAT is accounted for by the Irish business recipient on a reverse charge basis.)*
Passenger transport services (B2B and B2C)	Place of supply is where the passenger transport takes place.
Intra-Community transport of goods B2C	Place of supply is the place of departure.
Intra-Community transport of goods B2B	Place of supply is the place where the customer is established.
Ancillary transport services, valuations/work on movable property	Place of supply is where the services are physically carried out. *(Reverse charge for B2B)*
Restaurant and catering services	Place of supply is where the services are physically carried out.
Restaurant and catering services for consumption on board ships, planes and trains	Place of supply is point of departure.
Hiring out of means of transport (B2B and B2C)	For short-term hiring-out of means of transport, the place of supply is where the transport is put at the disposal of the customer. For long term hiring-out of means of transport, the place of supply follows the general rules. (Rules to change in 2013)

Note: There are to be changes to the rules for hiring out means of transport in 2013 and a significant change in 2015 to the place of supply for B2C services, which will shift the place of taxation from the place of the supplier to the place of the customer.

Cultural, Artistic, Sporting, Scientific, Educational, Entertainment or Similar Events and Services – Changes Effective from 1 January 2011

A clear distinction is made between the **provision** of a cultural, artistic, sporting, scientific, educational, entertainment or similar **service** and the **admission** to a cultural, artistic, etc. **event**.

Provision of a Cultural, Artistic, etc. Service
■ Where the supply of the services is to a business customer (B2B), the place of supply is where the business customer is established. The customer must self-account for the VAT on the reverse-charge basis.

- Where the supply of the service is to a non-business customer (B2C), the place of supply is where the suppler is established, and the supplier charges VAT to the customer at the appropriate rate.

Admission to a Cultural, Artistic, etc. Event

For both business (B2B) and non-business (B2C) customers, the place of supply of the right of **admission** to cultural, artistic, sporting, scientific, educational, entertainment, or similar events, and services ancillary to the admission, is where the **event actually takes place**. Charges for admission to such an event in Ireland will be liable to Irish VAT, **regardless** of whether the person paying the admission is a taxable person or a non-taxable person. Thus, a taxable person from outside the State, attending an event in Ireland, will pay Irish VAT on the admission charge and will not, if he/she is established in the EU, account for the VAT due on reverse charge basis in his/her own Member State.

Use and Enjoyment Provisions

The purpose of the use and enjoyment rules is to prevent double taxation, non-taxation or distortions of competition and to better reflect the place where service is actually received (which, in turn, is the place of taxation).

The section covers two types of situations:

- The place of supply of services provided in the State but effectively **used and enjoyed outside** the EU is deemed to be outside the EU.
- The place of supply of services provided by persons **established outside** the EU but effectively used and enjoyed **in the State** is deemed to be the State.

There are a number of areas specifically covered in section 35 VATCA 2010:

- The hiring out of movable goods – if the actual place of supply is outside the EU but the goods are used and enjoyed in the State, the place of supply is deemed to be the State.
- The hiring out of means of transport – if the actual place of supply is in the State but the goods are used and enjoyed outside the EU, the place of supply is deemed to be outside EU.
- B2C supplies of telecommunications, radio/television broadcasting or phone card – if the actual place of supply is outside the EU but the services are used and enjoyed in the State, the place of supply is deemed to be the State.
- B2C supplies of financial and insurance services, including reinsurance and financial fund management (but excluding the provision of safe deposit facilities) – if the actual place of supply is outside the EU but the services are used and enjoyed in the State, the place of supply is deemed to be the State.
- Money transfer services supplied to persons in the State by an intermediary on behalf of a principal established outside the EU – if the actual place of supply is outside the EU but the services are used and enjoyed in the State, the place of supply is deemed to be the State.

10.3 Amount on which VAT is Chargeable

10.3.1 General

In the case of the supply of goods or services and the intra-Community acquisition of goods, the amount on which VAT is chargeable is normally the **total sum** paid or payable to the person supplying the goods or services including all taxes, commissions, costs and charges whatsoever but **not including** the VAT chargeable in respect of the transaction. However, **section 38 VATCA 2010** introduces an anti-avoidance measure, which states that the **Revenue** may determine that the **value** on which tax is charged in relation to certain transactions **between connected persons** is the **open market value**.

10.3.2 Other

(a) Imports

VAT on imports is charged on the cost, **plus** transport cost, **plus** duty payable of the goods (customs value).

(b) Goods/Services Supplied otherwise than for Money

Where a customer agrees to pay the supplier in kind, the amount on which VAT is chargeable is the **open market** or arm's length value of the goods or services supplied.

In the UK case of *Boots Company plc v. ECJ*, it was decided that money off vouchers which were given to customers by Boots to enable them to buy other products at a discount did not form part of the consideration for the purchase.

(c) Credit Card Transactions

The taxable amount is the total amount actually charged to the customer by the trader. Any amount withheld by the credit card companies from their settlement with the trader forms part of the taxable amount.

(d) Special Schemes

Special schemes operate in relation to the sale by dealers and auctioneers of second-hand movable goods, works of art, collector's items and antiques. The principal feature of the schemes is that dealers and auctioneers effectively pay VAT only on their margin in certain circumstances.

A **special scheme** also operates in relation to the VAT treatment of second-hand motor vehicles. **Prior to 1 January 2010,** when a dealer purchased second-hand cars and agricultural machinery (including trade-ins), the dealer was entitled to take a credit for the imputed VAT and when the car or machinery was sold he had to account for VAT on the full price. **FA 2010** provides for the cessation of this scheme **from 1 July 2010** (with provisional arrangements for the period 1 January 2010 to 30 June 2010) whereby the dealer will account for VAT under the **margin scheme, i.e. the dealer will only account for the VAT on the margin or profit**. There will be no deemed input credit.

(e) New Motor Vehicles

The amount on which VAT is chargeable on a new motor vehicle is normally the price of the vehicle **before** Vehicle Registration Tax (VRT) is applied.

(f) Intra-community Services

The amount on which VAT is chargeable in relation to intra-Community services received from abroad will normally be the **amount payable** in respect of those services.

(g) Packaging and Containers

When goods are supplied packed for sale and **no separate charge** is made for the packaging in which the goods are contained, the rate of VAT chargeable is that **applying to the goods.** If containers are charged for **separately** from the goods, the transaction is regarded as consisting of separate sales of goods and of packages and **each** such **separate sale** is chargeable at the appropriate rate.

Where containers are returnable and a separate charge in the nature of a deposit is included on an invoice, the containers are regarded as being the property of the supplier and the **deposit** is **not** subject to VAT. VAT **is** payable on the value of containers which are **not returned** to the supplier. This VAT may be accounted for at the time when the containers account is being balanced and a charge is being raised by the supplier against the customer for the value of containers not returned.

(h) Postage and Insurance

Where a separate charge is made for postage and insurance and paid over in its **entirety** to the carrier or to the insurer on behalf of customers, suppliers may treat such charges as not being subject to VAT. If, for example, a trader charges an extra €1 for posting an order and such amount of postage is actually paid over, the €1 may be treated as exempt. Similarly, if a car hire company charges €50 for motor insurance, and that amount is actually paid over in full to insurers in the name of the lessee, the €50 may be treated as exempt. However, if a charge is made for posting and/or insurance, and a **lesser amount** is paid over by the supplier to the carrier or the insurer, the charge made to the customer is regarded as part of the total price of the goods/service supplied, and is subject to the VAT rate applicable to the goods/service in question.

(i) Mixed Transactions (Package Rule)

A "package" comprises of two or more elements that attract different VAT rates.

Composite Supply

Where there is a **principal element** and an **ancillary supply** (e.g. a story book and accompanying cassette), the VAT rate is that attaching to the principal element (i.e. the story book).

Multiple Supply

Where a number of supplies are **grouped together** for a single **overall** consideration, the consideration should be apportioned between the various supplies and taxed at the appropriate VAT rate.

(j) Bad Debts

Relief for VAT on bad debts is allowed, subject to Revenue's agreement, where bad debts have been written off after VAT has been accounted for on the supply.

10.3.3 Deductible VAT

In computing the amount of VAT payable in respect of a taxable period, a registered person may **deduct** the VAT charged on most goods and services which are used for the purposes of his **taxable business.** To be entitled to the deduction, the trader must have a proper VAT invoice or relevant customs receipt as appropriate.

While a deduction of VAT is allowable only on purchases which are for the purposes of a taxable business, a situation may arise where a **portion** of a trader's purchases may be for the purposes of the taxable business and the remaining portion for the trader's **private use** (e.g. electricity, telephone charges, heating expenses, etc. where the business is carried on from his private residence). It may also arise that inputs may be used for **both taxable and non-taxable** activities. In such cases, only the amount of VAT, **which is appropriate to the taxable business,** is deductible. Similarly where a trader engages in both taxable and exempt activities (dual-use inputs), it will be necessary to **apportion the credit** in respect of these dual-use inputs.

In general, VAT is deductible against a taxable person's liability in any of the following situations:

■ VAT charged to a taxable person by other taxable persons on supplies of goods (including fixed assets) and services to him.

■ VAT paid by the taxable person on goods imported by him.

■ VAT payable on self-supplies of goods and services provided that the self-supplies are for business purposes.

■ VAT payable on purchases from flat rate farmers.

■ VAT on intra-Community acquisitions.

- VAT payable under **reverse-charge rules** provided the goods or services are used for the purposes of his taxable business (e.g. goods which are installed or assembled in the State by a foreign supplier, etc.)
- **Qualifying Vehicles – section 62 VATCA 2010** allows any VAT-registered trader (other than motor dealers, car-hire companies, driving schools etc.) to recover **20%** of the VAT charged on the purchase or hire of vehicles **coming within VRT Category A**, subject to the following conditions:

  - The vehicle must have been registered on or after **1 January 2009**;
  - A maximum of **20% of the VAT** incurred on the cost or on the monthly hire/lease charge can be reclaimed;
  - VAT can only be reclaimed for vehicles that have a level of CO_2 emissions of less than 156g/km (i.e. CO_2 emission bands A, B and C);
  - At least **60%** of the vehicle's use must be for business purposes;
  - If the business is exempt from VAT (e.g. taxi, limousine and other passenger transport) then no VAT can be reclaimed. Partly exempt businesses can reclaim some, but not all, of the 20%;
  - If VAT is reclaimed on a vehicle purchased under this provision, some or all of the VAT must be repaid to Revenue if the vehicle is disposed of within **two years**;
  - There is no need to charge VAT on the disposal of the vehicle, even though VAT was reclaimed under this provision;
  - If the vehicle is sold or traded-in to a motor-dealer, the margin scheme for second-hand vehicles will apply.

10.3.4 Non-deductible VAT

No deduction is allowed in respect of VAT paid on expenditure on any of the following:

- The provision of food, drink, accommodation or other personal services supplied to the taxable person, his agent, or his employees, **except** to the extent that the provision of such services represents a taxable supply by the taxable person. For example where a hotel incurs expense in providing accommodation for its own employees, this would be a taxable supply and the VAT arising would be a deductible input. Note that **FA 2007** (effective 1 July 2007) allows a taxable person to claim VAT on "**qualifying accommodation**" in connection with the **attendance** at a "**qualifying conference**" by the taxable person or his representative. **FA 2012** amended **section 66(5) VATCA 2010** to remove the deductibility of VAT on conference accommodation where it was supplied under the Travel Agent Margin Scheme (TAMS). Where the accommodation is supplied and invoiced directly, the current right to a deduction for the VAT continues to apply.
- Entertainment expenses incurred by the taxable person, his agent or his employees.
- The acquisition, hiring or leasing of motor vehicles that are not "qualifying vehicles" (as above), **other** than as stock-in-trade or for the purpose of a business which consists, in whole or in part, of the hiring of motor vehicles, or for use in a driving school business for giving driving instruction.
- The purchase of petrol **otherwise** than as stock-in-trade.
- Expenditure incurred on food, drink, accommodation or other entertainment service, as part of an advertising service, is not deductible in the hands of the person providing the advertising service.
- VAT in respect of goods or services used by the taxable person for the purposes of an exempt activity or for the purposes of an activity not related to his business.

10.4 Cash Receipts Basis

VAT registered traders normally become liable for VAT at the time of the **issue** of **sales invoices** to their customers **regardless** of whether they have received payment for the supplies made. Accordingly, a trader must include in his January/February 2012 VAT return VAT on **all sales invoices issued** during January and February 2012. This is known as the **invoice basis of accounting** for VAT. Under the cash receipts basis of accounting, traders **do not** become liable for VAT until they have actually **received payment** for the goods or services supplied.

The cash receipts basis **does not apply** to transactions between **connected** persons. VAT on such transactions must be accounted for on the normal invoice basis. VAT on **property transactions** must always be accounted for on an invoice basis.

A trader who opts for the cash receipts basis of accounting is liable for VAT at the **rate ruling at the time the supply is made** rather than the rate ruling at the time payment is received.

For example, Joe, a trader operating under the cash receipts basis, made a supply of goods in December 2011 when the higher rate of VAT was 21%. He received payment of €1,000 for those goods in January 2012 when the higher rate had changed to 23%. Joe accounts for the VAT on the supply at 21% (i.e. €1,000 × 21/121 = €173.55) in his January/February 2012 VAT return.

In addition, where such a trader receives a payment from which PSWT or RCT has been deducted, the trader is deemed to have received the **gross amount due** and is liable to pay the **full amount** of the VAT due. For example, if an architect receives a payment of €800, being €1,000 less PSWT at 20%, he is deemed to have received €1,000 and must account for VAT on this amount.

Traders who opt for the cash receipts basis of accounting must **issue credit notes** for all discounts given to suppliers to ensure that a greater amount of VAT is not claimed by the purchaser than is paid by the supplier.

It should be noted that the cash receipts basis of accounting **only applies to sales and supplies** and VAT on purchases is still claimed on an invoice basis.

Entitlement to Cash Receipts Basis

The cash receipts basis of accounting for VAT may be used by traders engaged in the supply of taxable goods or services if:

- at least **90%** of the supplies are to **unregistered** persons; *or*
- the trader's turnover is not likely to **exceed €1 million** per annum (effective 1 March 2007).

Formal Election

Any VAT-registered trader who finds that he is eligible to use this basis of accounting and wishes to use it should apply to the local Revenue district for authority to do so. Traders may not change from the invoice basis of accounting to the cash receipts basis, or vice versa, without such authority.

Traders who are applying for VAT registration for the first time, and find that they are eligible for the cash receipts basis, should indicate in the appropriate box on the application form (TR1 or TR2) whether or not they wish to use it.

Change of Basis of Accounting

A trader who has been accounting for VAT on the cash receipts basis and now wishes to revert to the invoice basis (or who ceases to trade) will have to make an adjustment where a trader was authorised to account for VAT on the cash receipts basis, the adjustment for the VAT due must be made by reference to the **VAT due on outstanding debtors**.

10.5   Intra-Community Supplies of Goods and Services

10.5.1   Introduction

Following the introduction of the **Single Market** on 1 January 1993, the way in which VAT was charged on goods moving between EU Member States was changed.

The concept of import and export was **abolished** for such trade and replaced by a system of **intra-Community supply and acquisition** of goods. While the VAT treatment of most services supplied to traders in other Member States did not change, there were important changes relating to intra-Community goods transport and related services.

10.5.2   VAT on Purchases from Other EU Countries

VAT is **no longer** payable at the **point of entry** on goods imported from another Member State.

The treatment for **VAT** on **purchases** varies, depending on the taxable status of the purchaser.

(a) VAT Registered Traders

When an Irish trader purchases goods from a supplier in a Member State and these are dispatched to him in the State, the trader must provide the supplier with his Irish VAT number. Upon receipt and verification of this number, the supplier will zero-rate the goods in question. The trader then:

- becomes liable for VAT on the acquisition of the goods;
- declares a liability for the VAT in the VAT return;
- claims a **simultaneous input credit,** thus **cancelling** the liability (assuming the trader is entitled to full deductibility); and
- accounts for VAT on any subsequent supply of the goods in the normal manner.

Example

A shipment of wood is sold by a VAT registered trader in France to a VAT registered business in Ireland for €10,000, and delivered from France to Ireland by the supplier. The supply is charged at the zero rate out of France. The Irish company would then self-account for Irish VAT on the acquisition of the wood as follows:

		€
VAT on sales €10,000 @ 23%	=	2,300
VAT on purchases @ 23%	=	(2,300)

There is no net effect on the VAT liability since the VAT on the wood is recoverable by the trader.

Contrast this with a situation where the same trader buys a motor car in France for €10,000 and it is delivered from France to Ireland by the supplier. The supply is charged at the zero rate out of France.

The Irish company would then self-account for Irish VAT on the acquisition of the car as follows:

		€
VAT on sales €10,000 @ 23%	=	2,300
VAT on purchases	=	(0)
(assuming the car is not a "qualifying vehicle")		

In this scenario, the trader is not allowed to claim VAT on motor cars and there is a VAT liability on the transaction as a result.

(b) **Unregistered Traders**

Traders who are not registered for VAT in the State must pay VAT on their intra-Community purchases in the Member State of **purchase** at the VAT rate applicable there. Where the threshold of **€41,000** in respect of intra-Community acquisitions **is exceeded**, the trader must register for VAT in Ireland and account for the VAT in the manner described at (a) above.

(c) **Non-taxable Entities/Exempted Activities**

In the case of non-taxable entities such as Government Departments and exempted activities such as insurance companies or banks, VAT is payable in the Member State of purchase at the VAT rate applicable there. Again, if the threshold of **€41,000** in respect of intra-Community acquisitions **is exceeded**, the entity must register for VAT in Ireland and account for the VAT in the manner described at (a) above. However, as their activities are non-taxable/exempt, these entities **cannot claim input credits** and no Irish VAT is chargeable on a subsequent sale.

(d) **Purchases by Private Individuals**

The private individual pays the VAT charged by the supplier in the Member State and no additional Irish VAT liability will arise. This does not apply to **new** means of transport, e.g. boats, planes, motor cars. These items are liable to VAT in the Member State of the **purchaser**.

Where a private individual purchases goods through **mail order,** he must pay the VAT applicable in the **place of purchase** (e.g. goods purchased by mail order in Germany will be subject to German VAT).

10.5.3   VAT on Sales to Other EU Countries

The treatment for **VAT on sales** varies depending on the **taxable status** of the customer:

(a) **VAT Registered Customers**

Where a taxable person in Ireland **sells or supplies** goods to a VAT registered trader within the EU, the transaction will be **zero-rated** in Ireland and will be liable to foreign VAT in the Member State of the purchaser.

A VAT registered trader in the State may zero-rate the supply of goods to a customer in another EU Member State if:

- the customer is registered for VAT in the other EU Member State;
- the customer's VAT registration number (including country prefix) is obtained and retained in the supplier's records;
- this number, together with the supplier's VAT registration number, is quoted on the sales invoice; and
- the goods are dispatched or transported to that, or any other, EU Member State.

Where any of the above four conditions are not satisfied, the Irish supplier should charge Irish VAT at the appropriate Irish VAT rate (i.e. as if the sale had taken place between two Irish traders). If the conditions for zero-rating are subsequently established, the customer is entitled to recover the VAT paid from the supplier. The supplier can then make an adjustment in his/her VAT return for the period.

(b) **Unregistered Customers**

Where the customer is unregistered, the Irish supplier should charge Irish VAT. If their sales in the customer's home country are above the VAT registration threshold in that country, they will be obliged to register for VAT in that country and charge local VAT to their customers there.

10.5.4 VIES and INTRASTAT

VIES (VAT Information Exchange System)

When an Irish VAT-registered trader makes **zero-rated supplies** of goods to a trader in another EU Member State, summary details of those **sales** must be returned to Revenue on a quarterly or monthly basis. This return, known as the VIES return, is to enable the authorities in each EU Member State to ensure that intra-Community transactions are properly recorded and accounted for. The VIES return is made to the VAT Authorities in the **Member State of the exporter** and contains the following:

- The VAT number of each foreign Member State customer (this number can be verified with the Irish Revenue), and
- The total € value of sales to each customer in the quarterly (or monthly) period.

The return must be submitted by the 23rd day of the month following the end of the period covered by the return.

Section 83 VATCA 2011 stipulates that, from **1 January 2010, supplies of services** must now be **included** in VIES returns. **Monthly** VIES statements became **mandatory from 1 January 2010** where intra-Community supplies of goods **exceed €100,000** in any of the previous four quarters. This threshold is reduced to €50,000 from 1 January 2012. Irish VAT registered suppliers whose intra-Community supplies do not exceed the threshold may report **quarterly**.

Note: Where a trader has no exports to another Member State in a particular period, an "NIC" statement must be submitted for that period.

INTRASTAT VAT Return

This return system is designed to ensure that all **statistical data** relating to purchases and sales of goods (not services) between Member States continues to be available to each Member State and the EU Commission. Depending on the level of intra-Community trade carried out by each taxable person, there are two methods of making the necessary returns:

1. Where a trader's **acquisitions** from other EU Member States **do not exceed €191,000 annually** and the value of goods **supplied** to other EU Member States **does not exceed €635,000 annually**, then the appropriate disclosure can be made by way of the revised normal VAT 3 return. This form contains two boxes in which the trader inserts the value of exports and imports arising in the period covered by the VAT 3 return.
2. Where the €191,000/€635,000 limits are **exceeded**, then an **INTRASTAT** return, **in addition** to the normal VAT 3 return, must be prepared.

Where a trader **exceeds both limits**, then a separate INTRASTAT return must be prepared (in addition to the normal VAT 3 return) in respect of **both** exports and imports.

The INTRASTAT must be submitted to the Revenue not later than the 23rd day of the calendar month following the end of the month to which the return relates.

Category of Trader	VIES	INTRASTAT
Traders who **sell** to EU Member States	Complete VIES statement (Quarterly or monthly, annually in limited cases)	If value of sales outwards exceeds **€635,000** annually, complete a detailed INTRASTAT monthly return
Traders who **purchase** from EU Member States.	Do not complete (VIES statement applies only to exports)	If value of purchases inwards exceeds **€191,000** annually, complete a detailed INTRASTAT monthly return
	A 'Nil' declaration must be made where appropriate for a particular period.	

The information to be included in an INTRASTAT return includes:

1. Trader's name and address
2. Commodity code
3. Country of origin
4. Mode of transport
5. Nature of transaction
6. Invoice value (rounded to €)
7. Delivery terms
8. Statistical value
9. Nett mass in Kgs
10. Quantity

See Revenue's detailed **VIES and INTRASTAT Traders Manual** at www.revenue.ie

10.6 Imports/Exports from/to Non-EU Countries

10.6.1 Imports from Non-EU Countries

For VAT purposes, "imports" are goods arriving from non-EU countries. In this context, it should be noted that certain other territories (e.g. the Canary Islands and Channel Islands) are regarded as not being part of the EU for VAT purposes, and some other territories are (e.g. Monaco and the Isle of Man).

VAT is due at the **point of entry** on imports.

■ VAT is charged **at the same rate** as applies to the sale of the particular goods within the State and is charged at the point of importation. Zero-rated/exempt goods therefore attract no liability on importation.

■ VAT is payable **before** the imported goods are released by the Customs Authorities, unless the importer is approved for the Deferred Payments Scheme.

■ Eligibility under the **Deferred Payments Scheme** will permit payment of the VAT liability in respect of the goods on the **15th day** of the month **following** the month in which the VAT becomes due. Importers wishing to participate in the Deferred Payments Scheme must make an application to the appropriate Collector of Customs & Excise. Under the scheme, the Customs & Excise Authorities are authorised by the importer to initiate payment of the VAT by the issue of a direct debit voucher drawn on the debtor's bank. To qualify for this scheme, the importer must be able to obtain a guarantee from his bank that the VAT liability demanded for imports will be paid to the Customs Collector.

■ The **value** of imported goods for the purposes of assessment to VAT is their **value for Customs purposes**, determined on a delivery to State basis, together with any taxes, duties, and other charges levied inside the State on the goods, but not including VAT.

■ A VAT-registered person who imports goods during a taxable period is entitled to **claim credit** in their VAT returns for that period for the VAT paid or payable in respect of the goods imported. A taxable person who qualifies under the Deferred Payment Scheme and who imports goods on, say, 26 February, will pay VAT on 15 March and will recover the VAT on 23 March (date of VAT payment for Jan/Feb VAT return).

■ VAT-registered persons who are in a **permanent repayment position** as a result of VAT paid at the point of importation may be permitted to make **monthly** returns.

■ Goods imported into the Shannon Customs Free Airport from outside the State are not liable to VAT.

■ Manufacturers who **export 75%** or more of their produce are allowed to import raw materials and components (but not plant and machinery) **without** payment of VAT at the point of importation (**traders with 13A authorisation – see below**).

Example:
A car is imported into Ireland from Japan. VAT is charged at the point of entry on the total cost price including all applicable taxes and duties at the rate of VAT appropriate to the car.

Customs duty and VAT must be paid before the car will be released by Customs unless the Deferred Payment Scheme applies or a 13A authorisation is held.

10.6.2 Exports to Non-EU Countries

For VAT purposes, "exports" are goods directly dispatched to a destination **outside the EU**. In this context, it should be noted that, for VAT purposes, certain territories (e.g. the Canary Islands and the Channel Islands) are regarded as outside the EU.

The **zero rate** of VAT applies to **all exports**. A number of export type transactions and related services are also zero-rated, as are supplies of goods to VAT-registered traders in the Shannon Customs Free Airport.

A VAT-registered trader who supplies goods to the domestic market and **also** exports goods is entitled to an **input credit** or deduction for VAT invoiced to him on purchases for **both domestic and export sales**. The credit may be taken against the VAT liability on domestic sales. Normally a trader established in the State is not entitled to receive, from another VAT-registered trader, taxable goods free of VAT on the grounds that the goods are intended for export. However, see below for an exception to this rule under the **VAT 13A Scheme**. Traders who by virtue of the level of their exports are in a permanent repayment position may arrange with the Revenue to submit monthly returns to facilitate earlier repayment of input VAT.

Example:
A computer is made in Ireland and exported to the US. The place of supply is Ireland, and the supply is charged at the zero rate.

Zero-rating Under the VAT 13A Scheme

This scheme provides that a trader who derives **not less than 75%** of his annual turnover from supplies of goods out of the State can apply to Revenue to have most goods and services supplied to him and intra-Community acquisitions and imports made by him zero-rated. Revenue issue a certificate, usually for a two-year period, which is sent to all suppliers in order that purchase invoices are zero-rated. The zero-rating does not apply to the supply or hire of any passenger motor vehicles, the supply of petrol, and the provision of services consisting of the supply of food, drink, accommodation, entertainment or other personal services and other non-deductible purchases.

10.7 VAT Records

10.7.1 Records to be Maintained

A VAT-registered trader must keep **full records** of all transactions that affect his liability to VAT. The records must be kept up to date and be sufficiently detailed to enable a trader to accurately calculate liability or repayment and also to enable the Revenue to check the calculations, if necessary.

Purchases Records

The purchases records should **distinguish** between purchases of goods for **resale** and goods or services **not for resale** in the ordinary course of business. The records should show the date of the purchase invoice and a consecutive number (in the order in which the invoices are filed), the name of the supplier, the cost **exclusive** of VAT and the amount of VAT. Purchases at **each rate** must be recorded **separately**. The same information should be recorded in respect of imports, intra-Community acquisitions and services received.

Sales Records

The sales records must include the amount charged in respect of every sale to a registered person and a daily entry of the total amount charged in respect of sales to unregistered persons, **distinguishing in all cases** between transactions liable at each **different VAT rate** (including the zero rate) and **exempt** transactions. All such entries should be cross-referenced to relevant invoices, sales dockets, cash register tally rolls, delivery notes etc. Traders who are authorised to account for VAT on the cash receipts basis are also obliged to retain all documents they use for the purposes of their business.

Persons involved in intra-Community trade also have requirements in relation to retention of records as regards certain transfers of goods to other Member States.

10.7.2 Retention of Records

A taxable person **must retain** all books, records and documents relevant to the business, including invoices, credit and debit notes, receipts, accounts, cash register tally rolls, vouchers, VIES and INTRASTAT returns, stamped copies of customs entries and other import documents and bank statements. These business records must be retained for **six years** from the date of the latest transaction to which they refer, unless written permission from the Revenue has been obtained for their retention for a shorter period.

10.7.3 Information to be Included on VAT Invoices/Credit Notes

The Revenue imposes strict requirements on the information given on invoices and credit notes. This information establishes the VAT **liability** of the supplier of goods or services and the **entitlement** of the customer to an **input deduction** for the VAT charged.

Traders who issue invoices and credit notes, and persons to whom these documents are issued, should ensure that the documents **accurately represent** the transactions to which they refer. For example, if an incorrect rate of VAT is used on an invoice, both the supplier and the customer are liable for VAT at the correct rate, unless the supplier has **overcharged** VAT and is therefore liable for the total amount of VAT invoiced.

Form of VAT Invoice/Credit Note

A taxable person who supplies taxable goods or services to **another taxable person** is obliged to issue a VAT invoice showing the following:

- Name and address of the trader issuing the invoice;
- Trader's VAT registration number;
- Name and address of the customer;
- Date of issue of the invoice;

- Date of supply of the goods or services;
- Full description of the goods or services;
- Quantity or volume and unit price of the goods or services supplied;
- The amount charged **exclusive** of VAT (in €);
- The rate (including zero rate) and amount of VAT at each rate;
- The total invoice/credit note amount exclusive of VAT (in €).
- A trader who makes zero-rated intra-Community supplies is obliged, in addition to the above, to show the **VAT registration number of the customer** in the other EU Member State.

A taxable person is not required to issue a VAT invoice to an unregistered person, but may do so if he so wishes. If a VAT invoice is required to be issued, it must be issued **within 15 days** of the end of the month in which goods or services are supplied. Where payment in full is made **before** the completion of the supply, the person receiving payment must also issue an invoice within 15 days of the end of the month in which the **payment** was **received**.

10.7.4 Allowances/Discounts, etc.

When the amount of VAT payable as shown on an invoice is reduced because of an allowance or discount or similar adjustment, the trader who issued the VAT invoice must issue a credit note stating the amount of the reduction in the price and the appropriate VAT. This trader may then reduce his VAT liability by the amount credited in the accounting period in which the credit note is issued. Likewise, the customer or recipient of the credit note must increase his VAT liability by the same amount. All credit notes must contain a reference to the corresponding invoices.

Where a VAT-registered supplier and a VAT-registered customer **agree** in respect of a transaction **not to make any change** in the VAT shown on the original invoice, even though the price charged may subsequently be reduced, there is **no obligation** to issue a credit note in respect of the VAT. Such a practice saves trouble for both seller and purchaser. For example, if the discount taken by the purchaser is only on the goods, and the amount of VAT originally invoiced is allowed to stand, no adjustment for VAT is necessary and a VAT credit note is not required.

10.8 VAT Reverse Charge

Under the VAT reverse-charge rules, it is the **receiver** of the relevant supply and **not the supplier** who accounts for and pays over the VAT to the Revenue.

Under Section 16 VATCA 2010, VAT reverse charge applies to:

- NAMA and any NAMA entity;
- a taxable person in receipt of greenhouse gas emission allowances;
- a principal contractor in receipt of construction operations from a subcontractor subject to RCT;
- a taxable person dealing in scrap metal; and
- a taxable person in receipt of construction services from an accountable person who is **connected** to the taxable person **(FA 2012)** – effective from **1 May 2012**.

Procedures under VAT Reverse-charge Rule
- The supplier issues the recipient a reverse charge invoice that includes all of the information required on a VAT invoice, except the VAT rate and the VAT amount. It also includes an indication that it is the recipient who is accountable for the VAT.

- If there is prior agreement between the supplier and the recipient, the recipient may issue the reverse charge invoice, subject to agreed procedures being in place for the acceptance by the supplier of the validity of the invoice (e.g. invoice is signed by both parties).
- The recipient does not pay the VAT to the supplier but, instead, accounts for it in the VAT return for the relevant period in VAT on Sales (T1).
- The recipient can claim a simultaneous input credit in VAT on Purchases (T2) for that VAT if he has valid documentation and would have been entitled to an input credit if that VAT had been charged by the supplier.
- The recipient pays the supplier for the VAT-exclusive value of the supply, less RCT if applicable.

Example 1:

Allen Ltd is renovating a factory building for a manufacturing company. Allen Ltd invoices the manufacturing company in October 2012 as follows:

	€
Construction services	740,740
VAT @13.5%	100,000
Total	840,740

These services do not come within the reverse charge since Allen Ltd is not a sub-contractor to the manufacturing company for RCT purposes.

Burke, a building contractor, supplies services to Allen Ltd. Allen Ltd is the principal contractor and Burke is the sub-contractor.

Burke incurred €13,000 VAT on purchases in September/October 2012 for the purposes of his business.

Burke charges Allen Ltd €600,000 in September 2012 for the building services. Burke does not charge any VAT on this amount.

Allen Ltd VAT Return

Allen Ltd accounts for the VAT on the construction services from Burke. VAT chargeable on the services is €600,000 @13.5% = €81,000.

As the construction services provided by the sub-contractor to the principal were invoiced during September/October 2012, the VAT on these services is accounted for by reverse charge.

In its September/October 2012 VAT return Allen Ltd includes VAT €181,000 as VAT on sales (i.e. VAT on its own sales of €100,000 plus reverse charge VAT €81,000 on services received from Burke).

Allen Ltd can claim input credit for €81,000 reverse charge VAT in the same return.

Allen Ltd should pay Revenue €100,000.

Allen Ltd notifies Revenue of the gross payment to Burke (Payment Notification) online. Revenue issues a Deduction Authorisation, which states that RCT @ 35% should be deducted from the payment.

Allen Ltd should deduct RCT from the payment due to Burke (amount deducted €600,000 @ 35% = €210,000) and pay Burke net €390,000.

Burke's VAT Return

Burke does not account for VAT on the services supplied to Allen Ltd. As Burke only does work for a principal contractor, his VAT on sales figure is nil.

Burke is entitled to his input credit of €13,000.

He is entitled to a repayment of €13,000.

Example 2:

Axel Ltd supplies scrap metal to Breakers Ltd for €1,000 (excl. VAT). Both companies are registered for VAT.

Axel Ltd raises an invoice (or, if agreed, Breakers Ltd may raise the invoice), which shows that the recipient (Breakers Ltd) is accountable for the VAT. The VAT amount or rate is not shown on the invoice.

Breakers Ltd calculates the VAT (€1,000 × 23% = €230) and accounts for it in the VAT return for that period as VAT on Sales (T1). Breakers Ltd, subject to deductibility rules, can claim input credit, in the same return for that VAT (T2).

Questions (Chapter 10)

(See Solutions to Questions at the end of this text.)

10   Value Added Tax (VAT)

10.1   Registration and Information

Requirement

For VAT purposes, outline:

(a) the criteria for determining the obligation to register, and

(b) the records to be maintained and the information required to complete a return form.

10.2   Tax Point

Requirement

Outline the VAT rules for determining the tax point or time when a supply of goods or services is treated as taking place.

10.3   Records and Payment

Michael, a friend of yours, has recently set up business in Ireland selling computers. He has already registered for VAT.

Requirement

You are required to advise Michael on:

(a) what records he should keep for VAT purposes in relation to purchases and sales; and

(b) when VAT returns and related VAT payments should be returned to the Revenue Commissioners and what the consequences will be if he defaults.

10.4   John Hardiman

John Hardiman's business consists partly of the supply of VAT exempt services and partly of services liable to VAT at 23%. He is authorised by the Revenue Commissioners to account for VAT on the cash receipts basis (money received basis).

John's records for the VAT period September/October 2012 provide the following information:

(1) Sales and cash receipts:	€
Sales of services at 23% VAT (gross)	24,000
Sales of services exempt from VAT	2,000
Cash receipts relating to sales of services at 23% VAT (gross)	30,250
Cash receipts relating to sales of exempt services	3,000

(2) Purchases   €
    Purchases of goods and services at 23% VAT (gross)   6,150
    Purchases of goods and services at 13.5% VAT (gross)   2,270

(3) It has been agreed with the Revenue Commissioners that 10% of John's input credits relate to his exempt activities.

(4) Included in the purchases figures at (2) above are the following items:
    (i)   An invoice for the servicing of his motor car amounting to €160 plus VAT at 13.5%. It has been agreed with the Revenue Commissioners that the private use of his car is 25%.
    (ii) An invoice for the lease of the motor car referred to in (i) above. The invoice is for €300 plus VAT at 23%. The car is a "qualifying vehicle".
    (iii) An invoice for the purchase of stationery amounting to €123 was included with purchases at 23% VAT. A closer examination of the invoice revealed that it had no supplier VAT number listed and no details of VAT rates or amounts.
    (iv) An invoice for the building of a new office. The invoice was in respect of an instalment payment and amounted to €1,000 plus VAT at 13.5%.
    (v)   A petty cash voucher for postage, amounting to €64, was included with purchases at 23% VAT.

Requirement
On the basis of the above information, calculate the VAT liability/refund of John Hardiman for the VAT period September/October 2012.

10.5 Mr Byte

Mr Byte supplies computers to business and retail outlets. You are given the following information in connection with his VAT return for the period July/August 2012. All figures are **exclusive** of VAT.

	€
Invoiced sales July/Aug	100,000
Cash received July/Aug	75,000
Purchases invoices received July/Aug	40,000
Purchase invoices paid July/Aug	50,000

Other expenses

Stationery (23%)	6,000
Wages (exempt)	20,000
Electricity (13.5%)	2,000
Hotel bills (9%)	1,000
Rent (exempt)	2,400

Requirement
You are required to compute the liability to VAT of Mr Byte for the period July/August 2012 assuming he elects to account for VAT on the cash receipts basis.

10.6 Joe

Joe, who is a baker, supplies you with the following information from his books for the months of May and June 2012 (all figures are **exclusive** of VAT)

		May €	June €
Sales of bread	zero rated	10,000	8,000
Purchase of ingredients	zero rated	5,000	2,000
Expenditure on petrol	23%	1,000	1,000
Purchase of mixing machine	23%	–	6,000
Lease rentals – vans	23%	2,000	2,000
Bank interest	exempt	400	400

Requirement

You are required to compute the VAT liability for the period in question, and show the date on which the VAT returns should be submitted.

10.7 Voluntary Registration

Requirement

State the categories of persons who may apply for voluntary registration for VAT and discuss the reasons why such persons might choose to apply for voluntary registration.

10.8 General

Requirement

(a) Discuss the place where goods and services are deemed to be supplied for VAT purposes.
(b) Explain what you understand the term "self-supply" to mean for VAT purposes.

10.9 Andrew

Andrew opened a coffee shop on 17 March 2012 and the transactions undertaken during the first VAT period March/April 2012 were as follows:

Sales and Receipts

(1) Receipts in respect of sales of goods and services, inclusive of VAT @ 23%, amounted to €1,815 for the period.
(2) Receipts in respect of sales of goods and services, inclusive of VAT @ 13.5%, amounted to €2,837.50 for the period.

Purchases and Payments

(1) Purchases of stock for re-sale: €605 inclusive of VAT @ 23%
(2) Purchase of stock for re-sale: €334 @ zero rate VAT
(3) Purchase of tables and chairs: €440 plus VAT @ 23%
(4) Payment of rent to landlord: €373. No invoices have been received
(5) Purchases of second-hand cash register on three months credit. The invoice dated 3 March 2012 was for €665.50 in total and included VAT @ 23%.
(6) Payment of €200 plus VAT @ 13.5% to the tiler on 16 March 2012.
(7) On 5 March 2012, Andrew signed a lease for shop fittings requiring a monthly payment of €700 plus VAT @ 23%. The monthly payments are debited to Andrew's bank account on the 30th of each month.

(8)   Payment of €750 on account to a solicitor for legal fees on foot of a bill received for €1,452 inclusive of VAT @ 23%.

(9)   Purchase for the business of a commercial van for €9,840 inclusive of VAT @ 23%.

(10) Purchases of petrol for the van totalling €98 inclusive of VAT @ 23%.

All invoices relating to the above transactions have been received unless otherwise stated. Assume that Andrew was registered for VAT prior to incurring any expenditure.

Requirement
Calculate the VAT liability/refund for the VAT period March/April 2012.

10.10   HERMES Ltd

HERMES Ltd distributes pet food on the home and foreign markets. The following transactions were undertaken by the company during the VAT period March April 2012:

Sales invoiced to customers within the State	€250,000
Sales invoiced to customers in the US	€10,000

The above amounts are stated net of VAT. The VAT rate applicable to the company's sales is 23%.

During the same period, purchase invoices were received in respect of the following:

	Gross Invoice Value €	VAT Rate Applicable %
Stock purchased from suppliers in the State	233,700	23
Stock purchased from suppliers in the UK	50,000	23
Professional fees	6,150	23
Motor car leasing ("qualifying" car)	3,690	23
Motor car repairs	1,135	13.5
Computer	9,225	23

The amounts stated include VAT where charged.

Requirement
Calculate the VAT due for the period March/April 2012.
The computation of VAT return figures should be clearly laid out in your workings.

10.11   ELIXIR Ltd

ELIXIR Ltd operates an Irish based business selling materials for the repair and maintenance of yachts and small boats. During the VAT period of two months ended 31 October 2012, it recorded the following transactions:

Sales of services (exclusive of VAT)		€
Sales in Ireland		950,000
Sales to Spain (to Spanish VAT-registered customers)		320,000
Sales to non VAT-registered customers in the UK		25,000
Sales to VAT-registered customers in the UK		135,000
Sales to customers located in Singapore		46,000

Costs (inclusive of VAT where applicable)	VAT Rate	
Purchase of materials from Irish suppliers	23%	369,000
Purchase (imports) of equipment from German supplier	23%	200,000
Purchase of machinery locally	23%	246,000
Rent of premises *(Note 1)*	23%	18,450
Repairs and maintenance of office and equipment	23%	14,145
Audit and accountancy fees	23%	11,070
Diesel for staff vehicles	23%	5,535
Electricity and gas	13.5%	2,400
Salaries and wages	n/a	167,000
Advertising costs	23%	30,750

Note 1: VAT at the rate of 23% is included in the amount of the rent paid on the company's premises.

All of the above purchases of goods and services (except for wages, salaries and imports) are supplied by businesses which are registered for VAT in Ireland. The imports are purchased from a VAT registered business in Germany.

Requirement
Calculate the VAT payable by (or repayable to) ELIXIR Ltd for the VAT period ended 31 October 2012.

Taxation Reference Material for Tax Year 2012

Income Tax Rates

Single Parents (single, widowed or surviving civil partner) with qualifying children	Rate	Single/Widowed/ Surviving Civil Partner without qualifying children	Rate	Married Couple/Civil Partners	Rate
First €36,800	20%	First €32,800	20%	First €41,800/€65,600*	20%
Balance	41%	Balance	41%	Balance	41%

*Depending on personal circumstances of a married couple/civil partners

Income Tax Exemption Limits

Persons aged 65 years and over	Income Limit 2012
Married/Civil Partners	€36,000
Single/Widowed/Surviving Civil Partners	€18,000
Increase for Qualifying Children	**Increase in Exemption Limit for each Child**
First & second child	€575
Third & subsequent children	€830

Personal Tax Credits

Description	Non-Refundable Tax Credits 2012
	€
Single person	1,650
Married couple/civil partners	3,300
Widowed person/surviving civil partner:	
▪ With dependent children*	1,650
▪ Without dependent children	2,190
▪ In the year of bereavement	3,300
One-parent family (additional):	
▪ Widowed person	1,650
▪ Other	1,650
Widowed/surviving civil partner parent (additional):	
▪ First year after bereavement	3,600
▪ Second year after bereavement	3,150
▪ Third year after bereavement	2,700
▪ Fourth year after bereavement	2,250
▪ Fifth year after bereavement	1,800
Employee (PAYE) tax credit	1,650
Blind person	1,650
Both spouses/civil partners blind	3,300
Age credit (65 Years over):	
▪ Single/widowed person/surviving civil partner	245
▪ Married/civil partners	490
Incapacitated child	3,300
Dependent relative	70
Income limit	13,837
Home carer:	810
▪ Income limit lower	5,080
▪ Income limit upper	6,700

*Also entitled to Single-Parent Family Allowance

Tax Reliefs at the Standard Rate (2012 – 20%)

Rent Relief

	Rent Limit 2012 €	Max. Tax Credit 2012 €
Person **under** 55 years:		
Married/Widowed/Civil Partners	2,400	480
Single	1,200	240
Person **over** 55 years:		
Married/Widowed/Civil Partners	4,800	960
Single	2,400	480

Mortgage Interest Relief 2012

Interest Ceiling for First-time Buyers

Status	Ceiling	Rate of Relief Year 1 and 2	Max. relief available	Rate of Relief Year 3, 4 and 5	Max. relief available	Rate of Relief Year 6 and 7	Max. relief available
Single	€10,000	@ 25%	€2,500	@ 22.5%	€2,250	@ 20%	€2,000
Married/Civil Partnership/Widowed	€20,000	@ 25%	€5,000	@ 22.5%	€4,500	@ 20%	€4,000

Interest Ceilings for First-time Buyers for Tax Years 2012 to 2017

Year FTB loan taken out	2012 Ceiling @ Rate Single or Married /Widowed/Civil Partnership	2013 Ceiling @ Rate	2014 Ceiling @ Rate	2015 Ceiling @ Rate	2016 Ceiling @ Rate	2017 Ceiling @ Rate
2012	S: €10K @ 25% M/W/CP: €20K @ 25%	S: €10K @ 25% M/W/CP: €20K @ 25%	S: €10K @ 22.5% M/W/CP: €20K @ 22.5%	S: €10K @ 22.5% M/W/CP: €20K @ 22.5%	S: €10K @ 22.5% M/W/CP: €20K @ 22.5%	S: €10K @ 20% M/W/CP: €20K @ 20%
2011	S: €10K @ 25% M/W/CP: €20K @ 25%	S: €10K @ 22.5% M/W/CP: €20K @ 22.5%	S: €10K @ 22.5% M/W/CP: €20K @ 22.5%	S: €10K @ 22.5% M/W/CP: €20K @ 22.5%	S: €10K @ 20% M/W/CP: €20K @ 20%	S: €10K @ 20% M/W/CP: €20K @ 20%
2010	S: €10K @ 22.5% M/W/CP: €20K @ 22.5%	S: €10K @ 22.5% M/W/CP: €20K @ 22.5%	S: €10K @ 22.5% M/W/CP: €20K @ 22.5%	S: €10K @ 20% M/W/CP: €20K @ 20%	S: €10K @ 20% M/W/CP: €20K @ 20%	S: €3K @ 15% M/W/CP: €6K @ 15%
2009	S: €10K @ 22.5% M/W/CP: €20K @ 22.5%	S: €10K @ 22.5% M/W/CP: €20K @ 22.5%	S: €10K @ 20% M/W/CP: €20K @ 20%	S: €10K @ 20% M/W/CP: €20K @ 20%	S: €3K @ 15% M/W/CP: €6K @ 15%	S: €3K @ 15% M/W/CP: €6K @ 15%
2008	S: €10K @ 30% M/W/CP: €20K @ 30%	S: €10K @ 30% M/W/CP: €20K @ 30%	S: €10K @ 30% M/W/CP: €20K @ 30%	S: €3K @ 30% M/W/CP: €6K @ 30%	S: €3K @ 30% M/W/CP: €6K @ 30%	S: €3K @ 30% M/W/CP: €6K @ 30%
2007	S: €10K @ 30% M/W/CP: €20K @ 30%	S: €10K @ 30% M/W/CP: €20K @ 30%	S: €3K @ 30% M/W/CP: €6K @ 30%	S: €3K @ 30% M/W/CP: €6K @ 30%	S: €3K @ 30% M/W/CP: €6K @ 30%	S: €3K @ 30% M/W/CP: €6K @ 30%
2006	S: €10K @ 30% M/W/CP: €20K @ 30%	S: €3K @ 30% M/W/CP: €6K @ 30%	S: €3K @ 30% M/W/CP: €6K @ 30%	S: €3K @ 30% M/W/CP: €6K @ 30%	S: €3K @ 30% M/W/CP: €6K @ 30%	S: €3K @ 30% M/W/CP: €6K @ 30%
2005	S: €3K @ 30% M/W/CP: €6K @ 30%	S: €3K @ 30% M/W/CP: €6K @ 30%	S: €3K @ 30% M/W/CP: €6K @ 30%	S: €3K @ 30% M/W/CP: €6K @ 30%	S: €3K @ 30% M/W/CP: €6K @ 30%	S: €3K @ 30% M/W/CP: €6K @ 30%
2004	S: €3K @ 30% M/W/CP: €6K @ 30%	S: €3K @ 30% M/W/CP: €6K @ 30%	S: €3K @ 30% M/W/CP: €6K @ 30%	S: €3K @ 30% M/W/CP: €6K @ 30%	S: €3K @ 30% M/W/CP: €6K @ 30%	S: €3K @ 30% M/W/CP: €6K @ 30%

Interest Ceilings for Non-first-time Buyers

Status	Ceiling	Rate of Relief	Max. relief available
Single	€3,000	@ 15%	€450
Married/Widowed	€6,000	@ 15%	€900

Interest Ceilings for Non-first-time Buyers for Tax Years 2012 to 2017

Year NFTB loan taken out	2012 Ceiling @ Rate Single or Married / Widowed/Civil Partnership	2013 Ceiling @ Rate	2014 Ceiling @ Rate	2015 Ceiling @ Rate	2016 Ceiling @ Rate	2017 Ceiling @ Rate
2012	S: €3K @ 15% M/W/CP: €6K @ 15%	S: €3K @ 15% M/W/CP: €6K @ 15%	S: €3K @ 15% M/W/CP: €6K @ 15%	S: €3K @ 15% M/W/CP: €6K @ 15%	S: €3K @ 15% M/W/CP: €6K @ 15%	S: €3K @ 15% M/W/CP: €6K @ 15%
2011	S: €3K @ 15% M/W/CP: €6K @ 15%	S: €3K @ 15% M/W/CP: €6K @ 15%	S: €3K @ 15% M/W/CP: €6K @ 15%	S: €3K @ 15% M/W/CP: €6K @ 15%	S: €3K @ 15% M/W/CP: €6K @ 15%	S: €3K @ 15% M/W/CP: €6K @ 15%
2010	S: €3K @ 15% M/W/CP: €6K @ 15%	S: €3K @ 15% M/W/CP: €6K @ 15%	S: €3K @ 15% M/W/CP: €6K @ 15%	S: €3K @ 15% M/W/CP: €6K @ 15%	S: €3K @ 15% M/W/CP: €6K @ 15%	S: €3K @ 15% M/W/CP: €6K @ 15%
2009	S: €3K @ 15% M/W/CP: €6K @ 15%	S: €3K @ 15% M/W/CP: €6K @ 15%	S: €3K @ 15% M/W/CP: €6K @ 15%	S: €3K @ 15% M/W/CP: €6K @ 15%	S: €3K @ 15% M/W/CP: €6K @ 15%	S: €3K @ 15% M/W/CP: €6K @ 15%
2008	S: €3K @ 15% M/W/CP: €6K @ 15%	S: €3K @ 15% M/W/CP: €6K @ 15%	S: €3K @ 15% M/W/CP: €6K @ 15%	S: €3K @ 15% M/W/CP: €6K @ 15%	S: €3K @ 15% M/W/CP: €6K @ 15%	S: €3K @ 15% M/W/CP: €6K @ 15%
2007	S: €3K @ 15% M/W/CP: €6K @ 15%	S: €3K @ 15% M/W/CP: €6K @ 15%	S: €3K @ 15% M/W/CP: €6K @ 15%	S: €3K @ 15% M/W/CP: €6K @ 15%	S: €3K @ 15% M/W/CP: €6K @ 15%	S: €3K @ 15% M/W/CP: €6K @ 15%
2006	S: €3K @ 15% M/W/CP: €6K @ 15%	S: €3K @ 15% M/W/CP: €6K @ 15%	S: €3K @ 15% M/W/CP: €6K @ 15%	S: €3K @ 15% M/W/CP: €6K @ 15%	S: €3K @ 15% M/W/CP: €6K @ 15%	S: €3K @ 15% M/W/CP: €6K @ 15%
2005	S: €3K @ 15% M/W/CP: €6K @ 15%	S: €3K @ 15% M/W/CP: €6K @ 15%	S: €3K @ 15% M/W/CP: €6K @ 15%	S: €3K @ 15% M/W/CP: €6K @ 15%	S: €3K @ 15% M/W/CP: €6K @ 15%	S: €3K @ 15% M/W/CP: €6K @ 15%
2004	S: €3K @ 15% M/W/CP: €6K @ 15%	S: €3K @ 15% M/W/CP: €6K @ 15%	S: €3K @ 15% M/W/CP: €6K @ 15%	S: €3K @ 15% M/W/CP: €6K @ 15%	S: €3K @ 15% M/W/CP: €6K @ 15%	S: €3K @ 15% M/W/CP: €6K @ 15%

No relief is available for a qualifying loan taken out before 1 January 2004.

Medical Insurance

Age of Insured Person	TRS 2012
Up to age 59 years	Gross premium @ 20% (standard rate)
Additional age related tax credits:	Gross premium @ 20% (standard rate) **PLUS**
Greater or equal to 60 years but less than 65 years	€600
Greater or equal to 65 years but less than 70 years	€975
Greater or equal to 70 years but less than 75 years	€1,400
Greater or equal to 75 years but less than 80 years	€2,025
Greater or equal to 80 years but less than 85 years	€2,400
Greater or equal to 85 years	€2,700

Tax Reliefs at the Marginal Rate (2012 – 41%)

Employment of Carer for Incapacitated Person

The maximum deduction available is €50,000.

Revenue Job Assist

	Deduction for Self	Deduction for each Qualifying Child
Year 1	€3,810	€1,270
Year 2	€2,540	€850
Year 3	€1,270	€425

Pension Contributions

The maximum deductions on which tax relief may be claimed for pension contributions are:

Age	% of Net Relevant Earnings*
Under 30 years of age	15%
30 to 39 years of age	20%
40 to 49 years of age	25%
50 to 54 years of age	30%
55 to 59 years of age	35%
60 years and over	40%

*Subject to an overall "earnings cap" of €115,000

Employment and Investment Incentive

Maximum allowable of €150,000 per tax year up to 2013.

Film Relief

Maximum allowable of €50,000 per tax year.

Other Reliefs

Rent-a-room relief – income up to €10,000 p.a.
Provision of childcare services – income up to €15,000 p.a.

Motor Vehicles

Carbon Emission Categories

Car Category	Category A	Category B/C	Category D/E	Category F/G
CO_2 Emissions (CO_2g/km)	0g/km up to and including 120g/km	121g/km up to and including 155g/km	156g/km up to and including 190g/km	191g/km +

Motor Vehicle Benefit-in-Kind Scale

Annual Business Kilometres	Cash Equivalent (% of OMV)
24,000 or less	30%
24,001 to 32,000	24%
32,001 to 40,000	18%
40,001 to 48,000	12%
48,001 and over	6%

Specified Amounts for Motor Vehicles

There is a restricted cost of passenger motor vehicles for capital allowances and motor lease expenses restriction purposes, as follows:

Restricted Cost of Car for Capital Allowances	Maximum Allowed €
Provided for use:	
23 January 1997 to 2 December 1997	19,046
3 December 1997 to 2 December 1998	19,681
3 December 1998 to 30 November 1999	20,316
1 December 1999 to the basis period/accounting period ending on or after 1 January 2001*	20,951
1 January 2001 to 31 December 2001	21,586
1 January 2002 to 31 December 2005	22,000
1 January 2006 to 31 December 2006	23,000
1 January 2007 *et seq.*	24,000

*€21,586 applied to both new and second-hand vehicles. For second hand vehicles purchased in a basis period or accounting period ending before 1 January 2001, the restricted cost is €12,697.

■ Previous limits applied by reference to date expenditure incurred.

Restriction of Capital Allowances and Lease Expenses for Motor Vehicles

Car Purchased/Leased Prior to 1 July 2008
- Lease charge disallowed:

$$\text{Lease hire charges} \quad \times \quad \frac{(\text{List price} - \text{specified amount})}{\text{List price}}$$

- Capital allowances – restricted to the lower of cost or the specified amount.

Car Purchased/Leased after 1 July 2008
- Lease charge disallowed: leasing charges allowances are limited by reference to the CO_2 emissions of the cars.

Vehicle Category	Leasing Charges Restriction
A/B/C	$\text{Lease hire charge} \times \dfrac{(\text{List Price} - \text{Specified Amount})}{\text{List Price}}$
D/E	$\text{Lease hire charge} \times \dfrac{(\text{List Price} - (\text{Specified Amount} \times 50\%))}{\text{List Price}}$
F/G	Lease hire charge disallowed

- Capital allowances – limited by reference to the CO_2 emissions of the cars.

Vehicle Category	Cost of Car for Capital Allowances Restricted to:
A/B/C	Specified amount (regardless of actual cost)
D/E	Lower of specified amount or retail price × **50%**
F/G	No Allowance available

Capital Allowances

Plant and Machinery

Plant – expenditure on or after 1st April 1992 .... 15% / 10% straight line
Plant – expenditure on or after 1st April 1992 – cars............................. 20% reducing balance
Plant – expenditure on or after 1st January 2001 .... 20% straight line
Plant – expenditure on or after 1st January 2001 – cars .... 20% straight line
Plant – expenditure on or after 5th December 2002 .... 12.5% straight line
Plant – expenditure on or after 5th December 2002 – cars.................... 12.5% straight line

Industrial Buildings

IBAA (Industrial Buildings Annual Allowance)

Expenditure incurred on or after 1st April 1992   4% straight line

Hotels / Farm Buildings

Expenditure incurred on or after 27th January 1994   15% / 10% straight line

VAT

VAT Rate

Standard 23%
Reduced rate of VAT(1)... 13.5%
Reduced rate of VAT(2)... 9%
Flat rate for farmers 5.2%
Reduced rate (livestock, etc.)...................................... 4.8%

Preferential Loan – Benefit-in-Kind

Specified rate 2011 onwards:

- 5% in respect of qualifying home loans
- 12.5% in all other cases

PRSI

Effective from 1 January 2012:

Class A1 – Private and Public Sector Employments

Subclass	Weekly Pay Band	How much of weekly pay	All Income EE	All Income ER
AO	€38–€352 inclusive	ALL	Nil	4.25%
AX	€352.01–€356 inclusive	First €127 Balance	Nil 4%	4.25% 4.25%
AL	€356.01–€500 inclusive	First €127 Balance	Nil 4%	10.75% 10.75%
AI	More than €500	First €127 Balance	Nil 4%	10.75% 10.75%

Class S – Self-employed and Company Directors

Subclass	Weekly Pay Band	How much of weekly pay	All Income EE
S0	Up to €500	ALL	4%
S1	More than €500	ALL	4%

Universal Social Charge

Universal Social Charge – Rates and Income Thresholds 2012

(Where gross income is greater than €10,036 per annum (2011 €4,004))

PERSONS UNDER 70 AND NOT IN RECEIPT OF A MEDICAL CARD			INCOME LEVY
THRESHOLDS			
Per Year	Per Month	Per Week	Rate %
Up to €10,036	Up to €837	Up to €193	2%
From €10,037 to €16,016	From €837 to €1,335	From €193 to €308	4%
In excess of €16,016	In excess of €1,335	In excess of €308	7%

PERSONS IN RECEIPT OF A MEDICAL CARD OR OVER 70 YEARS			
Per Year	Per Month	Per Week	Rate %
Up to €10,036	Up to €837	Up to €193	2%
In excess of €10,036	In excess of €837	In excess of €193	4%

SELF-ASSESSED PERSONS UNDER 70 AND NOT IN RECEIPT OF A MEDICAL CARD	
THRESHOLDS	RATE OF USC
The first €10,036	2%
The next €5,980	4%
The next €83,984	7%
The remainder (> €100,000)	10%

SELF-ASSESSED PERSONS IN RECEIPT OF A MEDICAL CARD OR OVER 70 YEARS	
THRESHOLDS	RATE OF USC
The first €10,036	2%
The next €89,964	4%
The remainder (> €100,000)	7%

Report of the Employment Status Group – PPF

Introduction

This document has been prepared by the Employment Status Group set up under the Programme for Prosperity and Fairness (PPF).

The group was set up because of a growing concern that there may be increasing numbers of individuals categorised as 'self-employed' when the 'indicators' may be that 'employee' status would be more appropriate. The purpose of the document is to eliminate misconceptions and provide clarity. It is not meant to bring individuals who are genuinely self-employed into employment status. The remit of the group is contained in the PPF document at page 18, paragraph 9 as follows:

"The Office of the Revenue Commissioners and the Department of Social, Community & Family Affairs, in consultation with the Social Partners, will seek a uniform definition of 'employee' based on clear criteria, which will determine the employment status of an individual".

The group consisted of representatives from the following organisations:

- Irish Congress of Trade Unions
- Irish Business and Employers Confederation
- Revenue Commissioners
- Department of Social, Community and Family Affairs (now Department of Social Protection)
- Department of Enterprise, Trade and Employment
- Department of Finance.

Considerations

The group considered two approaches in their deliberations. They considered a legislative approach – to define in statute the traits or indicators of 'employee' status using criteria established by common law over many years. The other approach was to reaffirm the criteria as a Code of Practice and to distribute the material as widely to a relevant audience as possible.

It was felt by some members that a statutory definition would provide clarity for anyone dealing with or considering the issue of a person's employment status. It was felt by other members that the case law and criteria laid down by the courts over the years provided flexibility and that a statutory approach would interfere with that flexibility, while others felt that a statutory definition might prove detrimental to 'employee' status.

It was decided to issue the report as a Code of Practice which would be monitored by the Group with a view to reviewing the position within 12 months. While it was accepted by the Group that the Code of Practice does not have legislative effect, it was expected that its contents would be considered by those involved in disputes on the employment status of individuals or groups of individuals.

It was noted that the Revenue Commissioners and the Department of Social, Community & Family Affairs have already jointly produced a leaflet in September 1998 entitled **Employed or Self-Employed – A Guide for Tax and Social Insurance**. The Revenue Commissioners also produced a leaflet aimed at the construction industry but which would equally have general application. The Department of Enterprise, Trade & Employment also have a range of explanatory leaflets which, while not specifically relating to 'employee' status, set out comprehensively the rights of employees under different aspects of employment law.

This Code of Practice is also recommended for the consideration of all appropriate adjudication agencies where issues concerning employment status are the subject of a dispute.

Legal Background

The terms "employed" and "self-employed" are not defined in law. The decision as to which category an individual belongs must be arrived at by looking at what the individual actually does, the way he or she does it and the terms and conditions under which he or she is engaged, be they written, verbal or implied, or a combination of all three. It is not simply a matter of calling a job "employment" or "self-employment".

In the Irish Supreme Court case of *Henry Denny & Sons Ltd. T/A Kerry Foods v. The Minister for Social Welfare* (1997), the fundamental test as to whether a person who has been engaged to perform certain work performs it "as a person in business on their own account" was considered among other matters. This fundamental test was drawn from the UK case of *Market Investigations Ltd v. Minister of Social Security* (1969) which has received extensive judicial approval in this country as well as in the UK and other common law jurisdictions. This fundamental test in that case was amplified by a series of specific criteria, as follows. Does the person doing the work:

- assume any responsibility for investment and management in the business;
- otherwise take any financial risk;
- provide his own equipment or helpers; or
- have the opportunity to profit from sound management in the performance of his/her task.

From consideration of such tests one is better able to judge whether the person engaged is a free agent and has an economic independence of the party engaging the service.

In most cases, it will be clear whether an individual is employed or self-employed. However, it may not always be so obvious, which in turn can lead to misconceptions in relation to the employment status of individuals.

The *Denny* case, which is an important precedent in the area of whether a person is engaged under a contract of service (employee) or under a contract for services (self-employed), is of assistance because of the atypical nature of the engagement. The main features of the *Denny* case were:

- The facts were fully established and articulated and relevant legal principles applied by the Social Welfare Appeals Officer. The High Court or the Supreme Court did not disturb the decision.
- The employment was atypical – the person engaged was a demonstrator/merchandiser of food products in supermarkets.
- The employment was also casual in nature and would have included a pool of demonstrators to be drawn from.
- Because of the casual nature of the employment, 'mutuality of obligation' would have been an issue, i.e. whether or not the person engaged had an obligation to take each engagement when offered.
- The right of substitution was an issue albeit with the approval of the employer.
- The employment included fixed-term contracts.
- References were made to imposed conditional contracts.
- It was confirmed that the Appeals Officer was correct in deciding not to be bound by an unreported Circuit Court judgement, dealing with a similar issue under an unfair dismissal claim under employment law, which he did not agree with. The Appeals Officer was correct in considering "the facts or realities of the situation on the ground", i.e. to look at and beyond the written contract to arrive at the totality of the relationship. Certain statements included in the contract and other notes of engagement, such as:
  - "Deemed to be an independent contractor",
  - "It shall be the duty of the demonstrator to pay and discharge such taxes and charges as may be payable out of such fees to the Revenue Commissioners or otherwise",
  - "It is further agreed that the provisions of the Unfair Dismissals Act 1997 shall not apply, etc.",
  - "You will not be an employee of Kerry Foods", and
  - "You will be responsible for your own tax affairs",

were not contractual terms but that "they purported to express a conclusion of law as to the consequences of the contract between the parties".

In other words, the fact that such or similar terms are included in a contract is of little value in coming to a conclusion as to the work status of the person engaged.

Code of Practice in Determining Status

The criteria set out in the next paragraph should help in reaching a conclusion. It is important that the job as a whole is looked at including working conditions and the reality of the relationship, when considering the guidelines. The overriding consideration or test will always be whether the person performing the work does so "as a person in business on their own account." Is the person a free agent with from economic independence the person engaging the service?

Criteria on Whether an Individual is an Employee

While all of the following factors may not apply, an individual would normally be an employee if he or she:

- Is under the control of another person who directs as to how, when and where the work is to be carried out.
- Supplies labour only.
- Receives a fixed hourly/weekly/monthly wage.
- Cannot sub-contract the work. If the work can be sub-contracted and paid on by the person sub-contracting the work, the employer/employee relationship may simply be transferred on.
- Does not supply materials for the job.
- Does not provide equipment other than the small tools of the trade. The provision of tools or equipment might not have a significant bearing on coming to a conclusion that employment status may be appropriate having regard to all the circumstances of a particular case.
- Is not exposed to personal financial risk in carrying out the work.
- Does not assume any responsibility for investment and management in the business.
- Does not have the opportunity to profit from sound management in the scheduling of engagements or in the performance of tasks arising from the engagements.
- Works set hours or a given number of hours per week or month.
- Works for one person or for one business.
- Receives expense payments to cover subsistence and/or travel expenses.
- Is entitled to extra pay or time off for overtime.

Additional Factors to be Considered

- An individual could have considerable freedom and independence in carrying out work and still remain an employee.
- An employee with specialist knowledge may not be directed as to how the work is carried out.
- An individual who is paid by commission, by share, or by piecework, or in some other atypical fashion may still be regarded as an employee.
- Some employees work for more than one employer at the same time.
- Some employees do not work on the employer's premises.
- There are special PRSI rules for the employment of family members.
- Statements in contracts considered in the *Denny* case, such as:
  - "You are deemed to be an independent contractor",
  - "It shall be your duty to pay and discharge such taxes and charges as may be payable out of such fees to the Revenue Commissioners or otherwise",
  - "It is agreed that the provisions of the Unfair Dismissals Act 1977 shall not apply, etc.",
  - "You will not be an employee of this company", and
  - "You will be responsible for your own tax affairs".
  are not contractual terms and have little or no contractual validity. While they may express an opinion of the contacting parties, they are of minimal value in coming to a conclusion as to the work status of the person engaged.

Criteria on Whether an Individual is Self-employed

While all of the following factors may not apply to the job, an individual would normally be self-employed if he or she:

- owns his or her own business;
- is exposed to financial risk, by having to bear the cost of making good faulty or sub-standard work carried out under the contract;
- assumes responsibility for investment and management in the enterprise;
- has the opportunity to profit from sound management in the scheduling and performance of engagements and tasks;
- has control over what is done, how it is done, when and where it is done and whether he or she does it personally;
- is free to hire other people, on his or her terms, to do the work which has been agreed to be undertaken;
- can provide the same services to more than one person or business at the same time;
- provides the materials for the job;
- provides equipment and machinery necessary for the job, other than the small tools of the trade or equipment which in an overall context would not be an indicator of a person in business on their own account;
- has a fixed place of business where materials equipment etc. can be stored;
- costs and agrees a price for the job;
- provides his or her own insurance cover, e.g. public liability, etc.; or
- controls the hours of work in fulfilling the job obligations.

Additional Factors to be Considered

- Generally an individual should satisfy the self-employed guidelines above, otherwise he or she will normally be an employee.
- The fact that an individual has registered as self-employed or for VAT under the principles of self-assessment does not automatically mean that he or she is self-employed.
- An office holder, such as a company director, will be taxed under the PAYE system However, the terms and conditions may have to be examined by the Scope Section of Department of Social Protection to decide the appropriate PRSI class.
- It should be noted that a person who is a self-employed contractor in one job is not necessarily self-employed in the next job. It is also possible to be employed and self-employed at the same time in different jobs.
- In the construction sector, for health and safety reasons, all individuals are under the direction of the site foreman/overseer. The self-employed individual controls the method to be employed in carrying out the work.

Consequences Arising from the Determination of an Individual's Status

The status as an employee or self-employed person will affect:

- The way in which tax, PRSI and USC is payable to the Collector-General:
  - an employee will have tax, PRSI and USC deducted from his or her income; and
  - a self-employed person is obliged to pay preliminary tax and file income tax returns whether or not he or she is asked for them.

- Entitlement to a number of social welfare benefits, such as unemployment and disability benefits:
  - an employee will be entitled to unemployment, disability and invalidity benefits, whereas a self-employed person will not have these entitlements
- Other rights and entitlements, for example, under employment legislation:
  - an employee will have rights in respect of working hours, holidays, maternity/parental leave, protection from unfair dismissal, etc.;
  - a self-employed person will not have these rights and protection; and
- Public liability in respect of the work done.

Consequence for the Person or Company Engaging the Service of an Individual

In most instances, a person's work status will be clear. It is however crucial for a person or company to ensure that a person engaged to perform a service is correctly categorised as an employee or self-employed particularly where there is a doubt. There may, in certain borderline instances, be a divergence of opinion between the contracting parties assumptions and that of the Revenue Commissioners, the Department of Social, Community and Family Affairs or the adjudication systems established under employment and industrial relations legislation.

While it is accepted that the operation of the PAYE, PRSI and USC systems and compliance with the rights of employees under employment legislation creates an administrative burden for employers, the integrity of the systems very much depends on employers operating them correctly.

Under tax and social welfare law, if the status of 'employee' is found to be appropriate the person engaging the 'employee' is the accountable person for any PAYE, PRSI and USC deductible while that person was engaged (whether or not any deductions were made), together with appropriate interest and penalties that may arise.

There may also be penalties under various employment legislation for wrong categorisation of a person's employment status.

Deciding Status – Getting Assistance

Where there are difficulties in deciding the appropriate status of an individual or groups of individuals, the following organisations can provide assistance.

Tax and PRSI

The local Revenue office or the local Social Welfare office, (a listing of Revenue and Social Welfare offices is in the telephone book). Scope Section in the Department of Social Protection may also be contacted for assistance.

If a formal decision is required, relevant facts will have to be established and a written decision as to status issued. A decision by one Department will generally be accepted by the other, provided all relevant facts were given at the time and the circumstances remain the same and it is accepted that the correct legal principles have been applied to the facts established. However, because of the varied nature of circumstances that arise and the different statutory provisions, such a consensus may not be possible in every case.

Employment Appeals Tribunal

The purpose of the Employment Appeals Tribunal is to determine matters of dispute arising under the Acts relating to redundancy payments, minimum notice and terms of employment, unfair dismissals, protection of employees (employers' insolvency), worker protection (regular part-time employees), payment of wages, terms of employment (information), maternity protection, adoptive leave, protection of young persons, organisation of working time, parental leave, and protections for persons reporting child abuse. Disputes in relation to any matter arising under the above-mentioned legislation may be referred either directly, or on appeal (from a Rights Commissioner, where appropriate) to the Tribunal.

Labour Court

The main functions of the Labour Court are:

- to investigate industrial disputes under the Industrial Relations Acts 1946 to 1990, and to issue recommendations for their settlement;
- to make determinations on appeals against recommendations of equality officers, or for the implementation of such recommendations;
- to make orders in cases of dismissal under the Employment Equality Act 1998, and the Pensions Act 1990;
- to decide on appeals against recommendations and decisions of Rights Commissioners under the Industrial Relations and Organisation of Working Time Acts;
- to establish joint labour committees;
- to make employment regulation orders prescribing legally enforceable pay rates and conditions in employments covered by the relevant joint labour committees;
- to register employment agreements, which become legally binding;
- to register joint industrial councils; and
- to approve and register collective agreements under the Organisation of Working Time Act 1997.

Department of Enterprise, Trade and Employment

The Employment Rights Information Unit of Department of Enterprise, Trade and Employment may also be contacted for information on labour law issues. This Unit has a range of leaflets on employment law that are available on request.

Irish Congress of Trade Unions

The Irish Congress of Trade Unions is the single umbrella organisation for trade unions in Ireland representing a wide range of interests.

Irish Business and Employers Confederation

The Irish Business and Employers Confederation represents and provides economic, commercial, employee relations and social affairs services to some 7,000 companies and organisations from all sectors of economic and commercial activity.

Appendix 3

Tax Research and Preparing a Tax Case

Introduction

Taxation rules are determined from statutes enacted by the legislature, e.g. TCA 1997, or by interpretation of these rules by the Courts.

Under normal circumstances, most taxpayers have no reason to disagree with the notice of assessment issued by Revenue.

If a taxpayer **disagrees** with a notice of assessment or with a determination of the Revenue Commissioners in relation to income tax, he has the **right to appeal** against such an assessment or determination.

The most common reasons resulting in a case being listed for hearing before the Appeal Commissioners would include:

■ Disputes between the Inspector and taxpayer or his agent over the validity of items contained in the accounts/tax returns.
■ Disputes as to the interpretation of tax law or case law in relation to a particular item included in the accounts/tax return of the taxpayer.

Sources of Tax Law in Ireland

The following are the main sources of Irish tax law:

1. Statutory
The main source of statutory authority for direct taxes is contained in TCA 1997. This Act consolidates all Irish taxation legislation in relation to income tax, corporation tax, capital gains tax and tax administration.

Capital taxes such as stamp duty and capital acquisitions tax, are dealt with separately in the Stamp Duties Consolidation Act 1999 and Capital Acquisitions Consolidation Act 2003.

In addition, EU Directives form the basis of all national VAT legislation throughout the EU and are enacted into Irish law by:

- VAT Consolidation Act 2010; and
- VAT Regulations.

In the event of any inconsistencies, EU law takes precedence.

All taxes enacted into Irish law are available to search, view and print from the Office of the Attorney General at www.irishstatutebook.ie or from the Houses of the Oireachtas at www.acts.ie.

2.   Relevant Case Law

The law in Ireland relating to taxation is based on the Acts of the Oireachtas and is subject to judicial scrutiny.

Tax cases involve two distinct issues:

- the extent of a charge to taxation; and
- whether the facts are such to bring a taxpayer within that charge.

The Appeal Commissioners or a Court in determining these issues take account of previous decisions on relevant tax matters. Depending on the status of the courts handing down the decisions, the Appeal Commissioners or Court may be bound by these decisions. In the hierarchy of the courts, Supreme Court, High Court, Circuit Court and Appeal Commissioners, each is bound by decisions of a higher court but is not bound by their own decisions. A decision by a court on a point in any Act becomes part of the law on that point in question until overruled by a higher court or the passing of a new law.

In the past, Irish and UK taxation law were broadly similar and decisions in UK courts might be relevant to interpretation of a similar Irish Act. While the Irish courts may be influenced by decisions of UK courts, such decisions are not binding in Ireland.

In addition, the impact of European law through the European Court of Justice (ECJ) decisions is automatically taken into Irish law because of our EU membership.

Case law is reported through a variety of sources such as Tax Point, the service provided by Chartered Accountants Ireland whereby members receive reports and commentaries on recent Irish and ECJ tax cases. Butterworth's Irish Tax Reports or Irish Law Reports ("Lexis" on-line) are good reference points for all published cases since the foundation of the State. Many other legal and taxation reports and commentaries are also available.

You should also be aware that hearings of the Appeal Commissioners and Circuit Court are held in camera (not reported) so no reports are available unless published on a "no names" basis by the Court.

Procedure for taking a Tax Case

The most common reasons resulting in a case being listed for hearing before the Appeal Commissioners would include:

- Disputes between the Revenue and taxpayer or his agent over the validity of items contained in the accounts/tax returns.

■ Disputes as to the interpretation of tax law or case law in relation to a particular item included in the accounts/tax return of the taxpayer.

If a taxpayer is dissatisfied with a decision of the Appeal Commissioners, he may apply to have the case reheard before a judge in the Circuit Court or directly to the High Court on a point of law. The final court of appeal is the Supreme Court on a point of law against a High Court decision.

You should also read Section 9.4 for the procedures to be followed when taking a tax case to Appeal or Court.

Interpretation of Tax Law

The rules of construction which apply to statutes, including tax statutes, is a literal interpretation of what is actually said, with nothing read in or implied.

Interestingly, case law established three principles of interpretation of tax law:

■ words should be given their ordinary meaning,
■ where a word creates a penal or tax liability and there is ambiguity attached to it, then the word should be interpreted so as to prevent a fresh imposition of liability because it is oblique or slack; and
■ the judge can draw from his/her own experiences when deciding what words mean.

The Interpretation Act 2005 came into operation on 1 January 2006 and introduced a number of important points.

If a provision of the Interpretation Act appears to contradict a provision of another Act under examination, then that provision of the Interpretation Act will not apply.

The Act provides that where any provision is either obscure or ambiguous, or where a literal interpretation would be absurd or fail to reflect the plain intention of the Oireachtas, the provision is to be interpreted to reflect the intention of the Oireachtas, where that intention can be ascertained from the act as a whole.

This does not apply in the case of legislation which imposes "a penal or other sanction". The new approach is known as a "purposive" approach.

Putting a Tax Appeal Case Together

Consider the following client scenario:

Scenario 1

Angela Murphy was hired to dress pharmacy shop windows for a well-known beauty products company. She was provided with a list of sites to visit each week. She supplies her own transport and can schedule her week in conjunction with the manager of each pharmacy. She has received specialist training from the beauty products company but only the pharmacy manager reviews her work. She is paid by store and receives a mileage allowance in accordance with approved Civil Service rates. Your advice has been sought if she needs to be put on the payroll.

The process of building a case to support a client scenario begins with determining the facts of your case accurately.

The issue in this case is whether Angela Murphy is an employee of the company or an independent contractor.

1. Determine the facts of your case accurately:

   ■ Angela Murphy was hired by the company to provide display services for the company products in various pharmacies.
   ■ There was no direct supervision but she had to abide by the direction and authority of the pharmacy manager.
   ■ Her pay was determined solely by reference to the number of sites she visited.
   ■ It is unclear if she could engage a substitute though, since specialist training was provided, this would appear unlikely.

2. Then refer to tax statute. Review the ordinary meaning in the light of the facts in your case.

3. Provide supporting evidence for your interpretation in case law either through similar situations or similar interpretation.

   Using the *Henry Denny and Sons (Ireland) Limited v. Minister for Social Welfare* case, we can align the facts in this case to our particular circumstances.

   ■ The circumstances are quite similar.
   ■ A demonstrator was hired but not subject to direct supervision.
   ■ She was not entitled to sick pay and could not send a substitute.

   The High Court decision that the demonstrator was an employee was supported by the Supreme Court.

   The judge applied the control, reality and entrepreneurial tests from a number of cases, and mentioned the tests from the UK case of *Market Investigation Ltd v. Minister for Social Security* where the person performing the services performed them as a person in business on his own account in his decision.

4. Advise your Client
   In this case, the client should be advised that it would be advisable to have Angela Murphy treated as an employee for all aspects of her job.

Scenario 2

Your client, Bioscience Ltd, recently completed an extension to their factory and installed sensitive test equipment which required a sealed off room to house the equipment and maintain a dust and humidity free atmosphere. The room was constructed from partitioned panelling with sealed doors and artificial lighting. Your advice is sought on whether wear and tear allowance (12.5%) or industrial building annual allowance (4%) could be claimed on the partition panelling.

The process of building a case to support a client scenario begins with determining the facts of your case accurately.

The issue in this case is whether the panelling forms part of the setting (and therefore qualifies for IBAA) or whether it performs part of the function (and therefore qualifies for wear and tear).

1. Determine the facts of your case accurately:
   - The sensitive test equipment which required a special atmosphere to work properly
   - The panels created the setting in which this could be achieved

2. Then refer to tax statute. Review the ordinary meaning in the light of the facts in your case. Consider section 284 TCA 1997 as follows:

   Section 284 (1) Subject to the Tax Acts, where a person carrying on a trade in any chargeable period has incurred **capital expenditure on the provision of machinery or plant for the purposes of the trade,** *an allowance (in this Chapter referred to as a "wear and tear allowance") shall be made to such person for that chargeable period on account of the wear and tear of any of the machinery or plant which belongs to such person and is in use for the purposes of the trade at the end of that chargeable period or its basis period and which, while used for the purposes of the trade, is wholly and exclusively so used.*

   Section 284 (5) **No wear and tear allowance** *shall be made under this section in respect of capital expenditure incurred on the* **construction of a building** *or structure which is or is deemed to be an industrial building or structure within the meaning of section 268.*

3. Provide supporting evidence for your interpretation in case law either through similar situations or similar interpretation.
   Using the *O'Culachain (Inspector of Taxes) v. McMullan Bros* case, we can determine the facts in this case to our particular circumstances.

   - The company claimed wear and tear allowances on expenditure incurred on canopies in filling station forecourts as plant.
   - The canopies carried lit plastic advertising signs.
   - The canopies *provided functions other than mere shelter* such as attracting customers and product promotion.

   The High Court decision that the canopies did constitute plant and qualified for capital allowances was supported by the Supreme Court.
   In his judgement, Blayney J said "I must first look at the entire picture and satisfy myself as to the precise nature of the trade being carried on and then ask myself what precise function if any do the canopies fulfil, are they simply a place where business is carried on, or do they perform a function in the actual carrying on of a trade."

4. Advise your client
   In this case, the client should be advised that because the partition forms an integral part of generating accurate test results and therefore are not merely the setting in which the tests are performed, the items would qualify as plant (and wear and tear allowances can be claimed).

Scenario 3

Your client, Wimbledon Tennis Ltd, wants to boost sales of tennis racquets and proposes to give a voucher entitling the consumer to a free can of tennis balls with every tennis racquet bought. The racquet manufacturer has agreed to refund 50% of the cost of providing the free tennis balls. The racquets vary in price from €50 to €250 and the three-pack of tennis balls retail at €25. Your advice is sought on how to account for the VAT.

The process of building a case to support a client scenario begins as before with determining the facts of your case accurately.

The issue in this case is what value should be attributed to the can of tennis balls for VAT purposes.

1. Determine the facts of your case accurately:

    ■ The tennis balls are given free of charge and no consideration is received from the customer.

    ■ 50% of the selling price of the tennis balls is received from the racquet manufacturer.

2. Then refer to tax statute. Review the ordinary meaning in the light of the facts in your case.

    ***VAT Consolidation Act 2010, section 37** (Part 5, Chapter 1) – (1) The amount on which tax is chargeable by virtue of section 3(a) or (c) shall, subject to this Chapter, be the total consideration which the person supplying goods or services becomes entitled to receive in respect of or in relation to such supply of goods or services, including all taxes, commissions, costs and charges whatsoever, but not including value-added tax chargeable in respect of that supply,*

    ***VAT Consolidation Act 2010, section 19** (Part 3, Chapter 1) — (1) In this Act "supply", in relation to goods, means—*

    (a) the transfer of ownership of the goods by agreement.

    However this case is distinguished by reason of the tennis racquet consideration.

3. Provide supporting evidence for your interpretation in case law either through similar situations or similar interpretation.

    There are many cases dealing with the supply of money off vouchers for example, *Kuwait Petroleum Ltd v. C&E Commrs,* where vouchers were given with petrol entitling customers to redeem them for certain goods or services provided by Kuwait Petroleum. Kuwait claimed an input credit on the VAT on purchase of the goods on the basis that they were part of the original supply of petrol. However, the ECJ found that the goods were supplied on redemption of the vouchers and so were free of charge.

    Goods given free of charge are liable to VAT on their cost (usually given by way of disallowing the input credit on their purchase.)

    In the *Elida Gibbs Ltd v. C&E Commrs* case a refund from the manufacturer was deemed to be deducted from the original selling price in computing taxable amount.

4. Advise your client
    What would your advice be?

Note: A gift only arises where no consideration is received for it by the supplier. In such cases, where the cost of the gift is below €20, there is no output VAT due by the supplier, although input VAT is deductible.

Problems frequently arise when goods are supplied on a promotional basis either on their own or in conjunction with other supplies. A gift for VAT purposes is legislated for in Article 16 of Council Directive 2006/112/EC and section 21 VATCA 2010 and Regulation 27 VAT Regulations 2006. A gift only arises where no consideration is received for it by the supplier. In such cases, where the cost of the gift is below €20, there is no output VAT due by the supplier, although input VAT is deductible.

However, if there is a requirement for the customer to pay a consideration in connection with the receipt of an item, even if the supplier describes part of that item as a **"gift"**, or as being **"free"**, (for example "buy one, get one free", a free bar of chocolate with the purchase of a jar of coffee, a CD/promotional item with a newspaper/magazine), it does not come within the terms of a gift for VAT purposes. Where there is consideration, it is always referable to all the items supplied.

As regards "buy one, get one free" offers, the VAT analysis is that the consideration is referable to the supply of both items. There is no issue regarding which rate applies. As regards the free bar of chocolate (23% rate) with a jar of coffee (0% rate), assuming the bar of chocolate does not come within the de minimis rule, the VAT analysis is that the consideration is referable to both items, resulting in a multiple supply. As regards the supply of newspapers, magazines and periodicals when they are supplied together with, for example, a CD or other promotional item, Revenue regards all such supplies as multiple supplies for consideration in the course or furtherance of business. In these circumstances, the promotional item should not be treated as a gift. The total consideration payable must be apportioned for a multiple supply. However, the de minimis rule provided for by regulation may apply.

Chartered Accountants Ireland
Code of Ethics

Under the Chartered Accountants Ireland *Code of Ethics*, a Chartered Accountant shall comply with the following fundamental principles:

(a) **Integrity** – to be straightforward and honest in all professional and business relationships.

(b) **Objectivity** – to not allow bias, conflict of interest or undue influence of others to override professional or business judgements.

(c) **Professional Competence and Due Care** – to maintain professional knowledge and skill at the level required to ensure that a client or employer receives competent professional services based on current developments in practice, legislation and techniques, and act diligently and in accordance with applicable technical and professional standards.

(d) **Confidentiality** – to respect the confidentiality of information acquired as a result of professional and business relationships and, therefore, not disclose any such information to third parties without proper and specific authority, unless there is a legal or professional right or duty to disclose, nor use the information for the personal advantage of the Chartered Accountant or third parties.

(e) **Professional Behaviour** – to comply with relevant laws and regulations and avoid any action that discredits the profession.

As a Chartered Accountant, you will have to ensure that your dealings with the tax aspects of your professional life are in compliance with these fundamental principles. You will not be asked to define or list the principles, but you must be able to identify where these ethical issues arise and how you would deal with them.

Examples of situations that could arise where these principles are challenged are outlined below:

Example 1

You are working in the Tax Department of ABC & Co and your manager is Jack Wilson. He comes over to your desk after his meeting with Peter Foley. He gives you all the papers that Peter has left with him. He asks you to draft Peter's tax return. You know who Peter is as you are now living in a house that your friend Ann leased from Peter. As you complete the return, you note that there is no information regarding rental income. What should you do?

Action

As a person with integrity, you should explain to your manager that your friend Ann has leased property from Peter and that he has forgotten to send details of his rental income and expenses. As Peter sent the information to Jack, it is appropriate for Jack to contact Peter for details regarding rental income and related expenses.

Example 2

You are working in the Tax Department of the Irish subsidiary of a US-owned multinational. You are preparing the corporation tax computation, including the R&D tax credit due. You have not received some information from your colleagues dealing with R&D and cannot finalise the claim for R&D tax credit until you receive this information. Your manager is under pressure and tells you to just file the claim on the basis that will maximise the claim. He says, "It is self-assessment, and the chance of this ever being audited is zero." What should you do?

Action

You should act in a professional and objective manner. This means that you cannot do as your manager wants. You should explain to him that you will contact the person in R&D again and finalise the claim as quickly as possible.

Example 3

Anna O Shea, financial controller of Great Client Ltd, rings you regarding a VAT issue. You have great respect for Anna and are delighted that she is ringing you directly instead of your manager. She says that it is a very straightforward query. However, as you listen to her, you realise that you are pretty sure of the answer but would need to check a point before answering. What should you do?

Action

Where you do not know the answer, it is professionally competent to explain that you need to check a point before you give an answer. If you like, you can explain which aspect you need to check. Your client will appreciate you acting professionally rather than giving incorrect information or advice.

Example 4

The phone rings, and it is Darren O'Brien, your best friend, who works for Just-do-it Ltd. After discussing the match you both watched on the television last night, Darren explains why he is ringing you. He has heard that Success Ltd, a client of your Tax Department, has made R&D tax credit claims. Therefore, you must have details regarding its R&D. Darren's relationship with his boss is not great at present, and he knows that if he could get certain data about Success Ltd, his relationship with his boss would improve. He explains that he does not want any financial information, just some small details regarding R&D. What should you do?

Action

You should not give him the information. No matter how good a friend he is, it is unethical to give confidential information about your client to him.

Example 5

It is the Friday morning before a bank holiday weekend, and you are due to travel from Dublin to west Cork after work for the weekend. Your manager has been on annual leave for the last week. He left you work to do for the week, including researching a tax issue for a client. He had advised you that you were to have an answer to the issue by the time he returned, no matter how long it took. It actually took you a very short time and you have it all documented for him.

Your friend who is travelling with you asks if you could leave at 11 am to beat the traffic and have a longer weekend. You have no annual leave left, so you cannot take leave. You know that if you leave, nobody will notice, but you have to complete a timesheet. Your friend reminds you that the research for the client could have taken a lot longer and that you could code the five hours to the client. What should you do?

Action

It would be unprofessional behaviour and would show a lack of integrity if you were to charge your client for those five hours.

Suggested Solutions to Review Questions

1 Overview of Tax System

1.1 Pat and Una

Income Tax Computation of Pat and Una for 2012			
	Pat €	Una €	Total €
Total Income	15,000	47,000	62,000
TAX PAYABLE: (married persons)			
Una – First €41,800 @ 20%		8,360	8,360
Pat – €15,000 @ 20%	3,000		3,000
Una – Balance €5,200 @ 41%		2,132	2,132
Gross income tax liability	3,000	10,492	13,492
Less: tax credits			(6,600)
Net tax due			**6,892**

1.2 Paul and Jason

Income Tax Computation of Paul and Jason for 2012			
	Paul €	Jason €	Total €
Total Income	47,000	41,000	88,000
TAX PAYABLE: (civil partners)			
First €65,600 @ 20%			13,120
Balance €22,400 @ 41%			9,184
Gross income tax liability			22,304
Less: tax credits			(3,300)
Net tax due			**19,004**

1.3   Sean Paul and Norah

Income Tax Computation of Sean Paul and Norah for 2012	
	Total
	€
Total Income	88,000
TAX PAYABLE: (married one income)	
First €41,800 @ 20%	8,360
Balance €46,200 @ 41%	18,942
Gross income tax liability	27,302
Less: tax credits	(5,760)
Net tax due	21,542

2   Residence and Domicile

2.1   Hank

(a) 2010

TEST 1:	Did Hank spend more than 30 days in Ireland in 2010?	
ANSWER:	Yes, 226 days. Therefore, go to Test 2.	
TEST 2:	Did Hank spend 183 days or more in Ireland in 2010?	
ANSWER:	Yes; therefore, Hank is Irish resident for 2010.	

(b) 2011

TEST 1:	Did Hank spend more than 30 days in Ireland in 2011?	
ANSWER:	Yes, the full year. Therefore, go to Test 2.	
TEST 2:	Did Hank spend 183 days or more in Ireland in 2011?	
ANSWER:	Yes, the full year. Therefore, Hank is Irish resident in 2011.	

(c) 2012

TEST 1:	Did Hank spend more than 30 days in Ireland in 2012?	
ANSWER:	Yes, 121 days. Therefore, go to Test 2.	
TEST 2:	Did Hank spend 183 days or more in Ireland in 2012?	
ANSWER:	No. Therefore, go on to Test 3.	
TEST 3:	Number of days in Ireland in 2012 (if more than 30)	121
	Number of days in Ireland in 2011 (if more than 30)	365
	Total days in Ireland in current and previous years	468
QUESTION:	Did Hank spend 280 days or more in Ireland in 2011 and 2012?	
ANSWER:	Yes. Therefore, Hank is Irish resident in 2012.	
	(Note: Split year concession may be available. See **Section 2.7**).	

2.2 Kenji

(a) 2009	
TEST 1:	Did Kenji spend more than 30 days in Ireland in 2009?
ANSWER:	No, 15 days. Therefore, Kenji is not Irish resident for 2009.
(b) 2010	
TEST 1:	Did Kenji spend more than 30 days in Ireland in 2010?
ANSWER:	Yes, the full year. Therefore, go to Test 2.
TEST 2:	Did Kenji spend 183 days or more in Ireland in 2010?
ANSWER:	Yes. Therefore Kenji is Irish resident in 2010.
(c) 2011	
TEST 1:	Did Kenji spend more than 30 days in Ireland in 2011?
ANSWER:	Yes, the full year. Therefore, go to Test 2.
TEST 2:	Did Kenji spend 183 days or more in Ireland in 2011?
ANSWER:	Yes. Therefore Kenji is Irish resident in 2011.
(d) 2012	
TEST 1:	Did Kenji spend more than 30 days in Ireland in 2012?
ANSWER:	No, 16 days. Therefore, Kenji is not Irish resident in 2012.

2.3 Aurore

Tax Year	Resident	Ordinarily Resident
2011	Yes > 183 days	No
2012	Yes > 183 days	No
2013	Yes > 183 days	No
2014	No – fails 30 day test	Yes, as resident for three preceding years

For the years 2011 to 2014, Aurore is resident in Ireland and will be taxed on both her Irish salary and her salary paid in France if the latter is paid in respect of the performance of her duties as an employee in Ireland. The salary paid in France does not have to be remitted to be liable to tax in Ireland; it must be connected to the performance of Aurore's employment duties in the State. Any other income will only be taxed to the extent that it is remitted to the State.

For the tax year 2014, Aurore will be taxed on her Irish income, and on other income paid into the State, but will not pay tax on her French salary or other non-Irish income of less than €3,810 per annum. Aurore will continue to be ordinarily resident in Ireland until she has been non-resident for three years, i.e. until 2017.

2.4 Mr Harris

As Mr Harris is neither Irish resident nor Irish domiciled, he is liable only on income arising in Ireland and is not entitled to the married persons tax bands or to any tax credits.

	€
Schedule D Case V	37,000
€32,800 @ 20%	6,560
€4,200 @ 41%	1,722
	8,282
Less tax deducted at source from rent paid	(7,400)
Tax due	882
Note: Mr Harris' domicile is not relevant.	

2.5 Mr Klaus

SARP Relief 2012

SARP Relief:

Is relevant income > €75,000?

Salary €250,000 > €75,000 ⇒ eligible for SARP relief

Calculation of **Specified Amount:**

	€
Total income	272,500
Less: lower threshold	(75,000)
	197,500
Specified Amount @ 30%	**59,250**
Total income	272,500
Less: specified amount	(59,250)
Taxable income	213,250

Note: As Mr Klaus has paid PAYE on his total income, he will need to make a claim for a tax repayment of €59,250 @ 41% = €24,292.50.

3 Classification of Income

3.1 Ms Lola

Year of Assessment		Basis	Original Figure €	Final Figure €
2011	1st Year:	Actual 1/6/2011 – 31/12/2011 7/12 × €48,000	28,000	N/A
2012	2nd Year:	12 month accounting period ending in tax year 1/6/2011 – 31/5/2012	48,000	N/A
2013	3rd Year:	12 month accounting period ending in the year of assessment – year ended 31/5/2013	39,000	33,750 Note
2014	4th Year:	12 month accounting period ending in the year of assessment – year ended 31/5/2014	37,200	N/A
Note: Amount assessed in the second year (2012)			48,000	

Less: Actual profits for the second year

	(48,000 × 5/12) + (39,000 × 7/12)	42,750
	Excess	5,250
Final 2013 assessment: 39,000 – 5,250 =		33,750

3.2 Mr Charlie

Year of Assessment		Basis	Initial Figure €	Final Figure €
2011	1st Year:	Actual 1/5/2011 – 31/12/2011 44,800 + (2/12 × 54,400)	53,867	N/A
2012	2nd Year:	12 month accounting period ending in tax year y/e 31/10/2012	54,400	N/A
2013	3rd Year:	12 month accounting period ending in tax year Year ended 31/10/2013	53,600	53,467
Note: Amount assessed in the second year (2012) 54,400				

Less: Actual profits for the second year

(54,400 × 10/12) + (53,600 × 2/12) =   54,267

Excess   133

As the amount assessed for the second year exceeds the actual profits for the second year, a claim may be made for a deduction of €133 against the profits of the third year of assessment (2013):

y/e 31/10/2013	53,600
Excess for 2012	(133)
Final assessment	53,467

3.3   Jim – Commencement

Case II Assessments

			€
1st Tax Year 2011	1 May 2011 to 31/12/2011		
	8/12 × €48,000		32,000
2nd Tax Year 2012	12 month accounting period ending in tax year y/e 30/4/2012 =		48,000
3rd Tax Year 2013	Y/e 30/4/2013 =	(Note)	60,000
4th Tax Year 2014	Y/e 30/4/2014		9,600
Note: Profits assessable for second year, i.e. 2012:		48,000	

Actual profits for second year 2012: (48,000 × 4/12) + (60,000 × 8/12) = 56,000

Therefore, no reduction for third year 2013.

3.4   Donna Ross – Commencement

Case I Assessments

		€
1st Tax Year 2012	1 May 2012 to 31/12/2012	
	8/12 × €179,400	119,600
2nd Tax Year 2013	12 month accounting period ending in tax year y/e 30/4/2013 =	179,400

Donna Ross Income Tax Computation for 2012 and 2013				
		2012 €		2013 €
Schedule D Case I		119,600		179,400
Schedule E salary		20,300		–
Total Income		139,900		179,400
Tax (as single parent)				
36,800 @ 20%		7,360		7,360
Balance @ 41%	(103,100)	42,271	(142,600)	58,466
Less tax credits		(4,950)		(3,300)
PAYE paid		(3,902)		-
Income tax due		40,779		62,526

MEMO

To: Donna Ross   **Date: 3 January 2014**

cc:

From: Your Accountant   **Re: Taxable Trading**

I refer to our meeting last week. I have calculated your income tax liability for 2012 and 2013 at €40,779 and €62,526 respectively. The computations are attached.

I have considered the facts around your e-bay activity for 2010 and 2011. To be liable to income tax, your e-bay activity must constitute trading. There is no definition of trading in the Taxes Acts, and guidance is available in case law and the UK Royal Commission Rules. The rules or "Badges of Trade", for deciding whether you were trading are:

"Badge of Trade"	Your circumstances
Subject matter – if ownership does not give income or personal enjoyment, then sales indicate trading.	As your sales were of items bought originally for your enjoyment, this is not indicative of trading.
Length of ownership – short period indicates trading	The 2011 job lot purchase and sale had a very quick turnaround indicating trading.
Frequency – more over a long period indicates trading	Transactions appear infrequent and opportunistic, not indicative of trading.
Supplementary work indicates trading	As you didn't have an e-bay "shop" until 2012, there is no indication of an effort to obtain customers.
Circumstances, if opportunistic or unsolicited, refute trading	Sales until 2012 were opportunistic, and the items sold personal in nature. This would counteract the trading suggestion.
Motive	The evidence suggests the activity was merely a hobby until the business was established in 2012.

In deciding if trading is carried on, all rules are evaluated and the whole picture is taken into account. The overriding evidence in your case suggests that no trading took place during 2010 and 2011, and the activity involved an attempt to de-clutter your home.

3.5 Ms Dora – Cessation

Year of Assessment	Original Basis Period	Original Figure €	Revised Figure €	
2010	Year ended 31/5/2010	64,000	N/A	
2011	Year ended 31/5/2011	72,000	N/A	(Note 1)
2012	Actual 1/1/2012–31/12/2012	16,000	N/A	(Note 2)

Notes:
1. Actual Profits 2011
   $(72,000 \times 5/12) + (9,600 \times 7/12) = €35,600$, therefore no revision
2. Actual: $1/1/2012–31/12/2012 = €12,000 + (5/12 \times €9,600) = €16,000$

3.6 Mr Diego – Cessation

Year of Assessment	Original Basis Period	Original Figures €	Revised Figures €	
2010	Year ended 31/7/2010	32,000	N/A	
2011	Year ended 31/7/2011	60,000	N/A	(Note 1)
2012	Actual 1/1/2012–31/5/2012	20,000	N/A	(Note 2)

Notes:
1. Actual Profits 2011
   $(60,000 \times 7/12) + (40,000 \times 5/10)$ = 55,000
   Therefore, original assessment will not be revised
2. Actual Profits 1/1/2012–31/5/2012
   $40,000 \times 5/10$ = 20,000

3.7 Alex

		€
Final year 2012	$9/12 \times €240,000$	180,000
Penultimate year 2011	(Note)	78,000

Note: Actual profit 2011: $(24,000 \times 9/12) + (240,000 \times 3/12) = 78,000$

This figure will be assessed, as it is higher than the profits for the y/e 30/9/2011 of €24,000, which would have been originally assessed.

Alex Income Tax Computation for 2012	
	€
Schedule D Case I	180,000
Schedule E salary	15,000
Total Income	195,000
	continued overleaf

Tax as single person:	
32,800 @ 20%	6,560
Balance @ 41% (162,200)	66,502
	73,062
Less tax credits	(3,300)
PAYE paid	(3,485)
Income tax due	66,277

3.8 J. Cog

As J. Cog retired on 30 September 2012, his last year of assessment is 2012. The requirement is, therefore, to calculate his assessable income for 2011 and 2012. The tax years 2009 and 2010 don't change.

		€
2012	9/11 × 24,000 (9 months to 30/9/2012)	19,636
2011	y/e 31/10/2011	64,000 (Note)
2010	y/e 31/10/2010	65,000 – no change
2009	y/e 31/10/2009	40,000 – no change

Note: Actual profit 2011 (64,000 × 10/12) + (24,000 × 2/11) = 57,697. The 2011 assessment will therefore not be revised to an actual basis.

3.9 AB Partnership

Distribution of Profits				
	Total €	A €	B €	C €
Year ended 30/9/2008	20,000	10,000	10,000	Nil
Year ended 30/9/2009	25,000	10,000	10,000	5,000
Year ended 30/9/2010	30,000	12,000	12,000	6,000
Year ended 30/9/2011	30,000	Nil	15,000	15,000
Year ended 30/9/2012	35,000	Nil	17,500	17,500

Assessments will be raised as follows:			
A.	**Yr. of Assessment**	**Final Basis Period**	**Profits Assessable €**
	2008	y/e 30/9/2008	10,000
	2009	Actual (Note 1)	10,500
	2010 Cessation	1/1/2010–30/9/2010 (12,000 × 9/12)	9,000

Note 1:
2009 actual profits: (10,000 × 9/12) + (12,000 × 3/12) = 10,500. As this is higher than profits of the original basis period y/e 30/9/2009, actual profits will be assessed.

B.	Yr. of Assessment	Final Basis Period	Profits Assessable €
	2008	y/e 30/9/2008	10,000
	2009	y/e 30/9/2009	10,000
	2010	y/e 30/9/2010	12,000
	2011	y/e 30/9/2011	15,000
	2012	y/e 30/9/2012	17,500

C.	Yr. of Assessment	Basis Period	Profits Assessable €
	2008 Commencement	1/10/2008–31/12/2008 (3/12 × 5,000)	1,250
	2009	y/e 30/9/2009	5,000
	2010	y/e 30/9/2010 (Note 2)	6,000
	2011	y/e 30/9/2011	15,000
	2012	y/e 30/9/2012	17,500

Note 2:

2009: Actual profits: (5,000 × 9/12) + (6,000 × 3/12) = 5,250. As this is greater than the profits assessable for the second year, the third year does not require amendment.

3.10   June, Mary and Karen

Allocation of profits:						
	June	**Mary**	**Karen**	**Jill**	**Louise**	**Total**
	€	€	€	€	€	€
Y/e 30/6/2008	16,000	12,000	12,000			40,000
Y/e 30/6/2009	24,000	18,000	18,000			60,000
Y/e 30/6/2010	21,600	16,200		16,200		54,000
Y/e 30/6/2011	20,000	15,000		15,000		50,000
Y/e 30/6/2012	9,000	9,000		9,000	9,000	36,000
Six months to 31/12/2012	5,000	5,000		5,000	5,000	20,000

2008		€
June:	year ended 30/6/2008	16,000
Mary:	year ended 30/6/2008	12,000
Karen:	Actual (Note 1)	15,000
2009		
June:	Year ended 30/6/2009	24,000
Mary:	Year ended 30/6/2009	18,000
Karen:	Actual (Note 2)	9,000
Jill:	Actual (Note 3)	8,100
2010		
June:	year ended 30/6/2010	21,600
Mary:	year ended 30/6/2010	16,200
Jill:	year ended 30/6/2010	16,200

		€
2011		
June:	year ended 30/6/2011 (Note 6)	20,000
Mary:	year ended 30/6/2011 (Note 6)	15,000
Jill:	(Note 4)	14,400
Louise:	Actual (Note 5)	4,500
2012	(year of cessation – all partners on actual basis)	
June:	1/1/2012 – 30/6/2012 (9,000 × 6/12)	4,500
	1/7/2012 – 31/12/2012	<u>5,000</u>
		9,500
Mary:	As above	9,500
Jill:	As above	9,500
Louise:	As above	9,500

Note 1:

Karen:	2008: original assessment: Y/E 30/6/2008	<u>12,000</u>
	Actual profits 2008:	
	(12,000 × 6/12) + (18,000 × 6/12) =	<u>15,000</u>
	Penultimate year revised to actual.	

Note 2:

Karen:	2009: final year actual: 1/1/2009 – 30/6/2009	
	18,000 × 6/12 =	<u>9,000</u>

Note 3:

Jill:	2009 first year actual 16,200 × 6/12 =	<u>8,100</u>

Note 4:

Jill:	Second year 2010: assessment Y/E 30/6/2010	
	Actual profit for second year:	16,200
	(16,200 × 6/12) + (15,000 × 6/12) = Excess	
	Final third year assessment: 15,000 – 600 =	<u>(15,600)</u> 600
		<u>14,400</u>

Note 5:

Louise:	2011: First year actual: 9,000 × 6/12 = 4,500

Note 6:

There will be no revision of 2011 (penultimate year) profits to actual as actual profits were less than those assessed, i.e.:

June actual 2011 (20,000 × 6/12) + (9,000 × 6/12) = €14,500
Mary actual 2011 (15,000 × 6/12) + (9,000 × 6/12) = €12,000
Jill actual 2011 – as for Mary 12,000

3.11 Maeve

Income Tax Computation of Maeve		2012 €
Schedule D Case IV (Note 1)		10,714
Schedule E SW		11,976
Schedule F dividends (Note 2)		23,900
Total income		46,590
TAXED	Deposit interest €10,714 @ 30%	3,214
(widowed without dependent children)	€32,800 @ 20%	6,560
	Balance €3,076 @ 41%	1,261
	Gross income tax liability	11,035
	Less tax credits	(2,190)
	Less DIRT paid	(3,214)
	Less DWT paid	(4,780)
	Tax due	851

Note 1:

Schedule D Case IV		*Gross*	*DIRT @ 30%*
PTSB	6,300/0.70	9,000	2,700
Credit Union	1,200/0.70	1,714	514
		10,714	3,214

Note 2:

Schedule F Dividends		*Gross*	*DWT @ 20%*
Tyson	17,520/0.80	21,900	4,380
Holyfield	1,600/0.80	2,000	400
		23,900	4,780

Interest earned on long-term accounts in excess of €635 is subject to DIRT but should not be included in the income tax computation.

4 Computation of Taxable Income

4.1 Joseph Murphy

Computation of Tax-adjusted Case I Profit y/e 31 December 2012			
		€	€
Profit per accounts			9,874
	Add: Drawings (note)	8,500	
	Interest on VAT	1,121	
	Interest on PAYE	1,238	
			continued overleaf

	Depreciation	13,793	
	Subscription (political, football old folks, sports)	525	
	Repairs (6,480 – 2,335)	4,145	
	Bad debts - increase in general provision (7,975 – 5,100)	2,875	
	Legal fees (capital)	<u>1,009</u>	<u>33,206</u>
			43,080
Deduct:	Dividend from Irish Co.	2,813	
	National loan stock interest	2,250	
	Deposit interest	170	
	Profit on fixed assets	<u>5,063</u>	(10,296)
Case I Profit			**32,784**

Note: Disallow Mr Murphy's salary of €7,500 and the €1,000 holiday trip as these are drawings.

4.2 Andy Reilly

Computation of Tax-adjusted Case I Profit y/e 31 December 2012			€
Net Profit before Taxation			36,050
Add:	**Disallowed Expenses:**		
	Motor vehicles (Note 1)		2,400
	Depreciation	– Equipment	2,500
		– Vehicles	3,000
		– Office Equipment	900
	Construction of garages (capital)		3,150
	General bad debt provision		275
	Drawings		20,000
	Entertainment	– Holiday	1,200
		– Tickets (non-business)	300
		– Customer business meals	<u>1,200</u>
Case I Tax-adjusted Profit			**70,975**

Note 1: Disallowed Motor Expenses	€
Expenses for Andy Reilly's car	4,000
Disallow personal element 60% × €4,000	2,400

4.3 Tony

(a) Computation of adjusted profit for the 15 months ended 31 December 2012 and the 12 months ended 31 December 2013:

	15 months ended 31/12/2012		12 months ended 31/12/2013	
	€		€	
Net loss per accounts		(4,350)		(7,400)
Disallow:				
Depreciation	3,000		2,400	
General provision for bad debts	2,500			
Entertaining	1,500		700	
Political donations	100			
Charitable donations	50			
Interest on late payment of VAT	250		–	
Drawings	15,000		12,000	
		22,400		15,100
Adjusted profit		18,050		7,700
Allow:				
Reduction in general provision				
for bad debts		–		(500)
Adjusted profit		**18,050**		**7,200**

(b) Tony's Case I taxable profit for 2011:

2012 is Tony's second tax year of trading. An accounting period for a period in excess of 12 months ends in that year, namely the 15 month period ending 31 December 2012. Accordingly, Tony is taxable on the profits for the year ending on 31 December 2012. Taxable Case I profits for 2012 are therefore €18,050 × 12/15 = €14,440.

4.4 John Smith

Computation of Adjusted Profit for the 12 Months ended 30 April 2013			
		€	€
Profit per accounts			2,820
Disallow:			
Drawings (wages to self)		5,200	
Own PRSI		200	
Depreciation		1,250	
Motor expenses	(Note 1)	924	
Leasing charges	(Note 2)	1,994	
Extension		1,500	
		continued overleaf	

Provision for repairs		1,000
Interest on late payment of tax		120
Covenant to church	(Note 3)	260
Covenant to son		710
Retirement annuities		1,100
Life assurance		460
		14,718
		17,538
Less: Interest received		(390)
Adjusted trading profits		**17,148**

Note 1:

		Add back
Motor expenses	1,860	
Less: parking fine	(100)	100
	1,760	
Plus car insurance	300	
	2,060	
Less private element 40%	(824)	824
	1,236	
Total disallowed		924

Note 2:

		Add back
Lease charges on car	2,800	
Less private element 40%	(1,120)	1,120
Lease charges restriction (category D):	1,680	
$1,680 \times \dfrac{(25,000 - (24,000 \times 50\%))}{25,000} =$		874
		1,994

Emissions category D €24,000 – applies where vehicle leased on/after 1 July 2008

Note 3:
A donation in excess of €250 made to an eligible charity is given as a deduction from total income (in the income tax computation) and not as a deduction from Case I/II income.

Note 4:
The accrued bonus for the sales assistant should be added back if it remains unpaid six months after the year end.

4.5 Polly Styrene

Computation of Adjusted Profit for the Year Ended 31 December 2012		
	€	€
Profit per accounts		22,000
Disallow:		
Wages to self	8,000	
Light, heat and telephone (5/6 × 1,500)	1,250	
Repairs and renewals (extension to shop and general provision)	3,400	
Legal and professional fees	300	

Bad debts		(600)	
Travel and entertainment (1)		1,100	
Royalties		25,000	
Lease interest (3)		2,000	
Sundries (2)		1,549	
			41,999
Allow:			
Lease repayments (3)			(18,600)
Case I Adjusted Profits Year Ended 31/12/2012			45,399

Notes:

1. **Travel and entertainment**

Motor expenses (private 1/3 × 1,500)	500
Entertaining customers	600
	1,100

2. **Sundries**

Political party	1,000
Parking fines	49
Charitable donation*	500
	1,549

3. **Lease interest**

	€
Deduct total repayments for the year (allowable)	18,600
Add back lease interest deducted from profit	2,000

* Tax relief for the charitable donation will be claimed in Polly's personal tax return.

4.6 Jack and John

Case II computation			
Computation of Adjusted Profit	€	€	
Net profit Y/e 30/4/2012		46,000	
Add back:			
Disallowed expenses	26,000		
Partner salaries	41,000		
Partner interest	13,000	80,000	
Assessable profit		126,000	
Partnership Allocation	**Total**	**Jack**	**John**
Salaries (actual)	41,000	20,000	21,000
Interest (actual)	13,000	6,000	7,000
Balance (50:50)	72,000	36,000	36,000
Total	126,000	62,000	64,000
Case II Taxable Profits for 2012		**62,000**	**64,000**

4.7 Anthony and Sandrine Kelly (Investment Income)

Income Tax Computation 2012		Notes:	€	€
Income:				
Schedule D:	Case III – Anthony	(1)		900
	Case IV – Anthony	(2)	210	
	Case IV – Sandrine (Dresdner bank)		2,000	2,210
Schedule E:	Anthony		50,000	
	Sandrine		28,000	78,000
Schedule F	Gross dividend	(3)		3,125
Total/Taxable Income				84,235
Tax: (married, two incomes)				
	€2,210 @ 30%		663	
	€65,600 @ 20%		13,120	
	€16,425 @ 41%		6,734	20,517
Deduct:	Tax credits		9,900	
	DIRT €210 @ 30%		63	(9,963)
Net Tax Liability				10,554
Deduct:	PAYE paid – Anthony			(5,800)
	PAYE paid – Sandrine			(4,000)
	DWT			(625)
Tax due				129

Notes:

€

1. Case III Income:
   UK dividends net of UK tax   900

2. Case IV Income:
   Credit Union interest, ordinary deposit account   80
   AIB ordinary deposit account   130
       210

Interest on the medium term share account is exempt as it is less than €480.
Dresdner Bank interest of €2,000 may be treated as Case IV and taxed at the Case IV interest rate of 30% provided the tax due is paid on or before the filing date for the 2012 tax return (i.e. 31 October 2013).

3. Schedule F Income:
   Dividends net of DWT   2,500
   DWT @ 20%   625
   Gross   3,125

4.8   David Lee

David Lee – Income Tax 2012		€	€
Schedule D Case III			
Interest on government stock		1,130	
Income from Credit Union regular share account		<u>29</u>	1,159
Schedule D Case IV : 500 + 140 = 640 @ 100/70			914
Schedule E salary			<u>42,000</u>
Taxable Income			<u>44,073</u>
Tax:			
	€36,800 × 20% =		7,360
	€914 @ 30%		274
	€6,359 @ 41% =		<u>2,607</u>
			10,241
Less: personal tax credit		4,950	
DIRT	€914 @ 30% =	<u>274</u>	<u>(5,224)</u>
Tax Liability			5,017
PAYE deducted			<u>(4,900)</u>
Tax due			€117

Note: Interest from Post Office Savings Certificates is ignored, as these are tax-free.

4.9   Mr O'Reilly

			Properties			
			A	**B**	**C**	**D**
			Res	Comm	Res	Res
	Case V	Notes:	€	€	€	€
a.	Rent receivable during 2012		6,000	5,000	3,500	52
b.	Premium on lease	(1)		6,000		–
			6,000	11,000	3,500	52
Less:	Allowable expenses:	(2)				
	Bank interest	(1)	(4,125)	(3,000)	–	–
	Storm damage		–	(1,400)	–	–
	Advertising		–	–	(130)	–
	Roof repairs		–	–	–	(160)
	Blocked drains and painting		–	–	(790)	–
	Net rents		1,875	6,600	2,580	(108)

continued overleaf

Summary:	(3)	
Property A		1,875
Property B		6,600
Property C		2,580
Net assessable Case V 2012		€11,055

Notes:

1. Premium on Lease

Property A

Although the rent for December was not received until after the end of the tax year, it is still taken into account in 2012 as Case V is assessed on rents receivable. We assume he has registered the property with the PRTB. Section 97 TCA 1997 restricted the allowable interest on rental residential properties from 7 April 2009 to 75% of the amount incurred. Therefore, the interest allowable is:

$$(€5,500 \times 75\%) = €4,125$$

Property B

Let from 1 August 2012, i.e. 5 months @ €1,000 p.m. = €5,000

Assessable Portion of Premium:

$$€10,000 \times \frac{51 - 21}{50} = €6,000$$

Interest charge restriction:

$$(€3,600 \times \frac{5}{6}) = €3,000$$

Property C

$6,000 \times 4/12 = 2,000$	(4 months to 30 April)
$9,000 \times 2/12 = \underline{1,500}$	(2 months to 31 December)
$3,500$	

2. Allowable Expenses

Property B

Pre-letting expenses are not allowable.

These include bank interest paid in June 2012 of €1,800 and the interest relating to the period 1 July 2012 to 31 July 2012.

Expenses incurred in April and June are also disallowed as those are pre-letting expenses.

Property C

Although the property was vacant when the expenditure was incurred, this was only a temporary period of vacancy and the expenditure is allowed in full.

3. Summary

Losses on one property may be offset against the profit rents arising on other properties. However, the loss arising on property D is ignored for tax purposes as it is a "favoured" letting.

4.10 Sonya

(a) Property Income Assessable 2012

Rent Account 2012				
Property:	(1)	(2)	(3)	(4)
	€	€	€	€
Gross rents	16,000	8,000	9,600	4,500
Expenses	(4,300)	(1,200)	(800)	–
Interest	–	–	(1,400)	–
Net rents	11,700	6,800	7,400	4,500
Case V 2012	€30,400			

Notes:
1. The rent to be brought into account is that receivable in the tax year 2012 whether or not rent is actually received in the year, i.e. for Property 4 = 6/12 × €9,000.
2. The income from Property 5 is excluded on the grounds that the rent receivable under the lease, taking one year with another, is not sufficient to meet the allowable expenses connected with it. Losses may be accumulated and set off against future rental income from that property only.
3. Because all properties are commercial, no restriction is needed to interest and there is no requirement to register Property 3 with the PRTB in order to claim the interest paid.

(b) Tax Effects of Investments

   (i) *National Instalment Savings Scheme*
     Section 197 TCA 1997 exempts any bonus or interest payable to an individual under an instalment savings scheme.

   (ii) *Government Securities*
     Interest on Government securities is paid without deduction of tax and, accordingly, is assessable under Schedule D Case III on an actual basis.

4.11 Ray Houghton

Tax-free Element of Lump Sum

		€
(a)	Basic exemption €10,160 + (€765 × 18) =	23,930
(b)	May be increased to:	

		€	€
Basic exemption			23,930
Plus:		10,000	
Less: Tax free lump sum from pension scheme		(3,000)	7,000
			30,930

(c) May be further increased to SCSB, if greater:

$$SCSB = \frac{(A \times B)}{15} - C$$

A = Average of last three years' emoluments

B = Number of complete years of service

C = Tax-free lump sum from pension scheme

Therefore:

$$A = \frac{(€52,000 + €55,000 + €57,000)}{3} = €54,667$$

B = 18 years

C = €3,000

$$SCSB = [€54,667 \times \frac{18]}{15} - €3,000 = €62,600$$

As (c) results in the highest figure, the tax-free element of the lump sum is €62,600

Therefore, the taxable element is €2,400 (€65,000 − €62,600).

Mr Houghton			
Income Tax Liability 2012			
		€	€
Schedule E:	Salary 57,000 × 6/12		28,500
	Pension 18,000 × 6/12		9,000
	Termination payment	65,000	
	SCSB	(62,600)	2,400
Total/Taxable Income			39,900
Tax:			
	€32,800 @ 20%		6,560
	€7,100 @ 41%		2,911
			9,471
Deduct:	Tax credits		(3,300)
Net Tax Liability			6,171
Deduct:	PAYE paid		(7,000)
	Top slicing relief (Note1)		(352)
Tax refund due			**(1,181)**

Note: **Top Slicing Relief**

A = 2,400 × 41% = 984

P = 2,400

T = 42,100

I = 160,000

$$984 - (2,400 \times \frac{42,100)}{160,000} = 352$$

4.12   Mr Moran Termination

€

a.   Basic exemption €10,160 + (765 × 18)   23,930

b.   Increased basic exemption - not available as the tax-free pension lump sum of €19,000 received exceeds €10,000

c.   SCSB

$$A = \frac{37,250 + 34,500 + 32,625}{3} = 34,792$$

B = 18 years

C = 19,000

$$\left(34,792 \times \frac{18}{15} \right) - 19,000 = 22,750$$

As the basic exemption is higher than the SCSB, this is the exempt amount.

Lump sum	30,000
Less basic exemption	(23,930)
Taxable lump sum	€6,070

Mr Moran			
Income Tax Computation 2012		€	€
Schedule E:	Salary	28,500	
	Taxable lump sum	6,070	
Taxable Income			34,570
Tax @ 20%		6,914	
Deduct tax credits		(4,950)	
Net tax liability			1,964
Top slicing relief (note)			(738)
PAYE deducted			(2,200)
Tax refund due			(974)

Note:

Top slicing relief

$$6,070 \times 20\% = 1,214 - \left(6,070 \times \frac{7,800}{99,500} \right) = 738$$

4.13 Mr Lynch

Mr Lynch			
Income Tax 2012			
		€	€
Schedule E:	Salary		43,000
	Termination payment (Note 1)	30,000	
	Exempt (Note 1)	(27,810)	2,190
Total/Taxable Income			45,190
Tax	€32,800 @ 20%		6,560
	€12,390 @ 41%		5,080
			11,640
Deduct:	Tax credits		(3,840)
Net Tax Liability			7,800
Deduct:	PAYE paid		(6,000)
	Top slicing relief (Note 2)		(640)
Income tax due			1,160

Notes:

1. Lump sum: €30,000

   Exemption: (a) €10,160 + (€765 × 10)   = €17,810

                   (b) Increased basic exemption   €10,000

                       Total (a) + (b)   €27,810

                   (c) SCSB 10/15 × (43,000 + 35,000 + 30,000) ÷ 3

   $$= 10/15 \times \frac{108,000}{3} = €24,000$$

   As SCSB is lower than the basic exemption, the taxable element is (€30,000 – €27,810) = €2,190

      Pension contributions refund: they have been taxed at 20% under the usual arrangement and the figures will not impinge upon the computation of liability.

2. Top Slicing Relief

   $$2,190 \times 41\% = 896 - \left(2,190 \times \frac{9,700}{83,000}\right) = 640$$

4.14 Terence Flynn Termination Payment

Taxable Element of Lump Sum

		€
1.	Basic exemption €10,160 + (€765 × 15)	21,635
2.	May be increased by €10,000 less tax-free lump sum from pension scheme	
	Increased exemption	10,000
	Less: Tax-free lump sum from pension	Nil
		10,000
	Increased basic exemption	31,635

3. May be further increased to SCSB if greater.

$$SCSB = \frac{A \times B}{15} - C$$

A = Average of last three years salary

Year ended 30/9/2012	47,000
Year ended 30/9/2011	54,000
Year ended 30/9/2010	52,000
	153,000
Average (1/3rd)	€51,000

B = Number of complete years of service = 15 years

C = Tax-free lump sum from pension scheme = Nil

SCSB = €51,000 × 15/15	= 51,000

As SCSB is greater than the increased basic exemption, the taxable element of the lump sum is: €57,000 – €51,000 €6,000

Terence Flynn Tax Liability 2012					
Excluding Lump Sum	€	€	**Including Lump Sum**	€	€
Schedule E:			Total Income		
Salary from old job			As before		40,885
€47,000 × 9/12		35,250			
Unemployment benefit (note 1) (134 –13 = €121x8)		968	Lump sum	57,000	
Holiday pay		2,000			
Salary from new job			Exempt	(51,000)	6,000
€2,500 × 1		2,500			
Benefit in kind			Total/Taxable Income		46,885
€2,000 × 1/12		167			
		___	Tax		
Total/Taxable Income		40,885	€41,800 @ 20%		8,360
			€5,085 @ 41%		2,085
Tax					10,445
€40,885 @ 20%	8,177		Deduct:		
€0 @ 41%	0	8,177	Tax credits		
			As before		(4,950)
Deduct:			Net tax liability		5,495
Tax credits		(4,950)	Less: PAYE paid		(4,800)
			Top slicing relief (Note 2)		(737)
			Tax refund due		(42)
Net tax liability		€3,227			

Note 1:
The first €13 of weekly benefit is not taxable

Note 2:

The tax due on the lump sum if taxed in the normal manner
A = difference between the two figures i.e. 5,495 – 3,227 = 2,268

P = taxable lump sum = 6,000

T = total tax payable for past three years = 39,800

I = taxable income for past three years = 156,000

$$A - \left(P \times \frac{T}{I}\right)$$

2,268 – (6,000 × 39,800) / 156,000 = 737

Note:

Students should note that in their exam "A" in the formula for top slicing relief should be calculated the short way as outlined in previous solutions unless specifically requested to do otherwise.

4.15   Dermot O'Donnell

(a)

a.   Basic exemption €10,160 + (€765 × 15) = 21,635

b.   Increased basic exemption not available as tax free pension lump sum of €22,000 received exceeds €10,000

c.   SCSB

$$A = \frac{48,900 + 38,000 + 42,100}{3} = 43,000$$

B = 15 years

C = 22,000

$$\left(43,000 \times \frac{15}{15}\right) - 22,000 = 21,000$$

As the basic exemption is higher than the SCSB, €21,635 is the tax-free termination payment that can be made to Dermot O'Donnell.

Calculation of the lump sum:

	€
Compensation payment	40,500
Car	22,500
Lump sum	63,000
Less basic exemption	(21,635)
Taxable lump sum	41,365

(b)

Dermot O Donnell			
Income Tax Computation 2012			
		€	€
Schedule E:	Salary to September	37,000	
	Holiday pay	1,200	
	Salary to year end	4,200	
	Taxable lump sum	41,365	
Taxable Income			83,765
Tax payable:			
€36,800 @ 20%		7,360	
€46,965 @ 41%		19,256	26,616
Deduct tax credits			(4,950)
Net tax liability			21,666
Top slicing relief (note)			(13,200)
PAYE deducted			(10,400)
Refund due			(1,934)
Note:			
Top slicing relief			
$41,365 \times 41\% = 16,960 - (41,365 \times \frac{9,180}{101,000}) = €13,200$			

4.16 *Sid Harvey Benefit in Kind*

(a) Calculation of Taxable Benefit in Kind

CAR:

	€
OMV = €35,000	
Rate for 26,400 business km 24% =	8,400
Deduct: Fuel and insurance reimbursed	(1,300)
Sid's personal contribution €100 × 12	(1,200)
Final benefit-in-kind	5,900

Free use of apartment:

	€
Annual value 8% × €110,000	8,800
Add: Expenses paid by company	890
	9,690

Meals – exempt as provided free of charge to all staff

Loan – waiver of loan is treated as additional benefit in February 2012 of €1,000.

Loan interest − €1,000 × 12.5% × $\frac{1 \text{ month}}{12 \text{ months}}$ = €10

Note: Interest relief is not available to Sid in respect of the deemed interest paid as the loan was not a qualifying home loan as defined, i.e. the loan was not used for the purchase, repair, development or improvement of a principal private residence.

(b) Income Tax Computation For 2012			
		€	€
Schedule E Income :			
Salary 2012			40,000
Round sum expense allowance €100 × 12			1,200
Benefit-in-Kind:	Car	5,900	
	Apartment above	9,690	
	Meals	Exempt	15,590
Perquisites:	Loan waived	1,000	
	Deemed interest paid		
12 months	€1,000 × 12.5% × $\frac{1 \text{ month}}{12 \text{ months}}$	10	1,010
Gross Income			57,800
Tax payable (single):	€32,800 @ 20%	6,560	
	€25,000 @ 41%	10,250	
		16,810	
Basic personal tax credit		(3,300)	13,510
Deduct PAYE paid			(13,900)
Tax refund due			(390)

4.17 Terry

Benefit in kind:

Mortgage Loan

Preferential Loan

	€	
€125,000 × 5% =	6,250	
Less €125,000 × 2% =	(2,500)	Actual interest paid
Benefit in kind assessable	3,750	Deemed interest paid
Golf Club Loan		
Loan €10,000 × 12.5% =	1,250	Deemed interest paid
Company Car		
Cash equivalent percentage	18%	
(Business Km 36,000)		
€30,000 × 18% =	5,400	
Less reimbursement by employee 10,400 × 15c	(1,560)	
Benefit in kind assessable	3,840	

Taxable benefits:

Mortgage loan	€3,750	
Other loan	€1,250	
Golf club membership	€3,500	
Car	€3,840	
Total benefits assessable in 2012		€12,340

PAYE payable at 41%   €5,059 = cost of benefits provided

Terry – Income Tax Computation 2012		
	New Job	**Current Job**
	€	**€**
Schedule E salary	70,000	75,000
Benefit In Kind	12,340	0
Taxable Income	82,340	75,000
Tax (married - one income):		
€41,800 @ 20%	8,360	8,360
Balance @ 41%	16,621	13,612
	24,981	21,972
Deduct:		
Personal tax credits	(4,950)	(4,950)
Net tax liability	20,031	17,022
Net Pay Calculation:		
Salary	70,000	75,000
Deduct: Tax	(20,031)	(17,022)
	49,969	57,978
Add: Value of benefits:		
– Mortgage Interest saved (note 1)	3,750	0
– Car running costs (note 2)	9,580	0
Value received by Terry	**63,299**	**57,978**
Note 1: Mortgage		
Interest paid @ 5% €125,000 @ 5%		6,250
Interest paid @ 2% €125,000 @ 2%		(2,500)
Saving		3,750
		continued overleaf

Note 2: Car running costs	
Estimate current costs	10,500
Less reimbursed to bank (€1,560 – 41%)	(920)
Saving	9,580

4.18 Philip Stodge

Income Tax Computation 2012		
	€	
Schedule E:		
Salary (actual)	41,600	
Salary (spouse)	5,500	
Sales commission (actual earnings basis)	6,000	
Lump sum expense allowance 12 × €100	1,200	
	54,300	
Schedule E expense claim (Note 1)	(10,675)	
Total/Taxable Income	43,625	
Tax – married, two incomes:		
(€38,125 + €5,500 = 43,625) @ 20%	8,725	
Deduct: Tax credits	(6,600)	
Net tax liability	2,125	
Deduct: PAYE paid (€4,900 + €230)	(5,130)	
Tax Refund due	**(3,005)**	
Note 1: Schedule E expense claim 2012		
Motor car operating costs 2012	6,450	
Less: Related to private use (10%)	(645)	
Allowable running costs		5,805
Lease charges:		
Total lease charges	5,700	
Less personal element (10%)	(570)	
	5,130	
Less restricted amount:		
$5,130 \times (27,000 - \dfrac{24,000}{27,000})$	(570)	4,560
Other expenses tax year 2012:		
Total per schedule	910	
Disallow: Suits	(450)	
Correspondence course	(150)	310
Total allowable Schedule E expenses		10,675

Note: As Philip's car is a category B car, there is no further restriction to the lease allowances based on CO_2 emissions.

4.19 Frank

(a) Frank – Income Tax 2012		
	€	€
Schedule E		
Salary		50,000
Sales commission		8,000
		58,000
Schedule E expense claim (Note 1)		
Motor expenses	6,944	
Lease charges	0	(6,944)
Total/Taxable Income		51,056
Tax (single)		
€32,800 @ 20%	6,560	14,045
€18,256 @ 41%	7,485	
Deduct: Tax credits		(3,300)
Tax liability		10,745

Notes:

1. *Allowable motor expenses*

	€
Petrol	4,300
Insurance	1,500
Motor tax	1,480
Repairs and services	1,400
	8,680
Disallow private €8,680 $\times \dfrac{8{,}960 \text{ Km}}{44{,}800 \text{ Km}}$	(1,736)
Allowable	6,944

2. *Allowable lease charges*

	€
Total lease charges	6,600
Disallow personal element	
$6{,}600 \times \dfrac{8{,}960 \text{ Km}}{44{,}800 \text{ Km}}$	(1,320)
Less restriction (Vehicle Category F)	5,280
$5{,}280 \times \dfrac{(51{,}000 - 0)}{51{,}000}$	(5,280)
	0

(b)	New Arrangement		€
	Schedule E		
	Salary		50,000
	Sales commission (2/3)		5,333
	BIK (Note)		5,580
	Total/Taxable Income		60,913
	Tax		
	€32,800 @ 20%	6,560	
	€28,113 @ 41%	11,526	18,086
	Deduct: Tax credits		(3,300)
	Tax liability		14,786

Note:
Benefit in kind – car

Original Market Value		€31,000
18% (business 35,840 Km)		€5,580

After-tax position	**Option (a)**	**Option (b)**
Gross salary	58,000	55,333
Less tax	(10,745)	(14,786)
Less car running costs (8,680 1 6,600)	(15,280)	0
Net cash	31,975	40,547

Conclusion: Frank has more disposable income under option (b).

5   Capital Allowances and Loss Relief

5.1   Regina Briers

Computation	Motor Vehicles 12.5% €	Plant and Equipment 12.5% €	Total €
Asset cost	*12,000	2,500	14,500
Additions 2012		4,500	4,500
Cost of assets qualifying for capital allowances	12,000	7,000	19,000
WDV 1/1/2012	10,500	1,875	12,375
Additions y/e 30/4/2012			
(Basis period for 2012)		4,500	4,500
	10,500	6,375	16,875
Wear and tear 2012	(1,500)	(875)	(2,375)
WDV 31/12/2012	9,000	5,500	14,500

*Cost €35,000 – restricted to €24,000. Wear and tear allowance for the car is further restricted by 50%, i.e. €1,500 as the car is a Category D car for CO_2 emissions.

5.2 Lillian Hanney

Year of Acquisition	Cost €	WDV 1/1/2012 €	Wear and Tear 12.5% €	WDV 31/12/2012 €
2009	15,000	9,375	(1,875)	7,500
2010	9,000	6,750	(1,125)	5,625
2012	5,100		(637)	4,463
		16,125	(3,637)	17,588

5.3 Barney Connor

Tax Year of Acquisition	Cost	WDV 1/1/2012 €	Wear and Tear 12.5% €	WDV 31/12/2012 €
2008	10,000	5,000	1,250	3,750
2012 assets not in use	2,300			2,300
2012	9,920		1,240	8,680
		5,000	2,490	14,730
** The printer ink cartridges are not a capital item.				

5.4 Commencement Situation

Computation
First tax year for which business assessed: 2012
Basis period for 2012: 1/10/2012–31/12/2012

Second tax year for which business assessed: 2013
Basis period for 2013: 1/10/2012–30/09/2013

Asset bought and put into use during basis period for 2012.
Wear and tear allowances for 2012 and 2013 computed as follows:

	€	
Qualifying Cost	1,000	
Wear and tear 2012 @ 12.5% for 3 months		
(Length of basis period for 2012)	(31)	$(12.5\% \times 1,000 \times \frac{3 \text{ months}}{12 \text{ months}})$
WDV as at 31 December 2012	969	
Wear and tear 2013 @ 12.5% (basis period 12 months long)		
	(125)	
WDV at 31 December 2013	844	

5.5 Sean – Commencement Situation

Computation	€
Qualifying cost	10,000
Wear and tear 2012 @ 12.5% for 7 months	$(12.5\% \times 10,000 \times \frac{7 \text{ months}}{12 \text{ months}}$
(Length of basis period for 2012)	(729)
WDV 31/12/2012	9,271
Wear and tear 2013 @ 12.5%	(1,250)
WDV 31/12/2013	8,021

5.6 Joan O Reilly Commencement Situation

Computation

Basis period for 2012: 1/5/2012 – 31/12/2012 (8 months)

Basis period for 2013: y/e 30/4/2013

		Plant and Machinery 12.5% €
WDV	1/1/2012	–
Additions	1/5/2012–31/12/2012	9,000
(Basis period for 2012)		
Wear and tear 2012 (8 months)		(750)
WDV 31/12/2012		8,250
Additions 1/1/2013 – 30/4/2013		1,700
		9,950
Wear and tear 2013 (Note)		(1,337)
WDV 31/12/2013		8,613

Note

9,000 + 1,700 = € 10,700 @ 12.5% = € 1,337

5.7 Cormac Molloy – Annual Allowances Motor Vehicles

	€ 12.5% p.a.	Allow € 3/4	
Cost (restricted by 50%) (Category D car)	10,500		
Wear and tear 2012 @ 12.5%	(1,312)	984	(75%)
WDV 31/12/2012	9,188		

5.8 Joseph Ryan Wear and Tear Computation

	Motor Vehicles 12.5% €	Allow 2/3 €
Cost (restricted) 2012	24,000	
Wear and tear 24,000 @ 12.5%	(3,000)	2,000
WDV 31/12/2012	21,000	

Car cost restricted to €24,000

As the vehicle is emissions category C, no emissions restriction applies.

5.9 Dan Bell – Claim in a Continuing Business

Allowances Computation for 2012

	Motor Car 12.5% €	Allow 70% €	Office Equipment 12.5% €
WDV @ 1/1/2012			7,500
Acquired in y/e 31/12/2012	24,000		1,000
Disposals 2012			(7,500)
Wear and tear 2012	(3,000)	(2,100)	(125)
WDV 31/12/2012	21,000		875

Car cost restricted to €24,000
As the car is emissions category A, no emissions restriction arises.

Balancing Allowance (Charge) assessable:

Office equipment:	€
WDV 1/1/2012	7,500
Proceeds	(3,500)
Balancing allowance	4,000

Capital Allowance Claim	€
Wear and tear	2,225
Balancing allowance	4,000
Total 2012	**6,225**

5.10 Joe Bracken – Balancing Charge

Capital Allowance Computation 2012

		€
Proceeds:	$(20,000 \times \dfrac{24,000}{25,000} =$	19,200
WDV @ 1/1/2012 (Note)		(18,000)
Balancing charge		1,200
Business use 70%		840

New Vehicle Category C (use specified amount)	25,000

Workings

Motor car (Oct 09) allowable cost	24,000
Wear and tear 2010	(3,000)
Wear and tear 2011	(3,000)
	18,000

5.11 Fitzroy

Capital Allowances Computation for 2012

	Plant 12.5% €	Lorries 12.5% €	Motor car (1) 12.5% €	Total
Cost		26,000	25,000	
Cost (memo only)	10,000	20,000	24,000	
WDV 1/1/2012	8,750	0	15,000	23,750
Additions	50,000	20,000	0	70,000
	58,750	20,000	15,000	93,750
Disposals at WDV	0	0	0	0
	58,750	20,000	15,000	93,750
Wear and tear:				
Allowance 2012	(7,500)	(2,500)	(3,000)	(13,000)
WDV at 31/12/12	51,250	17,500	12,000	80,750
Wear and tear:				
Allowance 2013	(7,500)	(2,500)	(3,000)	(13,000)
WDV at 31/12/13	43,750	15,000	9,000	67,750
Balancing Charge / Allowance 2012				
WDV of plant sold		0		
Proceeds		2,200		
Balancing charge		2,200		
Cannot be offset as no replacement plant purchased.				
Asset sold for € 1,500 with a nil WDV ignored as proceeds < €2,000 as a balancing charge				

Summary

2012   €

Wear and tear 7,500 + 2,500 + (3,000 × 1/3) =	11,000
Balancing charge	(2,200)
Total allowances	8,800

2013

Wear and tear 7,500 + 2,500 + (3,000 × 1/3) =	11,000

Note 1:   **Motor Car (12.5%)**

Cost 16/7/2008, i.e. y/e

30/4/2009 (restricted) | 24,000
Wear and tear 2009 | (3,000) | (restricted 1/3 for business use)
WDV 31/12/2009 | 21,000
Wear and tear 2010 | (3,000) | (restricted 1/3 for business use)
WDV 31/12/2010 | 18,000
Wear and tear 2011 | (3,000) | (restricted 1/3 for business use)
WDV 31/12/2011 | 15,000

5.12 Sarah

Assessable Profits		
Tax Year	**Basis Period**	**Profits**
		€
2009	1/6/2009 to 31/12/2009	34,417 (7/12 × €59,000)
2010	Year ended 31/5/2010	59,000
2011	Year ended 31/5/2011	38,417 (Note)
2012	Year ended 31/5/2012	120,000
Note: Profits assessable for the second year		59,000
Less: Actual profits (€59,000 × 5/12) + (€46,000 × 7/12)		51,417
Excess		7,583
Final third year assessment: €46,000 − €7,583 = € 38,417		

Capital Allowances Computation				
	Equipment 12.5%	**Car 12.5%**	**Allow 60%**	**Total Wear and Tear**
	€	€	€	€
1/06/2009–31/12/2009:				
Additions	26,800	–	–	
Wear and tear (7 months)	(1,954)	–	–	(1,954)
WDV 31/12/2009	24,846	–	–	
Additions 2010	1,400	14,000		
Wear and tear 2010 (Note 1)	(3,525)	(1,750)	(1,050)	(4,575)
WDV 31/12/2010	22,721	12,250		
Wear and tear 2011	(3,525)	(1,750)	(1,050)	(4,575)
WDV 31/12/2011	19,196	10,500		
Wear and tear 2012	(3,525)	(1,750)	(1,050)	(4,575)
WDV 31/12/2012	15,671	8,750		
Note 1: (26,800 + 1,400) × 12.5% = 3,525				

5.13 Joe Bloggs: Case I and capital allowances

(a) Computation of taxable case/income for the year ended 31 December 2012		
	€	€
Loss per accounts to 31 December 2012		(310)
Adjustments – addback:		
Wages to self (drawings)	5,200	
Motor expenses 25% × 1,750 (private element)	437	
Light and heat 25% × 1,200 (private element)	300	
Christmas gifts (entertainment – n/a)	300	
Depreciation	900	
Covenant	105	
Cash register (fixed asset)	380	
Deposit on shelving (fixed asset)	1,000	
Display freezer (fixed asset)	600	
Flat contents insurance (private element)	100	
Hire purchase instalments	1,920	
Notional rent (drawings)	2,000	
		13,242
		12,932
Deduct: Hire purchase charges		(376)
		12,556
Deduct: Building society interest received	210	
Sale proceeds of equipment	1,500	(1,710)
Adjusted profits		10,846
Case I taxable income for 2012		10,846

(b) Capital allowances claim 2012	Motor car 12.5%	Allow 75%	Plant 12.5%
	€	€	€
WDV at 1/1/2012	5,250		1,250
Disposals	–		(1,250)
Additions:			
Cash register 1/2/2012	–		380
Shelving 10/2/2012	–		5,633
Freezer 1/3/2012	–		600
	5,250		6,613
Wear and tear 2012	(1,750)	(1,312)	(827)
WDV 31/12/2012	3,500		5,786

Balancing Charge /Allowance calculation	
Proceeds of sale	1,500
Less: WDV	(1,250)
Balancing charge – ignored as proceeds < €2,000	250
Capital allowances due	——
Wear and tear 1,312+ 827 =	2,139

5.14 Mr Goa and Mrs Statham Industrial Buildings

Mr Goa

2008   Basis period y/e 30/6/2008:

annual allowance of € 140,000 × 4% = € 5,600 claimed

2009   Basis period 30/6/2009 balancing charge as set out below:

	€
Sale proceeds (190,000 – 25,000)	165,000
WDV (140,000 – 5,600)	134,400
Balancing charge	30,600
Restricted to allowances actually claimed:	
(140,000 – 134,400)	5,600

Mrs Statham

Qualifying expenditure	140,000

2009 Basis period 1/5/2009–31/12/2009

$$\frac{8}{12} \times \frac{1}{25-1} \times €140,000 = 3,889$$

Basis period is less than 12 months

2010   Basis period y/e 30/4/2010

$$\frac{12}{12} \times \frac{1}{25-1} \times €140,000 = 5,833$$

2011   Basis period y/e 30/4/2011

$$\frac{12}{12} \times \frac{1}{25-1} \times €140,000 = 5,833$$

2012   Basis period y/e 30/4/2012

$$\frac{12}{12} \times \frac{1}{25-1} \times €140,000 = 5,833$$

5.15 James – IBAA Qualifying Items

Calculate eligible items

	€
Site purchase cost	0
Site development costs	5,000
Construction of factory	95,000
Construction of adjoining office	0 (Note 1)
Construction of adjoining showroom	0 (Note 1)
Total cost	100,000

Note 1:

The 10% rule for eligible items applies to the showroom and office as follows:

$$\frac{10,000 + 15,000}{(135,000 - 10,000)} = 20\%$$

IBAA @ 4% of 100,000 = €4,000

5.16 Mr Plant

Capital Allowances Computation 2012				
	Plant 12.5% €	**Motor Cars 12.5%** €	**Trucks 12.5%** €	**Total** €
Original cost (car restricted)	25,500	24,000	18,750	
WDV at 1/1/2012	15,937	9,000	14,062	38,999
Disposal at WDV		(9,000)		(9,000)
	15,937	0	14,062	29,999
Addition:				
New office furniture (1)	10,000			10,000
New truck (2)			25,000	25,000
New car (restricted to 50% Category D car) (4)		12,000		12,000
New machinery (3)*			–	
(Cost net of grant) (5)	20,000	–		20,000
	45,937	12,000	39,062	96,999
Wear and tear 2012	(6,938)	(1,500)	(5,469)	(13,907)
WDV at 31/12/2012	38,999	10,500	33,593	83,092
* There are no wear and tear allowances due for the milling machine or pump as they were not in use at the end of the basis period.				

Industrial Building Allowance (6): €

Original cost 75,000

IBAA 75,000 × 1/15 = 5,000

Extension to Factory Premises (7):

IBAA not due as extension was not in use at the end of the basis period.

Balancing Allowance Charge Computation – car:

		€
WDV at 1/1/2012		9,000
Sale proceeds:	$7,500 \times \dfrac{24,000}{26,000}$	(6,923)
		2,077
Balancing allowance	$1,702 \times 75\% =$	1,558

Summary of Capital Allowances 2012

Plant	6,938
Car (€1,500 × 75%)	1,125
Trucks	5,469
IBAA	5,000
Balancing allowance	1,558
	20,090

5.17 Janet

	Plant and Machinery 12.5% €	Motor Trucks 12.5% €	Vehicles Cars 12.5% €	TOTAL €
Original cost 1/1/2012	45,000	17,000	24,000	86,000
Additions at cost	25,000		48,000	73,000
Disposals at cost	(35,000)		(24,000)	(59,000)
Remaining cost	35,000	17,000	48,000	100,000
				–
WDV 1/1/2012	5,000	2,125	11,500	18,625
Additions y/e 31/5/2012	25,000		48,000	73,000
Disposals y/e 31/5/2012			(12,000)	(12,000)
	30,000	2,125	48,000	80,125
Wear and tear 2012	(4,375)	(2,125)	(6,000)	(12,500)
WDV 31/12/2012	25,625	–	42,000	67,625

Balancing allowances charges:

Machinery:	Sold for	14,000	
	WDV	Nil	
			Offset as
	Potential balancing charge	14,000	replacement

Replacement option:	49,000
	(10,000) Grant

	(14,000) Replacement Option	
Plant addition	25,000	
Balancing allowance charge on sale of car:	WDV	12,000
	Proceeds 12,500 × 24,000/24,000 =	12,500
	Balancing charge	500

Wear and tear is not due for the photocopier as it was not in use at the end of the 2012 basis period.

IBAA

Second hand industrial building $\dfrac{120,000}{25-11} = $8,571$ IBAA per annum.

Sale of office building: no balancing charge as the office would not have qualified as an industrial building.

Extension to industrial building: €70,000 × 4% = €2,800 IBAA per annum. The offices qualify for IBAA as they did not cost more than 10% of the overall cost.

Summary

	€
Wear and tear	12,500
Balancing charge	(500)
IBAA	8,571
IBAA	2,800
Total capital allowances due 2012	23,371

5.18 Linda Loss Relief

Assessment 2012

	€
Case I	–
Schedule E	80,000
	80,000
Less section 381 loss	(60,000)
Taxable income	20,000

5.19 Mr Jones Loss Relief

Assessment 2012

	€
Case III	25,000
Schedule E	50,000
Gross statutory income	75,000
Deduct: section 381 loss	(30,000)
Taxable income	45,000

5.20 Mr Fool – Loss Relief

This gives rise to a loss of €7,000 (27,000 – 20,000) which can be claimed under section 381.

		€
Profit y/e 31/12/2012		20,000
less capital allowances	(37,000)	
deduct balancing charge	10,000	(27,000)
Section 381 loss 2012:		(7,000)

Note

Capital allowances carried forward from previous year cannot be used to create or augment a section 381 loss claim directly. However, they may be used wipe out any current year balancing charges and to reduce current year profits and in this way may result in increasing a section 381 claim.

5.21 John – Loss Relief

2012	Section 381 claim is computed as follows:	€
	Tax-adjusted Case I profit y/e 30/9/2012	9,000
	Deduct: Capital allowances forward (limited)	(9,000)
	Net Case I	Nil
	Balancing charge	3,000
	Deduct: Balance of unused capital allowances forward	(600)
	Net balancing charge	2,400
	Deduct: 2012 capital allowances claim	(7,500)
	Section 381 loss (available to reduce total income for 2013)	(5,100)

5.22 Jim – Loss Relief

	2010	2011	2012	Total
	€	€	€	
Case I	Nil	17,000	50,000	
Deduct: Case I losses forward (section 382)	___	(17,000)	(1,000)	(18,000)
Assessable Case I	Nil	Nil	49,000	

Jim is obliged to take relief for the loss forward in the first year in which Case I profits from the same trade are available. This occurs in 2011 and results in a waste of his personal allowances/tax credits for that year. Jim would have preferred to defer relief for some of the loss until 2012 to avoid wasting his 2011 allowances/tax credits and to avail of relief at the higher rates of tax that will be suffered in 2012. Unfortunately, this is not permitted.

5.23 Basil Bond – Loss Relief

Assessments		€
2010	Case I	80,000
	Case IV	1,000
	Case V	20,000
		101,000
2011	Case I	Nil
	Case IV	1,200
	Case V	30,000
		31,200
	Less section 381	(31,200)
		Nil
2012	Case I	45,000
	Section 382 relief (37,000 – 31,200)	(5,800)
		39,200
	Case IV	1,200
	Case V	25,000
		65,400

6 Tax Credits and Reliefs

6.1 Joyces – Home Carer

(a) As only one spouse has income, they are entitled to the married couple, one income standard rate band. Their income tax liability for 2012 is as follows:

Income Tax Computation 2012	€	€
Taxable Income		46,000
Tax		
€41,800 @ 20% =	8,360	
€4,200 @ 41% =	1,722	10,082
Tax credits		
Basic personal (married)	3,300	
Employee	1,650	
Home carer	810	(5,760)
Tax liability		4,322

(b) If the home carer had income of €7,000 in 2013, i.e. above the income limit for the home carer tax credit in 2013, a home carer tax credit can still be claimed as the home carer was entitled to the tax credit in 2012. The maximum home carer tax credit claimable would be the tax credit claimed for the tax year 2012.

However, it will be more beneficial for the increased standard rate band to be claimed i.e. the tax saving by claiming the increased standard rate band (i.e. €7,000 @ (41%–20%) = €1,700) will be more than the reduction due to claiming the €810 home carer tax credit.

6.2 Roches – Home Carer

As both spouses have income, they are entitled to the increased standard rate tax band. As one spouse has income of less than €6,880, they also qualify for the home carer tax credit. If the increased standard rate tax band is claimed, their income tax liability for 2012 will be as follows:

Income Tax Computation 2012	€	€
Schedule E salary		46,000
Schedule F		6,000
Taxable Income		52,000
Tax		
€47,800* @ 20% =	9,560	
€4,200 @ 41% =	1,722	11,282
Tax credits		
Basic personal (married)	3,300	
Employee	1,650	(4,950)
Less refundable tax credit DWT		(1,200)
Tax liability		5,132
* The standard rate band of €41,800 is increased by the lower of €23,800 or the total income of the lower income spouse, i.e. €6,000 in this case.		

If the home carer tax credit is claimed instead of the increased standard rate band, their liability will be as follows:

Income tax computation 2012	€	€
Taxable income		52,000
Tax		
€41,800 @ 20% =	8,360	
€10,200 @ 41% =	4,182	12,542
Tax credits		
Basic personal (married)	3,300	
PAYE	1,650	
Home carer €810−(6000−5080)/2	350	(5,300)
Less refundable tax credit DWT		(1,200)
Tax liability		6,042

As their tax liability is lower if the increased standard rate tax band is claimed, they should claim the increased standard rate tax band instead of the home carer tax credit.

6.3   Mr Murray

Medical Expense	€
Mr Murray	80
Michael Murray	200
David Murray	210
Sean Ryan	650
	1,140

Medical expenses allowable for 2012 are €1,140. Relief is at the standard rate of 20% = tax credit of €228.

Mr Murray is also entitled to a deduction from net statutory income in respect of the €1,200 he pays towards nursing home care for his mother. Therefore, if Mr Murray's marginal rate of tax is 41%, tax relief @ 41%, i.e. €492, will be available. If the nursing home does not provide 24-hour nursing care on-site, then no deduction is available.

6.4   Rachel

(a) Rachel will be entitled to interest relief as a charge of €8,750 ((€10,000 × 6/12 × 100%) plus (€10,000 × 6/12 × 75%)) in 2012.

(b) Rachel's net relevant earnings for 2012:

	€
Case II	320,000
Less capital allowances	(10,000)
Less charges	(8,750)
Net relevant earnings	301,250
Premium paid	**75,000**
Maximum claim allowed:	
Net relevant earnings ceiling restricted to	115,000
Relief restricted to €115,000 × 25%	**28,750**

6.5   Mr Frost – Medical Insurance Premiums

Income Tax Computation 2012	€	€
Salary		46,000
VHI (gross)		1,200
Taxable income		47,200
Tax		
€32,800 @ 20% =	6,560	
€14,400 @ 41% =	5,904	12,464
Tax credits		
Basic personal	1,650	

Employee	1,650	(3,300)
		9,164
Tax deducted from VHI €1,200 @ 20%		(240)
Tax liability		8,924

6.6 Charitable Donations

A self-employed man makes a donation of €300 in 2012 to an eligible charity. He is entitled to deduct this amount is calculating his taxable income for 2012.

A PAYE taxpayer makes a donation of €300 in 2012 to an eligible charity. Assume the donor is single with no children and has taxable income of €38,000 for 2012. The donor is **not entitled to a deduction** for the donation made.

As the donor will have income of at least €300 taxable at 41%, the eligible charity is deemed to have received a donation from him of €300 after deduction of tax at 41%. **The eligible charity can then reclaim tax of €208 ((€300 × 100/59) – €300) from the Revenue.**

6.7 John – Loan Interest

John's income tax computation for 2012 will be as follows:

			€
Schedule E: Salary			75,000
Tax:	32,800 @ 20%	6,560	
	42,200 @ 41%	17,302	23,862
Less:	Basic personal tax credit		(1,650)
	Employee tax credit		(1,650)
	Mortgage interest relief	€ 3,000 × 15%	(450)
	PAYE deducted		(20,500)
Tax refund due			(388)

TRS does not apply to the mortgage interest paid by John as the residence in question is situated outside the State.

If this was the first mortgage in respect of which John had claimed relief and the loan had been taken out in June 2007, he would have been entitled to mortgage interest relief of €3,000 (€10,000 × 30%). If the mortgage was taken out prior to 1 January 2004, no relief would be available.

6.8 June

Income Tax Liability 2012

	€	€
Schedule E Income		
Salary	43,000	
Retirement annuity premium paid	(2,000)	41,000
	continued overleaf	

Widow's pension		<u>5,900</u>
Total income		<u>46,900</u>
Tax payable:		
€36,800 @ 20%	7,360	
€10,100 @ 41%	<u>4,141</u>	11,501
Tax credits:		
Basic personal tax credit (widowed)	1,650	
One-parent family tax credit	1,650	
Widowed parent (third year after year of death)	2,700	
Incapacitated child tax credits × 2	6,600	
Employee tax credit	1,650	
College fees (€3,000 − €1,125) @ 20%	375	
Rent relief €4,800 @ 20% (Max)	960	
Medical expenses €500 @ 20%	<u>100</u>	
Total tax credits due		(15,685)
Tax liability		(4,184)
Restrict as tax credits are non refundable		0
Less PAYE paid		(5,000)
Refund due		(5,000)

Notes:
(1) Medical expenses incurred for David of €500 are allowable. Expenditure incurred on eye test and spectacles for John is not allowable.
(2) The income received by John and Mary has no effect on June's entitlement to tax credits.
(3) VHI premium paid is ignored. Tax relief is given at source.
(4) The first €1,125 of college fees for a part-time course are not allowable.

6.9   John Fitzpatrick – Tax Credits

Income Tax Computation 2012	€	€
Schedule E:		
Pension (gross)		<u>29,400</u>
Tax Payable:		
€ 29,400 × 20%		5,880
Less Tax Credits:		
Widowed person tax credit	(2,190)	
Age tax credit	(245)	
Employee tax credit	<u>(1,650)</u>	
Total credits		(4,085)
Tax liability		1,795
Less PAYE paid		(1,900)
Refund due		(105)

Notes:
(1) Donation to eligible charity is ignored. Charity will claim back tax of €75, i.e. €300 ÷ 0.8 less €300 in respect of the donation.
(2) VHI premium paid is ignored as tax relief is given at source.

6.10 Jason and Damien

Income Tax Computation 2012	€	€
Schedule E Income/Taxable Income – pension (gross)		35,000
Tax Payable:		
€35,000 × 20%		7,000
Less tax credits:		
Basic personal tax credit - civil partners	(3,300)	
Age tax credit	(490)	
Employee tax credit	(1,650)	(5,440)
Initial tax liability		(1,560)
Income exemption limit €36,000 =>		(1,560)
Final tax liability		0
Less PAYE paid		(2,000)
Refund due		(2,000)

Note: It is the older civil partner's age that is relevant.

6.11 Bob

	2011 €		2012 €
Relevant Earnings	20,980		24,480
Less:			
Charges not covered by non-relevant income (3,000 – 1,160)	(1,840)	(3,000 – 1,195)	(1,805)
Net relevant income	19,140		22,675
Maximum allowable premium (30% in 2011, 35% in 2012)	5,742		7,936
2011: Premium paid	6,000		
Restrict to	5,742		
and carry balance of €258 forward to 2012.			
2012: Premium paid			4,000
+ Carried forward			258
Allow			4,258

6.12 Maria – Covenant

Maria's Income Tax Computation 2012		€
Schedule E salary		35,000
Less: Charges		
Covenant (€ 4,000/0.8)		(5,000)
Total income		30,000
Tax: 30,000 × 20% =		6,000
Less: Basic personal tax credit	(1,650)	
Employee tax credit	(1,650)	
		(3,300)
Add: Tax on covenant €5,000 × 20%		1,000
Tax liability		3,700
Less PAYE tax deducted		(4,400)
Refund due		(700)
Father's Income Tax Computation 2012		
Schedule D Case IV		5,000
Schedule D Case V		8,000
		13,000
TAX: 13,000 × 20% =		2,600
Less:		
Widowed person tax credit		(2,190)
Initial tax liability		410
Income exemption limit €18,000, thus tax liability =		nil
Less: Tax paid on covenant €5,000 × 20% =		(1,000)
Refund due		(1,000)

6.13 Robert O Sullivan – Pension and Charges

Income Tax Computation 2012		€	€
Schedule D Case IV (€1,600/0.70)			2,286
Case IV shares in lieu			800
Case V (Note 1)			3,019
Schedule E salary		84,000	
Less: Pension contribution (max 20% of Schedule E)		(16,800)	67,200
Schedule F	(Note 3)		6,500
GROSS INCOME			79,805
Deduct	Covenant brother (€3,200/0.8)		(4,000)
	Covenant father (Note 2)		(3,790)

Total income			72,015
Deduct			
	EII		(20,000)
Taxable income			52,015
Tax thereon:			
32,800 × 20% =		6,560	
2,286 × 30% =		686	
16,929 × 41% =		6,941	14,187
Less NRTC:	Basic personal tax credit	(1,650)	
	Employee tax credit	(1,650)	
	DIRT	(686)	(3,986)
Add: Tax on covenant paid (*Note 4*)			1,700
Tax liability			11,901
Less PAYE tax deducted			(13,780)
Less DWT (€ 6,500 × 20%)			(1,300)
Less medical expenses €845 @ 20%			(169)
Refund due			(3,348)

Note 1:

Computation of Case V income for 2012	€
Rental income	14,400
Less expenses:	
Mortgage interest (3,200 × 75%)	(2,400)
Management fee	(3,100)
Expenses	(2,600)
Capital allowances (2,250 × 12.5%)	(281)
Loss forward	(3,000)
Case V Income	3,019

Note 2:

Covenant to father is restricted to 5% of total income

Schedule D Case IV (€1,600/0.70)	2,286
Case IV	800
Case V	3,019
Schedule E salary	84,000
Less: Pension contribution (max 20% of Schedule E)	(16,800)
Covenant brother (€3,200/0.8)	(4,000)
Schedule F (*Note 3*)	6,500
TOTAL INCOME	75,805
Covenant to parent restricted to 5% of total income	3,790

Note 3:

Net dividend received from	
Independent News €5,200/0.8	6,500

Note 4:

Covenant paid to brother	4,000
Covenant paid to father	4,500
	8,500
Tax deducted 20% of €8,500 =	€1,700

7   Computation of Income Tax

7.1   Patrick and Helen

(a)   Joint Assessment

Income Tax Computation 2012	Patrick	Helen	Total
	€	€	€
Income:			
Schedule E	10,500	50,000	60,500
Schedule E - BIK	–	2,100	2,100
Total Income	10,500	52,100	62,600
Tax Calculation:			
€41,800 @ 20%		8,360	8,360
€10,500 @ 20%	2,100		2,100
€10,300 @ 41%	–	4,223	4,223
€62,600	2,100	12,583	14,683
Less: Non refundable tax credits:			
Basic personal tax credit (married)			(3,300)
Employee tax credits (× 2)			(3,300)
Tax Liability			**8,083**
Deduct:			
PAYE paid	(830)	(9,000)	(9,830)
Net tax refund			**(1,747)**

(b) Separate Assessment

Patrick Income Tax Computation 2012		€	€
Income:			
Schedule E			<u>10,500</u>
Tax Calculation:			
€10,500	@ 20%		2,100
Less: Non refundable tax credits:			
Basic personal tax credit			(1,650)
Employee tax credit			<u>(1,650)</u>
Excess tax credits transferred to wife			**(1,200)**
Deduct:			
PAYE paid			<u>(830)</u>
Net tax refund			**<u>(830)</u>**

Helen Income Tax Computation 2012		€	€
Income:			
Schedule E		50,000	
Schedule E - BIK		<u>2,100</u>	
Total Income			<u>52,100</u>
Tax Calculation:			
€41,800	@ 20%	8,360	
€10,300	@ 41%	<u>4,223</u>	12,583
€52,100			
Less: Non refundable tax credits:			
Basic personal tax credit			(1,650)
Employee tax credit			(1,650)
Tax credits transferred from husband			<u>(1,200)</u>
Tax liability			8,083
Deduct:			
PAYE paid			<u>(9,000)</u>
Net tax refund			**<u>(917)</u>**

Check:	*Patrick*	*Helen*	*Total*
Separate assessment	<u>(830)</u>	<u>(917)</u>	<u>(1,747)</u>
Refund per joint assessment:			<u>(1,747)</u>

(c) Single Assessment

Patrick Income Tax Computation 2012	€	€
Income:		
Schedule E		<u>10,500</u>
Tax Calculation:		
€10,500 @ 20%		2,100
Less: non refundable tax credits:		
Basic personal tax credit	(1,650)	
Employee tax credit	<u>(1,650)</u>	
	<u>(3,300)</u>	
Credits limited to tax liability		(2,100)
Deduct:		
PAYE paid		<u>(830)</u>
Net tax refund		<u>(830)</u>

Helen Income Tax Computation 2012	€	€
Income:		
Schedule E	50,000	
Schedule E - BIK	<u>2,100</u>	
Total Income		<u>52,100</u>
Tax Calculation:		
€32,800 @ 20%	6,560	
€19,300 @ 41%	<u>7,913</u>	
€52,100		14,473
Less: non refundable tax credits:		
Basic personal tax credit		(1,650)
Employee tax credit		<u>(1,650)</u>
Tax liability		11,173
Deduct:		
PAYE paid		<u>(9,000)</u>
Net tax payable		<u>**2,173**</u>

Note: Relief for VHI premium paid is given at source (TRS) so it is not included in the tax computations. Relief for mortgage interest relief is also given at source but, in this case, no relief is available as the loan was taken out prior to 1 January 2004.

7.2 Peter and Paul

Assessment as Single Persons for 2012					
Income Tax Computation 2012		Peter €	Paul €		
Income:					
Schedule E		50,000	26,000		
Tax Calculation:					
€32,800	@ 20%	6,560	5,200		
€17,200	@ 41%	7,052	–		
€50,000		13,612	5,200		
Less: non refundable tax credits:					
Basic personal tax credit		(1,650)	(1,650)		
Employee tax credit		(1,650)	(1,650)		
Initial tax liability		**10,312**	**1,900**	**12,212**	
Deduct:					
Year of registration of civil partnership relief (Note)		(703)	(130)	(833)	
PAYE paid		(10,300)	(2,050)	(12,350)	
Net tax refund		**(691)**	**(280)**	**(971)**	

Note: **Notional Joint Assessment for 2012.**

		Peter €	Paul €	Total €
Income:				
Schedule E		50,000	26,000	76,000
Tax Calculation:				
€41,800	@ 20%	8,360	–	8,360
€23,800	@ 20%	–	4,760	4,760
€10,400	@ 41%	4,264	–	4,264
€76,000		12,624	4,760	17,384
Less: non refundable tax credits:				
Basic personal tax credit (married/civil partners)				(3,300)
Employee tax credits (× 2)				(3,300)
Notional tax liability				**10,784**
Total under single assessment				**12,212**

"Saving"			1,428
Saving restricted to:			
€1,428 × 7/12 (months)			833
Split:	833 × $\frac{10,312}{12,212}$	833 × $\frac{1,900}{12,212}$	
Year of registration of civil partnership relief	€703	€130	€833

7.3 Mr and Mrs Thorne

1. **No change to Deed of Separation**

Mrs Thorne Income Tax Computation 2012		€	€
Income:			
Schedule E		35,000	
Case IV (€200 × 12)(Note)		2,400	
Total Income			37,400
Tax Calculation:			
€36,800	@ 20%	7,360	
€600	@ 41%	246	
€37,400			7,606
Less: non refundable tax credits:			
Basic personal tax credit		(1,650)	
One-parent family tax credit		(1,650)	
Employee tax credits		(1,650)	(4,950)
Tax liability			2,656

Note: maintenance payments specifically for children are ignored (i.e. €800 − €600)

2. **Deed of Separation changed**

Mrs Thorne Income Tax Computation 2012		€	€
Income:			
Schedule E		35,000	
Case IV Schedule D (€900 × 12)		10,800	
Total Income			45,800
Tax Calculation:			
€36,800	@ 20%	7,360	
€9,000	@ 41%	3,690	
€45,800			11,050
Less: non refundable tax credits:			
Basic personal tax credit		(1,650)	

One-parent family tax credit	(1,650)	
Employee tax credits	(1,650)	(4,950)
Tax liability		**6,100**

Comparison:

If the deed is not reviewed, Mrs Thorne's financial position is as follows:

	€
Maintenance payments (€800 × 12)	9,600
Salary	35,000
	44,600
Less: tax payable	(2,656)
Net income after tax	**41,944**

If the deed is reviewed, Mrs Thorne's financial position is as follows:

Maintenance payments (€1,000 × 12)	12,000
Salary	35,000
	47,000
Less: tax payable	(6,100)
Net income after tax	**40,900**

Mrs Thorne is worse off financially by €1,044 (€41,944 − €40,900) if the deed is reviewed.

7.4 Mr and Mrs Lynch

1. **Claim for joint assessment made for year of separation (i.e. election under section 1026 TCA 1997).**

As Mrs Lynch has income other than the maintenance payments, the separate assessment rules are used.

Mrs Lynch Income Tax Computation 2012	€	€
Income:		
Schedule E	15,000	
Total Income		15,000
Tax Calculation:		
€15,000 @ 20%	3,000	
€0 @ 41%	0	
€15,000		3,000
Less: non refundable tax credits:		
Basic personal tax credit	(1,650)	
Employee tax credits	(1,650)	(3,300)

Excess tax credits transferred to Mr Lynch		(300)
Tax liability		0

Mr Lynch Income Tax Computation 2012		€	€
Income:			
Schedule E		48,000	
Total Income			48,000
Tax Calculation:			
€41,800	@ 20%	8,360	
€6,200	@ 41%	2,542	
€48,000			10,902
Less: non refundable tax credits:			
Basic personal tax credit		(1,650)	
Employee tax credit		(1,650)	
Excess tax credits transferred from Mrs Lynch		(300)	(3,600)
Tax liability			**7,302**
Combined tax liability			**7,302**

Mortgage interest relief = NIL as loan was taken out before 1 January 2004.

VHI - tax relief given at source.

2. **No claim made for joint assessment for year of separation**

Mrs Lynch Income Tax Computation 2012		€	€
Income:			
Schedule E (1/7/2012 – 31/12/2012)		8,000	
Case IV (€600 × 6)		3,600	
Total Income			11,600
Tax Calculation:			
€11,600	@ 20%	2,320	
€0	@ 41%	0	
€11,600			2,320
Less: non refundable tax credits:			
Basic personal tax credit		(1,650)	
One-parent family tax credit		(1,650)	
Employee tax credit		(1,650)	
		(4,950)	

Restrict to amount needed to reduce tax liability to NIL		(2,320)
Tax liability		**0**

Mr Lynch Income Tax Computation 2012		€	€
Income:			
Schedule E - self		48,000	
Schedule E - Mrs Lynch (1/1/2012 – 30/06/2012)		7,000	
			55,000
Less: maintenance payments (€600 × 6)			(3,600)
Net Income			51,400
Tax Calculation:			
€41,800	@ 20%	8,360	
€7,000	@ 20%	1,400	
€2,600	@ 41%	1,066	
€51,400			10,826
Less: non refundable tax credits:			
Basic personal tax credit (married)		(3,300)	
Employee tax credits		(3,300)	(6,600)
Tax liability			**4,226**
Combined tax liability			**4,226**

As the assessable spouse in the year of separation, Mr Lynch is entitled to a married person's tax credits and tax bands.

3. **Claim for joint assessment made for the year following the year of separation**
    Same as 1. above

4. **No claim made for joint assessment for the year following the year of separation**

Mrs Lynch Income Tax Computation 2012		€	€
Income:			
Schedule E		15,000	
Case IV Schedule D (€600 × 12)		7,200	
Total Income			22,200
Tax Calculation:			
€22,200	@ 20%	4,440	
€0	@ 41%	0	
€22,200			4,440
Less: non refundable tax credits:			
Basic personal tax credit		(1,650)	

One-parent family tax credit	(1,650)	
Employee tax credits	(1,650)	
	(4,950)	
Restrict to amount needed to reduce tax liability to NIL		(4,440)
Tax liability		0

Mr Lynch Income Tax Computation 2012	€	€
Income:		
Schedule E - self		48,000
Less: maintenance payments (€600 × 12)		(7,200)
Net Income		40,800
Tax Calculation:		
€32,800	@ 20%	6,560
€8,000	@ 41%	3,280
€40,800		9,840
Less: non refundable tax credits:		
Basic personal tax credit	(1,650)	
Employee tax credit	(1,650)	(3,300)
Tax liability		**6,540**
Combined tax liability		**6,540**

As Mr Lynch's daughter only resides with her mother, Mr Lynch is not entitled to the one-parent family tax credit or tax band.

8 The PAYE System

8.1 Mary and Andrew

(a) Net pay receivable by Mary – August 2012

		€	€
Gross salary – this employment		2,200	
Gross salary per P45		16,310	
Cumulative gross pay to date			18,510
Cumulative SRCOP to date	€2,733	× 8	21,864
Tax @ 20%	€18,510	@ 20%	3,702
Cumulative tax credits to date	€275	× 8	(2,200)
Cumulative tax due to date			1,502

Less: Tax paid per P45				(1,208)
Tax due for August 2012				294
Net Salary for August 2012:				
Gross salary August 2012				2,200
Less:				
PAYE				(294)
PRSI	First €550 @ 0%	550	-	
	Balance @ 4%	1,650	66	(66)
		2,200		
USC: cut-off point 1	€837 × 8 @ 2%	6,696	134	
cut-off point 2	€498 × 8 @ 4%	3,984	159	
Balance	€18,510 − (€6,696 + €3,984) @ 7%	7,830	548	
Cumulative pay to date		18,510	841	
Less: USC paid per P45			744	(97)
Net pay for August 2012				**1,743**

(b) Total Gross Taxable Pay for Andrew – June 2012

			€
Benefit in Kind Calculation:			
Original market value of car			28,000
% applicable for annual business travel (km) of 51,200 – 8,000		43,200 km	12%
Cash equivalent	€28,000	@ 12%	3,360
Less: Annual amount paid to employer			(1,500)
Annual benefit-in-kind assessable			**1,860**
Gross taxable pay June 2012:			
June 2012 salary			4,167
BIK (monthly)			155
Gross taxable pay June 2012			**4,322**

8.2   Sean and New Ltd: BIK on Van and Emergency Basis

(a) Value of BIK on Van

OMV of van €17,500

	€
Cash equivalent 5% of €17,500	875
Less refunded by Sean	(120)
Annual BIK on van	755

Taxable BIK 2011 $\frac{(\ 6}{12ths)}$ 378

(b) (1) With PPS No

Gross wages – this employment	500.00
SRCOP	630.79
Tax at 20% (€500 × 20%)	100.00
Tax credits (€1,650/52)	(31.73)
Tax due for first week	68.27

PRSI: AL Rate

€500 – €127 = €373 × 4%	14.92
USC €500 @ 7% (emergency)	35.00
Total	49.92

Gross salary for August 2012	500.00
PAYE	(68.27)
PRSI	(14.92)
USC	(35.00)
Net pay for August 2012	381.81

(b) (2) Without PPS No

Gross wages – this employment	500.00
SRCOP	0
Tax at 41% (€500 × 41%)	205.00
Tax credits (€nil/52)	(0)
Tax due for first week	205.00

PRSI: AL rate

€500 – €127 = €373 × 4%	14.92
USC €500 @ 7% (emergency)	35.00

Gross salary for August 2012	500.00
PAYE	(205.00)
PRSI	(14.92)
USC	(35.00)
Net pay for August 2012	245.08

8.3 Paul

(a) Net pay receivable by Paul for w/e 17 October 2012 (Week 46) Temporary Basis		€	€

Gross salary – this employment	(39 × €21) + (11 × €21 × 1.5)	1,165.50	
Gross salary per P45 - do not use		0	
Gross pay to date			1,165.50

SRCOP to date	€803.85	× 1	<u>803.85</u>
Tax @ 20%	€803.85	@ 20%	160.77
Tax @ 41%	€361.65	@ 41%	<u>148.28</u>
			309.05
Tax credits this period	€95.19	× 1	<u>(95.19)</u>
Tax due to date (non-cumulative)			213.86
Tax paid per P45 – not used			<u>0</u>
Tax due for week 46			<u>213.86</u>

Net Pay for Week 46:

Gross pay for week 46				1,165.50
Less:				
PAYE				(213.86)
PRSI:	First @ 0%	€127.00	–	
	Balance @ 4%	<u>€1,038.50</u>	<u>41.54</u>	(41.54)
		<u>€1,165.50</u>		
USC:	€193 @ 2%	€193.00	3.86	
(Week 1 basis)	€115 @ 4%	€115.00	4.60	
	Balance @ 7%	<u>€857.50</u>	<u>60.03</u>	(68.49)
		<u>€1,165.50</u>		
Net pay for Week 46				<u>**841.61**</u>

(b) Net pay receivable by Paul for w/e 17 October 2012 (Week 46)
Cumulative Basis € €

Gross salary – this employment	(39 × €21) + (11 × €21 × 1.5)	1,165.50	
Gross salary per P45		<u>43,540.00</u>	
Cumulative gross pay to date			<u>44,705.50</u>
Cumulative SRCOP to date	€803.85	× 46	<u>36,977.10</u>
Tax @ 20%	€36,977.10	@ 20%	7,395.42
Tax @ 41%	€7,728.40	@ 41%	<u>3,168.64</u>
			10,564.06
Cumulative tax credits to date	€95.19	× 46	<u>(4,378.74)</u>
Cumulative tax due to date			6,185.32
Tax paid per P45			<u>(5,995.50)</u>
Tax due for week 46			<u>189.82</u>

Net Pay for Week 46:

Gross pay for week 46				1,165.50
Less:				
PAYE				(189.82)
PRSI:	First @ 0%	€127.00	–	
	Balance @ 4%	€1,038.50	41.54	(41.54)
		€1,165.50		
USC: cut-off point 1	€193 × 46 @ 2%	8,878	177.56	
cut-off Point 2	€115 × 46 @ 4%	5,290	211.60	
Balance	€44,705 − (€8,878 + €5,290) @ 7%	30,537	2,137.59	
Cumulative pay to date		44,705	2,526.75	
Less: USC paid per P45			2,458.30	(68.45)
Net pay for Week 46				**865.69**

9 Administration and Procedures

9.1 Mr Murphy

ABC

Accountants

Dear Mr Murphy,

Self-assessment

I refer to your letter of the 10th inst. requesting some information regarding the system of self-assessment.

Income Tax Returns and Surcharges

A taxpayer must submit a tax return whether or not he has been issued with a return form. The return must be submitted before 31 October in the year following the tax year; otherwise a penalty surcharge of up to 10% on the tax ultimately due is imposed.

A return for 2012 may be sent to the taxpayer after the end of the tax year requesting the taxpayer to enter on it details of income and capital gains from all sources, and to claim allowances and reliefs, for the tax year. The return will also request details of all capital assets acquired. An individual within the self-assessment system must submit his return on or before 31 October in the year after the tax year to which the return refers. Accordingly, a tax return for 2012 would normally have to be submitted before 31 October 2013.

However, as you have only commenced to trade in 2012, you have until 31 October 2014, the due date for the filing of your 2013 tax return, to file your 2012 tax return without incurring any penalties.

Note, however, that preliminary tax for 2012 must be paid by 31 October 2012 and the balance of the 2012 tax due is payable in full by 31 October 2013, even though your 2012 return is not due for filing until 2014.

Preliminary Tax

All taxpayers within the self-assessment system are required to pay preliminary tax by 31 October in the tax year. Accordingly, preliminary tax for 2012 must be paid on or before 31 October 2012.

If interest charges are to be avoided, preliminary tax must amount to:

(1) 90% of the final liability for the tax year; or

(2) 100% of the final liability for the preceding tax year.

Failure to pay preliminary tax by 31 October will result in interest accruing on the full liability from 31 October to the date the tax is paid. Also, even where a preliminary tax payment is made in time but proves to be less than 90% of the tax ultimately due (or 100% of the preceding year's liability, as adjusted for USC, whichever is lower) interest will run on the full underpayment at the rate of 0.0219% per day.

An individual may opt to pay preliminary tax by direct debit. If he chooses to do this, instead of paying 90% of the current year's liability or 100% of the adjusted previous year's, he has the option of paying instead 105% of the pre-preceding year's liability.

The direct debit payments are made on the 9th day of each month. For the first year in which a taxpayer opts to pay his preliminary tax by direct debit, he can opt to pay his liability in a minimum of three equal instalments in that year. In subsequent years, the taxpayer must pay his liability in at least eight equal instalments. If these conditions are satisfied, the person is deemed to have paid his preliminary tax on time. The Collector-General can agree to vary the number of instalments to be made, or agree to increase or decrease the instalments, after one or more instalments have been made.

Balance of Income Tax

An individual must pay the balance of his income tax due, after payment of preliminary tax, on the due date for the filing of his income tax return. Accordingly the balance of income tax due for 2012 must be paid on or before 31 October 2013.

For the tax year 2012, as this will be your first year to pay tax and file your return under the self-assessment system, you will not be required to make a preliminary tax payment on 31 October 2012. This is because you had no liability under the self-assessment system for the tax year 2011 so 100% of your prior year's liability is nil. Your total liability for 2012 is therefore due on 31 October 2013. You must pay your entire liability on or before this date if you wish to avoid interest even though you will not incur any penalties if your return for 2012 is not filed until 31 October 2014.

If you require any further information please do not hesitate to contact me.

Yours faithfully

ABC
Accountants

9.2   *Self Assessment*

(a)   **Returns of income**

All taxpayers must make a return of income on or before 31 October in the year following the year of assessment. Returns must be made whether requested or not and persons who fail to meet this requirement will be subject to a surcharge of up to 10% on the tax found to be ultimately due for the year. For the tax year tax year 2012 the return must be submitted by 31 October 2013. A person acting under the taxpayer's authority may submit a return on his behalf.

The return forms are concerned with establishing the two main features of a taxpayer's circumstances, namely the amount of his or her income and the reliefs claimed. Return forms for tax year 2012 will be sent to taxpayers after the end of 2012. Taxpayers must enter details of income from all sources for the period 1 January 2012 to 31 December 2012 and to claim allowances and reliefs for 2012. To protect himself from interest and penalties, the taxpayer should draw the Revenue's attention to any question of doubt concerning any item in the return using the "expression of doubt" facility.

(b)   **Payment of tax**

Preliminary tax is payable by 31 October in the year of assessment.

Failure to pay preliminary tax by 31 October will result in interest running on the full liability from 31 October to the date the tax is paid. Also, even where the preliminary tax payable is paid in time but proves to be less than 90% of the tax ultimately due for the year of assessment (or 100% of the previous year's liability, if lower) interest will run on the full underpayment at the rate of 0.0219% per day or part thereof.

An individual may opt to pay preliminary tax by direct debit. If s/he chooses to do this, s/he can pay the lower of:

1.   90% of the final liability for the year of assessment, or
2.   100% of the final liability for the preceding year of assessment, or
3.   105% of the final liability of the pre-preceding year of assessment

The direct debit payments are made on the 9th day of each month. For the first year in which a taxpayer opts to pay his preliminary tax by direct debit, he can opt to pay his liability in a minimum of three equal instalments in that year. In subsequent years, the taxpayer must pay his liability in at least eight equal instalments. If these conditions are satisfied, the person is deemed to have paid his preliminary tax on time. The Collector-General can agree to vary the number of instalments to be made or agree to increase or decrease the instalments, after one or more instalments have been made.

The balance of tax due for the year is payable on or before the due date for the filing of the return for the year. After the return of income has been submitted, a notice of assessment will be issued. If the balance of tax paid has been insufficient, the assessment will show a balance of tax payable.

Note: That returns and payments can be made on-line through the Revenue On-line Serivce (ROS). Taxpayers using ROS can avail of the extended deadlines for return and payment, provided both transactions are done on-line.

(c)   **Assessments**

In general, assessments will not be made until after a return has been submitted and will be based on the amounts included in the return. Where a person defaults in making a return or the Inspector is dissatisfied with a return, the Inspector may make an assessment.

If he is satisfied that all tax due has been paid, the Inspector may elect not to issue an assessment. He must however inform the taxpayer accordingly. The taxpayer has the right to require the Inspector by notice in writing to issue an assessment. A time limit of six years will apply to the making of an assessment where a full return has been made.

(d)   Appeals against assessments
Where an assessment is based on figures which differ from those which the taxpayer has included in his return, the taxpayer has the right of appeal. This must be notified in writing within thirty days of the issue of the assessment and the taxpayer must clearly and fully set out the matters under dispute. Failure to set out the grounds of the appeal properly renders the appeal void. Further, the taxpayer must also pay the amount of the undisputed tax within the same period. Appeals may be made outside the thirty day limit, but only if certain conditions are met, as follows:

(i) **Appeals within twelve months.** The Inspector must be satisfied that there was reasonable excuse and that application for late appeal was made without undue delay.

(ii) **Appeals outside twelve months**. In addition to satisfying the Inspector with regard to the above conditions, the taxpayer must also have made a full return of his income for the year concerned and have paid the full amount of the tax in the original assessment together with any interest which may be due on it. The Inspector must give his consent to the late appeal in writing. Late appeals will not be accepted where court proceedings have been instituted to recover the tax due until these are completed. Where the Inspector refuses a late appeal, there is a right of appeal against his refusal to be made within fifteen days to the Appeal Commissioners.

10   Value Added Tax (VAT)

10.1   *Registration and Information*

(a)   Obligation to register

A person is required to register for VAT if his turnover from the supply of taxable goods or services exceeds, or is likely to exceed, in any continuous period of 12 months whichever of the following limits is appropriate:

(i)   €37,500 in the case of persons supplying services,

(ii)   €37,500 in the case of persons supplying goods liable at the 13.5% or 23% rates which they have manufactured or produced from zero rated materials,

(iii) €35,000 in the case of persons making mail-order or distance sales into the State,

(iv)   €41,000 in the case of persons making intra-Community acquisitions,

(v)   €75,000 in the case of persons supplying both goods and services where 90% or more of the turnover is derived from supplies of goods (other than goods referred to at ii above), and

(vi)   A non-established person supplying goods or services in the State is obliged to register and account for VAT regardless of the level of his turnover.

In determining whether or not the relevant turnover threshold has been exceeded, actual turnover may be reduced by VAT on stock purchased for resale.

For example, in a twelve month period a trader purchases stock for €61,767 (including VAT of €11,550) and sells it on for €78,000. For the purpose of determining if the €75,000 threshold has been exceeded, the trader's turnover of €78,000 is reduced by VAT on purchases of stock of €11,550. Accordingly, his turnover is deemed to be €66,450. As this is less than the €75,000 threshold, he is not obliged to register.

No threshold applies in the case of taxable intra-Community services received from abroad and in the case of cultural, artistic, sporting, scientific, educational or entertainment services received from a person not established in the State. All such services are liable to VAT.

Suppliers of goods and services that are exempt from VAT, and non-taxable entities such as State bodies, charities etc, are obliged to register for VAT where it is likely that they will acquire more than €41,000 of intra-Community acquisitions in any twelve-month period.

(b)   Records and information

A taxable person must keep full and true records of all business transactions which affect or may affect his liability to VAT. The records must be kept up to date and must be sufficiently detailed to enable the trader to accurately calculate his liability or repayment, and for the Inspector of Taxes to check if necessary.

The record of purchases should distinguish between purchases of goods for resale and goods and services not intended for re-sale. The records should show the date of the purchase invoice, the name of the supplier, the cost exclusive of VAT and the VAT. Purchases at each date should be separated and similar records kept for imports.

The record of sales must record the amount charged in respect of every sale to a registered person and a daily total of the amounts charged in respect of sales to unregistered persons. Transactions liable at different rates must be distinguished as must exempt transactions.

All entries must be cross-referenced to the relevant invoices, cash register tally rolls, etc. which must be retained.

The bi-monthly, monthly or annual VAT return to the Collector-General must show the VAT charged on supplies (output tax), the VAT suffered on supplies, self-supplies, and imports used in the business (input tax), and adjustments to previous returns, and the net amount payable or repayable. The return should be on form VAT 3 and should be sent to the Collector-General within 19 days of the end of each tax period.

Input and output tax figures must be supported by the original or copy tax invoices. Records, including a VAT account, must be maintained for six years. A taxable person must keep a record of all taxable goods and services received or supplied, including any self-supplies and exempt supplies. It is not necessary to submit the supporting documentation with the return but it must be made available for inspection if required by the Revenue.

10.2   Tax Point

(a)   Unless a taxable person has been specifically authorised by the Revenue Commissioners to account for tax on the basis of monies received (cash basis), liability for VAT arises at the time when taxable goods or services are supplied. This general rule is, however, subject to a number of qualifications:

(i)   in dealings between taxable persons, tax becomes due on the date of issue of the tax invoice, or the date on which the invoice should have been issued if issue has been delayed;

(ii)   where payment in whole, or in part, in respect of a transaction was received before the date on which the VAT would normally be due, the VAT was due on the amount received on the date of receipt.

(b) Goods supplied on a sale or return basis are treated as supplied on the earlier of acquisition by the customer or when they are invoiced or paid for.

(c) If the services are supplied under a contract over a period during which periodic payments are made each payment will have its own tax point as under the general rule, the actual tax point for each payment will be the earlier of the date of the payment received or the issue of the tax invoice.

(d) Tax in respect of 'self-supplies' becomes due in all cases when the goods are appropriated or withdrawn from business stock or when the services are performed.

10.3 Records and Payment

(a) Records

A taxable person must keep full and true records of all business transactions which affect or may affect his liability to VAT. The records must be kept up to date and must be sufficiently detailed to enable the trader to accurately calculate his liability or repayment and for the Inspector of Taxes to check if necessary.

The record of purchases should distinguish between purchases of goods for resale and goods and services not intended for resale. The records should show the date of the purchase invoice, the name of the supplier, the cost exclusive of VAT and the VAT. Purchases at each rate should be separated and similar records kept for imports.

The record of sales must record the amount charged in respect of every sale to a registered person and a daily total of the amounts charged in respect of sales to unregistered persons. Transactions liable at different rates must be distinguished, as must exempt transactions.

All entries must be cross-referenced to the relevant invoices, cash register tally rolls, etc., which must be retained.

(b) If filing bi-monthly returns, the return must be submitted electronically (via ROS) by the 23rd of the month following the end of the two month taxable period, i.e. 23 March; 23 May; 23 July; 23 September; 23 November and 23 January.

If VAT is not paid within the proper time limit, interest will be charged at the rate of 0.0274% for each day or part of a day by which payment is late. In addition, the Revenue offences listed in section 1078 TCA 1997 apply to VAT as they apply to other taxes. They involve, for example, obtaining a refund of VAT on an illegal input credit, or suppressing a VAT liability. On summary conviction, any person who committed a Revenue offence is liable to a fine of up to €5,000 or to imprisonment of up to 12 months, or both. On indictment the penalty imposed can be up to €126,970 and/or imprisonment for a term of up to five years.

10.4 John Hardiman

	€
Sales: Cash receipts €30,250 × 23/123	5,656
Less: Purchases (note)	(1,202)
VAT due	4,454
Note:	
Total VAT on purchases:	
(6,150 × 23/123) + (2,270 × 13.5/113.5)	1,420

Not allowable:

(i) 160 × 13.5% × 25%	(5)
(ii) 300 × 23% × 80%	(55)
(iii) 123 × 23/123	(23)
(iv) N/A	–
(v) 64 × 23/123	(12)
	1,325
Less 10% exempt	(123)
VAT on purchases	1,202

10.5 Mr Byte

The VAT liability of Mr Byte for the period July/August 2011 is:

	VAT exclusive Amount €	VAT €	VAT rate
Sales	75,000	17,250	23%
Purchases:			
Purchases for resale	40,000	9,200	23%
Stationery	6,000	1,380	23%
Wages	20,000	–	(Note 2)
Electricity	2,000	270	13.5%
Hotel bills	1,000	–	(Note 3)
Rent	2,400	–	(Note 4)
VAT deductible		10,850	
VAT payable		6,400	

Notes
1. VAT is payable on the cash receipts basis, as sales are less than €1 million.
2. Services provided by employees are specifically exempt from VAT.
3. While VAT is payable at the rate of 9% on hotel accommodation, it is specifically not recoverable, except on "qualifying accomodation" in connection with the attendance at a "qualifying conference".
4. Rents in most cases are exempt from VAT. While a landlord may waive his exemption, it is assumed that he has not done so in this case.

10.6 Joe

Since Joe supplies goods at the zero rate of VAT, he will be in a permanent VAT repayment position. This means that he is entitled to submit monthly VAT returns on the 23rd day of each month in respect of the previous month's purchases and sales.

	VAT exclusive Amount €	VAT €	Rate €
May 2012			
Sales	10,000	–	(0%)
Purchases			
Ingredients	5,000	–	
Petrol	1,000	–	(Note 1)
Lease rentals – vans	2,000	460 (23%)	(Note 2)
Bank interest	400	0	
VAT recoverable		460	
June 2012			
Sales	8,000	–	(0%)
Purchases			
Ingredients	2,000	–	(0%)
Petrol	1,000	–	(Note 1)
Fixed assets	6,000	1,380	(23%)
Lease rental - vans	2,000	460	(23%)
Bank interest	400	–	
		1,840	
VAT recoverable May/June 2012		2,300	

Notes:
1. VAT arises at the rate of 23% on purchases of petrol but is specifically not recoverable.
2. VAT on the lease of vans is recoverable. VAT on the lease of passenger motor vehicles is restricted to 20% of the VAT if the vehicle is a "qualifying vehicle"; otherwise it is not recoverable.

10.7 *Voluntary Registration*

The following persons are not obliged to register for VAT unless they otherwise formally make an election to register:

(a) Persons whose turnover does not exceed €75,000 per annum, provided that 90% of their total receipts arise from the supply of taxable goods. The €75,000 registration limit is reduced to €37,500 for persons producing goods liable at the 13.5% or 23% rates from zero-rated raw materials.
(b) Farmers
(c) Persons whose supplies of taxable goods/services consist **exclusively** of the following:
  (i) Supplies of unprocessed fish caught in the course of a sea fishing business
  (ii) Supplies of machinery, plant, etc., which have been used by that person in the course of his sea fishing business
(d) Persons whose supplies of services do not exceed €37,500 per annum.

A person might choose to apply for voluntary registration if:

(a) He supplies goods or services to VAT registered persons. If he registers for VAT, he will get an input credit for his purchases. Although the sales would than be liable to VAT, VAT registered purchasers would be entitled to an input credit.

(b) He exports goods or deals in zero-rated goods, such as food. He would not have to pay VAT on his sales but he can claim a credit or repayment of any VAT invoiced to him on his business purchases.

Another category of person who might voluntarily register for VAT is a person who has not actually commenced supplying taxable goods or services but will soon become a taxable person. This will enable the trader to obtain credit for VAT on purchases made before trading commences.

10.8 General

(a) The place of supply of goods is deemed to be either:

 (i) In a case where it is a condition of supply that they are transported, it is the place where such transportation starts.

 (ii) In all other cases, it is where they are located at the time of supply (i.e. when ownership is transferred). Services are generally deemed to be supplied where the business making the supply is located. Where there is a provision of international services, the following rules are applied:

 (I) Services connected with immovable goods

 Services connected with immovable goods are deemed to be supplied where the property is located.

 (II) Transport services

 These are deemed to be supplied where the transport actually takes place. This rule applies to the transport of goods only. Passenger transport is exempt. If the transport of goods is part of a contract to export the goods physically outside of the State, then the transport service may be zero-rated.

 (III) Admission to cultural, artistic, sporting or entertainment services

 These are deemed to be supplied where the service is physically carried out.

(b) There is a self-supply of goods when a VAT registered person diverts to private or exempt use goods which he has imported, purchased, manufactured or otherwise acquired and in respect of which he is entitled to a tax deduction.

 Where this occurs, the VAT registered person is liable to VAT at the appropriate rate on the cost of the goods in question.

Valuation rules for the self-supply of services:

Where the supply consists of the private use of business assets, VAT is due on the cost to the taxable person of providing the service.

Where the supply is a non-deductible business service, then VAT is due on the market value of the service.

10.9   Andrew

Calculation of March/April 2012 VAT Return		VAT €
Sales		
(1)	Sales @ 23% (1,815 × 23/123)	339.40
(2)	Sales @ 13.5% (2,837.50 × 13.5/113.5)	<u>337.50</u>
		676.90
Purchases		
(1)	Stock for resale (€605 × 23/123)	113.10
(2)	Stock for resale (€334 @ 0%)	Nil
(3)	Tables and chairs (€440 @ 23%)	101.20
(4)	Rent (no invoice/exempt letting)	N/A
(5)	Cash register (€665.50 × 23/123)	124.45
(6)	Tiling (€200 @ 13.5%)	27.00
(7)	Shop fitting lease for two months	
	i.e. 30 March and 30 April; 700 × 2 @ 23%	322.00
(8)	Legal fees (€1,452 × 23/123)	271.50
(9)	Van (€9,840 × 23/123)	1,840.00
(10)	Petrol (non-deductible item)	<u>N/A</u>
		<u>2,799.25</u>
Net VAT refund due		<u>2,122.35</u>

10.10   Hermes Ltd.

Calculation of VAT Liability for March/April 2012		
VAT on sales	**Net of VAT**	**VAT Payable**
	€	€
Supplies in Ireland	250,000	57,500
Supplies to US	10,000	0
Purchases from UK (note 1)	50,000	<u>11,500</u>
VAT on sales		69,000
VAT on costs	**Net of VAT**	**VAT Claimable**
Purchase of stock from Irish suppliers	190,000	43,700
(233,700 × 100/123)		
Purchase of stock from UK suppliers (note 1)	50,000	11,500
Professional fees (6,150 × 100/123)	5,000	1,150
Motor car leasing (note 2) 3,690 × 100/123	3,000	138
Motor car repairs (1,135 × 100/113.5)	1,000	135
		continued overleaf

Computer (9,225 × 100/123)	7,500	1,725
Total VAT on purchases		58,348
VAT on sales	69,000	
VAT on purchases	58,348	
VAT payable	10,652	

Notes:

1. Where goods are purchased for business purposes from another EU Member State, the supplier will not charge VAT, provided he was given the VAT registration number of the EU purchaser. The purchaser must account for a notional amount VAT in the sales (reverse charge) and the purchases on his VAT return.
2. VAT charged on car lease is allowed at 20%, as the car is a "qualifying car".

10.11   Elixir Ltd

Calculation of VAT payable:

	Net of VAT €	VAT €
VAT on sales (output VAT):		
Supplies in Ireland (@ 23%)	950,000	218,500
Exports to Spain (to Spanish registered customers)	320,000	0
Exports to non VAT registered customers in the		
UK @ 23%	25,000	5,750
Exports to VAT registered customers in the UK	135,000	0
Exports to customers located in Singapore	46,000	0
		224,250
VAT EU acquisitions	200,000	46,000
VAT on sales		270,250

VAT on costs (input VAT)	VAT inclusive €	VAT content €
Purchase of materials from Irish		
suppliers (€369,000 × 23/123)	369,000	69,000
Purchase of machinery locally		
(€246,000 × 23/123)	246,000	46,000
Rent of premises (€18,450 × 23/123)	18,450	3,450
Repairs and maintenance of office		
and equipment (€14,145 × 23/123)	14,145	2,645
Audit and accountancy fees		
(€11,070 × 23/123)	11,070	2,070
Diesel for staff vehicles (€5,535 × 23/123)	5,535	1,035

Electricity and gas (€2,400 × 13.5/113.5)	2,400	285	
Salaries and wages	167,000	N/A	
Advertising costs (€30,750 × 23/123)	30,750	5,750	130,235
	NET	VAT	
EU acquisitions	200,000	46,000	46,000
VAT on costs			176,235
VAT payable			94,015

Author Index

ALSO AVAILABLE FROM KOGAN PAGE

ISBN: 978 0 7494 5242 1   Paperback   2009

ALSO AVAILABLE FROM KOGAN PAGE

STRATEGIC REWARD
Implementing more effective reward management

Michael Armstrong &
Duncan Brown

ISBN: 978 0 7494 5618 4   Paperback   2009

ALSO AVAILABLE FROM KOGAN PAGE

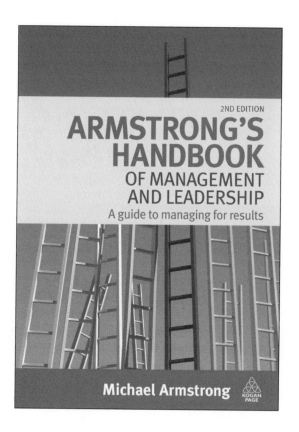

ISBN: 978 0 7494 5417 3   Paperback   2009

ALSO AVAILABLE FROM KOGAN PAGE

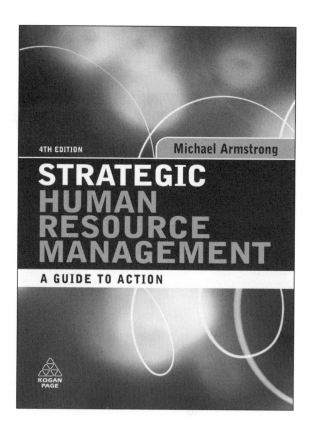

ISBN: 978 0 7494 5375 6   Paperback   2008

With over 42 years of publishing, more than 80 million people have succeeded in business with thanks to **Kogan Page**

www.koganpage.com

You are reading one of the thousands of books published by **Kogan Page**. As Europe's leading independent business book publishers **Kogan Page** has always sought to provide up-to-the-minute books that offer practical guidance at affordable prices.

KoganPage